Andrew Jackson
and the Politics of Martial Law

Andrew Jackson
and the Politics of Martial Law

Nationalism, Civil Liberties, and Partisanship

MATTHEW WARSHAUER

The University of Tennessee Press / Knoxville

Copyright © 2006 by The University of Tennessee Press / Knoxville.
All Rights Reserved. Manufactured in the United States of America.
First Edition.

This book is printed on acid-free paper.

Warshauer, Matthew, 1965–
  Andrew Jackson and the politics of martial law: nationalism, civil liberties, and partisanship / Matthew Warshauer.— 1st ed.
      p. cm.
Includes bibliographical references and index.

ISBN-13: 978-1-57233-548-6 (hardcover)
ISBN-10: 1-57233-548-3 (hardcover)

1. Jackson, Andrew, 1767–1845—Influence.
2. United States—Politics and government—1815–1861.
3. Martial law—United States—History—19th century.
4. Nationalism—United States—History—19th century.
5. Civil rights—United States—History—19th century.
6. Jackson, Andrew, 1767–1845—Military leadership.
7. Martial law—Louisiana—New Orleans—History—19th century.
I. Title.

E382.W28 2006
973.5'6092—dc22   2006007742

For my family. To the beach!

CONTENTS

ILLUSTRATIONS

ACKNOWLEDGMENTS

P|erhaps the best part about writing a book is finishing it. After years of work, any author realizes that it could not have been completed without the help and support of colleagues and friends. It is, therefore, with pleasure that I thank the many people who were part of making this book a reality. First and foremost is Mark E. Neely Jr., the McCabe Greer professor in the American Civil War Era at Pennsylvania State University. Previously an endowed chair of history and American Studies at Saint Louis University, Mark patiently and insightfully guided me as a young graduate student through "dissertation hell." Even after I completed my doctoral work, he continued to encourage and guide me through the revision process. I have no doubt that his students at Penn State have learned what I know: He's as great a teacher as he is a scholar.

I am also indebted to a number of accomplished scholars who read this book in the manuscript stage, challenged my interpretations, and offered important suggestions: Jonathan Atkins of Berry College; Daniel Feller, editor of the *Papers of Andrew Jackson* and professor of history at the University of Tennessee, Knoxville; David Heidler of the University of Southern Colorado; and Peter Onuf, of the University of Virginia. Two friends in Tennessee were also of particular help in the completion of the manuscript. Ann Toplovich, the director of the Tennessee Historical Society, read the entire manuscript, has been a steadfast supporter of my work on Jackson, and offered much appreciated friendship. Tom Kanon of the Tennessee State Library and Archives also read the manuscript and offered insights.

My colleagues in the History Department at Central Connecticut State University are also owed a sincere debt of gratitude. If anyone had told me at the start of graduate school that I would one day return to my alma mater and begin my teaching career, I would have thought them crazy. But return I did, and as a result I've been honored with wonderful colleagues and friends. In particular, I thank Norton Mezvinsky, who has been at CCSU for over thirty-five years, mentored me while an undergraduate, helped me to gain entry to graduate school, and as a senior scholar mentored me again when I came back to CCSU. If all that wasn't enough, he read the entire manuscript, too. Special thanks also go to Victor Geraci (now at the University of California, Berkeley), Katherine Hermes, Louise Williams, and Robert Wolff, all of whom have listened to me, though not without comment, blab on and on about Jackson. My students at CCSU are also owed thanks for challenging me to be a better teacher. In particular, I thank Joseph E. Camire III, a former graduate student who read the manuscript and offered suggestions.

Finally, I wish to thank my family, to whom this book is dedicated. There is little in life that is worth much if one doesn't have a family with whom you can enjoy the adventure. Thanks.

INTRODUCTION

I n 1841, while in retirement at the Hermitage, former president Andrew Jackson scrawled a letter to his old friend, military aide, and political protégé Maj. Auguste Davezac de Castera. The two had a long history, having served together in the famous Battle of New Orleans, the source of Jackson's national appeal and his road to the White House. Davezac had acted as General Jackson's adjutant general in the winter of 1814–15, a job for which the young Creole was well suited. He knew the Crescent City and was the brother-in-law of Edward Livingston, an acquaintance of Jackson's and an influential American in the polyglot culture of Spanish, French, and American citizenry. Livingston also served the general during this time by acting as his military aide and legal counsel. Both of these men, Davezac and Livingston, ultimately profited from their early relationship with the seventh president of the United States. Davezac received numerous appointments to foreign legations, and Livingston enjoyed a long and intimate friendship with Jackson that resulted in his appointment as secretary of state. In that pivotal position, Livingston crafted into words the president's steadfast commitment to Union during the Nullification crisis.[1]

Major Davezac received Jackson's letter while serving as a representative in the New York legislature. The war-worn general was in ill health at the time he wrote. At seventy-four, Jackson had reached a ripe age for anyone during this time of the Republic, let alone for a man who had survived so many campaigns, both military and political. He suffered from numerous medical complaints—tuberculosis, failing kidneys, weakness from frequent bloodlettings, a slow poisoning from mercury and calomel used as a medicinal—and there lay buried in his chest for almost forty years a duelist's bullet.[2] Yet even in this beleaguered condition, only four years from death, Jackson thought of politics. His letter to Davezac was more than a friendly note, the grumblings of a sick and dying old man.

Jackson looked back to the beginnings of his fame, to New Orleans, fully cognizant that one final battle had yet to be waged. In defending the southern coast from the most formidable British military force ever arrayed against the United States, Jackson had declared martial law, suspended the writ of habeas corpus, arrested civilians, censored the press, confiscated private property, and destroyed the same. In becoming America's greatest hero, Jackson also achieved what later became the notorious distinction of being the first U.S. general to ever impose martial law. The reason for his letter to Davezac stemmed from the one-thousand-dollar contempt of court fine Jackson had paid in March 1815 on the order of Dominick Augustan Hall, a federal district judge. A few weeks earlier, the iron general had arrested Hall for issuing a writ of habeas corpus on behalf of Louis Louaillier, a Louisiana state senator Jackson had imprisoned for criticizing the continuation of martial law in the aftermath of the January 8 victory in New Orleans. If it was not enough to stoke the ire of a federal judge with arrest, Jackson subsequently ordered his soldiers to escort Hall beyond the city limits with a letter banishing him until news of peace arrived or the British had left the Gulf Coast. Official news of the Treaty of Ghent, which ended the War of 1812, came only a few days later, and the general subsequently lifted martial law. Judge Hall promptly returned to New Orleans, launched a brief investigation, then demanded the hero's presence before the court.[3]

The Davezac letter focused on the return of the fine. Jackson had never believed the contempt ruling and ensuing fine to be legal or just, and he meant to have the money back, with interest, before he concluded his earthly career. He noted, "no one has ever brought to [the] view of Congress the iniquity and injustice of the $1000 fine with costs imposed on me by a vindictive judge." Jackson continued, "Congress is the only body whose action could wipe this stain from my memory, by a joint resolution ordering the fine, with costs and interests, to be

refunded." He finished the letter by remarking, "this is the only imputation that has not been by Congress expunged from the record. . . . I
cannot but regret that this stain upon my name, shall be permitted to
pass down to posterity."[4]

Davezac lost little time implementing the plan that Jackson had
devised. In January 1842, the major presented a motion in the New
York legislature to refund the fine, and from that body's discussion of
the issue, Senator Lewis Field Linn of Missouri began a national movement to return Jackson's money. Nor was he the only senator to prepare such a bill.[5] Why Jackson chose Davezac rather than some other
political foot soldier is a mystery. He could have easily turned to a representative from his home state of Tennessee. Perhaps it was simply a
matter of choosing someone intimately connected to the Battle of New
Orleans and someone who had benefited from years of presidential
patronage. Jackson may also have surmised that the bill would not
appear so self-serving if a representative from a northern state raised
the matter. Whatever the reason for choosing him, Jackson was surely
confident that Davezac would do as instructed and that the refund bill
would ultimately make its way to Congress. The letter and the ensuing
battle, then, reveal at least two things about Andrew Jackson: he was
obsessed with personal vindication and he was a shrewd, calculating
political operator who, even in retirement and close to death, wielded
tremendous political power. In one letter, the aged but still potent lord
of the Hermitage embroiled Democrats and Whigs in a two-year contest over nationalism, the Constitution, and civil liberties, all three of
which were intimately intertwined within the party power of the age.

The Jackson described here may seem foreign to historians of late.
Robert Remini has argued for years that Jackson was a "masterful politician" who over a lifetime of political contests continually honed his
skills.[6] Yet in the last thirty years, scholars have come to doubt such
assertions. Most recently, Andrew Burstein has raised doubts about
Remini's interpretations and Jackson's abilities. He was not, argues
Burstein, a skilled leader with a vision for America. Rather, Jackson
was obsessed only with his own shallow need for power and loyalty.
"His vanity was corrosive," offers Burstein. "The American conqueror
coveted nothing more and nothing less than dominion over the national
household." Burstein concludes that Jackson's "bluster" outweighed
his patriotism, he did not understand the "common good," his "political pronouncements" were irrational, and he was "a man of platitudes,

a mediocre intellect with a glamorous surface." Essentially, "historical imagination has contrived" Jackson as a "romanticized figure," insists Burstein, and "we can add [Jackson] to such story book heroes as Daniel Boone and Davy Crockett."[7]

Burstein's Jackson is the culmination of an idea that began with James C. Curtis's 1976 work, *Andrew Jackson and the Search for Vindication.* In this postmortem psychoanalysis, Curtis argued that Jackson had neither the patience nor the skill to assemble a national party, marshal congressional votes, or direct nuanced campaigns against the Bank of the United States or nullifiers. The portrait created is one of a virtual mad man with little political acumen, a man tormented by the premature deaths of his mother and brothers.[8] This attempt to define Jackson's character and impact on the age that bears his name inevitably influenced subsequent scholars. Donald B. Cole, in writing on Jackson's presidency, acknowledged his scholarly debt to Curtis and described the seventh president as a vacillating leader, "less sure of himself than imagined, a man more controlled by the political and economic forces of his age than the reverse." John F. Marszalek, in *The Petticoat Affair,* presented readers with "the poor orphan boy of the American Revolution" and continually reiterated Jackson's insecurity and need for reassurances.[9] The product of such portrayals is a Jackson out of control, lacking confidence, and exploding at any perceived threat, a man incapable of maneuvering amid the politics of the day.

The Andrew Jackson described by these historians and others is not the man who wrote Auguste Davezac in 1841. The Jackson in retirement at the Hermitage, and I believe throughout his life, was a man ingrained with supreme confidence in both his abilities and opinions. His success in military and political battles would most certainly have been impossible had he suffered the psychological impairment that some historians assert. He either possessed a considerable skill that allowed him to be victorious in both the military and political realm or he was the luckiest president in American history. It seems that a number of scholars have confused their dislike of Jackson and his policies with the idea that he was unintelligent or simpleminded. Whereas there is no doubt that Jackson was vain, as are so many formidable leaders, Burstein and Curtis go too far by arguing that the general had no vision for the nation's future and no political talent to achieve that vision. It is true that many of Jackson's conflicts most certainly stemmed from his firm and often overinflated belief in what was best for the nation and for those who surrounded him, yet his views were also grounded in a steadfast commitment to the preservation of republican government and the Union. If Jackson refused to tolerate criticism and constantly sought vindication, it was not because of some psychologically driven need to prove his right to survive, as James Curtis argued, so much as he was committed to proving that he was right. Jackson therefore engaged every campaign, be it military or political, with an intensity, passion, and skill that inevitably resulted in victory. The same was true of his final political feat. Once the general forwarded his orders on how best to reclaim his one-thousand-dollar fine, he embarked on a mission that included collecting evidence, directing Democratic troops, and assaulting his Whig enemies.

Jackson's desire for vindication, however, went beyond mere personal vanity. There is no question that he considered his legacy. He specifically noted his dismay that the stain of the fine would "pass down to posterity." Yet there were other significant, ideological issues at stake. Jackson always believed that declaring martial law at New Orleans had saved the city from capture and possible destruction. He never wavered on this point. In the immediate aftermath of the New Orleans victory, he journeyed to Washington to explain and justify his conduct. In the midst of the 1824 presidential contest, he noted that some in the nation believed him to be "a most dangerous and terrible man . . . and that I can break, & trample under foot the constitution of the country, with as much unconcern & careless indifference, as would one of our backwoods hunters, if suddenly placed in Great Britain, break game laws." He continued, noting, "it has been my lot often to be placed in situations of a critical kind" that "imposed on me the necessity of Violating, or rather departing from, the constitution of the country; yet at no subsequent period has it produced to me a single pang, believing as I do now, & then did, that without it, security neither to myself or the great cause confided to me, could have been obtained."[10] Years later, in an 1842 letter to his senatorial benefactor Lewis Linn, Jackson questioned, "I ask what general hereafter, if Neworleans was again threatened with invasion, let the real necessity be what it might, and the most energetic measures for its defense necessary, would hazard the responsibility, of adopting those energetic measures by which the Country could alone be defended, whilst the record of the fine and loss stared him in the face, inflicted upon me by an unjust judge for declaring martial law."[11] He repeated this point in numerous subsequent letters. He viewed the return of his fine as a larger statement about the legitimacy of violating the Constitution and civil liberties in times of national emergency. What Jackson wanted was a congressionally sanctioned precedent. The refund debates are, in part, the story of how such a precedent was created.

One might reasonably question why Jackson waited so long, some twenty-seven years, to push for the return of the fine and to set a precedent for emergency powers. Detractors may argue that it was sheer vengeance and narcissism that motivated him, noting that he did nothing to invoke a theory of emergency powers while president. Yet the fact is, he had other pressing matters to deal with while chief executive, none of which required martial law. Perhaps if nullifiers had pressed their case to its limits, Jackson may have taken more serious measures than the congressionally sanctioned Force Bill, but such an act never became necessary. It was only in retirement, while surveying a long career, that he focused on one final battle that needed waging and in doing so mixed personal and Union-minded goals. Ultimately, the length of time between Jackson's use of martial law and his pressing for a congressional precedent does not diminish the consistency or seriousness of his views on the need for emergency powers to safeguard the Union.

At the core of Jackson's belief was an imposing ideological conviction: the military could subvert civil liberties if doing so was imperative to the Union's survival. Such an idea stabbed at the heart of the Constitution's protection of liberty, the political ideology that shaped the colonies' battle for independence, as well as the continuation of that dogmatic republican ideology which guided Americans' constant fear of governmental and military power. This struggle between liberty and power was a staple of Revolutionary era political thought, and has commonly been referred to by historians as the "republican synthesis" or "paradigm." It is, perhaps, most commonly associated with Bernard Bailyn's 1967 work *Ideological Origins of the American Revolution*, in which he explained that the American colonists' understanding of the words "liberty" and "power" were heavily influenced by seventeenth-century English Commonwealth writers who warned of conspiracies perpetrated by the British government. Power was an aggressive, compulsive force that swelled beyond legitimate boundaries and trespassed on the citizens' liberties. Americans fought a war to maintain their liberty because they viewed English taxes and standing armies as attempts to rob colonists of their natural rights.[12]

In the wake of this Revolutionary fervor came the War of 1812. Many Americans touted the renewed hostilities with England as a second war of independence and cited British aggression on the seas as yet another example of unrestrained power. It was in the midst of fighting for their liberty against a foreign enemy that America witnessed the imposition of martial law in New Orleans. The military was, arguably, the most overt example of aggressive power. The irony, however, was that the founding fathers had always warned against standing armies as a source of despotism. Thomas Jefferson had been a stalwart advocate of the militia for this very reason. Yet Jackson led mainly a militia force and in declaring martial law proved that even an army of citizen-soldiers headed by a strong commander could endanger liberty.[13] Still, the larger issue revolved around the balance between the military and civilian spheres. A prominent American doctrine held that the military must remain subordinate to civil authority. Jefferson cited King George's violation of this principle among the list of grievances in the Declaration of Independence, and the belief was outlined in numerous state constitutions.[14]

Thus Jackson's desire for a precedent establishing the right of a general to suspend the writ of habeas corpus, impose martial law, and in doing so subvert all civilian authority represented a stark challenge to constitutional and republican protections of liberty. It also presaged the future of a doctrine of emergency powers, one that subsequent American leaders have not hesitated to invoke when the nation has been threatened with imminent danger. The formal political challenge to create such a doctrine did not, however, materialize until the congressional refund debates over Jackson's fine in the 1840s, more than twenty years after his imposition of martial law in 1814–15. In the immediate aftermath of the New Orleans episode, the government never officially investigated or reprimanded Jackson's conduct. In 1815, Secretary of War Alexander Dallas sent letters to the general questioning his use of the military, but neither Dallas nor President Madison desired to formally wrestle with the issue. In fact, it was Jackson who marched to Washington in the months following his victory to confront Dallas and ensure that the government understood the paramount need for military rule.[15] The secretary and president simply declined to pursue the matter. Such a decision most certainly stemmed from the swelling nationalism surrounding Jackson in the aftermath of the New Orleans victory and the desire to put behind them a miserable war that had few successes.

Madison's failure to act opened a gaping hole in the future protection of civil liberties. The refusal to challenge Jackson's conduct surely encouraged his belief that when it came to the nation's defense, extreme measures were justified. It also convinced the sometimes rash general that he had a license to bend the law to his uncompromising will. He did not hesitate to follow his notions of how best to protect the nation when only three years later, in 1818, he crossed into Spanish Florida to chastise Seminole Indians for attacking American settlements and in the process tried and executed two British citizens. In that instance, John Quincy Adams, then secretary of state, defended the general's conduct as national self-defense, justified by the law of nature.[16] By the time Jackson became president, he had fully embraced the idea that threats to the Union demanded rigorous action. Hence he battled the Bank of the United States, removed federal deposits, and threatened to hang nullifiers.

All of these episodes revolved around a single, steadfast Jacksonian principle: sanctity of the Union. Jackson's belief, cemented in his own blood as well as that of family and friends, is what inspired the famous Jefferson birthday dinner toast at which the general stared down arch nullifier John C. Calhoun and boomed, "Our Union: It must be preserved." Some scholars have viewed Jackson's unionist stance during the Nullification crisis as an unexpected and contradictory idea in relation to his views on states' rights, but in reality Jackson had always been staunchly unionist. As one early-twentieth-century historian wrote, "His political creed was preservation of the Union."[17] Whether the threat came from a British army or corruption within government, Jackson viewed them as equally dangerous to the survival of the United States. He had fought for the nation's independence during the American Revolution and from the turmoil and sacrifice of his youth came to understand that without constant vigilance, the Union would not survive. Awash in a sea of monarchy and despotism, the infant Republic required defenders who were willing to hazard everything to see it through to adulthood. Thomas Jefferson understood this point and embarked on an embargo policy in 1807 that included radical measures which violated civil liberties. He did so, as one historian noted, because he "believed that the nation lived in a continual crisis, the security of its republican institutions menaced internally and by foreign foes."[18] Jackson was no different, nor was he merely reacting to his own delusional inner demons about conspiracies. The dangers to the Union were real, and Jackson met them with resolve and ferocity. Historians who fail to recognize such points, refusing to acknowledge that Jackson, despite his many faults, was committed to the Union's survival, do a disservice to the nation's history. Even the general's opponents acknowledged his patriotism. It is one thing to disagree with Jackson's methods and conduct but something entirely different to conclude that he had no vision for America. To understand Jackson's devotion to Union, one need only read his Farewell Address, in which he dwelled on the importance of Union and the dangers facing it, or his last will and testament, in which he bequeathed to his nephew, Andrew Jackson Donelson, a commemorative sword given by the state of Tennessee, admonishing the young man that "he fail not to use it when necessary in support and protection of our glorious Union, and for the protection of the Constitutional rights of our beloved country should they be assailed by foreign enemies or domestic traitors."[19]

This portrait of Jackson as defender of the Union is hardly new. John William Ward's seminal text, *Andrew Jackson: Symbol for an Age*, explored the significance of Jackson's first great victory, entitling the book's initial chapter, "In the Beginning Was New Orleans." Ward insisted that "contemporary estimates of the Battle of New Orleans, at the very outset of Andrew Jackson's career, present in embryo the dominant conceptual strains which later characterize the fully developed symbol of Jackson." He achieved victory in a battle that most expected to be lost and in doing so secured the success of the Revolution. Ward explained the "moral blow" that America had been dealt during the War of 1812. With the nation's capital in ashes and British forces wreaking havoc throughout the Chesapeake Bay region, Americans expected little beyond more British punishment. "Into this atmosphere of gloom and doubt," wrote Ward, "burst the news of Andrew Jackson's crushing victory over the British before New Orleans." Americans, he continued, "were vicariously purged of shame and frustration. At a moment of disillusionment, Andrew Jackson reaffirmed the young nation's self-belief; he restored its sense of national prowess and destiny." As a result, Jackson came to symbolize American qualities of "nature," "providence," and "will." He became the representative and embodiment of American nationalism.[20]

Yet Jackson's symbolism went far beyond Ward's depiction. His appeal may have begun as a simple nationalist allure, a unity of sentiment among the people, but it did not take long for both Jackson and his many followers to build that nationalism into a formidable political power that carried him to the steps of the White House. Ward followed Jackson's symbolism throughout his career, to his death, utilizing numerous funeral orations to depict Jackson's and the age's particularly American qualities. Still, Ward never wholly grasped the intense partisan combat of the period or how it was influenced by Jackson and, in turn, how it influenced the general's image. Beginning in the early 1820s and fully developed by the 1830s, Jackson came to embody at least two strains of symbolism: he was viewed as both a hero and despot. Out of these two images, the symbol that best represented Jackson revolved entirely around one's party identity. To Democrats, Jackson was ever the hero and patriot, battling foreign enemies and corrupt domestic forces, each intent on grasping power and endangering the Union. Whigs, in turn, viewed Jackson himself as the greatest threat to the nation. Citing his abuse of the veto power and various questionably constitutional acts such as removal of the federal deposits from the Bank of the United States, Whigs dubbed the president King Andrew I. Thus the political combat of the second American party system directly fueled the duality of Jackson's image. One might argue that he became both a symbol and an antisymbol.[21] Yet the key was still New Orleans. For that famous battle revealed what Ward called the "embryo" of Jackson's symbolism. In the general's defense of New Orleans and his imposition of martial law lay the seeds of heroism and despotism.

Though Jackson's duality existed from the outset, the negative component of his symbolism was completely subsumed by nationalist euphoria following the New Orleans victory. The first tangible concerns over martial law did not develop until the midst of Jackson's 1824 and 1828 presidential bids. Some believed that his popularity in the initial election would wane rather quickly; he was, after all, a military man, not a politician. Yet as Jackson's support continued to rise and he appeared a genuine threat, opponents grasped at everything, even the previously sacrosanct New Orleans, to whittle the general down. To such challenges Jackson's supporters responded by wrapping the general in the still-potent nationalism of the battle, as they continued to do throughout his life. The sparring over martial law in the 1820s was to some extent a foreshadowing of what was to come when Jackson's refund bill appeared in Congress in 1842. The arguments in these election years hardly approached the development and complexity that they did some twenty years later during the debates, but they did reveal the extent to which partisanship influenced the dialogue over martial law and the future protection of civil liberties.

By the presidential election of 1840, the second American party system had come to fruition, with complex, highly organized political machines existing in virtually every state. It was into this Age of Party that Jackson's refund bill arrived. As the symbolic centerpiece of the system, Jackson divided people along sharply defined partisan lines. As historian Michael Holt has written, "Because few could remain neutral about Jackson, even after he left office, he injected an emotional context into the new party conflict at its birth. His name alone could polarize parties and energize supporters."[22] When the bill to refund Jackson's fine appeared, Democrats and Whigs seized it as a partisan tool to aid their respective parties. In such an atmosphere, there was little chance of engaging in a dispassionate dialogue about civil liberties versus military power or when paramount necessity might justify the use of extreme measures to save the Union. Though members of both parties expressed varying opinions over the complexities of republican ideology, the sanctity of the Constitution, and the question of "necessary" emergency powers, all of these issues were engulfed within the larger aim of party strategizing. Moreover, the debates in the 1840s were strikingly abstract. The nation's leaders argued about a military commander's power in times of danger when in fact the threats of the War of 1812 were a distant memory.

The partisanship connected to the refund bill was further exacerbated by its timing. The 1840 election marked the first presidential victory for Whigs, who had finally awoken to Democratic campaign strategies of fine-tuned political organization and the use of campaign symbols.[23] The Democratic defeat revealed organizational problems within the party, not the least of which was the loss of its greatest unifying symbol when Jackson retired in 1837. Though the Democracy had dominated the national political scene for years, the party was now in trouble. Writing in 1844, Thomas Ritchie, editor of the *Richmond Enquirer*, lamented, "For forty years . . . I have been Editor of a paper and never have I seen the . . . party in so much danger." Another party member, writing to Martin Van Buren, noted simply that the party was "in a bad way."[24]

The bill to refund Jackson's fine came in the midst of this political gloom. Whigs, sensing Democratic weakness and viewing everything through the lens of partisan maneuvering, were quick to sniff out a campaign ploy and charged the bill was merely a ruse to bring the old hero before the people once again and in doing so aid a faltering Democratic Party. Though this was not the actual impetus of the bill (Jackson had devised the refund legislation without this goal in mind), it did not take Democrats long to embrace such a strategy. Writing to Jackson at the outset of the refund battle, Francis Preston Blair, the general's longtime friend, political advisor, and editor of the Washington-based *Democratic Globe*, understood that the bill could be used to ignite the passions and nationalism of the people, noting, "I think it a good occasion to renew the impression on the public mind . . . [of] your glorious efforts in the last act of the war. . . . A revival of your military triumphs will give it [the Democratic Party] strength in its present contest with Federalism."[25] Following this strategy, Blair published some thirty-five articles in the *Globe* over the course of the debates in order to rouse interest in Jackson's struggle as well as the Democratic Party's role in fighting for the nation's preeminent hero and, hence, the Union itself.[26] Such a tactic on the part of Democrats brought forth petitions from private citizens and spurred party organization on the state level in the form of legislative resolutions.[27]

This attempt to utilize Jackson's popularity was nothing new for Democrats. When Jackson retired from the presidency, his party realized the need to transfer some of what historian Thomas Brown has called Jackson's "charisma" from the general to the party as a whole and thus to his successor, Martin Van Buren. Brown noted, "the literal meaning of charisma—was of course his generalship of the American forces in the Battle of New Orleans." Secondary charisma came from Jackson's defeat in the 1824 presidential election and the Jacksonian-inspired belief that the people's will had been thwarted by unprincipled politicians. Even in his own day, as Brown explained, Jackson's charisma, or symbolism, was used and expanded through "such devices as partisan speechmaking, barbecues, parades, and, of course, all manner of things made of hickory." Brown concluded that Jackson was "a symbol that proved of inestimable value in advancing his own fortunes and those of his party." Michael Holt forged a similar line of thought by insisting that party leaders consciously provoked conflict over Jackson to energize supporters. He gave as an example a movement by Pennsylvania Democrats in 1846 to recess the legislature on January 8 to celebrate the Battle of New Orleans, noting that the motion "had the desired effect of polarizing the parties against each other immediately."[28]

In light of such strategizing on the part of Democrats, there is little wonder that Whigs viewed the refund bill as little more than yet another maneuver to raise Jackson to the party's masthead and reap the rewards of his symbolism. This fact, along with the already prevalent partisan tension within the age of the second American party system, fueled a bickering and meanness that epitomized politics of the period. Yet at the same time, the nation's leaders clashed over one of the most fundamental doctrines in the Republic's history: the protection of liberty. The result is a complexity of partisan motivation steeped in the long-held tradition of republicanism. To some extent, Democrats and Whigs utilized the language of "liberty" and "power," well known to Americans of the day, for partisan advantage. In this sense, republicanism itself became a partisan tool manipulated for political profit.

Sorting out the often murky boundaries between party tactics and principled, ideological conviction is no easy task. Many political statesmen of the antebellum period were rhetorical geniuses who adeptly weaved their own and their party's goals within a broadly defined contextual framework that embraced the most cherished notions of constitutional government and American political ideals. One consideration in developing this book has been an attempt to determine the intersection between high-toned oratory and the more scheming political maneuvers utilized to gain and maintain party power. Admittedly, such a goal is at best elusive, at worst impossible, and it is made that much more difficult when wrestling with the ubiquity of republican ideology in the early Republic. It exists everywhere from the colonial period through the Civil War. Yet it is nonetheless fascinating and important to consider the extent to which partisanship shaped the use of republicanism as a mechanism for structuring political perception

One example is provided by the congressional refund debates, during which numerous politicians on both sides of Congress trumpeted the sanctity of liberty for partisan gain. This reality strikes hard against the notion that the tenets of republicanism were too hallowed and the nation's statesmen too steadfast in their devotion to sully the doctrine of liberty for mere party machination. Robert Remini, for example, insisted that "in the 1820s these ideals about liberty and virtue were not pious platitudes glibly uttered and devoid of substance and relevance. They had real meaning to the people of this dawning Jacksonian age and were not lightly bantered about by insensitive politicians. These ideas were the very soul of the nation, the principles upon which the political life of the American people depended." Remini is not alone in arriving at such conclusions. Harry Watson made similar arguments about the sanctity of republicanism when considering Jackson's presidency and the effects of the market revolution on the nation's economy and politics. "The President and his key spokesman meant what they said," he insisted. "Their ideas and actions were logically derived from their eighteenth-century heritage, especially from the still-vivid ideology of the American Revolution and its aftermath, as well as from the experience of their own lives."[29] Although there is no question that republicanism was the paramount ideology of the period, the extent to which it became infused with the rising politicking of the day is intriguing.

The understanding that republican ideology was utilized as a partisan tool is all the more important when considering the degree to which historians have identified it as a factor in the Civil War.[30] Writing of Abraham Lincoln's Republican Party, Michael Morrison noted, "Like every American politician stretching back to the pristine Washington, Republicans carefully, purposefully, identified their position with the revolutionary generation. . . . Speaking the language of republicanism, the Republican Party justified its cause." Yet it was not merely Republicans who embraced the ideology of liberty to better explain the political battles of their day. Southerners, too, viewed the tumultuous events of the 1840s and 1850s through the lens of republican understanding. Morrison develops this point in detail, declaring that "historians have been slow to explore fully the manner in which this commonly shared heritage was modified."[31] Yet the issue extends far beyond modification. Indeed, politicians were not modifying so much as they were manipulating republican ideology. As early as 1978, Michael Holt pointed to the idea that Republicans consciously used republican ideology to gain power, arguing that "the most successful tactic had been to pose as a champion of republican values and to portray the opponent as anti-republican, as unlawful, tyrannical, or aristocratic." He continued: "Republican politicians quite consciously seized on the slavery and sectional issue in order to build a new party."[32] In light of such assertions, and the evidence provided by the congressional refund debates, historians need to look more closely at the degree to which politicians, from the inception of the Constitution to the firing on Fort

Sumter, consciously manipulated the language of republicanism for party advantage.

Even when writing about parties in the midst of the Civil War, historians have focused on republicanism and insisted that one party or the other were better defenders of liberty. Speaking of northern Democrats, Jean Baker explained that an "antiauthoritarian tradition instilled apprehensiveness about liberty and a need to anticipate future encroachments." Thus, "as the war continued, Democrats did not abate their warnings. Nor did they change their position that civil liberties were the essence of Americanness." Joel Silbey made similar claims, insisting that the Democratic Party's protection of civil liberties during the war grew "out of an ideology rooted in their traditions and experiences and the perceptions developed in their past about the role and power of government."[33] The point here is not that such claims are entirely false. Rather, the importance is in attempting to determine the degree to which partisan strategizing was interwoven within the cries for fragile liberty and the charges that political opponents were despotic. One simply cannot discount the degree to which partisan animosity of Lincoln's Republican administration weighed into high-toned Democratic professions concerning the sanctity of liberty and writs of habeas corpus.

The fact is that a mere twenty years earlier, Democrats had been just as outspoken in their defense of Jackson's infringement of liberties and suspension of the writ of habeas corpus. They successfully concluded the general's refund bill in February 1844, passing it in the House on the January 8 anniversary of the Battle of New Orleans, and though the final bill did not include a word on the legality of martial law or the ideological and constitutional complexities of Jackson's actions, one could assume that its passage was an acknowledgment of the general's and of Democratic views. Indeed, there is formidable evidence to prove that the refund debates had a profound impact on military and legal opinions in the years following the debates. In essence, Jackson received his precedent. This is certainly the position held by Abraham Lincoln. Writing in 1863 to critics of his war policies, Lincoln cited the conduct of General Jackson and "its subsequent approval by the American Congress" as a justification for his own curtailment of liberties during the Civil War.[34] In the 1860s, it was Lincoln's turn to use Jackson's symbolic unionist appeal for political and nationalist effect.

Nor did Lincoln concern himself with the fact that his own former party, the Whigs, had battled Democrats over Jackson's suspension of civil liberties. Lincoln, along with Whigs who had participated in and lambasted Jackson during the 1840s refund debates, came to understand the importance of necessity and the role of military power in safeguarding the Union. Thus when it came to a doctrine of emergency powers, the main difference between Democrats and Whigs of the 1840s, and Democrats and Republicans of the 1860s, was who invoked such a doctrine. Partisanship was a key factor in all of the parties' professions over endangered liberty and the balance between military and civilian spheres. Hence the ultimate irony in the history of America's precedent for declaring martial law, of emergency presidential powers in time of war, and of the delicate equilibrium between military force and civilian authority is derived from political maneuvering over Andrew Jackson during the Age of Party. This is not to say that some of these partisans failed to believe in their professions over liberty, but it is a fact that party affiliation played an important role in such ideological disputes.

Thus the story of Andrew Jackson and martial law engages a variety of important subjects related to the early national period. At the most basic level, this book is about the other half of the New Orleans victory. Although numerous works have detailed the battle itself, none have investigated the specifics of martial law or how it followed Jackson throughout his career.[35] This history is particularly relevant as it relates to Jackson's character. The general may have been many things, among them stubborn, sometimes rash, and most certainly willing to seize power in order to gain victory, but he was certainly no fool. Nor was he the incapacitated, howling maniac that some historians have contended. Jackson was every bit as skillful a politician as he was a general. He never lost a military battle and rarely lost a political one.

This book is also about America's political, legal, constitutional, and military history as they relate to martial law. The congressional refund debates are a rich resource, and as such I spend considerable time discussing varying aspects of what legislators argued. As a result, there naturally exists some overlap between chapters. Yet the importance of distinguishing between the core arguments within the debates, I believe, warrants some repetition.

One of the important results of the debates was an evolution of emergency powers in the United States. Jackson was the first to impose martial law, and from his actions and the ensuing congressional debates a new theory developed. Prior to the debates, the term "martial law" had always denoted a set of rules for the military and was therefore synonymous with "military law." Neither term included military rule of civilians. Following the refund debates, however, a new definition entered legal and military treatises. The term "martial law" now empowered the military with emergency authority over civilians. Thus the strict, doctrinal balance between the military and civilian spheres was slowly chipped away so that in times of great danger, generals, the president, and even governors could declare martial law and infringe civil liberties if doing so ultimately safeguarded the nation. Such an understanding has inspired numerous curtailments of civil liberty: Abraham Lincoln during the Civil War, various governors during the labor unrest of the late nineteenth century, Woodrow Wilson with the Espionage and Sedition Acts of World War I, Franklin Delano Roosevelt's Supreme Court–condoned act of imprisoning Japanese Americans during World War II, and creation of the Patriot Act in the aftermath of the September 11 attack on the United States. These are but a few examples. A more detailed history of martial law and the curtailment of civil liberties is needed to more fully understand this subject for the late nineteenth through the twenty-first century.[36]

Intermeshed within the evolution of martial law is the nature of party power in the early Republic. The second American party system spurred the development of massive, highly organized party structures throughout the nation, and though some historians have recently questioned this "party period concept," arguing instead that antiparty sentiment, the role of third-party movements, and the overall social and cultural complexity of the nation during this era diminished the possibility of such power among two parties, the fact remains that Democrats and Whigs wielded significant influence on the overall dialogue of the period.[37] One way they did so was through the duality of Jackson's symbolic appeal. Old Hickory defined the partisan boundaries of the two-party system. He inspired either devotion or repulsion, and both parties utilized him as symbol or antisymbol in order to gain power. As such, Jackson as symbol was in many ways critical to the health and stability of the party system. Michael Holt has even gone so far as to argue that Jackson's retirement from office was one factor in why the two-party system of Democrats and Whigs disintegrated and a party system based on sectionalism arose, out of which erupted the Civil War.[38]

Clearly, then, the subject of symbolism and how it aids party power is also a component of this work. To many, Jackson represented the pinnacle of American nationalism. The Battle of New Orleans had invested him with the highest claims of patriotism and devotion to country. Jackson came to understand this early on. He used it to his advantage and for what he believed was in the best interest of the nation, invading Florida in 1818, riding into the White House in 1828, and challenging nullifiers in 1832–33, to name but a few episodes. Jackson's understanding of his own nationalist appeal is one of the items that made him a formidable politician and president. Subsequent presidents have embraced the same political use of nationalism. Lincoln focused on the sanctity of Union during the Civil War and in order to secure the nation's survival embraced martial law. Consider also the nationalism fomented by Franklin Roosevelt in the midst of the Great Depression. He utilized the overwhelming nationalist support of the 1936 election to challenge the Supreme Court's threats to his New Deal legislation much in the way that Jackson maneuvered his victory in 1832 as a mandate to remove federal deposits from the Bank of the United States. FDR also realized that engagement in World War II was impossible without nationalist sentiment, which arrived in the form of the 1941 attack on Pearl Harbor. Similarly, President George W. Bush could not possibly have engaged in a war against Iraq in 2002 or curtailed civil liberties with the Patriot Act without the nationalism spawned by the September 11 attack on New York's World Trade Center.[39] Essentially, history reveals that the limits of the Constitution can be challenged, and, more specifically, large-scale abridgements of civil liberties can be sanctioned when broad nationalism also exists.

Unlike many other politicians, Andrew Jackson had an amazing advantage when it came to maintaining his nationalist allure. With the Battle of New Orleans celebrated every year, the source of Jackson's nationalism was reinvested annually. During the interim, Democratic supporters raised hickory poles, held patriotic fêtes, and in doing so continually reminded Americans of Jackson, the hero of New Orleans. Thus even in retirement Andrew Jackson remained a potent political symbol who could raise the flags and fortunes of Democrats and Whigs. This is most certainly why the era is known as the Age of Jackson, rather than that of Calhoun, Clay, Adams, or any other mere politician.

CHAPTER 1

New Orleans under Martial Law

New Orleans invited invasion. The British attempted it in 1814–15, and in 1862, Union flag officer David G. Farragut entered the city successfully. Not only did the mighty Mississippi wend its way to the city's front door, but the myriad bayous and inlets leading from Lakes Bourgne and Ponchartrain, as well as the overland route from Mobile, left New Orleans ripe for the taking. Though Union troops captured the city during the Civil War, British forces during the War of 1812 were not so fortunate. Standing in their way was Maj. Gen. Andrew Jackson, commander of the seventh military district. The Tennessee general staged a stunning defense that saved New Orleans from the most formidable army ever arrayed against America. Yet victory did not come without costs. Concerns over spies and dissent within the largely foreign city prompted Jackson to proclaim martial law. In doing so, the fiery general achieved two firsts: he defeated an overwhelming enemy force, killing and wounding some twenty-two hundred British soldiers while sustaining only minimal American casualties,[1] and he became the first American general to supplant civil government with military rule. The first story is well known. The second remains all but a mystery. This fact is surprising considering the many volumes on both the War of 1812 and Andrew Jackson. One historian even noted that New Orleans was a critical beginning for Old

Hickory and was the beginning for his symbolic, national appeal.[2] Still, Jackson's conduct under martial law, the court case that ensued, and the controversial legacy that followed the general in later years have not been adequately explored.

It is particularly important that one understand the circumstances leading up to the declaration of martial law, as well as Jackson's conduct while the military was in power, the specifics of the court battle with Judge Dominick A. Hall, and the general's actions concerning a "mild rebuke" he received from President Madison. It is only after investigating these issues that one can begin to understand why the Battle of New Orleans was such a pivotal beginning for Andrew Jackson. For it was in the midst of saving the Crescent City that he revealed both the heroism and despotism that later came to be fully recognized in later years. At the heart of these competing ideals were classic republican antagonists, liberty and power. On the one hand, Jackson fought for American liberty. Yet he utilized a means to achieve victory which struck at the very heart of liberty and constitutionalism. There is little wonder why the martial-law episode followed Jackson throughout his life.

Martial Law Declared

Jackson did not declare martial law on a whim. For months prior to his arrival in New Orleans, he received urgent pleas from Governor William C. C. Claiborne and others within the city to take military control of the unsettled and significantly foreign population. "On the native Americans and a vast majority of the Creoles of the country, I place much confidence," wrote the governor in August 1814, "but there are others much devoted to the Interest of Spain, and whose partiality for the English, is not less observable than their dislike to the American Government."[3] Claiborne complained that the state legislature had in the past failed to respond to potential threats of rumored British invasions, and when he attempted to prepare the city, members of the legislature thwarted his plans. The governor subsequently wrote Jackson in September: "There is in this City a much *greater spirit of Disaffection* than I had anticipated." Others wrote the general that Claiborne was the problem, noting that "the total want of Confidence by all Classes of people, in the Chief Magistrate of the State, puts it in a truely [sic] alarming Situation." Some of Claiborne's complaints undoubtedly stemmed from longstanding political disputes. He had been governor since 1803, when Louisiana joined the Union as a territory, then was formally elected to the position upon statehood in 1811. During that time, political baggage had most certainly caused Claiborne to rail against those who he believed were not doing their part in preparing for the British invasion. The repeated and conflicting warnings served to prejudice Jackson's view of the inhabitants of New Orleans, especially the foreign population. "We have more to dread from Spies, and traitors, than from open enemies," he wrote Claiborne. "Vigilance and Energy is only wanting and all is safe."[4]

The turmoil in New Orleans was, of course, not the first time that conspiracies and plots presented a potential danger to the city. Aaron Burr's infamous attempt to separate the southern portion of the newly acquired Louisiana Territory in 1805–7 had prompted similar concerns. As a result of the warnings over Burr, Gen. James Wilkinson, who was also a longtime friend of Burr's and a co-conspirator, attempted to suspend the writ of habeas corpus and proclaim martial law. He was rebuffed by then–territorial governor Claiborne, who insisted that only the legislature possessed such an authority. Nonetheless, Wilkinson arrested suspects and those he considered accomplices, illegally transported some to the East Coast, defied writs of habeas corpus issued by an Orleans County judge, James Workman, and imprisoned the judge for actively engaging "in the nefarious projects." Workman stood trial and was ultimately acquitted. The result of Wilkinson's defiance of the writ of habeas corpus was the 1807 Supreme Court decision *Ex parte Bollman and Swartwout,* which declared that only the legislature could suspend the writ. Prior to this decision, who exactly could suspend the writ of habeas corpus was in some question. The Constitution allowed suspension, discussing it under article 9, section 2, noting: "The Privilege of the Writ of Habeas Corpus shall not be suspended, unless when in Cases of Rebellion or Invasion the public Safety may require it." Though this was stated under the section discussing the legislative branch, it was not clear that only the legislature had such an authority. During the Burr conspiracy, President Jefferson had undoubtedly assumed that only the legislature could do so and in fact requested that they suspend the writ in response to reports of Burr's activities in the West. Congress did not abide by the president's request.[5]

With this turbulent history in the not distant past, Claiborne and the citizens of New Orleans were eminently aware of threats to the city and the potential actions of the military. It was thus no small matter that Claiborne, who had refused the principle of a general suspending the writ of habeas corpus, changed his mind in light of the pending British invasion and the belief that spies and traitors abounded. Once Jackson arrived in the city on December 1, he immediately began preparations for the British assault. For two weeks he inspected the various routes into the city, judged their defensibility, and dispatched troops to warn of the enemy's arrival. He also contemplated the best course of action to control the disaffection reported by the governor. On December 10, the general wrote Claiborne, requesting him to "obtain the sence [sic] of the Legislature how far they will aid in erecting the works for the defence of the State." The request was not solely about money, for he added, "Should I be disappointed in the laudable feelings, that I am induced to believe pervades your whole Legislature, it is necessary that I should know it, that I may employ what means I have in my power for the best defence of this Section of the District that is intrusted for my care."

Claiborne must have engaged in a persuasive session with the legislature. On December 14, a joint resolution passed both state houses appropriating twenty thousand dollars to be expended under the governor's orders. Still, both Claiborne and Jackson remained suspicious, perhaps in part because the legislature refused to suspend the writ of habeas corpus in order to allow the impressment of seamen for duty on the American ships *Louisiana* and *Carolina*. The governor therefore requested the legislature to adjourn for two to three weeks. They refused, insisting that many reasons existed for continuing the session, not the least of which was that it would cost more to travel to their homes than remain within the city.[6]

The legislature's refusal to suspend their session, combined with distressing reports about spies, did little to allay Jackson's concerns over the loyalty of those in the city. Compounding his anxiety was the connection between certain citizens in New Orleans and those in the Spanish-ruled town of Pensacola, Florida. Spies had already been detected there, and, more important, the British had stationed troops in the Spanish fort, Barancas. Old Hickory ultimately solved the latter problem by invading the city in November 1814 and driving the English from the area, but in the meantime they had arrived below New Orleans and approached the Baratarian pirate, Jean Lafitte, to enlist his aid in capturing the city. Lafitte had cleverly stalled the British and informed members of the Louisiana legislature of the enemy's plan.[7] Yet the

British infiltration into the area alarmed the general, and on December 15 he published an address to the citizens: "The Major-General commanding has with astonishment and regret learned that great consternation and alarm pervade your city. . . . The General with still greater astonishment, has heard that British emissaries have been permitted to propagate sedi[t]ious reports amongst you." Jackson cautioned that "the rules and articles of war annex the punishment of death to any person hol[d]ing secret correspondenc[e] with the enemy creating false alarm or supplying him with provision." The regulations to which he referred were traditionally applicable to soldiers only, but the implication of Jackson's warning was that every "person," civilian or otherwise, would be held accountable to the military code of conduct. He subsequently announced that all citizens were expected to engage in the country's defense, declaring that "should the general be disappointed in this expectation he will separate our enemies from our friends. Those who are not for us are against us, and will be dealt with accordingly."[8]

This ominous warning foreshadowed the proclamation of martial law. Prior to publishing his address, Jackson contemplated imposing military rule and requested the legal opinions of two leading New Orleans attorneys, both of whom acted as his aides. Jackson's advisors, Edward Livingston and Abner Duncan, ultimately concluded that martial law suspended all civil functions and placed every citizen under military control. The lawyers disagreed, however, on the legality of the proclamation. Livingston believed that it was "unknown to the Constitution or Laws of the U.S." and thus "justified only by the necissity [sic] of the Case and that therefore the General proclaims it at his own risque and under his responsibility." Taking a decidedly different view, Duncan insisted that the constitutional provision authorizing suspension of the writ of habeas corpus impliedly permitted the operation of martial law and that it was the "guardian of the Public safety" who is "to judge of those cases provided for by the Constitution."[9] The question of martial law's legality was an important one considering that a key provision was suspension of the writ of habeas corpus. Though the Constitution did allow suspension, and the Supreme Court's decree in *Ex parte Bollman and Swartwout* ruled that only the national legislature had that authority to implement such an act, even that decision did not define or authorize the use of martial law as implemented by Jackson. Indeed, American law had no precedent for such an action. The nation's military and legal treatises referred to martial law as strictly a code of conduct for the military. It was synonymous with military law and not applicable to civilians. By the early nineteenth century, the British had evolved in their understanding of martial law so that it included the more extraordinary meaning of the term. Yet Americans, ever vigilant in their defense of liberty, shunned the notion of extreme military rule as invoked through martial law. Jackson, therefore, had no American precedent, no legal authority to make such a decree.[10]

Jackson did not quibble over the question of constitutionality presented by Livingston and Duncan. He was satisfied that martial law canceled all civilian authority and placed the city under military control. On December 16, he issued the proclamation. All who entered or exited the city were required to report to the adjutant general's office. Failure to do so resulted in arrest and interrogation. All vessels, boats, or other crafts desiring to leave the city required a passport either from the general, his staff, or Commodore Daniel T. Patterson. All street lamps were ordered extinguished at 9:00 p.m., and anyone found after that hour without a pass was arrested and held as a spy. New Orleans was officially an armed camp and General Jackson the only authority.[11]

The city buzzed with energy and trepidation as the military prepared for battle. Jackson ordered the bayous from Lakes Bourgne and Ponchartrain blocked and guards posted to warn of the enemy's arrival. Every slave, horse, ox, and cart was requisitioned for military use, and the general authorized the enlistment of all Indians within the district to serve on the same footing as the militia. Mayor Nicholas Girod received orders to "search every house and Store in the City, for muskets, Bayonets, Cartridge Boxes, Spades, shovels, pick axes, and hoes" and leave receipts for all items. Jackson also addressed the failure of some citizens to follow Governor Claiborne's muster order, warning that those failing to comply "shall be punished with the utmost severity." He then requested Girod to supply him with the name and age of every person under the age of fifty who was not yet enrolled in the militia. To ease the financial burden of those required to serve, the legislature passed an act suspending for four months all debt payments, seizure or sale of property, and any pending civil suits. Additionally, both state and federal judges closed their courts and released all prisoners without bail in return for their service in the militia.[12]

In the midst of these hurried preparations, Jackson was faced with an annoying dilemma. Accustomed to his premier status after serving as governor since 1803, William Claiborne quickly came to resent

Jackson issuing the declaration of martial law. From John Frost, Pictorial Life of Andrew Jackson, *1847.*

Jackson's domineering command. Essentially pushed aside by Jackson, Claiborne vented his injured pride in a letter to Secretary of War James Monroe. Assuring the secretary that he would follow Jackson's orders, Claiborne nevertheless whined about his "military talents" and requested that "General Jackson may be instructed to consider me as second in Command of the Forces to be employed within this State." Unable to await orders from Monroe, the governor drafted a heated note to Jackson requesting a private interview. Evidently, the meeting went poorly, for Claiborne did not receive the desired command. He never forgot the implicit affront to his self-proclaimed military prowess, but Jackson had little time to worry about the governor's wounded pride. On December 23, Maj. Gabriel Villeré reported that the British had surprised his post and entered the country with a large force through Bayou Bienvenue. Jackson immediately prepared an offensive. A question, however, remained: Had not he ordered all bayous blocked? How then could the enemy obtain entry? Writing his brother-in-law, Robert Hays, Jackson revealed his misgivings about the loyalty of the citizens in New Orleans: "*I fear the enemy obtained* their foothold through the treachery of the guard—they were of the . . . militia of the country." Major Villeré was later court-martialed for harboring and protecting the enemy and neglect of duty, a charge for which he was acquitted and of which Jackson approved.[13]

The Battle for New Orleans

For the next several weeks, Jackson's primary concern was defeat of the British army encamped beyond the Chalmette plain. His main line of defense stood directly in front of the Rodriguez canal, an abandoned mill race. Here the American forces erected a massive breastwork stretching from the Mississippi River on the west to an impenetrable cypress swamp on the east. In an attempt to build up the rampart, Jackson employed digging crews who were quickly hampered by the soggy Louisiana soil, which continuously slid back into the canal. As a result, the general ordered every inch of nearby picket fencing torn down and built into the breastwork as a support. In all, American forces destroyed some nine hundred acres of fencing valued at over $10,000. They also razed Negro houses, stables, chicken coops, and numerous other structures for fuel and to fortify their line. The damage to private property caused by Americans alone amounted to some $160,000. In addition to wood, Jackson's engineers added 250 bales of cotton confiscated from a nearby ship to help stabilize the rampart, but the ease with which the bales caught fire from British hot-shot forced their removal. Damage to the land on which the Americans made their stand was extensive. John Rodriguez, the owner of the famous canal, lamented that the military had done irreparable harm to his property and in the aftermath of the battle petitioned Jackson for redress.[14]

The extensive work and materials devoted to the breastwork proved successful on December 28, when the British launched a probing attack to gauge the American position, and again on January 1, when the two armies engaged in an artillery duel that shook the country for miles around. To the Americans' delight, the hastily constructed mud wall absorbed British cannon balls. Jackson's fortifications proved equally successful on January 8, when the enemy launched its main offensive. Attempting to storm the general's line, British forces were mowed down

"The Glorious Victory of New Orleans," engraving on cloth. The Historic New Orleans Collection, accession no. 1947.19i.vii.

by the well-directed American fire. Casualty figures showed the extent of the victory: Americans lost only six men with an additional seven wounded. British casualties reached nearly twenty-two-hundred.

Jackson's forces on the right bank of the Mississippi did not fair nearly as well. With no colossal barricade, and woefully ill equipped (a large portion of the men had no arms at all), the Kentucky Militia retreated before a small enemy force in what many observers described as a panic. Jackson, known for his quick temper, unleashed his disgust to the militia commander, Gen. David Morgan: "The want of Discipline, the want of Order, a total disregard to Obedience, and a Spirit of insubordination, not less distructive [sic] than Cowardice itself, this appears to be the cause which led to the disaster.—And the Cause must be eradicated or I must cease to command, and I desire to be distinctly understood, that every breach of Orders, all want of discipline, every disattention of duty will be severely and promptly punished." Jackson's reprimand revealed his uncompromising and at times harsh view of duty, and though he berated Morgan, he also perceived the vulnerability of the general's command and sent a brief order directing him to "destroy every house, and remove the fences in front of your position which may in the slightest degree interfere with its defence." Jackson acknowledged that "altho I feel great pain at the destruction of private property, and the infliction of individual injury, yet when the imperious dictates of public duty require the sacrifice I am not allowed to hesitate."[15] This almost fanatical sense of duty marked the majority of Jackson's life, both military and political. It also revealed his ability to see the larger picture regarding necessity and the periodic need for drastic actions.

The loss on the right bank was not Jackson's only difficulty during the engagements. On December 28, as a sea of red coats rolled toward the American lines, he received word from his aide Abner Duncan that the legislature was prepared to capitulate in fear of a British victory. Jackson, expressing disbelief and harried by the approaching enemy, sent orders for "the governor to make strict inquiry into the subject, and if true to blow them [the legislature] up." As he sped his way toward the city, Duncan, perhaps from the excitement of the campaign, exaggerated the order. Rather than merely inquiring into the legislature's actions, Claiborne posted guards and refused entry to the legislative hall. The moment Jackson learned of the mistake he rescinded the order, but the damage was already done. The legislature launched an investigation and issued a report blaming Duncan for overstepping his authority and Alexander DeClout, the man who informed Duncan of the alleged capitulation, for making false reports. Jackson was exonerated of wrongdoing. Nevertheless, he viewed the investigation with annoyance and a degree of paranoia. On the envelope of a letter in which the legislature requested him to order DeClout to appear before a committee, Jackson wrote, "This will show that the Legislature of Louisiana endeavored to withdraw officers from the defence of important posts to which Genl. Jackson had assigned them, thus trying by every means to frustrate his designs for the defence of the City while the enemy were in sight." Clearly, Jackson never trusted the legislature. Nor were the legislators enthralled with him. In a formal address thanking the various officers for their valiant service, Jackson's name was excluded.[16]

Martial Law Continued

The ghastly battle of January 8 was the enemy's final attempt on New Orleans. With hundreds of bodies strewn about the Chalmette plain and a large part of their command either dead or wounded, the British had little alternative but to retreat. On January 18, they silently and quickly slipped back to the awaiting British fleet. The next day, Jackson investigated the abandoned camp, then quickly penned a letter to James Monroe, noting that "there is but little doubt that his [the British army's] last exertions have been made in this quarter, at any rate, for the present season." "I hope, however," he continued, "I need not assure you that wherever I command, such a belief shall never occasion any relaxation in the measures for resistance."

Jackson, always fervent about duty, remained true to his word. For the next two months New Orleans prepared for a battle that never came. The general increased fortifications, ordered further obstruction of the bayous, and, to the regret of many, continued martial law. Jackson apparently had real concerns that the British would attempt another assault upon the city. In a letter to Claiborne, the general reported the capture of a British sailor who told of a fleet expected to arrive with reinforcements numbering fifteen thousand and a plan to attack New Orleans by land.[17] Jackson also continued to have concerns over the loyalty of those within the city, and he therefore kept an especially tight rein. Those without passes were quickly arrested and delivered to the guardhouse at the city hotel. Within ten days of declaring martial law, so many individuals, both soldiers and citizens, had been arrested that Mayor Girod wrote to Jackson complaining that "before two days the Guard House shall be full." Some citizens gained release by signing up for immediate militia duty, while others were freed after brief interrogations.[18]

In a number of cases, however, citizens languished in jail for weeks. Three such instances involved little more than being in the wrong place at the wrong time. Arrested on January 14, James Hotz (or Holtz), a plantation owner, was held until March for allegedly aiding the enemy. Originally stopped for having no pass, Hotz explained that he was trapped behind enemy lines and acknowledged that the British had visited his home on a number of occasions. The arresting officer determined that because the British did not capture Hotz, "I take it for granted that this man is a friend to our enemy. It seems he has remained peasibly on his plantation without attempting to do any-thing for the defense of his country." In a similar case, Joseph Suares, a private in the Louisiana Militia, was arrested and tried for "reliev-ing the enemy with victuals" as well as "holding correspondence with and giving intelligence to the enemy." In actuality, Suares was cap-tured by a party of British dragoons and forced to drive cattle to the enemy camp. The unfortunate militiaman was found not guilty by a court-martial on January 27 but was nevertheless held in the guard-house until the end of February. James Sterling, a civilian, was caught in an equally disagreeable and, if it were not for the seriousness of the outcome, comical situation. Captured by the British, he was in trans-port to the enemy fleet when Americans seized the boat. Rather than gaining his liberty, Sterling was lumped together with the British and thrown in prison.[19] Other civilians had similar problems while either attempting to aid the American forces or abide by the rules of martial law. James Berns, a volunteer discharged in October from the Maryland Militia, hurried to New Orleans with arms and ammunition only to be arrested on the pretext of being an enemy alien by birth. J. Davidson also had difficulty upon his arrival. A mate on a ship, Davidson explained that he feared entering the city because he was not a naturalized citizen. Once in New Orleans, he reported to the mar-shal's office, which was closed. He was soon arrested and, after being held for four days, told that he must bear arms, "as," he reported, "I must be considered as a friend or a foe." Though willing to serve, Davidson explained that his two brothers were soldiers in the British army and that he did not wish to fight because they might be a part of the British force at New Orleans. Davidson learned later that his broth-ers were not in Louisiana, and he subsequently requested release to join the militia.[20]

Military rule in New Orleans made every citizen a potential vic-tim of martial law, and although their arrests were unfortunate, men such as Suares, Berns, and Davidson at least had the benefit of being charged with a crime. Not all citizens were so lucky. From the begin-ning of February to early March, the military incarcerated well over thirty men without stating any crimes or violations. Some remained in confinement for this entire period and were listed on one morning guard report as "Citizens Without Charges."[21] Though they had few avenues of redress, not all of these men sat quietly in prison. Writing to General Jackson, an exasperated William D. Perry complained, "I have been Confined in Neworleans Guardhouse now twenty days doing no good for myself nor my country. I have not heard of any Charge against me if there is no Charge I hope your Excellency will be so good as to have me liberated . . . if there is any Charge against me your Excellency will Please to be so Condecending as to Inform Capt Chaveaux what Security your Excellency will require for my appearance at Court martial, if no Security can be taken I beg your Excellency will have me brought before yourself or the court for trial." Evidently, Perry's plea proved successful, for he was not listed on the following guardhouse report. Some residents of New Orleans went to rather extreme lengths to secure their freedom. One even wrote to Jackson's wife, Rachel, requesting her influence with the general. Foreign prisoners also had no compunction about writing letters to gain their release. On February 17, four Spaniards penned a second letter to Jackson, relating, "Some days ago we had the Honor to address to your Excellency, a Petition wherein we stated our Imprisonment & the Innocence of our cause." Ironically, the author begged Jackson to speak with the pirate, Capt. Jean Lafitte, who had boarded the men's boat at sea, apparently in an act of piracy, and thus could give "ample information" about their voyage.[22]

Desertion and mutiny among American troops prompted even more arrests. No longer perceiving a threat to their city following the January 8 victory, the citizens of New Orleans desired a return to the their former lifestyles. The rigors as well as diseases of camp life did not appeal to a citizenry motivated only by imminent invasion. Just as important, the spring planting season had arrived and fields needed tending. Even more ominous was the fear of possible slave insurrections while so many plantation owners served in the militia. Governor Claiborne therefore wrote Jackson on January 31, reporting that "applications [are] being hourly addressed to me by the militia officers of the state" and requesting discharge of their troops. Jackson, still intent on defending New Orleans, promptly denied the requests. As a result, over the next two days he received numerous reports of soldiers who had "absented" themselves from service. Though Claiborne insisted that he recalled the troops, Jackson felt compelled to lecture the governor about duty and warned that "subordination must exist in an army or it becomes worse than a mob—and it now appears, that coertion and punishment must be resorted to Enforce subbordination and prevent desertion, and neglect of duty. . . . A Just

punishment awaits all who for a moment forget themselves."[23] Seeing
danger in the general's words, Claiborne reiterated that he recalled all
troops, but remarked, "I see however *many obstacles* to this organization in the way you advise. Obstacles growing out of the militia Laws
of the State, and of *a nature so serious,* that I wish the opportunity of
explaining them to you, in person."

The governor's meeting to save the citizens of New Orleans from
militia duty proved no more successful than his attempt to force his
"military talents" on the general. And never one to make idle threats,
Jackson approved the arrest of some one hundred soldiers for offenses
ranging from desertion and mutiny, to drunkenness and sleeping on
duty. Two of the more serious cases involved the arrests of Sgt. Solomon
Brumfield and Pvt. James Harding. Both were apprehended on February 3, the very day Jackson promised punishment for deserters.
Scheduled for court-martial on February 17, Harding wrote to Jackson,
explaining that he had been denied leave to aid his wife, who was
evicted from their home, and subsequently deserted only to help
her. The private's plea did not stop the trial, and both Harding and
Brumfield had real cause for concern. Less than a month earlier
Jackson had approved the execution of six militia men for mutiny
during the Creek campaign. Ultimately found guilty for "disobedience
to orders, mutiny, desertion and using abusive and contemptuous language to their captain," both men were sentenced to be executed, a
verdict that Jackson sanctioned once again. After receiving numerous
letters and petitions, however, the general reversed the decision on
March 1, the scheduled day of execution. Both men were released, along
with James Hotz.[24]

The massive arrests for neglect of duty and desertion failed to sway
the citizens of New Orleans, and in mid-February Jackson attempted
to shock them into vigilance by declaring that "the enemy are still hov-
ering around us & perhaps meditates an attack." The general order had
little effect. Requests for dismissal from the militia continued to pour
in.[25] For the city's inhabitants, the Battle of New Orleans was over and
the need for unity and military zeal had retreated with the British. Ever
wary of being thrown in prison for desertion by the iron Jackson, a
number of citizens attempted using their ethnicity as an excuse for dismissal. Spaniards and Frenchmen barraged their respective consuls
requesting certificates of citizenship to exempt them from active military duty. Both Diego Morphy, the Spanish consul, and Chevalier de

Tousard, the French consul, approved the requests. Morphy subsequently wrote Jackson on February 17 demanding that he honor the certificates. Though it is unclear how many certificates Morphy issued, Tousard dispensed some 158 from February 11 to the beginning of March. Ironically, Tousard had noted in a January 6 letter to Jackson that he "had inspired a confidence that has united all parties and shades of opinion." Moreover, prior to the battle Tousard took pride in declaring that only one Frenchman had requested exemption from duty, noted that he had fulfilled his duty as consul by sending the man's name to the general, then announced that "the proclamation of Martial Law put an end to my duties in that respect."[26]

Tousard obviously changed his mind in light of continued military rule. It is not clear what Jackson did about militiamen claiming Spanish citizenship, but his response to the myriad Frenchmen was clever, immediate, and harsh. The general's staff combed through the city's voting rosters to determine whether the supposed French citizens had participated in city and state elections and thus in Jackson's view acted as American citizens. Following the brief investigation, Jackson released from militia duty all those who he believed to be legitimate French citizens. The uncompromising general promptly banished them from New Orleans with orders not to return until the restoration of peace or the enemy had left American waters. Tousard implored Jackson to reconsider his order, but it was not until he received a request from officers in the famed Louisiana Uniformed Battalion that the general rescinded his banishment order. Tousard, however, was forced to vacate the city.[27]

In the midst of the certificate controversy, Jackson's troubles worsened when an erroneous report of peace reached the city and was published in the *Louisiana Gazette*. He immediately wrote the editor, denying the rumor. Moreover, revealing his suspicions concerning the article's source, Jackson remarked that it would be a disgrace to surrender defenses because of "newspaper publications—often proceeding from ignorance but more frequently from dishonest design." He then directed that all further such publications be approved. Outraged by the military's blatant censorship, the editor published both the order and a protest in the paper's next edition: "Every man may read for himself, and *think* for himself; (Thank God! our thoughts are as yet unshackled!!) but as we have been *officially* informed that the city of New-Orleans is a *camp,* our readers must not expect us to take the liberty of expressing our opinion as we might in a *free* city."[28]

On February 24, William Claiborne joined the growing movement against military rule. The governor's motives were many. He not only wanted to punish Jackson for past insults, but the two had for some time been arguing over the return of slaves carried away by the British. After informing the general of a planned delegation to the English fleet to negotiate the slaves' return, Claiborne received a threatening reply from Jackson: "That is a subject on which you nor the Legislature as such has any power over . . . be assured if either the assembly or yourself attempt to interfere with subjects not belonging to you, it will be immediately arrested." Incensed by Jackson's message, the governor blasted the continuation of martial law in a heated letter to Louisiana attorney general Stephen Marerceau: "I can no longer remain a Silent Spector of the prostration of the Laws.— I therefore request you Sir, without loss of time to repair to this city, and resume your official duties . . . and on receiving information of any attempt of the Military to seize the person of any Private Citizen, not actually in the Military Service of the United States, you are specially instructed to take for his protection, and for avenging the Injured Laws of this State such measures as your knowledge of the Laws will point out." Claiborne also penned a wave of letters to James Monroe detailing the numerous arrests and the "misunderstanding" between the general and the legislature. He declared that the "violence" of Jackson's character "casts a Shade" upon his victory, "and in this Capitol he has observed a Course of Conduct which cannot be easily excused, much less justified by those who feel a proper regard for the rights of others."[29]

Clearly, tensions within the city were mounting, and perhaps in acknowledgment of this fact, Jackson allowed Brig. Gen. Stephen Hopkins, the commander at Lafourche, to dismiss the majority of his force on February 25. Yet Jackson was still not ready to release the entire militia, even though rumors of the peace treaty signed at Ghent circulated throughout New Orleans. Ever cautious, the general warned that ratification must come from both governments before peace is assured and in the meantime a defeated but still hostile British army remained within striking distance. Such warnings continued to fall upon deaf ears.

The United States versus
Major General Andrew Jackson

Jackson's attempt to rally the citizens of New Orleans was met with open defiance on March 3, when an article appeared in the *Louisiana Courier*. Responding to Jackson's order banishing French citizens, the author, "A Citizen of Louisiana of French Origin," declared

> it is high time the laws should resume their empire; that the citizens of this State should return to the full enjoyment of their rights; that, in acknowledging that we are indebted to General Jackson for the preservation of our city and the defeat of the British, we do not feel much inclined, through gratitude, to sacrifice any of our privileges, and, less than any other, that of expressing our opinion of the acts of his administration; that it is time the citizens accused of any crime should be rendered to their natural judges, and cease to be brought before special or military tribunals, a kind of institution held in abhorrence, even in absolute governments; that, after having done enough for glory, the moment of moderation has arrived; and, finally, that the acts of authority which the invasion of our country and our safety may have rendered necessary are, since the evacuation of it by the enemy, no longer compatible with our dignity and our oath of making the Constitution respected.[30]

Here was a direct challenge to General Jackson's authority. Yet he did not erupt in a rage or react hastily. Rather, he thought carefully about his next course of action and, after ascertaining the author's identity from the newspaper's editor, waited two days before issuing arrest orders for state senator Louis Louaillier. Moreover, believing that Louaillier was merely one actor in a larger conspiracy, Jackson prepared for a move by the local magistrate, including in the orders that "should any person attempt serving a writ of Habeas corpus to arrest the prisoner Louaillier from confinement immediately confine the person making such attempt." The second order showed the general's shrewd foresight. For on the very day of Louaillier's arrest, attorney Pierre Louis Morel, a witness to the arrest, petitioned Dominick Augustan Hall, a federal district judge, for a writ of habeas corpus. Apparently, Morel first solicited Appellate Court Justice Francois-Xavier Martin but was denied because Martin noted that his court handled appeals only and thus lacked authority to issue the writ. Judge Hall, who was originally appointed to the position of federal judge by Thomas

Jefferson in 1804, also questioned whether he had the authority necessary to aid Louaillier. The arrest had occurred entirely within the boundaries of Louisiana, and thus the case was a state matter and Hall was a
federal judge. Still, he ultimately acquiesced, perhaps in part because
state judge Joshua Lewis was enrolled in the militia and could not be
reached immediately.[31] Upon learning of Hall's action on the evening
of the fifth, Jackson wasted no time in arresting him for "aiding and
abetting and exciting mutiny within my camp." Moreover, he seized the
writ from the court clerk and, noting a change made on its date (Hall
had mistakenly written the sixth then changed it to the fifth), questioned
what the "juggling" was about. Showing his penchant for paranoia,
Jackson insisted that Hall's action was part of a larger conspiracy and
that the alteration was "evidence of a personal, not judicial interference." Jackson insisted that Judge Hall "approved his [Louaillier's] conduct and supported his attempts to excite disaffection among the
troops." To head off further plots, the general issued a proclamation to
the people and repeated his belief in a conspiracy: "The commanding
general is responsible for the safety of this section of the union; and it
shall be protected against every design of the enemy, in what manner
soever he may shape his attack, whether it be made by the known and
declared foe, or by the pretended and deceitful friend. . . . The lurking
traitor is now laboring to feed fresh fuel, a spirit of discontent, disobedience and mutiny, too long secretly fomenting." Jackson added that all
officers and soldiers should arrest individuals inciting mutiny or sedition, and they indeed followed these orders. James Hollander, a civilian, was arrested for "insubordination and mutiny in camp" after publicly supporting Louaillier's article and denouncing Jackson.[32]

While Louaillier and Hall languished in the same jail cell, Jackson
was faced with more distressing news. Daily expecting word of the
peace treaty from Washington, he suffered only disappointment on
March 6 when a post rider arrived and, because of an unexplained mix-
up, carried only orders to raise two more regiments of volunteers. Yet
the rider also bore a letter from the postmaster general directing all
on the post route to aid the rider because he carried news of peace.[33]
Refusing to accept such an unofficial communication, Jackson continued martial law.

On March 8, John Dick, a federal district attorney, attempted to
rescue Louaillier and Hall by petitioning First District Court Judge
Joshua Lewis for a writ of habeas corpus. Jackson responded to the

new writ in customary fashion. He promptly ordered the arrest of both Dick and Lewis, though he later countermanded the order, perhaps after deliberating upon the admirable militia service of both men. On the same day, though he had still received no official word of peace, Jackson relaxed military rule by releasing the militia from duty and allowing all vessels to travel freely.[34] Not all citizens enjoyed the good news. Continuing to feel the general's wrath, Louaillier faced a court-martial on March 7 for mutiny, exciting mutiny, general misconduct, being a spy, illegal and improper conduct and disobedience of orders, writing a willful and corrupt libel, and, finally, unsoldierly conduct. The senator refused to recognize the jurisdiction of the military court and opted to remain mute throughout the trial. Even the military tribunal, headed by Gen. Edmund P. Gaines, questioned its jurisdiction in the case as well as the nature of the charges. The court subsequently ruled that the defendant could be tried on the fifth charge only, illegal and improper conduct and disobedience to orders. Even this ruling was a comical, though serious, twisting of the facts. Louaillier had never been a member of the militia and thus was not technically subject to military orders. Rather, he had continued his role as senator, helping to procure supplies and money for the city's defense. Louaillier's acquittal after only one day of hearings revealed the flimsy nature of the military's case. Jackson's ire, however, was not so easily dismissed. Disapproving the court's decision, the general kept the senator in prison and gave a comprehensive definition of martial law that explained Louaillier's guilt:

> Martial law, being established, applies, as the commanding general believes, to all persons who remain within the sphere of its operations, and claims exclusive jurisdiction of all offences which aim at the disorganization and ruin of the army over which it extends. To a certain extent it is believed, it makes every man a *soldier;* to defend the spot where chance or choice has placed him, and to make him liable for any misconduct calculated to weaken its defence. . . .
> Decide with the accused, no army can be safe, no general can command. Disaffection and disobedience, anarchy and confusion, must take the place of order and subordination—defeat and shame, of victory and triumph.[35]

Most likely expecting a similar decision if Hall faced military trial, Jackson opted instead to banish the magistrate from the city. On March 11, he wrote Hall: "I have thought proper to send you beyond the limits of my encampment, to prevent you from a repetition of the improper conduct for which you have been Arrested and Confined; and to order that you remain beyond my chain of centinals, untill it is announced by proper authority that the ratification of the treaty between Great Britain and the U. States has been made, or the enemy shall have left the Southern Coast." Hall did not have long to wait. Just two days later, on March 13, news of peace arrived. Jackson immediately revoked martial law and released as well as pardoned all prisoners, both military and civilian. The city and its inhabitants were finally free.

The Battle of New Orleans, however, was far from over for Jackson. After suffering eighty-nine days of military domination, the civil magistracy prepared to demonstrate its rightful supremacy. Hall returned to the city and promptly turned the tables on the general, summoning him to court for interfering with judicial authority. The ensuing case, *United States v. Major-General Andrew Jackson*, allowed the judge to vindicate both his judicial station and his injured pride. More important, the case ultimately revolved around Jackson's authority to declare and enforce martial law. Upon his initial arrival in the city, Hall met with John Dick and determined the strategy for punishing Jackson. On March 21, the judge began taking depositions from various witnesses and on the twenty-second ordered Jackson to appear in court to show

> why an attachment should not be awarded against him for contempt
> of this Court, in having disrespectfully wrested from the Clerk afore-
> said an original order of the Honorable the Judge of this Court, for
> the issuing of a writ of habeas corpus in the case of a certain Louis
> Louallier [*sic*], then imprisoned by the said Major General Andrew
> Jackson, and for detaining the same; also, for disregarding the said
> writ of habeas corpus, when issued and served; in having imprisoned
> the Honorable the Judge of this Court; and for other contempt, as
> stated by the witnesses.[36]

After two delays at the request of Jackson's attorneys, John Reid, Abner Duncan, and Edward Livingston, the general appeared in court on March 27 dressed in the plain garb of a common citizen. His counsel utilized the postponements well, for in answer to the contempt charge they posed a variety of motions questioning the legal procedure in the case as well as an elaborate defense of the need to declare and enforce martial law. Hall, however, refused to be circumvented. Uninterested in entertaining the attorneys' justifications, the judge flatly refused to hear the argument. He instead issued a ruling severely restricting the general's ability to defend himself: "1st. If the party objects to the jurisdiction, the Court is ready to hear. 2d. If the party's affidavit contains a denial of the facts sworn to, or if he wishes to show that the facts charged do not, in law, amount to a contempt, the Court is ready to hear it. 3d. If the answer contains any thing as an apology to the Court, it is ready to hear. 4th. If the party be desirous to show that by the Constitution or laws of the United States, or in virtue of his military commission, he had the right to act as charged in the affidavits, the Court is ready to hear." Hall then stated that the court would pose a number of interrogatories that the general could object to individually, on the grounds that it is improper, or he could simply deny the facts charged. The judge also addressed indirectly one of the defense's motions. From the outset Jackson's attorneys argued for a jury trial because the case involved a criminal prosecution. (Jackson argued later that Hall acted illegally by sitting in his own case.) Brushing the argument aside, Hall acknowledged both that the case was the first of any importance for contempt since the court's establishment and, more important, that one of the causes of the contempt was the imprisonment of the judge. He saw, however, no conflict of interest in deliberating on his own case. He subsequently ordered Jackson to appear before the court on March 31 to answer the interrogatories.

On the assigned day, the now-besieged general entered the courtroom to the cheers of a large crowd. So raucous was the assembly of Jackson supporters that Judge Hall contemplated postponing the proceedings. Upon hearing this, Jackson quickly rose, insisting, "there is no danger here, the same arm that protected from outrage this city, against the invaders of the country, will shield and protect this court, or perish in the effort." Hall then posed his list of nineteen questions, all of which Jackson refused to answer, instead calling for the judge to pass sentence.[37] Hall obliged by fining Jackson one thousand dollars.

The Second Battle of New Orleans

The court case was now over. Jackson refused money collected by some of the city's residents as a reimbursement for the fine and instead suggested that it be applied to widows and orphans of the battle. The general's more magnanimous side shined brightly in both this refusal

and an impromptu speech outside the courthouse in which he lauded
the supremacy of the civil power. Though Jackson may have been sincere in his support of military subordination to civil rule, he certainly
had no love for Judge Hall. And the battle was by no means over. The
general, intent on proving his conduct correct, regrouped, launching
his first counter-offensive by publishing in several papers the defense Judge Hall disallowed in court. Jackson not only reiterated that
Hall was in league with Louaillier to incite mutiny and desertion
within the camp but also accused the judge of cowardice and spread-
ing fear throughout the countryside. He also described the rampant
disaffection reported by Claiborne and insisted that the governor and
many other influential citizens, including Hall, urged the proclamation
of martial law. When the trial began, Jackson in fact requested a written affidavit from Gen. David Morgan to prove this assertion.[38]

By denying Jackson's defense in court, Judge Hall had ignored a
major aspect of the case and in fact disregarded one of his own instructions in which he challenged the general "to show that by the Constitution or laws of the United States, or in virtue of his military commission, he had the right to act as charged." (The judge's refusal to
allow an answer revealed that revenge may have outweighed justice
in the contempt proceedings.) Jackson's defense focused on this very
question by arguing that necessity called for extraordinary measures
that sometimes exceeded the technicalities of law. He noted that even
the legislature, by regulating commerce, an act permissible by the
federal government only, and Judge Hall, by discharging prisoners
and closing the court during a regular session, had engaged in illegal
acts for reasons of necessity. The general insisted that his conduct
stemmed from a regard for the public good and that he had not overstepped his authority. His duty as a military commander, he argued,
was to protect American citizens and property. He believed, as Abner
Duncan had advised prior to the proclamation of martial law, that the
"guardian of the Public safety" was the judge of inherent necessity.
Because Jackson deemed martial law necessary, it, along with all acts
performed under it, such as seizure of the habeas corpus writ and the
arrest of Judge Hall, were legal. The general's defense counsel explained that martial law was meant to supercede all civilian powers as
well as suspend personal liberty and the security of private property.
And, noting that "the civil magistrate is the guardian of those rights,"
they declared that "martial law was therefore intended to supersede

the exercise of his authority so far as it interfered with the necessary restriction of those rights, *but no further.*"

Jackson's published defense, with its slap at Hall's patriotism and the charges of conspiracy, did not go without a response. On April 15, the incensed judge published a reply in the *Louisiana Gazette*, asserting that "all this cant of the judge's exciting mutiny and desertion was a mere pretext under which he [Jackson] might put down the judicial authority of his country, and excuse his other outrageous and illegal proceedings." Furthermore, Hall insisted that he was never consulted on the subject of establishing martial law and never "approved of martial law as since exercised by general Jackson."[39]

Jackson left New Orleans on April 6 for his return trip to the Hermitage. Still, the turmoil over his conduct was far from over. On the twelfth, the newly appointed secretary of war, Alexander J. Dallas, wrote Jackson, informing him that "representations have been recently made to the President, respecting certain acts of military opposition to the civil magistrate, that require immediate attention, not only in vindication of the just authority of the laws, but to rescue your own conduct from all unmerited reproach." Dallas questioned the arrest of Louaillier and Hall, noting that the president viewed the subject with "surprise" and "solicitude," requested a "full report," and stated his presumption that "every extraordinary exertion of military authority has ceased, in consequence of the cessation of all danger, open or covert, upon the restoration of peace." Here was more than a mere "traitorous" judge questioning the general's authority and imposing an unjust and illegal fine. The secretary's letter was, in Jackson's view, tantamount to an official sanction, and he replied immediately, enclosed his formal defense, and noted, "I shall feel satisfaction in going into a more particular examination & defence of my several acts when my accusers can be known. . . . I have but little doubt they will be found to belong to those who would have betrayed their Country, or skulked from its defence." Dallas's letter was actually no surprise to Jackson. Ever the shrewd tactician, the general had planned for just such an occurrence. Prior to his departure from New Orleans, he had requested Commodore Patterson to furnish a statement supporting martial law and attesting that it was approved by the city's leading men.[40]

His honor and reputation questioned, Jackson went on the offensive. He planned not only to visit Washington and present his case to the president, and Congress if need be, but also to demand the impeachment of

Dominick Hall. On July 1, Jackson received yet another letter from Secretary Dallas expressing concern over the "extraordinary exercise of military authority," and though he acknowledged the general's "patriotic motives," Dallas noted, "the President would willingly abstain from any further remarks upon the subject, were he not apprehensive, that the principle of your example, and the reason of his silence, might be hereafter, misunderstood, or misrepresented."[41] Dallas's comments revealed the most imposing aspect of Jackson's conduct: the creation of a precedent. Madison was indeed faced with a dilemma. Though Washington was threatened with an imminent attack and ultimately burned, neither the president nor Congress went to the extreme of suspending the writ of habeas corpus and imposing martial law. What then justified Jackson's precipitate action? Madison never answered the question. Still reeling from his own unpopularity in connection with the war, the president had the alternative of chastising a newly crowned national hero and in doing so upholding the supremacy of the civil law or letting the entire episode rest. The choice was clear. Dallas informed Jackson that the president deemed it unnecessary to enter into a "critical examination" at the present time. Nevertheless, the secretary, perhaps in an attempt to safeguard Madison's silence, outlined the government's views in relation to "extraordinary" military measures:

> The military power is clearly defined, and carefully limitted [sic], by the Constitution and laws of the United States; but the experience of the best regulated Governments teaches us, that exigencies may sometimes arise, when (as you have emphatically observed) 'Constitutional forms must be suspended, for the permanent preservation of Constitutional rights.' . . . To enforce the discipline and to ensure the safety of his garrison, or his camp, an American Commander possesses indeed, high and necessary powers; but all his powers are compatible with the rights of citizens, and the independence of the judicial authority. If, therefore, he undertake to suspend the writ of Habeas Corpus, to restrain the liberty of the Press, to inflict military punishments, upon citizens who are not military men, and generally to supersede the functions of the civil magistrate, he may be justified by the law of necessity, while he has the merit of saving his country, but he cannot resort to the established law of the land, for the means of vindication.[42]

Though sugar-coated, Dallas's memorandum was still censure. The essence of the secretary's letter was that though necessity sometimes existed, Jackson had nonetheless gone beyond the Constitution and was therefore on his own. Such a view could not have been a surprise to the general. His able counselor, Edward Livingston, had given a very clear legal opinion of martial law, advising Jackson that it was "unknown to the Constitution or Laws of the U.S." and therefore "justified only by the necissity of the Case and that therefore the General proclaims it at his own risque and under his responsibility." Dallas's and Livingston's opinions presaged a view of martial law that in years to come became a major sticking point between the general's defenders and opponents: necessity versus sanctity of the Constitution.

Andrew Jackson did not like the stark reality of his superior's letter and thus continued preparations for his trip to the nation's capital. In early September, he wrote Dallas of his future arrival and again expressed his desire for a full investigation; Jackson also enclosed the opinion of Commodore Patterson supporting martial law.[43] The general arrived in Washington on November 16 and hurried to the secretary's office. According to John Reid, who accompanied Jackson, Dallas insisted that "the president, as well as all the heads of departments, were so sensible of the great, the inestimable services he had rendered his country, & the wisdom of the measures he had pursued for this purpose, that they neither required nor wished any further explanation." Though Reid's account is undoubtedly that of an admirer and future biographer, Jackson also wrote that "the administrators of the Govr are perfectly contented with *all* my conduct before Neworleans."[44] Jackson left for Tennessee on Christmas Eve satisfied that he had successfully defended his use of martial law.

The Hero versus the Despot

The government's lack of interest in exploring the civilian arrests and destruction of property in New Orleans fit the nation's mood at the time. Americans focused only on the conclusion of a miserable war and the glory in which it ended. Jackson's popularity was, in fact, never greater. Everywhere the general turned he was honored with waves, salutations, and invitations to celebrations and banquets. Little wonder that enterprising men with their fingers on the political pulse of the nation soon considered placing the hero in the running for the presidency. In this respect, the Battle of New Orleans was a distinct beginning for Old Hickory, launching him to national fame and ultimately the White House. And as the means of achieving that victory, martial law tells us much about Jackson's character. He possessed the ability not only to act decisively and lead brilliantly but also, if he believed it necessary, to lay aside the Constitution and undermine the most fundamental notions of American political ideology: the balance between civil liberty and military power. Nor was this latter trait stemmed by the government. Opting instead for political expediency, Madison's failure to formally investigate Jackson undoubtedly fed the general's iron will and sense of unlimited authority. Indeed, such attributes were exceedingly apparent in later episodes such as Jackson's invasion of Florida in 1818, and his war on the Bank of the United States. Still, though martial law was laid to rest following the immediate conclusion of the war, it nevertheless remained a black spot on an otherwise brilliant campaign, and political enemies inevitably resurrected the inglorious accounts of military rule when it suited their need for electoral advantage; key times were during Jackson's run for the presidency in 1824 and 1828, as well as the 1840s congressional debates on refunding the general's fine. Moreover, the question of a precedent remained. Martial law in New Orleans, when debated in the 1840s, not only influenced the very definition of the term but also was cited by Abraham Lincoln when Civil War ignited the nation. It is only after investigating what occurred under the dictates of martial law that one can begin to understand why Jackson's conduct was so easily criticized in the years that followed. In a nation obsessed with liberty and civilian authority, the idea of military rule struck a tender nerve. America's most fundamental notions of liberty and power were threatened when the military went unchecked.

Still, there exists the larger question of whether Jackson was justified in his declaration of martial law, as well as its continuation in the aftermath of the British retreat. Viewing the issue in purely constitutional terms, there is no question that Jackson acted illegally. Yet this does not necessarily satisfy the issue of necessity, as Jackson's supporters argued later. Can one violate civil liberties if doing so saves the government that provides those civil liberties? There is no doubt that Jackson believed the warnings from Governor Claiborne and others regarding the internal dissension and spying within New Orleans. Such threats were compounded by the daily expectation of attack by a massive British army, part of which had recently burned the nation's capital. These factors, along with the singular importance of New Orleans as a port city, made Jackson's remedy of martial law understandable. At the very least, Jackson wanted the city's populace to fear him more than the impending British army. He succeeded. The key issue is that Jackson, as the commander of the region, believed that his best recourse was to impose martial law. He believed that it was the only way to prepare for the invasion. However much one might like to disdain Jackson for military rule, he did in fact save the city in a victory that was unprecedented and perhaps impossible without martial law.

The next question is the duration of martial law. Should Jackson have kept the military in force for some three months? Should he have arrested a state senator and federal judge after the battle had been won and the enemy retired? Jackson clearly went to excesses. Always a domineering commander, he believed that once in charge he was the sole authority. Surely, Jackson could have handled the Louaillier and Hall matter more sensitively. The senator and judge posed no real threat to Jackson's military authority. Still, Jackson believed that fomenting dissension with New Orleans among an already fractious population was dangerous and threatened the city's security. And to be fair to Jackson, he had no idea whether the British might attempt another attack from a different route. Even after the heavy losses suffered on January 8, the British army was still considerably larger, better trained, and better equipped than Jackson's. To a large degree, the general had been lucky. Had the British not been hemmed in by the swamp and the Mississippi River, they would undoubtedly have flanked Jackson and the battle's outcome might have been quite different. Even with news of peace, Jackson could not realistically relax his preparations until official word of the treaty arrived. Imagine the history if he had canceled martial law, released his troops, then suffered a surprise British attack and lost the city. Jackson would have been lambasted as a fool.

Ultimately, Jackson did acquiesce to the civil authority, something that he did not have to do. He could very easily have left the city and thwarted Judge Hall's attempt to bring him before the court. Finally, the unconstitutionality of martial law could have been dealt with decisively by President Madison. He could have made a statement or even sent a letter to Congress expressing his concerns over martial law and the dangers of the military overriding civil government but at the same time exonerated Jackson for any evil intentions. Madison, however, failed to do so, opting instead to ignore the matter. Had Madison acted, though this is purely speculative, he might have settled some of the issues over martial law that Democrats and Whigs argued about in later years.

CHAPTER 2

Jackson as a Military Chieftain:
The Presidential Elections of 1824 and 1828

T he splendor of the New Orleans military campaign overshadowed Andrew Jackson's use of martial law. Americans reveled in an unprecedented nationalism in which Old Hickory was rocketed to the lofty heights of national hero. Congress unanimously passed resolutions commending the general. George M. Troup of Georgia, a member of the House Committee on Military Affairs, which drafted the resolutions, lavished the victorious hero with eloquent praise: "I cannot sir, perhaps language cannot, do justice to the merits of General Jackson." State legislatures throughout the Union followed suit, passing declarations lionizing Jackson. The people clamored to see him wherever he went. Jackson was even commemorated in song. Described as the Era of Good Feelings by some historians, American nationalism was never greater in the history of the young Republic.[1] Is it any wonder that President Madison and Secretary of War Dallas dropped the martial law episode like a stone? Better to let the matter sink into oblivion than face Jackson's certain defense by the people. Thus the turmoil surrounding Jackson's conduct virtually disappeared in the wake of peace. Yet it was not laid to rest forever. Politics has a way of digging up the past and placing it under the microscope of electoral competition. When Jackson's name appeared on the roll for the office of president, opponents pulled out their shovels and exhumed the general's record.

Anti-Jackson forces raised the specter of martial law and insisted that civil authority had been unalterably damaged at the hands of military tyranny. The delicate balance between civil liberty and military power, they argued, was subverted by Jackson's actions in New Orleans. The general's followers rallied in support of both Jackson and martial law, claiming that military rule in the Crescent City was a simple matter of necessity. Rather than harming liberty, they insisted, the general's forceful actions sustained it.

Concerns over the fate of liberty were direct reflections of the nation's inherent republican political ideology. The founders had instilled in the citizenry an almost desperate fear of military power. Yet ideological concerns were also infused, even led, by an overarching partisan motivation. Virtually no one expressed anxiety over martial law in the years between its use and Jackson's bid for the presidency, and even when he entered the 1824 election, serious criticism did not come until it seemed possible he could win. Thus charges that Jackson was a military chieftain who threatened the nation's liberty were prompted as much by increased competition within the quickly burgeoning second American party system as by any sudden concern for the Revolutionary generation's legacy.

Nor were the critics of Jackson and martial law the only ones who manipulated the people's trepidation over the balance between liberty and power. Jackson's supporters also latched onto martial law and in doing so revealed the extent to which republicanism could be utilized as a partisan tactic. Rather than downplay the general's military trans-

Replicas of the gold medals given to Jackson by Congress for his victory in the Battle of New Orleans. The dies for the medals were created by Moritz Furst and are 2.5 inches in diameter. Congress approved their creation on February 27, 1815, and Jackson received them in a ceremony at the White House on March 16, 1824. Author's collection.

gressions, supporters embraced the charges of military chieftain, aver-
ring that the boldness and decisive action shown by Jackson as a military commander were essential qualities for a president. Jacksonians
asserted that liberty could best be protected by military power and
pointed to martial law as proof.[2] Such an argument would have been
unthinkable under the political assumptions of the Revolutionary War
era. Yet this was a new period, a party period in which clever politicians reconstructed republican ideology for partisan purposes.

To be perfectly clear, readers need to understand that important
ideological issues were involved in the political battles over Jackson
and martial law. These issues, however, were engaged in a decidedly
abstract manner, distanced from the dangers of 1814–15, and permeated with partisan strategizing. As such, there existed no larger, deeply
thought-out theoretical or ideological design to revise American notions
of military power. The campaign tracts defending the general's use of
martial law had a rather shallow, ad hoc quality because Jacksonians
were often responding to a laundry list of charges posed by opponents.[3]

And the laundry list revealed that many anti-Jacksonians were
equally superficial in their discussion of martial law. It was merely
one stone among many thrown in an attempt to knock Jackson from
the presidential race. Pamphleteers filled their presses by dredging
up every unseemly, potentially controversial episode in Jackson's past.
Historians have done well in documenting issues such as the Seminole
Affair, Jackson's marriage woes, and his involvement in dueling. Yet
martial law has remained largely neglected even though the majority
of anti-Jackson authors raised the issue as not only an example of the
general's unfitness for the presidency but also a threat to civil government and liberty.[4] Always at the heart of opposition literature was the
question of Jackson's temperament. Opponents described him as hate-
ful and rash, pointing to his execution of militiamen and military rule
in New Orleans as prime examples of a far too martial demeanor.

The Danger of a "Military Chieftain": The Opposition Speaks

One of the first anti-Jackson attacks came in 1818–19 by an anonymous
author calling himself "Algernon Sydney" (an echo from the commonwealth tradition). Originally produced as letters to the *Richmond*

Enquirer, the work was republished in 1830 as a pamphlet. The author identified himself only as a "Citizen of Virginia," and it is uncertain whether his identity was ever publicly known. Henry Clay, however, certainly came to know that Sydney was actually Benjamin Watkins Leigh, a lawyer from Richmond who later became a devout anti-Jacksonian.[5] As a U.S. senator in 1834, he advocated restoring the federal deposits to the Bank of the United States and delivered a fiery speech in response to President Jackson's protest of the Senate's censure for removal of the deposits. Later, Leigh refused Virginia's instructions to vote in favor of Thomas Hart Benton's expunging resolution which called for the removal of the Senate censure. Unlike his fellow senator, John Tyler, who resigned rather than vote for the resolution, Leigh retained his seat in defiance. It was an action that was quite characteristic of the aristocratically minded Virginian. He abhorred the very notion of a democracy in which the rabble directed affairs and once sneered at the idea that the "peasantry of the west" possessed any political abilities whatsoever.[6]

What started in 1818 as disgust over Jackson's imperious actions grew to hate in ensuing years. *The Letters of Algernon Sydney* revealed the seeds of this enmity. Leigh opened the work by commenting on "the violence that has marked the character and conduct of General Jackson." Focusing directly on martial law, the author noted the "acquiescence" by the government, particularly President Madison, and apathy on the part of the public "have filled my mind with amazement, indignation and alarm." Leigh devoted seven of the pamphlet's eleven pages to denouncing Jackson's military rule in New Orleans: "Turn your eyes now to the principal scene of General Jackson's glory: happy, if it were not also the scene of unrestrained violence and tyranny." After narrating the history of Jackson's conduct, the cancellation of civil liberties, the arrests of Louaillier and Hall, and the defiance of judicial authority, Leigh asked whether the hero was reprimanded for his violent and illegal acts. "No!" declared the author. "History that records his ninety days tyranny, records also, that his whole conduct stands unquestioned to this day, as if it were the regular exercise of undoubted authority." President Madison, lamented Leigh, in no way obviated "the dangerous consequences of the example."[7] This last point was something upon which many of the general's opponents directed their pens. Because the government never formally questioned Jackson's use of martial law, the "example" lingered as a potential precedent.[8]

THE LETTERS

OF

ALGERNON SYDNEY,

IN

DEFENCE OF CIVIL LIBERTY

AND

AGAINST THE ENCROACHMENTS

OF

MILITARY DESPOTISM,

WRITTEN BY AN EMINENT CITIZEN OF VIRGINIA, AND
FIRST PUBLISHED IN THE RICHMOND ENQUIRER
IN 1818–19.

TO WHICH ARE ADDED, IN
AN APPENDIX,

The remarks of Mr. Ritchie as referred to by the author of
" Algernon Sydney" in page 3 of this pamphlet.

WITH AN

INTRODUCTION
BY THE PRESENT PUBLISHER.

RICHMOND:
PRINTED AND PUBLISHED BY T. W. WHITE.
::::::::::
1830.

Title page of The Letters of Algernon Sydney, *by Benjamin Watkins Leigh, 1830.*

In some respects, Benjamin Leigh's letters were an anomaly, much like the man himself. Unlike later works dealing with military rule in New Orleans, Leigh's was not written specifically for a presidential election. It also appears to be the first pamphlet chastising Jackson for martial law and warning of his military exploits. This, in part, was also why Leigh opted to write under the pseudonym Algernon Sydney rather than expose himself to the hero's popularity. Pen names were a common device for those who wanted to influence the citizenry but shield themselves from potential backlash. Leigh was no different, and especially because he was a southerner—Jackson's popularity was greatest in the South—the Virginian had good reason to fear retribution at the hands of the general's adoring public.

Algernon Sydney's remonstrance was both fitting and timely. In March 1818, the iron general had marched into Florida, essentially overthrown the Spanish government, court-martialed two British citizens, then hanged one and shot the other. The action not only breached an international treaty but also was potentially a violation of the Constitution for declaring war without congressional approval. Shades of martial law in New Orleans abounded, and there is little doubt why Leigh recognized such a clear tie between the two incidents. Jackson was at it again. And even though the Seminole Affair was the catalyst for the Sydney letters, Leigh spent more time dissecting martial law in New Orleans than on Jackson's conduct in Florida. It is reasonable, though Leigh does not say it outright, that the general's unchecked actions in New Orleans permitted his later invasion of Florida. Algernon Sydney opined that "example and precedent are of mighty wonderful influence in the affairs of men."

Benjamin Watkins Leigh was not the only American to express concern over Jackson's foray into Florida. James Monroe's cabinet was thrown into disarray, as the members debated whether the general should be censured. Secretary of State John Quincy Adams was the only advisor who defended Jackson, arguing that he acted out of national self-defense and therefore his conduct was sanctioned by the law of nations. Interestingly, such arguments were precisely what some Democrats raised when discussing martial law during the 1840s congressional refund debates over the return of Jackson's fine. During the debates, however, Jackson and Adams were implacable foes, and in the 1840s Adams scoffed at the idea of justifying martial law under the dictates of self-defense. Florida was a different matter. The wily,

Massachusetts-born politician calculated that Jackson's invasion of Spanish territory could aid the secretary in his contentious negotiations with Spain over the western boundary of the Louisiana Territory. Adams, therefore, threw his weight toward Jackson in the Seminole controversy because it served larger political desires.[9]

Some members of the House and Senate were not as liberal in their willingness to approve Jackson's conduct in Florida. Both houses of Congress appointed committees that ultimately issued reports critical of the general. In the House, representatives spent several weeks debating whether to sanction the report from the Committee on Military Affairs and ultimately voted against it. In the midst of the battle, virtually every representative, even those who objected to Jackson's actions, realized the importance of treading carefully when it came to the Hero of New Orleans. Jackson's supporters, abundantly aware of his nationalist appeal, lauded his unparalleled services and chastised those who attempted to cast a shadow over his fame. "A nation should preserve its glory," warned Alexander Smyth of Virginia, "and, as the glory of a nation is composed of the aggregate of the fame of individuals, to tarnish the character of the most distinguished hero of the United States, of the present age, is to tarnish the glory of the nation." He added, "Let me assure you that the American people will not be pleased to see their great defender, their great avenger, sacrificed."[10] Jackson's critics, though many undoubtedly looked to him with some degree of admiration for the Battle of New Orleans, took such admonitions seriously, never forgetting to give Jackson the proper respect due America's hero. Speaking for the House Military Affairs Committee, Thomas Nelson noted "your committee must here, in justice to their own feelings, express their extreme regret, that it has become their duty to disapprove the conduct of one who has, on a former occasion, so eminently contributed to the honor and defence of the nation, as had Major General Jackson." Nelson also noted gingerly that the committee engaged in a "temperate expression" on the subject.[11]

The fact that Algernon Sydney's letters made such a clear connection between the Seminole Affair and martial law caused two congressmen to address the matter directly. Alexander Smyth, commenting on the letters that were published in one of his home state's newspapers, remarked in a decidedly scoffing tone, "Some youth . . . has been writing for the public prints." Smyth announced that "the conduct of General Jackson, at New Orleans, during the invasion, when he declared martial law in force, has been mentioned as indicating an inclination to exert unnecessarily arbitrary power." Smyth answered the charge by insisting that "an excuse for the General will be found in the imminent danger of the loss of the country, whose inhabitants had not then given any decisive evidence of attachment to the United States, and which was invaded by a powerful army. If martial law may be declared in force on any occasion, a more fit occasion can seldom arise."[12] Smyth's justification was supported by James Tallmadge of New York, who, though he believed martial law unconstitutional, recognized its importance: "I felt and gratefully acknowledge that to him we owe much of our national character, and the security of a valuable portion of our territory, yet I do not forget that even on that occasion he overstept his power. I was disposed to forgive. The evils which he averted and the blessings which he conferred upon us, were some atonement for the violated majesty of the Constitution."[13] Nothing more was said about martial law. Certainly no one in the House dared take up Benjamin Watkins Leigh's line of attack. Martial law and the Battle of New Orleans were intertwined. To criticize one was, by connection, a condemnation of the other. And, as Jackson's supporters had warned, the famous battle was intimately tied to the nation's reputation. As a result, legislators spoke of New Orleans with reverence, and critics for the most part shied away from martial law, even though, as Leigh had accurately pointed out, it was a fitting parallel to the Seminole Affair.

Even Jackson's most vocal and cutting opponent in the Congress refused to broach the subject of martial law. Henry Clay delivered a fiery speech on the Seminole Affair in which he chastised the general as a dangerous "military chieftain." Yet the degree of Clay's ardor was in part fueled by the threat Jackson posed in future presidential elections. As one historian noted, Jackson "could easily rival Henry Clay of Kentucky for western votes and William H. Crawford of Georgia for Southern votes. Because of this he invited the kind of surgical stroke by master politicians that would cut him down to size. . . . Naturally they disguised their intentions and their motives. Not until the Florida question came up for debate in the House did Clay publicly reveal his envy of the 'military chieftain.'"[14] Clay, an imperious rhetorician, laid siege on the general. The Kentuckian could have utilized essentially the same speech if he thought it prudent to attack Jackson for martial law. He hoped gentlemen would "deliberately survey the awful position on which we stand. They may bear down all opposition; they may

even vote the general public thanks; they may even carry him triumphantly through this house. But, if they do, in my humble judgment,
it will be a triumph of the principle of insubordination—a triumph of
the military over the civil authority—a triumph over the powers of this
house—a triumph over the constitution of this land. And he prayed most
devoutly to Heaven, that it might not prove, in its ultimate effects
and consequences, a triumph over the liberties of the people." Like
Algernon Sydney, Clay pondered future dangers: "Precedents, if bad,
were fraught with the most dangerous consequences."[15] The connection was so obvious, yet still no reference to martial law even though
it was a far greater threat to American citizens. Clay was no fool. He
understood that berating the general for invading foreign territory was
far different from raising questions about the most stupendous military victory in the nation's history. Yet even an attack on Jackson's
conduct in Florida held risks, as one of Clay's friends warned after the
House speech: "Your late speech on the Seminole war, in which you condemn the conduct of Genl. Jackson, is disapproved of by some—and
some of your friends are apprehensive that you may lose friends as a
consequence."[16] Attacking Andrew Jackson's military exploits was serious business, even for a politician of Henry Clay's stature. Yet the "disapproval" expressed by some of Clay's friends was also helped along
by Jackson, who, revealing that he too could wage political warfare,
mailed copies of the speech to friends in the West and encouraged publication in local newspapers. "I hope the western people will appreciate his conduct accordingly," wrote the general. "You will see him
skinned here, & I hope you will roast him in the West."[17]

There is little wonder why Clay did not toy with the sanctity of New
Orleans. He and his followers, always with their eyes on the White
House, opted to avoid future conflicts with Jackson. At the outset of
the presidential campaign, in fact, Clay was never really sure that
Jackson's candidacy would move beyond Tennessee, noting "it is uncertain whether it has been stimulated to produce division in the West, or
was intended as a mere compliment to the Genl. from his own state."
The Kentuckian's friends assured him, "Gen J will decline eventually—
The public esteem him *only* for his military energy—He is too much of
a Soldier to be a civilian."[18] When Jackson's popularity as a candidate
widened, even into Kentucky, Clay and his supporters continued to
express doubt about Old Hickory's ability to ultimately win a nomination. Still, they considered the general's appeal when strategizing for

Clay's candidacy: "Believing as we do that Gen Jackson will not finally be a candidate we have deemed it bad policy to give the Slightest offence to his friends in general as it will be very easy to turn the large majority of the people in your favour when he is out of view."[19] Henry Clay's presidential aspirations necessitated silence. The degree of that silence, however, was directly weighted with the 1824 presidential contest.

More significant rumblings about Jackson's military conduct arose only after he entered the executive race in 1823, and the more pointed attacks began when it seemed that he might actually win.[20] Albert Gallatin, Jefferson's former secretary of the treasury, for example, wrote a friend in May 1824, remarking, "Whatever gratitude we owe him [Jackson] for his eminent military services, he is not fitted for the office of first magistrate of a free people." "He entertains," continued Gallatin, "very sincere but very erroneous and most dangerous opinions on the subject of military and Executive power. Whenever he has been instrusted [sic] with the first, he has usurped more than belonged to him; and when he thought it useful to the public, he has not hesitated to transcend the law and the legal authority vested in him." But Gallatin also understood Jackson's immense popularity and feared that the people would be "dazzled by military glory."[21]

The voices of doubt became louder in the winter of 1824–25. The November election had resulted in no clear winner, and even though Jackson had received the most popular and electoral votes, he had not achieved the requisite number to win the presidency. The question devolved to the House of Representatives, where Jackson's future, as well as that of John Quincy Adams and William Crawford, lay in the hands of the nation's congressmen (Henry Clay was eliminated because he failed to achieve a spot as one of the top three electoral vote recipients). The election had clearly slid toward Jackson, and as a result Clay felt it unavoidable to raise the general's military record. "What I would ask, should be the distinguishing characteristic of an American statesman?" wrote Clay in a letter to a friend. "Should it not be a devotion to civil liberty?" continued the Kentuckian. "Is it then compatible with that principle, to elect a man, whose sole recommendation rests on military pretensions?"[22] As the struggle over the presidency continued, Clay expressed astonishment and, finally, turned his attention to the source of Jackson's popularity: "I cannot believe that killing 2500 Englishmen at N.Orleans qualifies for the various, difficult and complicated duties of the Chief Magistracy." Is it not wrong, he continued, "to establish the dangerous precedent of elevating, in this early stage of the Republic, a Military Chieftain, merely because he has won a great victory?"[23] The question was not rhetorical. Clay made his query with the full intent of publication so that Americans themselves could ponder the question. Yet he did not take the chance that the nation's citizens might come to the wrong conclusion. Fearing that Jackson might win the House vote, Clay utilized his considerable political skill and position as Speaker of the House to keep Jackson from delivering an inaugural address. The infamous "corrupt bargain" in which Clay allegedly bartered the presidency to John Quincy Adams in exchange for appointment as secretary of state not only squashed Jackson's quest for the executive office in 1825 but also yielded the general's undying enmity.

If Henry Clay thought that this was the end of the matter, or of Jackson's march to the White House, he had sorely underestimated his opponent. Jackson returned with a vengeance, leveling his guns not only on the corruption connected to the campaign but also on Clay's criticism of the "Military Chieftain." Writing to Samuel Swartwout in the month following the House election, Jackson responded to the attack: "Mr. Clay has never risked himself for his country. . . . He who fights, and fights successfully, must, according to his standard, be held up as a 'military chieftain.'" Then, beating a nationalist drum, Jackson paralleled his military service to someone that no man dared malign. "Even Washington," he insisted, "could he appear again among us, might be so considered, because he dared to be a virtuous and successful soldier— a correct man, and an honest man." Clearly, Jackson could at times match Clay's shrewdness. Indeed, he did not miss the opportunity to further justify his past conduct as a military leader. Revealing absolutely no regret for constitutional infractions, he stated flatly that should necessity again demand such action, he would not shrink from the responsibility: "I have as you very well know, by some of the designing politicians of this country, been charged with taking bold and highhanded measures; but as they were not designed for any benefit to my self I should under similar circumstances not refrain from a course equally bold. . . . If these opinions and sentiments shall entitle me to the name and character of a Military Chieftain I am content so to be considered."[24]

Though such a statement could be viewed by opponents as extreme and perhaps dangerous in a society obsessed with safeguarding liberty, the general balanced his message by insisting that the purity of

his motives absolved him of wrong doing. His virtue clearly established, Jackson added the crowning touch by expertly flipping Clay's
"Military Chieftain" label. Old Hickory proved himself to be an able
politician. His letter was, of course, printed so that America could see
the depth of his patriotism.

If there was any certainty following the bizarre circumstances of
the 1824 contest, it was that the succeeding election ensured rabid, no-
holds-barred, sucker punching. Certain that Jackson was the candidate
to beat, opponents opened a deafening fire in which they bombarded
him for stealing another man's wife, dueling, killing militiamen, invading Florida, and trampling upon civil liberties in New Orleans. As a
result, the election of 1828 in which Jackson ran against incumbent
John Quincy Adams was one of the dirtiest in American history. Still,
though his supporters fired away, Clay avoided any direct assaults,
even when friends reminded him directly that in New Orleans Jackson
had taken "away the liberty and lives of persons, in spite of the writ
of Habius corpus, and trial in a fair and legal way." Referring back to
1819 and Benjamin Watkins Leigh, Clay merely lamented, "What has
become of the eloquent pen of Algernon Sydney?"[25]

If Henry Clay continued to remain silent in the hopes of someday
gaining the executive office, Jackson's other opponents relished in the
opportunity to attack. And because the stakes were now so high, the
control of the executive department, many of Jackson's critics felt no
compunction about broaching the subject of martial law and the previously untouchable Battle of New Orleans. The passage of years since
the famous battle may also have made the matter less sensitive. When
targeting martial law, the opposition proved remarkably resourceful.
It was not only important what Jackson's critics said, but who delivered the message. And who better to decry the arbitrary arrests and
military dictatorship in New Orleans than Louis Louaillier, the very
senator punished by the uncompromising general.

Addressing a large crowd within his native state in 1827, Louaillier
declared that "one of the candidates for the Presidency of the United
States has violated our constitution and our laws." Noting that Jackson
had leveled charges of treason against him, Louaillier challenged the
audience: "If I succeed in proving that these accusations are utterly
unfounded; that the General has been unjust; that his acts were arbitrary, and stand unjustified by any consideration of public utility, I
shall have a right to infer that he is unworthy of the Supreme Magis-

Caricature of Andrew Jackson as Shakespeare's Richard III.
"Methought the souls of all that I had murder'd came to my tent."
Hurja Papers, Tennessee Historical Society Collections, Tennes-
see State Library and Archives.

tracy to which he aspires." After giving a detailed account of the despotism perpetrated under martial law, Louaillier, borrowing Clay's
epithet, denounced Jackson as a "military chieftain" who "laid a
fearless and sacrilegious hand upon the interpreter of the law," Judge
Dominick Hall. The former Louisiana senator concluded, "this General, although skilful [sic] and brave, possesses none of the qualities
which you ought to require in all the successors of washington." It
appeared that two could raise the memory of America's first hero. In
attacking Jackson, Louaillier combined nicely both personal and political agendas. Jackson's supporters, in fact, laughed at Louaillier's pro-
fessed "patriotism" and argued that he had "tamely" suffered "the imputation of treachery to rest upon his character, for thirteen years."[26]

The denial of Jackson's likeness to Washington was a common theme in opposition literature, both because the general himself had compared his life and conduct to Washington's and because Jackson's supporters often compared the two generals. In response to such analogies, one anonymous author fumed that "the great and gallant Washington, whose name has been too often profaned, by using it in connection with Gen. Jackson's, never once proclaimed martial law; neither was a militiaman ever shot by his order."[27] Disputing Jackson's claim to Washington-like qualities was only one of several themes contained in opposition pamphlets and newspaper articles. Critics argued essentially seven points regarding Old Hickory's conduct in New Orleans and his military exploits in general: (1) military victories alone did not make one fit for the presidency, (2) Jackson possessed an irascible temper, (3), the military was subordinate to civil authority, (4) Jackson violated the Constitution by declaring martial law, (5) Jackson remained a threat to our civil liberties, (6) there existed the danger of a precedent for future military commanders to declare martial law, and (7) what does it say about the nation if Jackson is rewarded with the presidency for trampling upon the laws?[28]

Always highlighted in the opposition pamphlets was Jackson's irritable and uncontrollable temper. It was easy to do. Jackson's past lent itself to criticism. But unlike Algernon Sydney's early pamphlet, these later anti-Jackson works combined the discussion of Jackson's brutish behavior with his unsuitability for public office. Writers talked of duels, executions, and, of course, New Orleans. In a book-length biography of Jackson, one author, calling himself "a free man," devoted an entire chapter to martial law. Criticizing Jackson's claim of necessity, the author lamented, "We wish it had not been so, and that every step of our hero's course had not conveyed pregnant proof of his unfitness to exercise civil-power. On the contrary, his conduct puts us in mind of the exasperated rhinoceros, wreaking his fury on every object that presents itself." Another writer denounced Jackson's "vindictiveness and cruelty," noting that he possessed "a total want of talent or acquirements, suitable for civil office."[29] Questioning the validity of Jackson's claim to the presidency was an important strategy for opponents, often allowing them to get at the heart of his popularity. "The answer is obvious and palpable," declared one critic speaking before an assembly in New York. It is "the Battle of New Orleans." The speaker continued, "The monstrous doctrine is then publicly avowed that the gaining of a single battle is a sufficient qualification for the highest *civil office*."[30] Other critics cut much closer to the bone, making sure that the general's greatest victory was intimately tied to his illegal declaration of martial law: "It is unfortunate for him, that the military achievements which first gave general celebrity to his character, gave publicity also to his vices and errors."[31]

The heightened political competition of the 1828 election had opened the door to criticizing Jackson for martial law in New Orleans. The once-sacred battle, a subject around which even Henry Clay tiptoed carefully, was no longer off limits. Critics now focused directly on Jackson's indifference to civil liberties at the very same time that he was achieving military glory. At an anti-Jackson convention in Richmond, Virginia, one orator declared that the general "has been unmindful of the subordination of military to civil power, and has violated the law and the constitution—by declaring martial law at New Orleans."[32] The pamphlet produced by the convention contained not only the speaker's denunciation of martial law but an appendix that included a copy of the 1814 martial law proclamation, as well as an article from the *New York Advertiser* retelling the New Orleans episode and criticizing Jackson for his tyrannical conduct. Arguing along the same lines, another critic insisted "it was never intended by the constitution to give any military chief discretionary power to interfere with the civil rights of the people." Yet it appears, continued the author, that "in the face of our government, and in the midst of a people who admit no power above the laws, an individual has been permitted with impunity, under the color of military authority, to sport with the lives and liberties of our citizens."[33] If Jackson's unabashed destruction of the nation's liberties while a general were not enough, what, argued critics, would occur if such a tyrant reached the office of the presidency? Surely Americans could see the distinct pattern in Jackson's past: the execution of militia men, martial law in New Orleans, the invasion of Florida. All of these episodes, warned opponents, exhibited a willingness to usurp power and trample liberty. "If elected President, the constitution entrusts him with the command of the navy and army of the United States," warned the *New York Advertiser*: "We have seen, that when at the head of only a small body of men he was able to suspend the operation of all civil law in a very important district of the country, establish the supremacy of military power, and under its influence, exercised acts of the most unqualified oppression and injustice.

What might be expected from his irascible temper, his lawless ambition, his fierce and vindictive spirit, when clothed with the immense power which the constitution reposes in the chief magistrate of the nation?"[34]

Considering Jackson's near victory in the 1824 election and the continuation of his immense popularity afterward, questions about his suitability were not hypothetical. Opponents recognized the very real threat he posed to their own candidate, John Quincy Adams, and thus grasped at every item that could cast a shade of doubt. The immediacy of the campaign even allowed attacks on the once untouchable New Orleans victory. The strategy made sense. Jackson's greatest strength was also his greatest weakness. His popularity was a product of grand, but decidedly troubling and often illegal military exploits. Opponents scrambled to expose the illegality and hence strip the exploit of its nationalist splendor. While maintaining their own devotion to liberty, they attempted to implant the worst in the minds of citizens: "We should, indeed do great injustice to the virtue of our people, the circumstances of our country, and the value of our government, if we indulged in the idle fear, that an open attack upon our liberties, made with any military force, which Gen. J. could probably command in the course of his Administration, would bring us under the yoke of his power. . . . We would bid a proud defiance to his power, if he should so dare our liberties."[35]

With such bold, impassioned, and somewhat absurd declarations, anti-Jacksonians attempted to strike fear into the voters and defeat the general's march to the White House. For on the election, they warned ominously, depended the very soul of America's political ideals. Maintaining that civil authority remained supreme and the citizens' rights of the utmost importance, one anti-Jacksonian lamented, "What will be the moral effect of the direct sanction given to these offenses, by rewarding the offender with the first honor of the nation?" "Can we preserve our love and reverence for institutions," continued the speaker, "which we suffer to be violated, not only without censure, but with applause?"[36] Another adversary insisted that "republicans cannot elevate such a man to office without laying the axe to the root of the Tree of Liberty!"[37]

Anti-Jacksonians engaged in a masterful campaign in which they placed the election in the light of a life-or-death struggle for American liberty. Citizens could save the nation only by voting against the despot of New Orleans; then they must join the effort to censure Jackson, however belatedly, for his conduct in New Orleans because such a pre-

cedent might cause future military men to emulate Jackson's dangerous example. Summing up the viewpoint succinctly, a speaker at an anti-
Jackson meeting in Philadelphia, cautioned, "Fellow citizens, it is evident, that whatever powers Gen. Jackson could rightly exercise over the
people of Louisiana, some other General might as justifiably claim to
exercise over *us;*—and that those who justify him in such proceedings
must be content to hold their liberty of speech and personal security *at
the will* and by the *sufferance* of the military power."[38] Making the warning even more forcefully, another opponent declared that "to acquiesce
in his guilt, would be establishing a precedent, which in some future
period, might encourage an exertion of military power, that in case of a
long protracted war, might prove fatal to liberty."[39]

The pangs over precedents and the dangers posed by Jackson's
use of martial law were about thirteen years late. During the interim,
virtually no one, save Algernon Sydney, lamented Jackson's actions in
New Orleans. Even the president and secretary of war turned a blind
eye to the dangers of martial law. Prior to Jackson's bid for the presidency the Battle of New Orleans was sacrosanct, a national trophy to
be revered. No one dared malign this great American battle or the man
who achieved it. The first rumblings over the general's military demeanor came in the wake of the Seminole Affair, when opponents con-
nived against Jackson as much because of his celebrity and potential
candidacy as from any ideological misgivings over constitutional
transgressions. The movement against Jackson grew bolder only after
he proved to be a true contender. An exasperated Henry Clay touched
on the source of Jackson's popularity, and in the midst of the ensuing
struggle for the executive office, opponents, many of them writing
anonymously, took on the nation's hero for his use of martial law.
Depicting Jackson as an enemy to civil liberties, political opponents
presented the 1828 election as a trial for the American people. On one
side existed republican simplicity: virtue of character, devotion to the
laws, and preservation of the citizens' rights against despotic rule. On
the other side stood the overbearing power of a "military chieftain,"
the antithesis to fragile liberty. "If our republic is to be saved from
the disgrace and ruin with which it is threatened," concluded one opponent, "you must be persuaded, my fellow citizens, by the veneration
which you owe to the constitution achieved by valor and cemented by
the purest blood of patriotism . . . to oppose by all lawful means, the
election of Andrew Jackson."[40]

Andrew Jackson:
Defender of the Nation, Savior of Liberty

If Andrew Jackson's opponents utilized the military chieftain charge and martial law in New Orleans to derail the general's momentum toward the White House, supporters proved equally adept at keeping the presidential train on the tracks and fully stoked. Pro-Jackson adherents from around the country took to the podium and pen in order to advocate and defend Old Hickory. Like the anti-Jackson attacks, the vast majority of works came about in the aftermath of the 1824 election fiasco. Jackson had proven himself a viable candidate, and once the opposition opened up their big guns, supporters happily returned fire. Focusing on Jackson's military record and martial law in New Orleans, they heralded the assets of a "military chieftain," lauded his devout patriotism, and argued that the nation could never repay his services. The presidency, of course, would go far in demonstrating American appreciation. Jackson's supporters also revealed cunning and boldness in their campaign, insisting that military power actually sustained liberty and thus a military commander understood better than virtually anyone the importance of its defense. This revelation was a stunning alteration of accepted republican political thought, and the motivation was tied directly to Jackson's election.

Not all pro-Jackson works were written post election of 1824. John Henry Eaton, for example, spearheaded the publicity for Jackson's initial campaign. Eaton's involvement was fitting. A close friend and former military aide to the general, Eaton was from Tennessee and for some time had been a diehard Jackson supporter. Appointed to the U.S. Senate in 1818, he took a personal role in Jackson's candidacy, even finishing Jackson's first biography, begun by John Reid in 1817. The biography was ultimately published in 1824, yet it was not Eaton's first public discussion of Jackson's merits. In 1823, Eaton authored a series of thirteen anonymous letters to Philadelphia's *Columbian Observer* in which he broached a variety of issues related to Jackson. In 1824, the various tracts were published in a single pamphlet, *The Letters of Wyoming,* in which Eaton developed further the popular national symbol of Jackson created at New Orleans.[41] The letters also sounded a ringing defense of martial law and Jackson's devotion to liberty: "While the storm of battle raged—while a well-trained army hovered on our shores, and every patriot trembled at the result of a contest, on which was staked the only remnant of liberty that existed on earth,

Jackson stood forth, the Champion, the Defender, the Deliverer of his Country, and closed our war with a brilliancy that lighted a smile on the brow of every patriot. . . . The Constitution and Liberty of the country were in imminent peril, and he has preserved them both!"

Eaton consistently hammered away at the patriotism inherent in the general's protection of America. "He has saved, defended, and shielded his country," thundered Eaton. "Storms and perils he has breasted, and borne her in safety through her angry trials."[42] It was this very devotion that required Jackson to impose martial law. Eaton insisted that potential traitors littered the streets of New Orleans. It was a place "where treason reposed, and where disaffection stalked abroad, until hopes, in the bosom of the sternest patriot, scarcely lingered. All was distrust, doubt, uncertainty and fear: there was neither union nor harmony, nor concert of action." Clearly, insinuated Eaton, internal discord was the greatest threat to the city. *Letters of Wyoming* made it appear as though the British were in fact a minor problem compared to the internal struggles plaguing the city. "With warmth of feeling, and glowing fire of soul," continued Eaton, "he entered on the seemingly forlorn and hopeless effort."[43] Considering this dire state of affairs, argued the former aide, Jackson's declaration of martial law was fully justified: "High handed measures and caution alone could have secured to him beneficial results." And the only thing that mattered was that "they [beneficial results] were secured." Eaton admitted that the general "did violate the constitution; of this none have ever doubted, nor has Jackson himself pretended to say otherwise." (Jackson and some followers later reversed their position and argued the constitutionality of his conduct.) But those same "strong measures" saved the city. Thus, in Eaton's opinion, "Jackson stood forth, the Champion, the Defender, the Deliverer of his Country." In a rather paradoxical twist, Eaton argued that rather than a threat to the nation, Jackson's violation of the laws solidified his devotion to them. "Let the nation answer then," he challenged, "where amongst them is there a republican like andrew jackson? Does he love his country? Let a head grown grey, a constitution impaired in the service of the country, declare!" Such lofty assertions were a novel attempt to juxtapose unconstitutional acts with unflagging patriotism, a parallel that subsequent Jackson supporters happily exploited. Eaton concluded, "Jackson's pretensions on the score of fidelity and attachment cannot be questioned and to him a debt of gratitude is due, which this nation can never fully repay."[44]

To fill out the picture of Jackson as the devoted patriot, Eaton paid special attention to the importance of military men in general, especially the value of electing one to the presidency. And who better to hold up than the father of the nation, George Washington? The first lines of the *Letters* began with a sort of tribute to Washington, noting gleefully, "he was a military man." Eaton followed quickly with Jackson's devotion to the country and emphasized his title, "*The Hero of Orleans.*" Eaton compared the two generals no less than ten times throughout the work and at one point, in the midst of describing martial law, pushed the parallel to extremes: "washington would have done the same." The only problem, of course, is that Washington never declared martial law. Yet this fact was of little consequence in a campaign tract oozing with praise and designed to lionize Jackson as a national hero. At the core of such comparisons was a reverence for liberty and a connection to the Revolution. Eaton made sure to point out that Jackson had fought in the War of Independence and even argued that because of that service he deserved the presidency. "To this high office Jackson has superior claims," extolled Eaton. "Remember, he was of the Revolution!"[45]

Washington as a military man, the fight for independence, and the idea of liberty were intimately connected. Eaton's attempt to place Jackson in the same category was clever, but not nearly so bold as the claim that those who fought for liberty on the battlefield were best suited to defend it in the civil arena: "Who that has feelings of gratitude, and loves the land he dwells in, will fear to trust the directions and affairs of this country, to him, who has protected and defended, and saved it." Eaton also rejected the notion that a military man might be dangerous to the nation, and in fact reveled in Jackson's fierce military demeanor, declaring, "A wonderful manifestation of violence and temper, to be sure! God grant, should peril again assail us, that we may find some bold commander ready and willing to make precisely as strong a demonstration of his temper as did Jackson."[46] Such an image was potentially dangerous in a nation obsessed with the protection of liberty. A violent, temper-driven military man at the head of a powerful army was traditionally the antithesis of liberty in a Republic. In campaigning for the general, Eaton had rewritten one of the principle tenets of the Revolutionary era. The quickly rising Age of Party, with partisans on both sides maneuvering for political gain, allowed Eaton to argue effectively that liberty was best protected by power.

The *Letters of Wyoming* were a masterful work designed to smooth over some of Jackson's past acts and advertise his value to the nation. Certainly one of the episodes that required explanation was New Orleans. As the source of Jackson's heroism, the famous battle resonated as a shining example of American ability and nationalism. Yet it was also fraught with danger. Eaton realized the necessity of making the New Orleans victory immune to criticism, and he therefore addressed martial law directly, twisting it into another example of Jackson's self-sacrifice for the good of the nation and, hence, his inherently virtuous character. Eaton was so successful in this endeavor that one historian noted, Americans "doubtless went to the polls with Eaton's image of Jackson—or an image influenced by Eaton's—in their minds."[47]

Because of their impact, the *Letters* became a model of how to write a campaign pamphlet. Thus it is no surprise that subsequent Jackson defenders followed in John Eaton's rhetorical footsteps. Isaac Watts Crane, while speaking before a crowd in Philadelphia, declared that if Jackson "erred" in declaring martial law, "it was from motives of patriotism and regard to the public good." "Having like Washington, fought for liberty," insisted Crane, "[Jackson] knows its value and how to appreciate its blessings."[48] The parallels between Wyoming and Crane could not be more apparent; both focused on extinguishing criticism of martial law by virtue of Jackson's devotion to the public. The connection to the first father was also highlighted, as it was in most pro-Jackson pieces.[49] And, once again, there was the incredible insistence that a military man could best defend liberty. Crane even connected the military and civil authorities more closely, arguing that a commander's expertise was not incompatible with civil government. The nation, in fact, would benefit from having such a man in the White House: "Those who advocate him as General, but not as President, ought to consider, that as President every part of our country would be benefitted and derive protection from his military talents, his sagacity and vigilance."[50]

Subsequent pro-Jackson campaign literature was both advertising and an attempt to explain away charges made by the opposition. The content of these pieces, like the opposition works, covered a broad spectrum of the hero's past: duels, marital problems, and Florida. Still, the overwhelming majority of his supporters discussed New Orleans and martial law to some degree and usually devoted considerable time to the issue.[51] Also connected to such discussions was Clay's "military chieftain" charge and Jackson's allegedly violent temper. Foremost among the general's advocates was an anonymous pamphleteer named "Aristide," later identified as William P. Van Ness, a Jackson man from New York. Van Ness devoted his entire work to Jackson's first invasion of Florida in 1814 and his subsequent defense of New Orleans. The author immediately revealed his intention of vindicating Old Hickory's reputation by announcing in the preface, "If I shall establish the fact, and I think I shall do it most conclusively, that Gen. Jackson did those things *only* which could have saved the country, he must be acquitted of all blame." "If he be exonerated from censure," continued Van Ness, "then must he be applauded for his foresight, wisdom, and prudence; and these high qualities added to his universally admitted virtues of patriotism and valour."[52] Van Ness's pamphlet was a melodramatic diatribe that often launched into outright hagiography: "Matchless hero! Incomparable man! Brave and skillful in war, generous and benevolent in peace. The records of chivalry, the pages of history do not furnish a more exalted character than thine!"[53]

If Van Ness added flair and saccharine to lauding Jackson, the New Yorker proved equally adept at piling it on when denigrating the general's foes. Only the "disaffected and wicked," the "base and degenerate," the "villains," and "bad men," he trumpeted, protested against martial law during its use. "The good and patriotic advised it," insisted the author. Keeping with this theme, he accused Senator Louaillier and Judge Hall of conspiring to interfere with military authority. (Jackson had made the same point during his formal defense against the contempt charge.) Van Ness even compared the actions of Jackson and the judge in the face of the impending British attack and scoffed, "Hall fled like a slave."[54] Attacking supposed traitors in Louisiana was actually a clever way of both turning the spotlight away from Jackson and justifying his actions at the same time. Thus other supporters adopted the same strategy. Nathan Felton, speaking before a crowd in Concord, New Hampshire, posed a simple question to his audience: Who was it who denounced Jackson in New Orleans? "Louaillier," he cried, "a traitor, whom Jackson detected and arrested in his treachery; a wretch, who hated the Constitution, and would have sold his Country. . . . As well might the character of Washington be impeached by the testimony of Arnold."[55] In such diatribes it did not matter that Louaillier had been a staunch defender of his state, voted for defense measures, and only ran up against Jackson after what the senator felt was the unnecessary continuation of martial law.

Nor did the general's defenders stop at denouncing men like Judge Hall and Senator Louaillier as conspirators and turncoats. The treachery went further than resisting Jackson's authority in New Orleans. Notwithstanding Jackson's justified and patriotic violation of the law, Judge Hall was actually the one who had subverted the Constitution by refusing Jackson's right to a trial by jury. Moreover, Hall had engaged in conduct that was beyond his purview. Critics insisted that because Louaillier's arrest occurred within Louisiana, it was strictly a state matter. As a federal judge, Hall had no authority to issue a writ of habeas corpus. Indeed, Judge Hall himself had questioned his power to perform such an act.[56] Such arguments hit upon important constitutional points. The first dealt with the power of the judiciary to punish contempt and the second disputed Hall's jurisdictional authority to sit in judgment of the general (these issues arose again in the 1840s refund debates). This maneuver on the part of Jackson's supporters revealed an adroit attempt to place the burden of constitutionality upon the judge rather than Jackson. Still, exposing Hall's supposedly unconstitutional acts entered the complicated realm of legalese, and Jackson's partisans much preferred sticking to more basic, clearly understood points. Comparing Jackson to Washington was one such strategy. Making the support of martial law and of Jackson a matter of patriotism was another. The reverse, of course, as was shown with the attacks upon Hall and Louaillier, was that anyone criticizing Jackson was unpatriotic. "The man, whose bosom does not swell with pride at the recollection of his [Jackson's] brilliant exploits," announced one speaker before a crowd in New York, "possesses not an American heart." Maj. Henry Lee, son of Henry "Light Horse Harry" Lee, made a similar implication, announcing, "I am . . . satisfied, that no friend to his country, can lay his hand on his heart and say, he [Jackson] did not perform" his duty.[57]

Lee's work, *A Vindication of the Character and Public Services of Andrew Jackson in reply to . . . Electioneering Calumnies*, was written specifically to combat the anti-Jackson literature produced by the opposition. Originally encouraged by Duff Green, editor of the Washington-based *Telegraph*, Lee embarked on his mission with Jackson's full consent and even visited the Hermitage to utilize the general's papers.[58] Like *The Letters of Wyoming*, Lee's work began as a series of newspaper tracts. And again, like Eaton and other pro-Jackson authors, Lee confronted the need to defend Jackson's declaration of martial law. As the source of his national appeal, the New Orleans campaign, every aspect of it, had to appear beyond reproach. Lee therefore expounded upon the "the great law of self-defense," insisting that Jackson acted properly when "superseding the less essential and elementary provisions of law." Explaining further the relationship between military and civil authority, he insisted that the latter is sometimes temporarily incompatible with the nation's safety, "hence the well known maxim of the civil law, *Inter arma silent leges* [In the midst of arms laws are silent]."[59] In making these points, Lee offered two different, though not incompatible, concepts to justify the necessity of declaring martial law. Each idea was targeted at a different audience. The average reader easily comprehended the law of self-defense. When danger threatened one's person or property, a degree of force was justified to end the threat. Invoking Latin phrases such as *Inter arma silent leges*, on the other hand, was directed at educated Americans who grasped the underlying technicalities of constitutions and civil versus military power. This is not to say, however, that the theory of self-defense did not contain its own theoretical complexities. Derived from the law of nature, the notion of self-defense, when applied to New Orleans, did more than merely justify martial law; self-defense made Jackson's conduct legal. John Locke's treatise on the law of nature made clear that it existed prior to and was not superseded by any social contracts or man-made legal systems. Moreover, the use of force while defending one's self was among the most fundamental of human rights. Many nineteenth-century politicians could readily cite from Emer de Vattel's *Law of Nations; or, Principles of the Law of Nature*, which explained the grounds upon which a nation could engage in acts of self-defense.[60]

Lee's second explanation, *inter arma silent leges*, seemed to go a step further, calling for the suppression of civil law when military necessity existed. Lee announced the Latin maxim as though it was an acknowledged and accepted doctrine to which all must bow. Those who have subsequently utilized the famous decree, even up to the present day, hold the same view. Yet the original meaning of *inter arma silent leges* was absolutely identical to the law of nature's notion of self-defense. In 52 b.c.e., Cicero announced that the law of nature was ingrained in every individual and when violence is intended a person may use any means to secure safety; he followed with the famous statement, "For laws are silent when arms are raised." Cicero's declaration considered individuals, not nations. Still, the logical extension was that the law of self-defense applied to both, nations as well as individuals.

A

VINDICATION

OF THE

CHARACTER AND PUBLIC SERVICES

ANDREW JACKSON;

IN REPLY TO THE

RICHMOND ADDRESS, SIGNED BY CHAPMAN JOHNSON,

AND TO OTHER ELECTIONEERING CALUMNIES.

———

ORIGINALLY PUBLISHED IN THE NASHVILLE REPUBLICAN.

AND ATTRIBUTED TO

MAJOR HENRY LEE,

OF VIRGINIA.

———

BOSTON :
True and Greene, Printers......1828.

Title page of A Vindication of the Character and Public Service of Andrew Jackson, *by Maj. Henry Lee, 1828.*

Where and when the maxim escalated to a justification for suppressing all civil authority in the midst of war is an utter mystery, and one that requires historical study.[61] Henry Lee's use of the Latin phrase did not engage such subtleties. Rather, it was intended solely to impart some higher legality for martial law. It was merely one more argument why Jackson was right and everyone who opposed him was wrong.

The seemingly intricate aspects of *inter arma silent leges* were abandoned by most pro-Jackson writers in favor of the much more comprehensible argument of self-defense. It is unclear who among the writers first adopted the theory of self-defense, but once introduced, a number of authors gladly capitalized on the strategy. "God of nature!" declared William Van Ness, "shall not the child rescue his parent from death, though he commit a breach of the peace in the attempt? It is the first law of nature." Pushing the point further, and again criticizing Judge Hall, Van Ness queried, "Did not the Judge know that there is a legal and moral justification for homicide?"[62] The obvious implication was that Jackson had an innate right to impose martial law in defense of the nation. Nathan Felton, a pro-Jackson speaker in New Hampshire, touched even more specifically on the preeminent authority of natural law: "Constitutions and Treaties, and Laws, may be disregarded, without violating them, under the rigorous demands of necessity." "Our own lives, and the lives of our fellow creatures may be preserved," declared Felton," at the expense of our liberty, and of the lives and liberties of those who would destroy them."[63] With the promulgation of such doctrines, Old Hickory's actions in New Orleans were transformed from despotism and lawlessness into the highest form of patriotism and natural rights.

Jackson's campaign spokesmen were also faced with Henry Clay's damning "military chieftain" epithet. The unflattering picture that it might create in the minds of voters necessitated a response. Jackson himself had attempted to spin the barb into something beneficial, but doing so required more than a single retort. Thus Jackson's adherents worked feverishly to not only counter Clay's charge but also capitalize on it. And it was indeed a group effort, for nearly every Jackson partisan addressed the subject, and many went to great lengths. Part of the strategy was continuing the comparison between George Washington and Jackson as military men. Supporters also utilized John Eaton's forceful advocacy of military prowess. In doing so, they not only attempted to discredit Clay's notion of a dangerous military man but also altered the Revolutionary era conception that liberty was at the mercy of an ever-encroaching power, especially in the form of standing armies and despotic military officers. The Jacksonians embraced the good "military chieftain" who battled for the nation's liberty and juxtaposed him against the self-serving politician motivated only by thirst for political office. Accepting Clay's title, William Van Ness declared that Jackson "is just in all his actions; honourable in all his engagements; temperate in his habits, and benevolent in his sympathies. he loves his country more than he does his life! . . . Such a man is andrew jackson, the military chieftain." Van Ness attacked Clay and his "retainers" for criticizing the general and questioned why they treated the hero with such disrespect in light of his valuable military services. "Because he stood in the way of that gentleman at the last election, *and will at the next*," thundered the author. Then, playing on the Kentuckian's charge, Van Ness mocked, "It displeased that gentlemen [Clay] that the *people* should *dare* to prefer Andrew Jackson, the 'military chieftain,' to him, Henry Clay, the *civil chieftain*."[64]

Equally resolute in his defense of Old Hickory's military record, a New Hampshire supporter insisted that there was "something due to him on the score of military renown" and dismissed the idea that he posed a threat to liberty: "Is there danger of him, who regardless of life and property, has fought and bled for the liberties of his country, that he will turn traitor to the very freedom and independence he has assisted to establish?" On the contrary, "there is more danger to our civil liberties from the artifices of one such man as John Q. Adams or Henry Clay, ready to stretch the Constitution to any dimension, so it may suit their purposes of patronage [than from] all the military men that have lived, now live, or will live in this country for a century."[65] Isaac Hill, Jackson's chief political henchman in New Hampshire, made the same implication, arguing that the general's great victories were "enough to establish the fame of a self-taught 'military chieftain' and to render harmless and contemptible the rival ambition of a mere state-fed office-hunter."[66] Jackson's supporters engaged in an adept game of political juggling. Jackson was no longer a dangerous military man who threatened liberty by force of arms. He was now a shining example of patriotism who exercised beneficial military power to secure liberty and safeguard the nation. This was, of course, a remarkable juxtaposition to the negative attributes of a professional politician who sought office merely to expand his own unquenchable power. Such men would

never place their own reputation on the line and sacrifice themselves
in the way that Jackson did, argued supporters. William Van Ness challenged, "Would the Hartford Convention men have done this? . . . Would
the dark-souled Webster have done it? or the *Hon. Josiah Quincy*, or
any other of the *present distinguished friends of the Hon. Henry Clay*,
have done it, or the Arch Sophist himself? Would any of these have ven-
tured and suffered what this patriot and gallant warrior did at the time,
for his exposed and bleeding country? No; I answer! And shall he be
condemned for it, or forgotten for it? No! I Repeat."[67]

The political intent of such comparisons was obvious. None of the
pro-Jackson partisans bothered to mention that Henry Clay was one
of the principal War Hawks who advocated hostilities with England in
order to defend American sovereignty. Nor did they note that the Kentuckian helped to end the war by serving as a Ghent peace commissioner. Clay certainly did not partake in the notorious Hartford convention. Far from giving him any credit for services to the nation, Clay
was condemned as the worst sort of danger to the nation; he was a
politician.

The speeches and pamphlets written in favor of Jackson's bid for
the presidency in 1824 and 1828 reaffirmed his status as the Hero of
New Orleans. The darker side of the famous victory, martial law, was
expertly managed so that it actually added to the glory of the victory
and revealed Jackson's devotion to the nation. Jackson's partisans concluded that the nation could never repay the hero for his services, but
raising him to the presidential chair would certainly go far in erasing
a portion of the country's debt. Nor was this all, for this approach was
the friendlier of the pro-Jackson messages. The other shamed voters
into supporting the hero by labeling anyone who opposed martial law,
and thus Jackson, a traitor. Such tactics, as well as the ability to redi-
rect the massive criticism aimed at the general's conduct in New
Orleans revealed the boldness and expertise of his many supporters.
They not only addressed the difficulties of martial law but also pro-
moted them as assets. Especially significant was the troubling argument that liberty was best defended by military power. John Eaton
went to the furthest extreme, declaring that a violent temper was an
asset for a commander. Such ideas rubbed hard against the Revolutionary conception of liberty and power. The nation's founders had
always identified power as a threat to liberty, and thus constant vigilance was required to maintain a delicate equilibrium. Jackson's adher-

ents essentially exploded this idea, arguing instead that power protected liberty and a military commander, the embodiment of power, was best suited to defend the nation's liberties. Revolutionary republicanism was shaped by supporters to aggressively politic for Andrew Jackson. The fact that a long-held political tradition was manipulated by campaign strategy revealed the extent to which adherents would go in advocating Jackson's bid for the presidency. Yet arguments championing military power held potentially dangerous consequences. Pro-Jackson writers had only General Jackson in mind when making such arguments and therefore necessarily avoided the opposition's warning that martial law created a precedent that other commanders might follow. Though Jackson's followers could insist that he was a virtuous and patriotic general, they could hardly vouch for the character and conduct of future military officers.

The battle for the presidency in 1824 and 1828 revealed strikingly new, negative images of Andrew Jackson. As the Hero of New Orleans, Jackson had always basked in the famous victory. It was the source of his national appeal. Having saved the nation's honor during its darkest hour, Jackson was for the most part untouchable by any politician with an ounce of common sense. President Madison and Secretary of War Armstrong certainly thought it wise to allow the problems of martial law to fade away rather than face the potential ire of Jackson's adoring public. If there were others who viewed martial law with concern, they too remained silent. Indeed, no one raised any questions until Benjamin Watkins Leigh's anonymous Algernon Sydney letters on the Seminole Affair and martial law. Yet Leigh's criticism of New Orleans, as much as Leigh himself, was atypical. True, Henry Clay made his famous military chieftain charge during this same time period and repeated it in the dispute over the election of 1824, but the political wheeler and dealer from Kentucky never openly disavowed the means to gain victory at New Orleans, and following the risky speech on the Seminole War he was counseled to keep his mouth shut. It was only in exasperation that he broached the question of whether killing redcoats was a proper qualification for the executive office. Martial law, however, was still off limits, even though it was so closely tied to Jackson's conduct in Florida. Only when Jackson proved himself a viable candidate did New Orleans and martial law suddenly fall victim to attack. The motivation was decidedly partisan. Opponents unleashed a torrent of criticism concerning Jackson's martial despotism and, with the banner of "military

chieftain" held high, attempted to squelch Old Hickory's hopes of political victory. The belated calls for safeguarding liberty from the hands
of a powerful and dangerous military despot were as much for political effect as any ideological considerations. The growing partisan enmity
that arose in tandem with the flourishing new party system ensured
that ideology was infused with politicking. Thus politicians found it not
only easy but effective to manipulate for their own purposes the long-
held Revolutionary tradition of safeguarding liberty against aggressive
power.

CHAPTER 3

The Congressional Refund Bill: A Partisan Battle

I n the wake of Andrew Jackson's presidential victories in 1828 and 1832, few bothered to mention the specter of martial law. Arguments over civil liberties and dangerous precedents for future uses of military power faded in light of much more tangible concerns. The Eaton Affair, bank veto, removal of federal deposits, and subsequent Senate censure, as well as Nullification, gripped the attention of the general's opponents. Why bother with an episode that occurred in 1815 when it seemed that King Andrew I, as Whigs called him, threatened the very fiber of the Republic while he occupied the White House? The battle over martial law thus ceased for a time, but it did not disappear forever. When Senator Lewis Field Linn of Missouri introduced in March 1842 a bill to refund with interest Jackson's one-thousand-dollar fine for contempt of court, a battle ensued that stretched some two years over three sessions of Congress. Ironically, Senator Linn originally expected the refund bill to generate little opposition and even wrote Jackson to that effect: "My opinion is it will pass without a dissenting voice—but it may be otherwise."[1]

The Missouri senator's motivation for introducing the refund bill, as well as the "otherwise," loom as integral questions in the history of the congressional refund debates. Why, after some twenty-seven years,

did Linn suddenly deem it important that the general receive reimbursement? Of equal importance, what actually happened to the bill in
the Senate and House? Connected to this question is why Whigs engaged
in such steadfast resistance. To the first of these inquiries, Jackson historians have surmised that Democrats broached the refund legislation
primarily in regard to the general's dire financial circumstances.[2]
Jackson was flat broke. His adopted son, Andrew Jackson Jr., was a
poor businessman and a notorious spendthrift. The result was excessive debt for Jackson. It was only through the favor of friends such as
Francis Preston Blair and Jean-Baptiste Plauché that Jackson avoided
bankruptcy.[3]

To explain away the introduction of the refund bill solely or even
primarily because of Jackson's precarious financial situation is, however, incorrect. It was Jackson himself who not only desired but also
orchestrated the very means of attaining the congressional refund. In
retirement at the Hermitage, Jackson looked back over a long military
and political career in which he claimed victory after victory. He
crushed the Indian tribes of the South, devastated the British at New
Orleans, slew the Monster Bank, and silenced the traitorous Nullifiers.
For these accomplishments he received the accolades and votes of
the people. Even when Whigs attempted to sully his triumphs, as with
the Senate censure for removing the federal deposits in 1834, Jackson's
supporters ultimately overcame, in the general's view, such mean-
spirited partisan attacks. Thomas Hart Benton successfully expunged
the Senate censure in 1837. Yet on Old Hickory's greatest military victory, New Orleans, there remained a shadow: Dominick Hall's contempt
fine. Jackson, ever jealous of his reputation, wanted that blight removed. Thus his 1841 letter to Auguste Davezac, in which Jackson complained, "I cannot but regret that this stain upon my name, shall be permitted to pass down to posterity," was the beginning of the general's
campaign for vindication.[4] In both the choice of Davezac as legislative
messenger and the subsequent battle for the refund bill, Jackson revealed a shrewdness and political skill that some historians have dismissed. In reality, he knew exactly how to work the political system in
Washington. Jackson also understood his nationalist appeal and expected it to help aid his quest. Another component of Jackson's motivation was establishing a precedent for the future use of emergency powers should the nation again face imminent danger. This aspect of the
debates, however, is discussed in a subsequent chapter.

Senator Linn's assumption that the refund bill would elicit little dissent was decidedly naïve in light of the vitriol that defined Jackson's relationship with Whigs. The party evolved in direct opposition to what they considered Jackson's freewheeling abuse of power, specifically in regard to the bank issue. The very name "Whig" harkened back to eighteenth-century commonwealth English radicals who wrote in opposition to monarchical power. To Jacksonian era Whigs, the general epitomized dangerous, kingly rule. It was Jackson himself, during his tenure as president and long after, who stood as a key figure in party warfare. As one historian astutely noted, "He made the issue one of supporting or opposing Jackson, and consequently he even more than his policies became the dominant issue of his presidency. . . . His name alone could polarize parties and energize supporters."[5] Even in retirement, Jackson's political symbolism remained potent. And though Democrats originally argued that they broached the refund bill in the interest of justice to the general, insisting that any breach of law on his part was mitigated because of virtuous intentions in saving New Orleans, they quickly awakened to the bill's potential political power. Support or opposition for the refund was a defining factor between the parties, and Democrats made sure to herald the New Orleans victory, insisting that the refund was a national obligation to the aging hero. As the general's supporters had done when discussing martial law in the midst of his run for the presidency, Jackson was lionized for his devotion to the nation. This time, however, the political capital was not for Jackson. Rather, the Democratic Party itself needed reenergizing. After a devastating loss in both the presidential and congressional elections of 1840, Democrats were left treading political water. The refund bill, with all of Jackson's heroism tied to it, could not have arrived at a better time. Jackson's name was paraded before the people prior to the approaching congressional elections and during the initial planning for the 1844 presidential contest. Whigs certainly did not miss this fact.

Ironically, Democrats did not broach the refund legislation with such a clearly partisan, electioneering goal in mind. Their initial arguments focused on justice to Jackson and the improper sentence of Judge Hall. And though the issue of Hall's conduct quickly became a sticking point between the two parties, when Lewis Field Linn originally proposed the refund he hoped that opposition might never come. Whigs, however, rallied in defense of the judiciary, adding amendments clarifying that the bill made no determination regarding the legality of Judge

Hall's or Jackson's actions. Whigs also charged that the refund was a mere ploy to raise Jackson's name before the people in anticipation of the pending elections. The Whig assertion was like a lightning bolt for Democrats, who quickly recognized the potential boon that lay before them and the power of stringing the legislation along so that they could lambaste Whigs for their bitter opposition to the Hero of New Orleans. In a letter to Jackson, Francis Preston Blair, a friend, former political advisor, and editor of the Washington-based *Daily Globe*, articulated beautifully the newly found tactic, noting that "the Democracy are making the conduct of the Whigs in relation to it [the refund bill] a question before the people in the pending elections—how they will feel it. . . . I think it a good occasion to renew the impression on the public mind [of] your glorious efforts in the last act of the war. . . . A revival of your military triumphs will give it [the Democratic party] strength in its present contest with Federalism."[6]

Thus the battle over Jackson's refund exploded onto the political scene. Charges and countercharges abounded, each side attempting to paint the other as manipulative and insincere. And the stakes could in deed be high. At least one legislator lost his reelection bid to the Senate and other politicians felt pressure as a result of the refund battle. When studying the political history of nineteenth-century America, one must not lose appreciation for the everyday bombast and rhetoric of partisan debate. This was an era of language and high-minded oratory in which the sharp tongues of the nation's leaders cut into one another, figuratively bloodying their foes. The victor in these contests commanded formidable political power; the loser was often relegated to political oblivion. This was especially true with the maturation of the second American party system in which a highly organized political structure existed in virtually every state. Thrust into this Age of Party was Jackson's refund bill. The ensuing debates stand as a testament to the political expertise of Democrats and Whigs, for both parties attempted to manipulate the bill and Jackson as a symbol for electoral gain.

To be sure, the refund bill was but one among many issues that tested the will and power of the competing parties. Whigs and Democrats continued to battle over the nation's banking system, and to make matters worse for Whigs, President John Tyler, who was a former Democrat and had risen to the executive office only after William Henry Harrison's untimely death, consistently vetoed the party's bills to charter the national bank. Other major topics of the period were the Bankruptcy Act of 1841 and the Whig Tariff of 1842.[7] Where exactly Jackson's refund bill fit into the equation in terms of political importance is difficult to determine with certainty. Jackson, Francis Blair, and other Democrats certainly believed that it would cause major problems for Whigs, but the reality of this assertion is not entirely clear. There are specific instances in which the refund bill had a decided impact, but these dealt with one state or person and thus do not reveal the extent to which the issue impacted the parties in the nation as a whole. Though one may never be able to determine without question the degree to which voting on one specific measure among many might influence a party's fortunes, Whigs and Democrats who fought over Jackson's refund argued as though it was the biggest issue facing the nation.

Andrew Jackson as Political Mastermind and the Advent of the Refund Bill

Andrew Jackson was no political simpleton. His mission to remove the contempt fine from his military record reveals both organization and an understanding of politics. Jackson not only devised the strategy for removal of the fine but also kept close watch on the refund bill throughout the congressional battle. Distinctly aware of his popular appeal, Jackson fully expected the refund issue to hurt his opponents once the debates began to rage. And he did all that he could to ensure that the bill passed and his enemies paid for their opposition. Letters poured forth from the Hermitage. Jackson collected evidence, forwarded it to supporters, and made certain that Democrats refused to yield on *his* understanding of how the fine should be refunded. Moreover, Jackson, in at least one instance, ensured that a political enemy who argued against the refund lost his Senate seat. The fine issue was Andrew Jackson's final vindication, his last, masterful political feat.

Jackson made first mention of the fine in an 1839 letter to his nephew, Andrew Jackson Donelson. Noting that attending the annual Battle of New Orleans celebration held in Louisiana was impossible due to insufficient funds, the general added, "I have sacrificed both property and health in the salvation of Neworleans, paid $1000 fine and costs, and the Legislature thereof has never attempted to have that unjust sentence removed by resolutions and memorial to congress to have the fine and costs restored to me with interest."[8] There is little doubt that Jackson had given the fine considerable thought. Since the day it was imposed he bristled at the actions of Judge Hall, wrote disparaging letters to a Louisiana newspaper, and marched to Washington fully prepared to confront the president and defend martial law. Jackson even contemplated the removal of Hall from the federal bench but ultimately let the matter drop. Still, his pride was not to be toyed with, and the fine ate like a canker on his ego. When he first devised the specific plan to erase the fine is uncertain, but the 1839 letter to Donelson is the first known written expression. Jackson's solution for removal was clear. Congress must rescind the fine. With this strategy in mind he wrote to Auguste Davezac, who served as a representative in the New York legislature.[9] As he had done in the letter to his nephew, Jackson outlined clearly the method for the refund: "Congress is the only body whose action could wipe this stain from my memory, by a joint resolution ordering the fine, with costs and interests, to be refunded."[10]

Though Jackson made first mention of the fine in relation to his dire financial situation, concern for his seemingly battered image and defense of martial law as an act of necessity were of paramount importance. Writing to Lewis Linn, Jackson refused to accept any refund if the final bill contained Whig amendments that placed censure on his conduct, or upheld that of Judge Hall: "I have to repeat, that no circumstances under which I could be placed would induce me to accept of such a dishonorable boon, as the one proposed, by my enemies, in the amendment to your bill."[11] To Jackson, the refund was about bigger issues than mere money; his national fame and the nation's future security were in question.

In January 1842, Major Davezac brought the refund issue before New York's legislature, and from there it made its way into Congress with the help of Lewis Linn.[12] As proposed by Linn on March 10, 1842, the bill was "to indemnify Major General Andrew Jackson for the damage sustained by him in the discharge of his official duties in the city of New Orleans, in the year 1815, and which proposes that the fine of a thousand dollars with costs imposed upon that officer by Judge Hall shall be refunded to him, with legal interest."[13] Party members in fact raced to present the legislation. Senator Benjamin Tappan of Ohio, who was as devoted to Andrew Jackson as his younger brothers Arthur and Lewis were to the mission of abolition and moral reform, announced

Lewis Field Linn. Courtesy of the Library of Congress.

that Ohio "was in the process of putting forth resolutions independent of Missouri's actions and that had the Governor of Ohio sent them sooner, Ohio would in fact have been the state that put forth the bill."[14]

The Twenty-seventh Congress, in which the refund, Senate Bill 12, came to light, was firmly controlled by Whigs. The party's dominance was significant in the Senate, with 28 seats to the Democrats' 22, and commanding in the House, with 145 seats to the Democrats' 98.[15] How Lewis Linn ever believed that the refund might sail unmolested through this bastion of Whiggery is a mystery. Indeed, such a notion was an ironic twist on the tenacity of Democratic Party warfare in preceding years. Most Whigs were certainly not willing to back away and view the bill in a nonpartisan light.

Whigs had learned party tactics all too well from their opponents and, seeing Democratic blood in the wake of the 1840 presidential contest, descended on the bill. After charging that it involved setting aside the decision of a federal judge, Whigs pushed for referral to the Senate Judiciary Committee, on which only one of the five members was a Democrat.[16] Not surprisingly, the committee quickly issued a negative report and in doing so fired the first shot in a partisan battle that stretched from March 1842 to February 1844. Democrats were, of course, irked at the committee report, especially Robert Walker, a senator from Mississippi and the single Democrat on the Judiciary Committee. Walker informed the Senate that he was ill and confined to his bed while his fellow members deliberated on the matter and was unaware that they had even written a report. Had he known, Walker insisted, he "would have asked the privilege of making a minority report." Suffice it to say, he continued, "[I] do not concur in any part of the report which has been made." Walker objected that the commit-

Thomas Hart Benton. Courtesy of the Library of Congress.

tee had acted unfairly, insisting, "it is nothing more than an act of justice that the money should be refunded; and I believe that it will be perfectly accordant with the opinions of an overwhelming majority of the American people."[17]

Next to rise from the Democratic phalanx was Thomas Hart Benton, the seasoned Jacksonian from Missouri who had so ably commanded the movement to expunge the Senate's censure of Old Hickory for removal of the federal deposits from the Bank of the United States. "Every consideration of justice and right requires us to reverse the sentence, and to expunge the censure which it implies," thundered Benton.

Yet Old Bullion, as he was known, also insisted that "the fine was illegal [and] imposed by an irritated judge, for a supposed contempt of his own authority." In making such an argument, Benton widened the scope of the debate. Whigs, in fact, had expressed concern over a possible challenge to the judiciary and for that very reason argued that it should be forwarded to the Judiciary Committee. As a result of Benton's remarks, Whigs rallied in defense of the courts and, necessarily, Judge Hall. John J. Crittenden of Kentucky, a member of the Judiciary Committee, remarked that Congress "should be extremely cautious in doing an act which would degrade the judiciary of the country, or imply that the law is of little consequence."[18] John Henderson, a Whig from Mississippi, therefore proposed the following amendment: "*Provided always,* That nothing in this act shall be construed to be an expression of the opinion of Congress as to the legality of the proceedings of the judge in inflicting the fine, but that this shall be deemed and taken to be an additional expression of the sense of Congress of the high consideration in which they hold the achievement of General Jackson in the defence of New Orleans, and of the services rendered by him and his companions in arms on that memorable occasion."[19]

Alexander Barrow of Louisiana quickly offered a modification; he requested a paragraph declaring that Congress did not question the fidelity of the citizens of New Orleans. The bill was now becoming unwieldy in the eyes of its originator, and thus Linn insisted that his resolution said nothing about the legality of anything connected to the fine and that Barrow's addition belied the very reason for martial law. Disaffection, stated Linn, did exist in New Orleans. Barrow ultimately withdrew his proposal after feeling the bill's political heat, remarking that he had "consulted with friends" and "at their suggestion, as well as under the conviction that the citizens of New Orleans stood in no need of this reassertion of their fidelity."[20] Henderson's amendment, however, remained, and on May 25 the Senate voted it down by the narrow margin of twenty-two to twenty. Democrats voted as a solid block, whereas two Whigs, William Archer of Virginia and Oliver Smith of Indiana, crossed party lines. Immediately after the vote, Archer clarified his stand on the issue, declaring that he could never support a bill that restored a legally imposed fine. If it was a donation to the general, added Archer, that was another matter.[21]

Whigs did not cease in their attempt to modify the bill, and on the very same day that the first amendment was voted down, Richard Bayard of Delaware put forth another proposal, that "this act shall not be construed as an expression of the opinion of Congress upon any judicial proceedings or legal questions growing out of the declaration of martial law by General Jackson during the defence of New Orleans." The amendment passed by the razor-thin margin of twenty-three to twenty-two, with one Democrat and one Whig crossing lines, but the final legislation was lost because the vote on engrossing the bill for a third reading, as per congressional rules, failed.[22] Thus Democrats succeeded in scuttling the refund legislation with what many viewed as an obnoxious Whig amendment.

In the midst of this wrangling, Democrats again tried to act the part of nonpartisans. Attempting to diminish Whig opposition, William King of Alabama expressed hope that "no political feeling may enter into this question, but that it may be decided upon its merits." King echoed the patriotism so well connected to the Battle of New Orleans, remarking that Jackson's "glory is identified with the glory of his country, and will live in the hearts of his countrymen while one patriotic feeling remains." The strategy was clever, though hardly novel. Democrats had always attempted to defend Jackson by shielding him under the umbrella of New Orleans. And to be sure, there was no reason to stop. Thus King trumpeted the glory of Jackson, asking, "Where is the man, with an American heart in his bosom, who will stand forward and condemn him?"[23] Nor was King alone in walking this well-worn path. James Buchanan also advised that he "did not think this was a case which ought to produce any party excitement." Rather, continued the senator, this is a measure to "render justice where justice is due." Buchanan added, however, that "it may not be said with more justice, that a deep stain will remain upon the character of his country, until it is wiped away by refunding the whole sum, principal and interest,

Charles Magill Conrad. The Historic New Orleans Collection, accession no. 1970.11.123.

to the uttermost farthing. . . . I am more mistaken than I have ever been, if there will not be one enthusiastic and united feeling throughout the country, without the distinction of party, in favor of refunding this money."[24] Democratic avowals of avoiding partisan rancor were subtly disingenuous. They had not yet identified the potential political power of the bill for upcoming elections, but the constant allusions to glory and patriotism unquestionably influenced the debates and put Whigs on the defensive. The Democratic formula was fairly simple. True Americans, those who were patriotic, reveled in Jackson's victories and therefore would without hesitation desire to refund his fine. If this was the case, all who opposed the refund were unpatriotic or, worse, traitors to American glory.

Whigs attempted to avoid such arguments by focusing upon the tangible problem of voiding a judicial decision, something they had raised when the bill was first introduced. Charles Magill Conrad of Louisiana explained that he knew well the history of martial law in his state and at the time of its use "angry discussion" had ensued.

He continued that the manner in which the refund had been requested forced the Senate to confront an important principle. "Congress," he warned, "is called upon to reverse the judgment of a competent tribunal, on the ground of its illegality." This was a serious matter, argued Conrad, and problematic because he "had always entertained the opinion that the imprisonment of Judge Hall, and the resistance of General Jackson to the process of the court, were acts of arbitrary power, entirely unjustifiable in themselves, and not excusable on any plea of *public necessity*." This was a powerful statement and one that haunted the senator in the months that followed. Conrad also turned to the question of the bill's motivation and the Democratic insistence that it should not be a party measure. Acquiescing to the "sincerity of these professions," Conrad nevertheless concluded that he "could not help suspecting that party considerations were lurking at the bottom of this disinterested movement."[25]

To Conrad's and other Whigs' arguments that the refund legislation involved the judiciary and Judge Hall, Silas Wright, the veteran senator from New York, responded that if Whigs "will divest themselves of political prejudices, and look at the proposition as it is," the "legality of the course of the Judge is not drawn in question, his protection does not call for it." Thus Whig opposition stemmed from another source. Wright put the question plainly: "Will they, then, permit political feelings and prejudices, having their origin in events long since arising, to influence their action upon a question like this? Had General Jackson never been in public life since the defence of New Orleans, do they believe that a voice would have been raised, or a vote given, against this bill in its original form?" Wright's arguments were largely correct, but his expectations were not. There is no question that some Whig opposition stemmed primarily from hatred of Andrew Jackson, yet to believe that Whigs would cease the party battles that Democrats themselves had helped to foment was unrealistic. In the aftermath of 1840, Democrats suddenly wanted Whigs to operate according to some sort of mythic partisan rule book. Not surprisingly, Whigs viewed such appeals as a party ploy and correctly recognized that Democrats were attempting to condone Jackson's conduct in New Orleans. Refusal to accept the bill with amendments revealed that the

Democrats' definition of justice included a justification of Jackson's actions in New Orleans and, by implication, a condemnation of Judge Hall's. This is exactly what the general wanted, both vindication and a precedent, and it was directly through his guidance that Democrats became clear on the conditions under which Jackson would accept the money. With the party battles lines clearly drawn, the first attempt to pass the bill died with the end of the Twenty-seventh Congress' second session.[26]

Following the debates carefully from the Hermitage, Jackson was incensed at the Judiciary Committee report and Whig amendments. He grumbled in a letter to Francis Preston Blair, "I have just seen Berrien's report on the case of the fine imposed by judge Hall—he may be applauded for his party zeal."[27] The general followed with a letter to his nephew Andrew Jackson Donelson, noting, "it is evident that these well read jurists [Judiciary Committee] acted from combined party principles to defeat the bill by [adding what is] to me the insulting and degrading amendment."[28] Jackson also wrote that he "would not touch one cent of the money under that odious and insulting bill," and then, in classic Jackson style, thundered, "When I approach Congress it is to demand justice not to beg it. I only appeal to my god for acts of special grace, not man."[29] In a later letter to Blair, Jackson denounced Berrien as a "hypocrit [sic]" and insisted that his opposition to the fine was a result of his dismissal from the presidential cabinet in 1831. Berrien had formerly served as Jackson's attorney general and was jettisoned with the rest of the cabinet in the midst of the Eaton Affair, in which many of the cabinet members and their wives ostracized Margaret Eaton, the wife of Secretary of War John Eaton.[30]

Jackson was also disgusted with the conduct of Charles Conrad, who, insisted the general, had previously supported martial law and been "one of my greatest advocates and approved my whole course." Jackson argued further that Conrad had denounced the conduct of Judge Hall as "tyranicol [sic], illegal, and unjust."[31] Conrad had, in fact, been a member of the Democratic Party and a Jackson supporter until the Bank War, when President Jackson vetoed the bill to recharter the Bank of the United States and removed the federal deposits. As a result, Conrad jumped ship. Previous speeches by Conrad in support of the general and martial law have not been found, though there are many letters to Jackson from Louisiana residents supporting the general's assertion that Conrad was previously a zealous supporter.[32] And if there was one thing that Andrew Jackson could not stomach it was disloyalty, whether in military or political affairs. On such men the general exacted the harshest punishments. Militia men during the 1813–14 Creek Wars learned this all too well when Jackson tried and subsequently executed six deserters. John C. Calhoun also understood the pitfalls of crossing Jackson when, during his first administration, it became apparent that Calhoun had hidden his lack of support for the general during the 1818 Seminole Affair. Calhoun's punishment was expulsion from the party.[33] Jackson viewed Charles Conrad's unforgivable treachery with the same revulsion and desire for revenge. Writing to Blair in June 1842, the general accused Conrad of hypocrisy and urged publication of the letter to "shew Conrad in his true colours, and not a very enviable hue." Jackson also noted that many supporters had written him expressing disgust at Conrad's course, and, revealing his still powerful political influence in the state, added, "I mistake the feelings of the Democracy of Louisiana, if Mr. Conrad, & Mr. Barrow ever get back to the Senate when there [sic] term expires."[34]

By the end of the month, Blair notified Jackson that his letter had been published and had "given the greatest satisfaction to your friends."[35] Yet Jackson was not even close to fulfilling his vengeance upon Conrad, remarking to Blair, "I think that when fairly brought before the Senate & the people will make Mr. Conrad, Barrow & Co. feel for their course, as those men ought, who abandon principles of Justice & truth for party purposes." A short time later Jackson followed with yet another letter explaining that he had received a communiqué from Maj. E. G. Butler, Conrad's brother-in-law, explaining, "Conrad had by his speech in the Senate practically destroyed himself." Jackson concluded by announcing confidently, "I think Mr. Conrad will long regret becoming the tool to that sick hypocrit Berrian [sic], and that vindictive Federalist Bayard." Blair responded that he would put the information to good use and assured the general, "I will never cease to expose on all proper occasions Conrad's tergiversation and self centered ideas in relation to your conduct."[36] Senator Conrad had good reason to worry. His term expired in March 1843, and election for the seat was quickly approaching at the end of 1842. If Jackson possessed as much influence as both he and Blair claimed, Conrad was in trouble.

Jackson and Blair looked to the next session of Congress for victory. Blair wrote Jackson, "You may rest satisfied that the next congress will pass the Bill and probably with a censure of the Judge's decision." The editor also discussed the Democratic strategy that would force Whig approval of the refund, explaining that "the Democracy are making the conduct of the Whigs in relation to this Bill a question before the people pending the elections, and they will feel it." And while Blair reconnoitered with party members in Congress in preparation for the next offensive, the general also organized for battle. "Between this and the meeting of Congress," he wrote Blair, "I intend having all the facts of this case before you." Blair, ever the dutiful political soldier, reported back, "I will devote myself at the next session to see that Federalism is brought to choose again between the gallantry that serve and the treachery that would have betrayed our country during the last war."[37]

The Refund Battle Continues:
The Third Session of the Twenty-seventh Congress

At the beginning of December, in the third session of the Twenty-seventh Congress, Lewis Linn introduced a new resolution to refund Jackson's fine. This time, however, Linn attempted to avoid problems that ensued in the previous session by moving that the bill not be referred to any committees.[38] Yet Whigs still held the majority, and once again the Judiciary Committee seized the refund legislation. Troubled that the bill might fall victim to Whig animosity a second time, Linn rose to the floor just days before Christmas and declared that "this bill must pass. The American people have willed it. It is not with them a party question. All go for it—Jew and Gentile, Democrat and Whig; and it should be done promptly." He even argued that it was particularly fitting that a Whig-dominated Congress refund Jackson's fine, "to act with justice and magnanimity, and do the deed themselves; the more magnanimous from the bitter political war that has been waged for so many years."[39] The senator's plea had little effect. Shortly after the new year, Berrien and his compatriots returned the bill with considerable revisions, including changing the title from "A bill to indemnify Major General Andrew Jackson for damages sustained in the discharge of his official duty" to "A bill for the relief of Major General Andrew Jackson." The committee also changed the language of the bill so that the refund's main thrust was "in consideration of the distinguished military services." Nothing could have enraged Jackson more.

The change in title emasculated the bill and made the general sound like some sort of miserable pauper.[40]

Whigs were certainly not oblivious to the refund bill's political importance. As Blair and Jackson had discussed, Democrats were heralding the New Orleans victory and attempting to make the refund a matter of patriotism in connection to the famous battle. Democrats had always used the victory as a sort of cloak in which they protected the general from the attack of enemies. In light of this strategy, Whigs played a potentially dangerous game in opposing the legislation. Yet in reality it was Whigs themselves who provided Democrats with partisan fuel by opposing the refund, and in the aftermath of the second congressional session the Democrats came to understand and savor this fact. The harder Whigs fought the bill, the longer Jackson, with all of his nationalism, remained before the people and more political capital was given to Democrats. Still, Whigs continued, believing from the outset that the refund was nothing but a slick Democratic ploy to raise Jackson's name before the people in anticipation of the coming presidential election. Thus to Lewis Linn's plea for justice and magnanimity, Jacob Miller of New Jersey questioned why Democrats had let the matter sleep for a quarter of a century. He answered his own question:

> It was because they had no conviction that it was necessary, either in support of General Jackson's character, or of their own continuation in power. But now there was a necessity to catch at everything calculated to have a bearing on the presidential election of 1844. It was for this that it was now proposed to take back the hero of New Orleans to the scene of his military glory, with all Congress at his heels. . . . It was . . . a mere movement at a critical time, to make political capital out of the sympathies of a grateful people, for a meritorious officer whose glory was even yet thought capable of lighting his successor to the Presidency once more from the seat from which he had descended."[41]

Miller's statement must have thundered through the halls of the Senate. Here was an impressive charge—that the entire refund issue was a mere Democratic conspiracy for electoral advantage. This, of course, was not the case initially. It was Jackson who forced the legislation, and he did so not because of his party's desperate need for an issue on which to rally but because of his own wounded pride and the belief that emergency measures were warranted in times of imminent danger. Still, Democrats were not fools, and the refund ultimately did become an issue on which they believed the party could be reinvigorated. Part of the Democratic strategy was to continue heralding the patriotic motivations behind the bill and thus capitalize on Jackson's nationalism. Arthur Bagby of Alabama therefore rose to the floor and once again made the Democratic plea that Whigs not block the legislation because of partisan animosity. He "appealed to the Senators on the other side to discard the idea of party management and party tactics" then, following what was now an almost scripted Democratic proclamation, implored his opponents "to look upon it as became every American Senator, and every American citizen with a patriotic breast in his heart."[42] The appeal was brilliant. From one side of his mouth Bagby spoke of avoiding party rancor, and from the other side he disingenuously played the game of Jackson as the embodiment of American glory.

From mid-December to February 1843, senators wrangled over the refund bill, arguing about the title, some attempting to replace the Judiciary Committee amendment with that proposed by Senator Henderson during the previous session and others proposing statements about contempt of court. These maneuverings came to a head on February 21, when the bill, with the Judiciary Committee amendment, came up for a vote. With party lines well defined, the hostility was apparent, and no one felt the pressure more than Charles Conrad. He undoubtedly understood that his previous speech had raised eyebrows in Louisiana and that as a result Jackson was on the hunt for retribution. Conrad also knew that during the previous session his fellow senator, Alexander Barrow, had hastily withdrawn his modification because of pressure from home. With tensions running high, Conrad let his tongue slip, blurting out that he "was perfectly tired and disgusted with the eternal subserviency and sycophancy displayed by the worshippers of this political idol." Linn sprung to the floor, demanding to know if he or any other senators were charged with "sycophancy." Conrad quickly retreated rom the charge, assuring Linn that the remark was not directed at any member of the Senate. The question was then taken and the refund bill passed as amended. Yet it did not survive. The legislation still required House concurrence, and in that chamber, too, tempers flared in the midst of a war over Jackson and the refund of his one thousand dollars.

Though Lewis Field Linn ignited the refund battle by introducing a bill in the Senate, the first mention of the refund actually occurred in the House of Representatives when the single representative from Michigan, Jacob M. Howard, a Whig, presented resolutions from the Michigan legislature "instructing their Senators and requesting their Representative in Congress to use their efforts to procure the passage of a law directing that the fine imposed on General Andrew Jackson, while commanding the army of the United States at New Orleans, near the close of the late war with Great Britain, of one thousand dollars, by the judge of the United States for the district of Louisiana, for an alleged contempt of his authority, be refunded to General Jackson, with costs and interest from the day of the payment of said fine."[43] That Michigan acted first is of no great importance, nor is the fact that Howard was a Whig. News of Maj. Auguste Davezac's January 1842 proposal in the New York Assembly spread rapidly throughout other states in the Union, and within days of Lewis Linn's March 10 Senate bill both houses of Congress received numerous state resolutions as well as private petitions from citizens.[44] Many Whigs, like Howard, were required to present the resolutions.[45] Over the course of the long debates, some eighteen states sent instructions and memorials to Congress and one territory debated the matter.[46]

All of the initial resolutions sent to the House in March 1842 were laid upon the table until Charles Jared Ingersoll, the man who ultimately became Jackson's champion in the lower chamber, presented another memorial on April 11 and succeeded in referring the matter to the Judiciary Committee of which he was a member. Shortly thereafter, on June 17, the committee reported bill 503, "A Bill for the relief of General Andrew Jackson. *Be it enacted by the Senate and House of Representatives of the United States of America in Congress assembled,* That there be paid to General Andrew Jackson, of Tennessee, of any money in the Treasury not otherwise appropriated, the sum of one thousand dollars, being the amount of the fine paid by him while commanding the American forces at New Orleans, in the year one thousand eight hundred and fifteen."[47] Though the bill certainly included the wrong title, for the "relief," and said nothing about interest, it was nevertheless the starting point for the House debate.

Yet even the Judiciary Committee's bill was slow going. It languished most of the summer in 1842 and was blocked by Whigs for discussion in late August, thus remaining idle at the end of the second session.[48] Still, talk of Jackson's refund swirled in Washington, and in his Second Annual Message to Congress, delivered on December 6, President Tyler closed his address with a recommendation that Jackson's fine be refunded: "The defence of New Orleans, while it saved a city from the hands of the enemy, placed the name of General Jackson among those of the greatest captains of the age, and illustrated on the brightest pages in our history. Now that the causes of excitement at the time have ceased to operate, it is believed that the remission of the fine, and whatever of gratification that remission might cause the eminent man who incurred and paid it, would be in accordance with the general feeling and wishes of the American people."[49]

Tyler also attempted to appease Whigs by noting that the bill should not be a reflection on the judicial branch and reasserted the supremacy of the civil authority. Though one might expect a president to have some sway with Congress, Tyler had little. He was, after all, an accident, rising to the executive office only as a result of William Henry Harrison's untimely death after a mere month in office. A former Democrat turned Whig, Tyler was hated by his former party and equally loathed by his new one. It is no surprise that Whigs paid little attention to the message and once again blocked discussion of the refund bill one week after Tyler encouraged Congress to pass it.[50]

By the start of the new year, some House Whigs revealed their steadfast animosity. Thomas Arnold, from Jackson's home state of Tennessee, remarked that he "presumed the principal motive with gentleman who brought forward bills and resolutions on this subject, was, that they might make an harangue in favor of the Old Hero." James Meriwether of Georgia followed suit, acknowledging that "the people had called aloud for the remission of the fine . . . but the call was got up by interested politicians."[51] With the constant stonewalling by House Whigs, Democrats began to show frustration. Finally achieving the floor, an exasperated William Gwin of Mississippi remonstrated that he was "of the opinion that the dominant party in this House intended to give the go-by to the bill." He continued that the bill had been "permitted to sleep" for months and that he "had tried to, from day to day, to get this bill up in committee for consideration; but the majority pertinaciously refused to take it up."[52] To Gwin's complaint came a response from Caleb Cushing, a Whig representative from Massachusetts. Surprisingly, Cushing commiserated on the delay and counseled his fellow congressman to remember that Jackson was no longer the president and therefore he should be considered a "historical personage" who had added to the glory of the nation. "It seemed," continued Cushing, "that it became them to regard that man, and to regard this measure, above all things, in relation to an historical personage and to honor the country as connected with that great event, and not in regard to the changeful vicissitudes that might embarrass the mind, arouse the passions, or gather around him either the reproach or applause of the transitory party passions of the hour."[53]

If Cushing seemed to have reached a sense of disinterest in the matter, his fellow Bay State representative, John Quincy Adams, had not. Rising from his seat, Adams shot back at Cushing, remarking that the bill was unquestionably a party matter and noted that its "prime mover" was Major Davezac, "who introduced it as a Democratic measure, and as one of the first fruits of the Democratic triumph in the State of New York." Adams counseled his colleagues not to pass the refund without a "thorough discussion," then belittled what he viewed as the fawning sanctity connected to the Battle of New Orleans, announcing, "But God forbid that he [Adams] should say a word in disparagement of that day, or of the person to be honored and profited by this donation." The former president then charged to the heart of the matter. Referring to the movements in the Senate in favor of the refund, he remarked that a bill had been passed, but "it was rejected by General Jackson's friends, because it did not contain a condemnation of the judge who imposed the fine."

Adams also noted that he had seen a letter from Jackson that said "he would not have received a dollar unless the character of the judge was blasted."[54] The next day, on January 6, Adams continued his onslaught by recommending an amendment to the Judiciary Committee's original bill. Like the amendments in the Senate, Adams suggested including a statement that Congress was not making any determination on the judicial branch that imposed the fine. But whereas the Senate bill stopped at merely protecting Judge Hall and the power of the judiciary, Adams went further by questioning Jackson's use of military power: "And that the said [Judiciary] committee do further report their opinion, whether the declaration of martial law by General Jackson, at New Orleans was within the competency of his official powers, by the laws of war, without violation of the Constitution of the United States; and if so whether his imprisonment of Dominick A. Hall . . . and his arrest and his subjection of Louis Louaillier . . . to trial by a court martial . . . were justifiable acts of martial law, and not an abusive exercise of despotic and arbitrary power."[55] Adams also wanted

John Quincy Adams. Courtesy of the Library of Congress.

the committee to consider whether or not congressional approval of the refund bill sanctioned Jackson's use of martial law.

Adams's comments revealed his still formidable political acumen. An experienced political operator, he proved to be a thorn in the general's side. If Democrats thought that they could sneak the bill by Adams, they were sorely mistaken. Adams, in fact, went directly after the Democrats, charging that the bill was nothing more than a partisan plot. He also referred to President Tyler's comments in his Annual Message that the people of the nation desired the refund, sneering, "[I] would not deny that the American people wished this fine to be paid back. It might be so. At least a portion of them wished it—a portion commonly called 'the Democratic party.'" Adams then made a blistering charge. "Much had been said about setting up the Presidency at auction," he remarked, and "if auctioneering was to elect the next President, this measure . . . was one of the best auction schemes that had entered into the campaign." The only reason that Democrats supported the bill, he argued, was because "the goodwill of General Jackson was courted by all the divisions of the Democratic party. . . . Every effort made in its behalf was traceable to auctioneering for the Presidency." Adams even asserted, though it was only a "rumor," that the Democratic presidential nominee was to be decided by Jackson and thus all "suitors" were after "the good-will or neutrality of Gen. Jackson."[56] If these accusations were not enough, Adams concluded his harangue by questioning the lame-duck President Tyler's supposedly impartial motives in recommending the bill's approval.

Congressman Adams's speech was an open declaration of war against House Democrats. And though he had little but speculation on which to base his charges there was undeniably a hint of truth, especially if one looks ahead to the presidential election of 1844 in which Martin Van Buren lost his bid for the party's nomination because of his negative stand on the annexation of Texas and the subsequent loss of Jackson's support. In Van Buren's place came James K. Polk, an advocate of Texas annexation backed by the aging Jackson. Old Hickory's favor did count. As for Tyler's motivation, Adams may have been on the mark there as well. Tyler had a long history of animosity toward Jackson and had left the Democratic Party specifically because of the general's handling of Nullification and the Bank War. While a senator, Tyler had lambasted Jackson for invading Florida in 1818, voted in favor of Senate censure for removal of the federal deposits, and ultimately resigned his seat rather than vote for expunging that censure. He was also the only Democrat to vote against Jackson's Force Bill during Nullification. That Tyler, who was clearly a lame-duck president badly in need of political support, would suddenly change his mind about Jackson and deem him worthy of the nation's thanks stinks of beggary.[57]

To such charges as those posed by John Quincy Adams, Democrats did not remain silent for long. Within a few days Kentucky representative William Orlando Butler fired back. One of Jackson's former military aides during the Battle of New Orleans and a longtime friend of the general, Butler's connection to Jackson assured Democrats of an electrifying response. Beginning slowly, he turned the table on Adams, insinuating that it was Whigs who were making the refund a party matter. "I see with equal pain and surprise," he announced, "that this simple proposition, which ought to depend upon truth and justice alone, is fast assuming, if it has not already assumed, a decided party character." Butler's mild suggestion that the bill may have become a party matter was a conscious understatement. He knew full well that party lines had been sharply drawn on the issue and recognized the potential damage to Whigs if they could be branded as unpatriotic. Butler therefore set out to bloody his opponents. He naturally heralded the New Orleans victory as "that immortal page in his country's history" and denied that the Democratic Party initiated the refund bill for political capital. Still, he was more than happy to capitalize on its political nature now that it had become a partisan issue that might favor Democrats. "Nothing could please me more than to witness the party bias attempted to be given it," remarked Butler. Will the Whig Party, he continued, "with all its knowledge and talents, never have the wisdom to appreciate the American people? Lay this question before them at the next canvas, and you will at least learn that ingratitude and injustice to those who have freely periled their lives in defence of their country form no part of their character."[58] Butler clearly basked in the Whig opposition with the expectation that it would hurt them in the coming elections. After challenging Whigs on the issue of patriotism, he turned his sites directly on Adams. Responding to the assertion that the bill was merely a campaign scheme and that Jackson was going to choose the next Democratic presidential candidate, Butler remarked wryly, "I will not pretend to decide what influence General Jackson may have in future President-making [but it is] well known—and to none better than the venerable gentleman [Mr. Adams] himself— that the old hero, in his day, was esteemed a most capital President-breaker."[59] The slap at Adams's 1828 defeat to Jackson was not lost on House members. Butler then went for the jugular, the "corrupt bargain" charge that had haunted Adams throughout his career. It is fair to presume, announced Butler, from "rumor" of course, that another former president, Adams, may have some influence in choosing the Whig presidential candidate. If this is correct, continued Butler, "I would advise him, by all means, when that interest is disposed of, to adhere to the good old 'rumored' precedent of 1824—or perhaps, sir, sealed proposals will suit quite as well."[60] Butler's stinging words had exactly the desired effect. That night Adams confided in his diary that William O. Butler had "discoursed for nearly an hour and a half in glorification of Jackson, and in malignant slander upon me." Adams added that the bill "has got to be a mere party football" and Democrats were "attempting to carry the measure by storm." He lamented that they would probably succeed.[61]

Butler was mistaken if he believed that hacking away at John Quincy Adams would silence Whig opposition. John Minor Botts of Virginia returned to the party's primary charge that the bill was little more than a campaign strategy, counseling his colleagues, "Let it be borne in mind, too, that this was the first Whig Congress that had sat for years; and further, that it was the last Congress that would sit prior to the convention that was to nominate the candidate for the Presidency." "The conclusion, therefore, was inevitable," charged Botts, "that the whole proceeding was to purchase the political support of General Jackson for one or the other of the aspirants."[62]

House members spent far less time on the refund legislation than their colleagues in the upper chamber, yet the debates were no less heated. From the outset, Democratic congressmen were particularly annoyed that Whigs stalled the bill for so long. Not much changed in the third session. Though William Gwin succeeded in opening debate for a brief period in January 1843, he failed in his efforts to open further discussion on February 20 and again on March 3, the last day of the Twenty-seventh Congress' final session. Thus the bill died.

Jackson's Political Influence
and the Ramifications of the Refund Bill

In the midst of the debates in both the Senate and House of Representatives, Andrew Jackson remained vigilant in his quest for vindication. He made sure to funnel a virtual river of documents and letters to Francis Blair in Washington, where the editor of the *Globe* selected some for publication and passed on others, per Jackson's instructions, to supporters in Congress. The two men also coordinated strategy, determining which of Jackson's followers would write certain tracts in support of the refund bill and who would explain the necessity and legality of martial law. They also gauged the damage the movement might do to the nation's Whigs. Following the dispatch of one set of documents, Jackson wrote Blair, remarking, "I hope you will see that the whole papers, and my friends Dr. Linn & Benton & Wright in the Senate, and Mr. Ingersol [*sic*], johnson & brown in the House be acquainted with the real facts of the case." In a subsequent letter, Jackson transferred additional materials and again requested that supporters in Congress be supplied with necessary documents: "I wish you to shew the enclosed to my friend Linn, & Ingersol, and that they should be advised of the papers in Mr. Kendall's possession—that if the question comes up, that if necessary, they may carry the war into africa."[63] Blair followed Jackson's orders without delay, reporting, "I have conferred with Mr. Kendall and Mr. Ingersol relative to the best mode of employing the record of papers you have forwarded. . . . Mr. Kendall has agreed to expose the treason, cowardice, fraud and forgery you had to encounter [in New Orleans] in a Series of articles."[64] Shortly afterward, Amos Kendall, a former Kitchen Cabinet advisor to President Jackson, published an article titled "General Jackson's Fine" in the *Democratic Review*. Old Hickory aided Kendall by sending, via James K. Polk, affidavits and other official papers concerning the conflict with Judge Hall.[65]

For the most part, Jackson entrusted the battle to his partisans in Washington, writing Blair, "I feel safe that my honor & fame is safe in your hands and Mr. Kendalls, and Mr. Ingersol is an able counseller . . . and Senator Linns, & other friends."[66] Yet notwithstanding this firm confidence in his followers, the general found it impossible to remain silent while the war raged in Congress. On a number of occasions he wrote to Blair, Linn, and Kendall for the express purpose of having the correspondence published and, in Linn's case, entered into the official congressional debate.[67] Preparing a letter for Linn, Jackson drafted a heated note to his nephew, Andrew Jackson Donelson, who acted as secretary and often rewrote the general's letters: "I want a costic [*sic*] but decorous criticism upon the conduct of the Whiggs incorporated in my letter to Doctor Linn. . . . Add as much spice to the criticism as your genius can [summon] forth." Moreover, the general, understanding his still powerful symbolic and political appeal, added that such a letter "will arouse the whole democracy in the United States and greatly aid in the downfall of the Whiggs." He also singled out particular Whig politicians, noting that his letter "will prostrate Talmage [*sic*] in Newyork, Berian [*sic*] in Georgia and Barrow and Conrad in Louisia[na]."[68]

As debate in both chambers of Congress came to a close in February 1843, Blair and Jackson had come to appreciate fully the potentially powerful political impact of the refund legislation. Rather than focusing on immediate passage, as they had done in the aftermath of the second session, they now understood that the prolonged debate might aid the Democratic Party in contests across the Union. Blair defined the strategy in a letter to Jackson:

the federal leaders under the influence of blind feeling & their high toned principles resist the right of instruction as well as the consent of national sympathy & affection for you, and are thus rendering themselves more & more obnoxious to the country everyday. In this way the delay & opposition the Republicans here encounter in their efforts to expunge Halls nefarious sentence against you, are all calculated to do good to our party, as well as to your fame.—and it will prove to be, I have no doubt, a potent Democratic ingredient in the next presidential canvass in as much as throughout the next session it will enter into the Congressional elections which will all turn in some degree upon the presidential question which they will so much effect. In this way you will become blended intimately with the prospects for the individual whose pretensions you favor & so serve him most essentially. For these reasons I am not sorry that Whiggery has thrown obstacles in the way of the passage of the refunding bill this session.[69]

The charges put forth by some Whigs, most notably John Quincy Adams, had come to fruition. Democrats were now fully cognizant of the political possibilities connected to the refund bill. In a follow-up letter to the general, Blair again discussed the timing of the bill's passage and anticipated victory for Democrats in coming congressional elections: "I would rather pass it in the next session with a full Democratic Congress, than now by Federal votes. . . . I don't want them to have the credit, in history, of passing this measure of Justice to you at this Coonskin Congress." After the third session ended, Blair wrote Jackson once again, expressing satisfaction that Congress concluded without passing the refund bill: "I was really glad that the coon congress learned too late to do themselves so much good as the passage of the Bill would have done. It would have redeemed them in some sense."[70] Lewis Linn also wrote Jackson, noting the fateful consequences awaiting Whigs if they continued their resistance to the bill. "It has proved to them a *thorny* subject to handle," he remarked, and "the fact is, the Whigs had better be in hot haste to do justice in this matter or you will kill off with the people a Hecatomb of their great men, yet."[71]

Blair, Linn, and Jackson fully expected Whig opposition to exact a heavy toll on the party, yet the result at the polls is not easily gauged. Though Democrats took control of the House with 139 seats to the Whigs' 81, and gained 1 seat in the Senate so that they trailed Whigs 23 seats to 29, there exists no clear indication that the refund bill was the prime motivator in the majority of elections.[72] Other important issues were also at stake, including arguments over banking, tariffs, and bankruptcy legislation. With that said, one can nevertheless point to examples in which the refund bill played a decided role in a candidate's future.

Jackson had predicted early on that Charles Conrad of Louisiana would pay for his "treachery." Of course, the general helped to exact that retribution by writing to friends and poisoning the legislative waters in Louisiana. Shortly thereafter, Conrad failed to gain reelection, and Henry Piere, of New Orleans, wrote Jackson on January 9, 1843, announcing, "C. M. Conrad has received the punishment he so highly deserved, he has been expelled from the Senate where he so meanly tried to throw a stigma on the man who once he venerated in common with his fellow citizens." John Slidell, a new Democratic congressman from Louisiana, also commented on Conrad's loss, noting, "he was a candidate for re-election, and yet, in derogation of what may almost be an established usage, he was set aside. . . . And why? Because a considerable portion of his own party strongly disapproved of his course in relation to this bill." A historian of Louisiana politics noted, "Conrad quixotically undermined his own chances by blaspheming Louisiana's savoir, Andrew Jackson," and that "Conrad's impolitic vote against the measure raised the ire of both Democrats and Whigs in Louisiana."[73]

Even Conrad's brother-in-law, E. G. W. Butler, wrote to the stricken senator, explaining that he too hoped Conrad would not be reelected to the Senate. Butler insisted that he played no part in the outcome of the election but noted that the Louisiana legislature "were influenced mainly, if not entirely, by their disapprobation of your conduct toward the saviour of Louisiana" and that the matter was made worse by the fact that the legislature had recently sent resolutions and instructions requesting that Congress pass the refund bill. "These proceedings," he wrote, "especially when taken in connection with the instructions upon the subject from the various State Legislatures, the pronouncements by you that [these resolutions were the] result of 'sycophancy and subserviency,' must lead to a very different conclusion from that at which you have arrived; and I am very sorry that they have produced no change in the sentiments uttered by you upon the floor of the Senate." Butler also commented that the Louisiana legislature had recently debated Jackson's use of martial law and its duration, approving the necessity of both.[74]

Auguste Davezac, the originator of the national refund movement, also followed the Democratic victories in the Louisiana congressional elections, writing to Jackson, "To your friends it has been a subject of greater honest exultation from the well known fact, that these [Democratic victories] were made under the auspices of your name; and in vindication of your fame. Every candidate, offered to the people who was known to have voted in Congress, in contradiction of the express will of the nation . . . was repudiated by a high minded people."[75] Conrad's fellow senator, Alexander Barrow, survived the election only because he immediately withdrew his modification to the bill and thereafter remained silent. He was also among only a handful of Senate Whigs who voted for the bill's final passage in the Twenty-eighth Congress.[76]

Other senators also tread carefully. At least one gave serious consideration to how he should handle the bill and ultimately resigned rather than get caught in the political sniping. John C. Calhoun had remained conspicuously silent while the refund debate raged around him, rising only once in January 1843 to present resolutions from the South Carolina legislature in support of the refund.[77] The senator dared not speak in regard to the bill, mainly because he had larger issues on his mind, namely, the 1844 presidential race. Calhoun had coveted the executive office since the beginning of his career. Opting to run for the vice-presidency in 1824 and again in 1828, he surmised that only time stood in his way. Yet in the midst of Jackson's first term, the two men had an ugly falling out that forced the South Carolinian's expulsion from the party. Set adrift, he flourished in the one-party rule of South Carolina, but that did not help his quest for the presidency. One solution was a broad-based southern party, but Calhoun's movement was slow going in the entrenched two-party system that existed throughout the nation. Remaining firmly committed to southern rights and the protection of slavery, he viewed control of the White House as a means to achieve his goals.

Calhoun may very well have looked at the 1844 contest as his last chance, and he therefore worked especially hard to return to the Democratic fold and cultivate a broad following. As one biographer wrote, "Not since 1822 had so concerted an effort been made, either by his friends or himself, to win the presidency." When discussing strategy on how best to deal with the Democratic Party front runner, Martin Van Buren, Calhoun was warned to avoid any open rupture in the party.[78]

Robert Barnwell Rhett, a hot-tempered South Carolinian, and one of three brothers who made up the "Regency," a political group that counseled Calhoun, watched for anything that might endanger his chances. Rhett set up a pro-Calhoun paper in Washington called the *Spectator* and remained vigilant in his warnings that enemies would set "traps" in an "attempt to sow dissensions amongst the Democratic Party, and kill you off." Keeping a keen eye on the refund debates and the danger of running into a problem with Jackson, Rhett advocated resignation rather than potential trouble over the refund bill:

> To vote with the Whigs to rescind this resolution, expunging a censure on Genl Jackson, will be restoring the censure. The Whigs controlling the majority will of course, so put it, as to put you in the worse position. A vote with them on this question will revive all the old feuds. . . . Your prospects for the Presidency will utterly expire under the question. . . . If you could consistently with truth and honour, go with the Democratic Party, on this question, your return to the Senate altho surrounded with difficulties, might do no irreparable injury. . . . [But since this is a problem] my mind is therefore clear, in the judgment, that it is impolitic, and will probably be fatal, for you to expose yourself any farther in the Senate, to the cross-fire of your enemies. . . . I am now satisfied that it is your unquestionable policy and duty to keep out of the Senate, at the approaching Session.[79]

Rhett's letter could not have been clearer. The refund bill was a probable disaster and Calhoun had spent far too much time building support for 1844. He resigned on March 3, 1843, the last day of the Twenty-seventh Congress.[80] The move came as a shock to many friends, and as one historian noted, "even if they approved his presidential candidacy, [they] were bewildered by his resignation. He deprived himself of his most effective forum and left his greatest enemy, Benton, in command of the Senate."[81] Calhoun was, however, merely calculating with a larger goal in mind. Wary of once again falling within Jackson's shadow, he avoided conflict and even attempted to appease the aging hero. In a campaign biography and a subsequent book of speeches, Calhoun opted to ignore certain conflicts with Jackson. As one Calhoun biographer explained it, there were "no speeches from the early period, except Calhoun's maiden effort in the House. . . . That he would consign his early speeches on the bank, the tariff, and internal improvements was scarcely surprising; it was more interesting, certainly, that he omitted his speech of May 6, 1834, in reply to Jackson's protest against the censure resolutions, along with all subsequent speeches against the Expunging Resolution [for removal of the bank deposits]. Both *Life* and *Speeches* seemed designed to placate the grey eminence at the Hermitage, who had yet to declare himself on the Democratic ticket."[82] In light of such facts, Calhoun's resignation from the Senate, due to the dangerous political shoals that lay beneath Jackson's bill, was exceedingly prudent.

Victory in Site: The Refund Bill Passes

The start of the Twenty-eighth Congress promised new life for Jackson's refund. Democrats held a commanding lead in the House, and it was there, rather than the Senate, where the debate returned to the political scene. Jackson's followers marched in full force, making the refund their first order of business. On December 6, only three days after the start of the session, Charles Ingersoll introduced House bill 1: "A bill to refund the fine imposed on General Andrew Jackson. Be it enacted by the Senate and House of Representatives of the United States of America in Congress assembled, That the sum of one thousand dollars, paid by General Jackson as a fine imposed on him at New Orleans, the 31st day of March A.D. 1815, be repaid to him, together with interest, at the rate of six per cent a year, since then, out of any moneys in the treasury not otherwise appropriated."[83] This time Ingersoll made sure that the bill fit the general's expectations. It was no longer for his "relief," as it had been in Ingersoll's original bill, and the congressman also included interest.

There was little doubt that the House would act quickly. Whigs, no longer in the majority, could not stall as in the previous Congress. Yet in the highly unlikely possibility that the bill might founder, Democrat John Slidell of Louisiana rose to the floor and announced resolutions from his state's legislature requesting Congress to refund the fine during the current session, and should that not occur, Louisiana was prepared to act by refunding the fine with interest.[84] The resolution was mainly symbolic, for Democrats had already mapped out their victory, waiting until near the end of the month so that a short debate could take place, and then they would approve the bill on January 8, the anniversary of the Battle of New Orleans. The spectacle of such an affair would be replete with all the nationalist fanfare that Democrats could desire.

Some Whigs, of course, still attempted to throw up road blocks. On December 29, the day debate began, Alexander Stephens of Georgia proposed an amendment which stated that the bill was not a censure on Judge Hall. Ingersoll responded as Democrats always had, remarking that nothing in the bill implied censure and thus the amendment was unnecessary.[85] And though House Whigs could not slow the legislation with modifications, they could at least blast away at their opponents. Daniel Barnard of New York, following the line of argument that John Quincy Adams had initiated, declared, "this bill was to be passed for effect on the approaching Presidential election, and not because it was just." Then, making reference to John Slidell's resolutions, he asked, "How was it that the State of Louisiana had waked up to this 'great act of justice,' now at this day? How was it that she now showed the most extraordinary zeal for the character of General Jackson?" To the congressman's queries came a voice from the floor: "Because she is now a Democratic State." Of this, Barnard had no doubt. He insisted that the entire matter was fodder for Democratic power. This bill, he exclaimed, was "in obedience to party—in obedience to the high behest of party—and for the purpose of effect on party." Barnard's only hope was that the Whig-dominated Senate might put the brakes on the refund, and thus he warned Democrats that though "they might pass this bill here . . . they could not lick it into any shape that would suit the other branch of Congress."[86]

Perhaps sniffing out imminent victory, some Democrats revealed a degree of giddiness and began to sermonize and fawn over Jackson. Insisting the bill was "no party question," John Dawson, another new member from Louisiana, piled saccharine praise upon the general and his blessings to America:

> These blessings, Mr. Chairman, have been preserved and maintained to us and our children by the spirit of a wonderful man—Andrew Jackson. Gallant Spirit! He stands before the world a spectacle of moral greatness—vast in his intellectual endowments, stupendous in his calm and invincible courage; in peace, as gentle as the morning breeze; in war, as fearless and irresistible as the spirit of the mountain storm. No; this is no party question. The honor of every citizen of the United States is at stake. Every lover of Freedom should come forward, and promptly rebuke the axiom that republics are ungrateful.[87]

To such blatant homage, Whigs responded with rhetorical force, proving that they too could engage in elocution that made nineteenth-century debate famous for its brilliant oratory. Joseph Peyton of Tennessee sneered at Democrats, insisting that the bill was merely a "humbug" and "you are now poor, bankrupt, humble, timid; and like drowning men, you are catching at straws." Of the coming presidential question upon which the bill really revolved, and the likely candidacy of Martin Van Buren, Peyton evinced scorn: "Mr. Van Buren was a mere political parasite, a branch of mistletoe, that owed its elevation, its growth—nay, its very existence, to the tall trunk of an aged hickory; but so soon as it was attempted to transplant it and force it to live upon its own resources, independent of hickory sap, it withered, and died; and you now find out that the only mode of reviving it again . . . is to call to its aid the strength and support and sustenance of the same old hickory." "This," Peyton concluded, "is the secret of all this clamor about this fine. It's intended for political effect, for political capital, and for no other purpose under the sun."[88]

Whigs clearly understood the symbolic importance of raising Jackson's name before the people. This was the very reason why they had opposed the bill in the first place. Yet rather than stopping the Democratic movement, Whigs actually helped to fan the partisan fire. And though they repeatedly identified the Democratic strategy, it was to no avail. The damage was already done. Some Whigs were therefore left with nothing but sarcasm. Addressing his opponents' desire to pass the measure on the anniversary of the Battle of New Orleans, Robert Cumming Schenck, a newly elected representative from Ohio, noted acerbically that "the people of this country generally now have ascertained that Mr. Van Buren did not actually fight the battle." Yet, continued Schenck, "when I reflect upon the peculiar connexion of Mr. Van Buren with the scenes of New Orleans, and with this tribute of justice to the old hero, and of the way in which it is all expected by his friends to operate on the public mind, I cannot forbear to urge upon you, instead of this 8th of January, the *first day of April,* for your festivity."[89]

Democrats too could engage in caustic, mean-spirited debate. In response to Joseph Peyton's remark about "humbugs," John McClernand of Illinois roared, "without the aid of humbugs, their [Whig] gaunt and famished frames would not have been fattened and glutted upon the spoils of office, being the reward for their victory in the election of 1840."[90] Ultimately, Democrats simply continued to hammer home their argument of Jackson the hero, patriotic America, and the political impact of the refund bill on those who refused to do justice. Lewis Steenrod of Virginia put it plainly, noting that this "bill, above all other bills of the session, is the bill by which the American feeling of this Congress (not the party feeling, sir) will be tested. General Jackson is too fully identified with the freedom and the glory of the country, not to justify the application of this test to the recorded vote of this Congress."[91]

With their domination in the House and their strategy clearly planned, Democrats succeeded in bringing the refund bill up for a vote on January 8, 1844. The victory was a landslide. Democrats voted in block, and some twenty-nine Whigs crossed party lines. The bill now devolved to the Senate, where Whigs still held a slim majority. On January 9, the upper chamber received news of the House bill and promptly referred it to the Judiciary Committee, where John Berrien still served as chairman.[92] While the committee took the bill under consideration, state resolutions continued to pour in. Democrat Daniel Sturgeon of Pennsylvania spoke on behalf of his state's legislature, noting that the resolutions he presented were the third set sent from Pennsylvania. Whigs also presented memorials from their home legislatures. Albert White of Indiana presented resolutions and remarked that he was not wholly opposed to paying justice to Jackson but had voted against the refund "in consequence of the ungracious manner in which it had been brought forward, and the political aspect which it had assumed."[93]

On January 30, Berrien returned the bill from the Judiciary Committee with what was now the standard Whig strategy: "Provided, that nothing in this act shall be construed to express or imply any censure of the conduct or character of the Hon. Dominick A. Hall, by whom the fine was imposed." Democrats also responded with their standard; the bill said nothing about Judge Hall and thus the modification was needless. The amendment failed.[94] Many Whigs ultimately resigned themselves to the fact that Jackson's bill was a fait accompli, especially in light of the state resolutions ordering support for the bill. This, in fact, became the bigger issue for a number of Whigs. The "right of instruction" had been a matter of dispute for some years. The controversy stemmed from the belief, held mainly by Democrats, that because state legislatures appointed senators they were subsequently obliged to abide by the state's instructions. State resolutions invariably "instructed" senators but "earnestly requested" popularly elected representatives to support a given measure. Democrats supported the doctrine both because it helped to maintain popular control of government and, more practically, because refusing to follow instructions often required a senator to resign his seat, thus making it available to an opponent.[95]

By the 1840s, the tide of partisan competition reached such a height that senators no longer felt compelled either to obey instructions or resign their office. Thus, angry over the refund issue, New Jersey's William Dayton represented the Whig view when declaring, "I utterly deny the binding force of these instructions. . . . In my judgment, it is a doctrine at variance both with the letter and the spirit of the constitution." The senator's statement of principle, however, was largely motivated by who instructed him. "When I find myself instructed by the party now in the ascendant in the New Jersey legislature, I am constrained to" refuse compliance. Since 1838, Whigs dominated both the council and assembly of New Jersey, but in 1843 Democrats won both houses of the legislature and promptly sent a resolution to Congress instructing senators to support the refund bill.[96] Angry over the thought of acquiescing to Democratic commands, Dayton refused to vote for the bill. Nor was he alone. Dayton's fellow senator, Jacob Miller, also refused to vote for the bill and denounced the right of instruction, as did Michigan's William Woodbridge.[97] Interestingly, one of the largest previous arguments over the right of instruction stemmed from the debates over expunging Jackson's censure for removal of the federal deposits.[98]

Whig opposition to the refund bill was petering out. Many members of the opposition simply wanted to rid themselves of the now obnoxious legislation. At least one new member of the Senate lamented that the previous Whig Congress had not passed the measure when it first arose. Outlining the Democratic strategy beautifully, Ephraim Foster of Tennessee discussed his perceptions of the refund when it first came to his attention:

> I could not help thinking how wise it would be in my political associates at the Capitol to give the *coup de grace* to the whole stratagem, by freely assenting to the passage of the law. Gentlemen on the other side of the chamber may smile at these remarks if they please. They know how much weight they are entitled to; and I imagine some of them believed, with me, that a dead lion was not

without its terrors; and that some political capital might be made
of this bill, if it were opposed or rejected by a whig Congress. Let
it go now, sir. I have seen enough of it, and have no objection. I shall
satisfy myself, if I do not gratify the friends of the measure, by voting to keep down all immaterial obstructions, facilitating the passage
of the law, and relieving the country forever from the agitation it
has produced.[99]

If only Senator Foster had occupied his seat during the previous
Congress. Perhaps he might have ended the battle sooner and deprived
Democrats of the partisan gem that fell in their laps. At any rate, Senate
Whigs acquiesced on February 14, 1844, and two days later President
Tyler signed the bill into law. Jackson received a much needed $2,732.90
and the heartfelt congratulations of many supporters.[100]

Francis Blair and his commander at the Hermitage fully expected
the refund to pass during the first session of the twenty-eighth Congress and following the vote in the House, Blair wrote Jackson in anticipation of final victory: "None but the very malignants among the coons
dared to vote against it. It will certainly pass the Senate, the Clay men
are afraid to take the millstone of a vote against it, into the deep waters
of the next canvass. They know that it would sink them." Once the
Senate ultimately rid themselves of the bill that had caused them so
much turmoil, Blair wrote to Jackson again, this time noting that the
Whigs were "so mollified by the force of public opinion, that they voted
for it against their convictions and wishes!!" It was, insisted Blair, "the
fear of the effect in the approaching presidential election [that] cured
their obstinacy."[101] Thus Andrew Jackson received his vindication. He
also earned it by expertly shuffling the entire matter into and through
the Congress. Old Hickory devised the refund legislation and watched
it carefully for the two years in which his Democratic soldiers did
battle on his behalf. To his lieutenants, Francis Preston Blair, Lewis
Linn, Charles Jared Ingersoll, and Amos Kendall, the general supplied
ammunition in the form of letters and official documents. Success was
ultimately due to the skill of his army in Congress, but behind every
victory there existed a skilled commander.

Yet Jackson's desire for vindication became far more than a mere
quest for congressional absolution. Democrats revealed a moment of
partisan paradox by expecting that Whigs would willingly acquiesce to
an act of justice for Jackson. The party battles of the age made such a
notion unthinkable. The fruition of the second American party system,

marked by rabid competition, virtually ensured that Whigs would view the refund legislation as nothing more than a Democratic ploy. As a result of the hard-fought log cabin and hard cider campaign in 1840, Whigs appreciated the tremendous impact symbols had on the electorate and they therefore opposed the refund bill in an attempt to deprive Democrats of a unifying symbol. Unfortunately, the strategy backfired. Whigs, in what can only be described as complete irony, handed Democrats a powerful electioneering tool. It is unclear whether the Democratic victories in the 1844 congressional elections were motivated primarily by Whig opposition to the bill, but a few instances reveal the undeniable impact of opposing Jackson and the power of nationalism embedded within his image and the New Orleans victory.

CHAPTER 4

Liberty, Power, and Partisanship:
The Debate over Republicanism in the 1840s

A ndrew Jackson's mission to force the refund issue into Congress was not solely about personal vindication. As much as he looked to posterity with concern for his legacy, Jackson also considered the future security of the Union. That security, he believed, necessitated the ability of commanders during war time to take emergency and perhaps extraordinary actions to safeguard the nation. Thus in the general's mind, declaration of martial law was justifiable and should be available to other military commanders in times of imminent danger. The problem was that such an idea stood in stark contrast to the safeguards of liberty guaranteed by the Constitution as well as the republican legacy that had guided the young Republic since its birth.

Such ideological complexities certainly were not lost within the halls of Congress. Though Democrats and Whigs figuratively bludgeoned one another in an attempt to gain from Jackson's political symbolism, they also engaged the important question of whether a general could legitimately violate civil liberties. The subordination of military power to civil authorities was a mainstay of American political thought. In the Declaration of Independence, Thomas Jefferson blasted the king for rendering "the Military independent of and superior to the Civil Power," and virtually every state Constitution written from the nation's founding up to 1842 said something to the effect that the military shall remain subordinate to civilian authority.[1] Such doctrines stemmed from the still-potent Revolutionary era belief that aggressive power must be kept in check and that standing armies posed perhaps the greatest overt danger to liberty. Thus martial law rubbed hard against American notions of freedom and balance of power. Any military commander, let alone the imperious Jackson, posed a potential threat to the people's liberties. Other than an outright military coup over a civilian government, martial law was the most formidable military threat to the people's rights.

The general's party faithful were in a difficult position. Like virtually all Americans of the era, they were wed to the belief of military subordination to civil authority. Defending Jackson flew in the face of the nation's republican traditions. Glorifying the Battle of New Orleans and Jackson's heroism, as Democrats had done since 1815, could go only so far. If Democrats expected victory in the refund battle, they had to justify martial law. One way to do so was focus upon competing ideological traditions. The law of nature, like republicanism, served as a cornerstone of American political thought. Just as Jefferson had represented republican ideals in the Declaration of Independence when he lamented the subversion of civil authority by military power, he also championed the "Law of Nature and of Nature's God." The two ideologies worked in concert to inform American sensibilities about society and government. The nation's leaders were eminently familiar with the writings of John Locke and with Emer de Vattel's *Law of Nations; or the Principles of the Law of Nature.* One aspect of the law of nature was the right of self-preservation, or self-defense, which allowed an individual to engage in any means necessary, even murder, to defend his own life or that of a loved one. Democrats simply transferred this universal understanding to the right of a nation to engage in the same type of self-defense. In doing so, they argued that the law of nature existed long before and superceded a written Constitution.

At the most basic level, arguing the law of nature was profoundly simple; most anyone understood the basic concept of self-preservation. Yet in the hands of Democrats the law of nature became a complex jumble of varying and sometimes contrasting ideas. Some argued that necessity allowed Jackson to declare martial law, but that it was without question unconstitutional and was utilized at the general's own peril. In this sense, Jackson's conduct fell under the scrutiny of the nation's rulers and they needed to decide whether his actions stood justified. If one accepted this idea, Whigs and Democrats were engaged in just such a discussion. Other Democrats disagreed, insisting that necessity not only allowed but authorized the use of martial law even though the Constitution did not. In this sense, the law of nature existed as a parallel power to the nation's written laws. Some Democrats went even further, announcing that because the law of nature was older than the government it superceded all constitutions and written law. Other party members asserted that martial law was actually consistent with the Constitution because it allowed suspension of the writ of habeas corpus. More radical elements of the party went to extremes, stating bluntly that they cared not whether the Constitution was violated so long as Jackson saved New Orleans. At the most tangible, nontheoretical level, the many Democratic points of view were distinctions without a difference. The result was support of Jackson and recognition of martial law.

Democratic arguments also related to the conduct of Judge Hall. If, for example, martial law was legally in force, Hall had no authority over Jackson. Thus no writ of habeas corpus should have been issued and the ensuing conflict with military authority should not have occurred. If one accepted this view, Jackson's fine was illegal. But this was a rather extreme position and one that most Democrats did not advocate. In fact, many party members acknowledged Hall's services to the nation and his defense of civil authority.

Ultimately, Democrats came to no consistent conclusion regarding why martial law was legal or, at the very least, why it was not a violation of the Constitution. Moreover, some party members believed it was merely enough to justify martial law's necessity and not engage the question of legality. Attempting to glean some sort of clear ideology regarding emergency powers is, therefore, impossible. Still, the discussions in Congress were without question a broader and more in depth consideration of the matter than what had occurred in the midst of Jackson's campaigning for the presidency when political supporters and opponents shallowly engaged some of the ideological and constitutional issues surrounding martial law. Additionally, the tenor of the debates had more weight specifically because it was the nation's leading men engaging the issue.

Whether Democrats argued that military rule was merely justified, fully legal, constitutional or unconstitutional, the results were extreme:

the suppression of civilian authority by the military. In the end, the only common Democratic goal was justifying Jackson and winning passage of the refund bill. In the process, Jackson's adherents set a potentially dangerous precedent for the nation's future. And to be sure, this is exactly what Jackson wanted. In constant contact with particular supporters, the general made clear his position on the necessity of emergency powers in a time of war and those views were injected directly into the debates.

It was the very idea of a precedent that motivated some Whigs to confront the refund bill and demand amendments. Some Whigs believed that returning Jackson's fine with no official congressional statement on the matter was tantamount to sanction. Yet even on the issue of a precedent Whig party members were not in agreement, and Democrats had the same problem. The various members of both parties disagreed on the danger of such a precedent, or even if one would ultimately derive from the debates. Some argued strongly that there are times of national emergency when the form of law is suspended so that it might ultimately survive. Hence the Latin maxim *Inter arma silent leges*. The question of dire military emergency and the people's rights is a debate that has and continues to last in discussions of civil versus military authority. Acknowledging the idea that necessity can unleash the dangers of military authority was and is difficult to accept in a nation obsessed with a fear of power.

That many Whigs issued forlorn predictions about the nation's future should martial law gain approval by Congress comes as no surprise, both in terms of the nation's ideological legacies and the Whig party's hatred of Andrew Jackson. Rather than a hero, argued some, the general was a monster who usurped the most fundamental American beliefs. Most Whigs argued that he had no authority to declare martial law, and taking the matter further, they insisted that Jackson should have defended New Orleans with only the means authorized by the Constitution. Taken at face value, one might conclude that such assertions revealed an unwavering adherence to the Constitution and the most basic of American political tenets that placed civilian power above that of the military. In this sense, Whigs appeared as the steadfast defenders of republicanism and American law. For a few this may be true, but for other members of the party there existed a decided lack of consistency regarding martial law. Additionally, Whigs refused to acknowledge the rather dire circumstances that precipitated Jackson's declaration of martial law. In doing so, they ignored the realities facing Louisiana in 1814–15. Whigs also split along clearly geographic lines. Southerners revealed a continuing reverence for Jackson's services to the South and West, whereas northerners evinced a diehard, partisan opposition to the general that at times over ran their supposed principled defense of liberty.

Essentially, the key to understanding the varied, nuanced approaches to martial law presented by Democrats and Whigs is in accepting the impossibility of separating partisan motivation from ideologically based arguments. The myriad discussions sounding the depths of constitutional law, civil versus military power, the law of nature and concepts of necessity abounded within a politically charged arena. With both parties looking carefully toward the pending congressional and presidential elections, the ideological complexities of martial law were to a significant degree subsumed by partisan strategizing. This is not to say that the nation's leaders failed to address important ideas about the limits of military power. Still, the essential point is in recognizing that discussions of balancing civilian liberties and military power occurred under the looming shadow of Andrew Jackson, a partisan symbol that stirred the deepest of passions in the Age of Party.

Andrew Jackson, Martial Law, and the Beginning of the Senate Debate

There is little doubt that Andrew Jackson declared martial law on December 16, 1814, with the belief that it was necessary for the salvation of New Orleans. He had received letters from numerous residents, including Governor William C. C. Claiborne, warning of disaffection, spying, and conspiracy. These internal problems, compounded by a fractious and multiethnic community made the threat of a large British invasion all the more ominous. There is also no doubt that Jackson possessed the military might to shut down the city and force obedience. Legality remained the only question. Did he have the constitutional and or military authority to suspend the writ of habeas corpus and impose martial law? Even Jackson was uncertain and therefore turned to his newly acquired aides, Abner Duncan and Edward Livingston, both well-respected lawyers from New Orleans. Yet what Jackson received was hardly conclusive. Duncan theorized that the constitutional provision

authorizing suspension of the writ of habeas corpus impliedly sanctioned the use of martial law. Hence it was technically legal. Livingston
disagreed, insisting that martial law was "unknown to the Constitution
or Laws of the U.S." He explained that necessity alone justified such
an action, and even then the commander utilized such a power at his
own risk and responsibility. Alexander Dallas, the secretary of war in
1815, later confirmed Livingston's view.[2]

Duncan's and Livingston's disagreements over legality represented, to a degree, the varied distinctions posed by the nation's leading statesmen in the 1840s. Many legislators agreed on what martial
law actually did, but disputed Jackson's right to impose it. Benjamin
Tappan led the Democratic charge in the Senate only days after Lewis
Linn introduced the legislation, confidently announcing that "the law
of self-preservation is paramount to all other laws, with States as with
individuals. 'In the midst of arms the laws are silent.' I admit that the
right to declare martial law must be placed on the ground of necessity
alone, but of that necessity the Commanding General was the sole
judge."[3]

Tappan's argument was potentially explosive. Though he had managed to decisively step around the constitutionality of martial law, he
had also placed into the hands of Jackson, or any general, the authority to decide the extent of military necessity and power needed to impose military rule. Tappan's reasoning was based on the most fundamental notion of the law of nature, that of self-preservation. This idea
was fully in accordance with the writings of John Locke and Emer de
Vattel, both of whom occupied revered positions in the minds of
American statesmen. Indeed, there were few American politicians who
could not cite some aspect of Locke's and Vattel's work.[4] As an important cornerstone of American law, the law of nature was exactly the
justification that Democrats needed in order to approve Jackson's use
of military power.

If one accepted Tappan's reasoning, martial law was not necessarily constitutional, but it was not unconstitutional either. The nation's
statutes, including the writ of habeas corpus, were merely circumvented by a greater truth: the law of self-preservation. After presenting the authority of such doctrines, Tappan logically progressed to the
issue of Jackson's fine. The fact that martial law existed, explained the
senator, meant that "Judge Hall's authority was suspended." Thus, concluded Tappan, the fine "was wrongfully and illegally exacted."[5]

James Buchanan. Courtesy of the Library of Congress.

Senator Tappan's pointed argument was hardly a delicate discussion of civil liberties and the potential dangers of some freewheeling military commander in the nation's future. Subsequent Democratic senators, however, tread more carefully on the substantial issues at hand. James Buchanan of Pennsylvania calmly acknowledged that "strictly speaking, we admit he had no Constitutional right to make this declaration, but its absolute necessity for the purpose of defending the place amply justified the act." Furthermore, continued Buchanan, it was "indispensable to the safety of New Orleans that it should be converted into

a military camp. . . . If, then, the necessity of the case justified the declaration of martial law—and this must be admitted by all—what followed as a necessary consequence? Why, that the exercise of the civil
authority should cease, at least so far as was necessary to the defence
of the city." In this sense, Jackson was justified in arresting Judge Hall.
Buchanan explained, "Even though Judge Hall might have been acting
under a mistaken sense of duty, from the obvious necessity of the case,
would not the General be obliged to treat him, too, in the manner which
he did?"[6]

Buchanan's views undoubtedly possessed a degree of logic. Yet be-
side the fact that some Whigs simply refused to buy into the argument
of necessity, others questioned how far the military needed to go in
defense of the city. Jackson, after all, arrested Senator Louaillier and
Judge Hall well after the British had vacated the immediate area, and
southern Whigs in particular questioned Jackson's conduct under martial law rather than martial law itself, arguing that he went beyond
what was necessary.

On the whole, Senator Tappan and Buchanan made relatively brief
comments justifying martial law. A fuller, more detailed exposition on
the law of nature and the notion of overriding necessity came from
the bill's originator, Lewis Linn. Rising to the floor of the Senate, the
Missourian tried to temper the growing party acrimony: "It is possible . . . that the Judge and the General, in the discharge of their peculiar duties, may have both been right." If Linn gained any ground with
this olive branch, he surely lost it by bluntly announcing, "*We all know
that the General was right*." Still, Linn tried to avoid battles over Judge
Hall by insisting "an investigation into the motives or the acts of Judge
Hall is uncalled for; and I will not contribute to such an investigation."[7]
What Linn really wanted to focus upon was the justification of
Jackson's conduct. The senator therefore placed the matter in what he
believed were the simplest terms: "The question is in a nutshell: Was
the declaration of martial law necessary to aid in saving the 'beauty
and booty' of New Orleans?—was it declared for the public good?"[8]
This no one could deny, answered Linn, and thus "duty required him
[Jackson] to establish martial law." For Senator Linn, Jackson's actions
were not merely a matter of necessity, which in itself exonerated the
general, but even more notably, a question of duty to the nation, his
own command, and the salvation of New Orleans. "Many emergencies
arise in war—and some in peace—," he explained, "in which the high

civil and military servants of the people are, from *necessity*, compelled to 'take the responsibility' of doing some act, for the safety of the country, which is beyond the pale of their ordinary duties, and . . . beyond the law."[9]

For Linn, the case was elementary: Jackson could not have saved the city without martial law. Pointing to the clarity of such a view, Linn expressed surprise at Whig opposition. He also insisted that there existed ample precedent supporting Jackson's conduct and a subsequent indemnification by Congress. Still, Linn opined, "I did not anticipate that gentlemen would take a course which would render them [other precedents] necessary." He then called in what he believed was the big gun. "I have one now before me," he continued, "from a source to which Senators will attach a sincere veneration."[10] None other than Thomas Jefferson had delivered an opinion on military officers surpassing the bounds of law. Commenting on events during the infamous Burr conspiracy in 1807, Jefferson had declared that when a grave and menacing danger threatened the nation and her citizens, it

> constituted a law of necessity and self-preservation; and rendered the salus populi supreme over the written law. The officer who is called to act on this superior ground does, indeed, risk himself on the justice of the controlling powers of the Constitution; and his station makes it his duty to incurr [sic] that risk. But those controlling powers, and his fellow-citizens generally, are bound to judge according to the circumstances under which he acted. . . . It is incumbent on those who accept of great charges, to risk themselves on great occasions, when the safety of the nation, or some of its very high interests, are at stake. . . . But the good officer is bound to draw it at his own peril, and throws himself on the justice of his country, and the rectitude of his motives.[11]

Jefferson's reasoning was not altogether different from his argument concerning the legality of the Louisiana Purchase. In 1803, he had explained that when the chief executive or legislature engage in an act beyond the Constitution and "risking themselves like faithful servants," they must "throw themselves on their country" for approval.[12] Lewis Linn certainly expected Jefferson's words to hush, perhaps even cow Whig opposition. The Sage of Monticello made a strong defense of extraordinary military powers. Yet Jefferson's advocacy was certainly no blank slate for commanders. They could override the Constitution during times of emergency, but only at their own peril. It was up to the "controlling powers," the nation's legislators, to determine whether the emergency actions were acceptable. Whigs could reasonably argue that this is what they were attempting.

Moreover, there was also a question regarding Jefferson's opinion of General Jackson. Like most Americans, Jefferson rejoiced in the New Orleans victory and never mentioned martial law specifically, yet he did note in an 1824 letter that Jackson "had very little respect for laws or constitutions" and "is a dangerous man."[13] The fact that Jefferson had no great love for Andrew Jackson is of little importance regarding the larger issue of extreme necessity and military authority. The truth is that Jefferson's reasoning did support Jackson's actions, with the important caveat that such conduct was subject to Congress' and the people's approval. Yet Jefferson also went further in his support of extraordinary military action. In an 1808 letter, one Lewis Linn most likely did not have because he surely would have utilized it, Jefferson expanded his view of emergency powers, noting that "under the maxim of the law itself, that *inter arma silent leges,* that in an encampment expecting daily attack from a powerful enemy, self-preservation is paramount to all law. . . . There are extreme cases where the laws become inadequate even to their own preservation, and where the universal resource is a dictator, or martial law."[14]

Jefferson's argument in this case was potentially more extreme and certainly more forceful. There existed no qualifications about subsequent approval. True, both letters included the core idea of self-preservation as a higher law, but the later letter specifically endorsed martial law and matched later Democratic arguments that this higher law did not conflict with the Constitution. Linn, however, did not go to such extremes, opting instead to focus on earlier precedents in which Congress had absolved military commanders.

There were numerous instances, explained the senator, in which military officers had exerted power by arresting or detaining civilians, ultimately been fined, but later indemnified by Congress. Linn listed a series of examples: in 1818, Maj. General Jacob Brown was reimbursed for a fine after he imprisoned a civilian found near the military camp and suspected of traitorous designs; in 1823, Col. Robert Purdy was indemnified for a fine issued after arresting an individual caught near the garrison; and in 1823, Lt. Robert Stockton captured and detained a vessel and its crew. He was later fined and, again, indemnified by Congress. Senator Linn made special note of one particular case that occurred in 1818. A Captain Austin and Lieutenant Wells were fined some six thousand dollars for confining nine individuals suspected of treachery to their country. Not only were these two officers reimbursed for their losses, but the secretary of war at the time, John C. Calhoun, spoke forcefully on their behalf. "I would respectfully suggest," he insisted, "that there may be cases, in the exigencies of war, in which, if the commander should transcend his legal power, Congress ought to protect him, and those who act under him, from consequential damages." Linn's brief discussion of these various cases revealed that precedents existed in which Congress refunded money to military officers. "Cases in point might be further multiplied," he insisted, "were it deemed necessary, to show the entire willingness of the Government, at all times, to protect its faithful officers and agents in the discharge of their official duties."[15] Adding the opinion of Calhoun, a presidential cabinet officer at the time, certainly did not hurt matters. Whether Senator Calhoun was in attendance during Linn's speech is unknown, but he was doubtlessly aware that his previous remarks were entered as a defense for Jackson. No matter, Calhoun remained silent.

The fact that the government had refunded money to military officers was an important item that Linn rightfully pointed out. There were remarkable similarities between those cases and Jackson's. Yet there also existed a rather obvious difference. None of those officers had declared martial law. And whether Jackson was actually fined for imposing martial law or refusing to abide by Judge Hall's writ of habeas corpus, a matter that later speakers focused upon, the fact is that both were integrally tied to one another. However much Linn might have wished it, the fine was not a simple matter. Nevertheless, he continued to insist that any officer, including Jackson, should be protected if a law was violated while in the service of country. Linn concluded his speech by imploring that the general's fine should be refunded, for "it will tend to smooth his way to the grave, by showing that the Senate of the United States looked upon his conduct at New Orleans as justifiable—his motives as pure—and as an example to future generals to do likewise under similar circumstances."[16]

Focusing on the justification of Jackson's actions and the purity that inspired him were, perhaps, reasonable points. Announcing that the Senate should set a precedent for future declarations of martial law was not, especially considering that many of the bill's opponents expressed concern over that very issue. Yet Linn had actually focused

upon this point in greater detail during a speech delivered a week earlier. "Exigencies like those which existed at New Orleans may again
arise," he explained, "and a commanding general ought not to be de-
terred from taking the necessary responsibility by the reflection that
it is in the power of a vindictive judge to impair his private fortune,
and place a stain upon his character which cannot be removed."[17] Linn
not only made an off-hand criticism of Dominick Hall, something the
senator insisted was unnecessary, but also advocated the sanction of
future, extraordinary military action. This latter point was forceful and
showed an understanding of the necessity that military commanders
sometimes faced. What the point was not, however, was Lewis Linn's.
Andrew Jackson had, through a series of letters to the senator, hammered away at an officer's need to utilize all necessary measures: "I
ask what general hereafter, if Neworleans was again threatened with
invasion, let the real necessity be what it might, and the most energetic measures for its defense necessary, would hazard the responsibility, of adopting those energetic measures by which the Country could
alone be defended, whilst the record of the fine and loss stared him in
the face, inflicted upon me by an unjust judge for declaring martial
law."[18] Linn clearly ensured that the general's views made their way to
the Senate, and as such they are yet another example of the degree to
which Jackson influenced the proceedings. Nor were the general's
views ignored. Several Democrats, for example, also argued that the
bill would send a message to future commanders.[19] Still, not all Democrats agreed. Congressman John Dawson of Louisiana, for example,
insisted "there is nothing in this case which can tempt future officers
to a similar hazard."[20]

Another of Jackson's great champions in the Senate continued the
argument on the paramount nature of self-defense and the power of
military officers. Robert Walker, the lone Democrat on the Judiciary
Committee, asserted that the refund bill did not actually involve the
power of a military commander to declare martial law. Rather, the bill
was, as many of Jackson's supporters argued, merely a matter of justice and said nothing about martial law. Yet because the issue of a commander's authority had arisen, Walker declared, "in time of war, and
of imminent public danger, it may be the duty of the commander to
arrest those regarded as spies, or mutineers, within the limits of his
camp." This was Jackson's situation, he insisted, and therefore his declaration of martial law "was not merely excusable, but justifiable. It

was demanded by a great and overruling necessity." Walker then focused more specifically on martial law and the question of its implicit violation of the Constitution, stating, "the law which justified the act, was the great law of necessity; it was the law of self-defence. This great law of necessity—of defence of self, of home, and of country—never was designed to be abrogated by any statute, or by any constitution."[21] Walker's view was remarkably similar to that espoused by Benjamin Tappan. Both senators held that under the law of nature, self-preservation did not actually run in opposition to a nation's laws. Rather, the two worked in combination. Thus the question of martial law as constitutional or unconstitutional was to a large degree moot.

Other Democrats concurred and went even further in explaining the relationship between the necessity for martial law and the sanctity of the Constitution. Perry Smith, the sole Democratic legislator from Connecticut, began with the rather standard understanding of the right of self-defense inherent in the law of nature.[22] Smith questioned, "What is martial law, as enforced at New Orleans by General Jackson, but physical power which our common Creator has given us for self-preservation; and which every man, and all men, have always exerted; and which no society or Government has ever dared to impair and much less to take away?" With the issue posed so clearly, he went on to extrapolate further on the intrinsic similarity between an individual's right to fight off an aggressive assailant and the right of a nation to do the same. In light of this most basic entitlement, Jackson "did no more than any other citizen, or every other one of the United States, might have done, to prevent a violation of our territory by a public enemy." Smith even argued that Jackson, in keeping with any individual's right of defense, could have declared martial law in his capacity as a private citizen. The senator did not bother to elaborate on how a civilian goes about declaring martial law, but in accepting the fundamental privilege provided by the law of nature, he concluded that Jackson had not overstepped any American laws: "General Jackson violated no law; nor did he, in making his defence, transcend his powers, or abuse those of the civil department of our Government."[23] Here was a clear statement on the legality of Jackson's conduct.

Senator Smith did not, however, stop there. Once on the subject of laws and Constitution he offered a logical scenario of the situation that has plagued those who have argued and continue to argue about transcending laws in order to ultimately save them. "The great crime in his defence of New Orleans," he announced, "is that he trampled upon our sacred Constitution. But, I would ask, what is our Constitution worth, when our country is gone? And what was the defence at New Orleans, but a struggle for our country?" Depending upon one's point of view, one answer to Smith's question is that New Orleans did not represent the entire country and that if the city had fallen, it did not mean that the remainder of the nation was also lost. In such a case, the Constitution remained intact. Was this not the situation at Washington when the British invaded and put the capital city to the torch? Another point of view, of course, is that some believed the British planned on taking and keeping New Orleans. They did not have this sort of design on Washington and thus the comparison is not entirely valid. Better to put the Constitution aside in order to save an important port city than lose it forever to the enemy.

In addition to discussing constitutionality, Smith also focused directly upon the conflicting ideologies inherent in Jackson's use of martial law. Republican thought was a tradition that warned of aggressive power, especially in the form of military usurpation, and the supremacy of civil authority was touted as a bulwark of American government. Yet the law of nature was an equally revered tradition. As many Democrats insisted, it preceded and continued alongside written laws. Yet Smith went further. He not only addressed the issue of martial law's legality but also focused specifically upon the intersection of republicanism and the law of nature: "When both the civil and military powers are in healthy action, I readily agree to the principle that the military is subordinate to the civil power. But I know of no instance where physical power may not be exerted to prevent the commission of a crime, or for the suppression of a crime, or to protect an individual from an assault." Smith concluded that it is "the law paramount to all others, either political, civil, or international—the law of self-preservation I refer to."[24] The key to the senator's view was "when" the civil and military powers are in healthy action. In the case of New Orleans they were not, he argued. Thus when such a conflict arose, it was the law of nature to which one turned, not the Constitution.

Democratic senators revealed a wide degree of latitude regarding the intricacies of the law of nature. Yet though they differed over whether or not martial law was strictly constitutional, they did not quibble over its effect; necessity authorized and justified Andrew Jackson's imposition of martial law. As a result, the nation was obligated to return the general's fine with interest. Nor were senators alone in such views. Democrats in the House of Representatives were equally adamant in their support of Old Hickory. They raised many of the points discussed in the upper chamber but also expressed a greater degree of radical thought.

The Battle in the House

At the forefront of the House debates over the fine was Charles Jared Ingersoll, a congressman from Pennsylvania and a minority member of the Judiciary Committee. Ingersoll, in fact, became so involved in the refund issue that he took to the pen and wrote an extensive treatise titled *Gen. Jackson's Fine: An Examination into the Question of Martial Law; with an Explanation of the Law of Contempt of Court.* The work actually devoted more space to discussing the extent of the judiciary's contempt power than on the law of nature and legality of martial law. Francis Preston Blair, always Jackson's conduit for publicity and political action, published the work and assured Jackson that a copy would be sent to every member of Congress as well as every state legislature.[25] Like others who were heavily involved in Jackson's cause, Ingersoll received ample assistance from Jackson and Blair.[26]

Like many of his colleagues in the Senate, Ingersoll based the justification of martial law squarely upon the idea of self-defense. He continually reiterated that just as any person possessed an inherent right of self-protection, so too did a nation. In such cases, it is necessity alone that authorized action. For Jackson, the issue of necessity was that much more paramount because of the threat posed by a hostile invasion force. Ingersoll made it clear that the general violated the civil law but that the demands of the situation required extraordinary measures; and the greater the threat, the more extreme the defensive action. As Ingersoll explained it, the "blast of war stiffens the sinews to severer control, burns houses, seizes chattels, imprisons men; as danger increases, necessity keeps pace with it, till all common law may be superceded for self-preservation. . . . This power, unconstitutional, enormous, and formidable, General Jackson took upon himself."[27] The congressman's view of martial law in the pamphlet was an extension of his earlier House speech in which he announced that martial law "was nothing more than extreme necessity" and that "a declaration of war authorizes every species and contrivance of destruction, as the inevitable means of ulterior good."[28]

Not all House Democrats embraced Ingersoll's admission that martial law was unauthorized by the Constitution. Rather, the arguments, as in the Senate, ran the gamut of martial law's unconstitutionality, to its consistency with the Constitution, to the law of nature as paramount to all written laws. Aaron Brown of Tennessee, for example, argued that "in no case does the law of necessity abrogate the Constitution. It only rises above it, but yet stands consistent with it." Arguing a slightly different point of view that pushed aside any consideration of constitutionality was James Belser of Alabama, who insisted that there are certain cases "above human regulations, and controlled only by the great rule of nature. These rights were inherent in man; they existed antecedent to the formation of governments or the adoption of constitutions." Belser's fellow representative from Alabama, William W. Payne, agreed. Insisting that martial law was predicated on the "grounds of self-defence which were paramount to all written constitutions and laws," the congressman went a step further by addressing the inherent conflict between the law of nature and that of the republican tradition that informed the American understanding of the balance between liberty and power: "There was scarcely a constitution which did not expressly declare that the military was subordinate to the civil power, and the Constitution of the United States contained the same doctrine. Yet, notwithstanding all this, it did not follow, that in time of war, a case might not arise in which it was justifiable—nay, in which it was essential—that a commander should assume the responsibility of declaring martial law."[29]

These varying interpretations justifying martial law were all related to fear over impairing the Constitution. The line of difference between men such as Brown and Belser was actually razor thin. One maintained that martial law was consistent with the Constitution, whereas the other simply dismissed such a consideration because the law of nature was paramount. The end result of the two views was exactly the same; both congressmen justified martial law without belittling the Constitution. In the midst of these varying theories, some Democrats expressed skepticism over Whig concerns of a damaged Constitution, and in doing so revealed the intense partisan animosity that permeated the refund debates. Andrew Kennedy rose to the floor, announcing, "I doubt not, Mr. Chairman, there are men in and out of this House who are honestly opposing the passage of this bill, for fear they may commit an infraction on the civil authorities of this country; but I at the same time as little doubt that there are those, here and elsewhere, who are making this a pretext for their opposition." Commenting on other constitutional disputes of the period, John Dawson of Louisiana cut more deeply into Whigs by remarking condescendingly, "But I hear the cry of a violated Constitution. Whence comes this cry? Surely, such devoted patriots, such lovers of the Constitution, are not the advocates of a national bank; of a high protective tariff; of national internal improvements; of a distribution of the proceeds of public lands; and the abolition of slavery in the South?"[30]

By 1844, with Democrats in full control of the House, Andrew Jackson's political foot soldiers knew that their victory was secure. Thus the first week of January witnessed an intensified series of speeches, some of which bordered on radical notions concerning the Constitution and the tender balance between civil and military power. Lewis Steenrod of Virginia, for example, began, as had many of his colleagues, by heralding the supremacy of the law of nature over the Constitution. Yet he also went a step further, thundering, "I have not patience to examine the lawyers' books to answer whether this great cause of freedom was maintained according to the constitution." He then advocated a decidedly radical view: "I would say, away with the inviolability of the constitution, with the perfectibility of the law, when it would surrender an empire, and subject its citizens to be immolated on its holy altar."[31] Here was not the reasoned discussion put forth by men like Perry Smith, who questioned the worth of the Constitution if the country was lost. Steenrod also had harsh words about Judge Hall, charging that "he prostituted his station in acting on the sentiments and feelings of an Englishman; that as an Englishman, and not as a United States judge, he sought to entrap an American general, who had driven back an English invasion." Though a variety of sources do support the argument that Hall was English born, Steenrod's invective, as well as his statement about the Constitution, revealed a degree of animosity and excitement that bordered on absurdity.[32] Steenrod, perhaps caught up in the impending Democratic victory, expressed his views with an indecorous, blunt extremism. Nor was he alone.

Stephen Douglas, a freshman congressman from Illinois, rose to the floor and in doing so made his debut speech in the national Congress. Like Andrew Kennedy, Douglas believed "the charge of exerting arbitrary power and lawlessness . . . have been so often made and reiterated for political effect." Still, he ably answered those who believed that martial law was unconstitutional. First of all, he explained, Jackson's "duty, as prescribed by the Constitution and laws, as well as the instructions of the War Department, was to defend the city and country at every hazard." Because this was the case, continued Douglas, "he had a right to declare martial law, when it was ascertained and acknowledged that nothing but martial law would enable him to defend the city and the country." If this logic was not enough to convince the opposition, Douglas followed the path of his many col-

Stephen Douglass. Courtesy of the Library of Congress.

leagues, insisting that inherent necessity "was the great, first law of nature, which authorizes a man to defend his life, his wife and children, at all hazards, and by every means in his power." Up to this point, the young congressman's speech, though well articulated, was nothing out of the ordinary. This, however, quickly changed. Douglas took on a mocking tone and ultimately joined Lewis Steenrod in extremism:

> It is more prudent to deal in vague generalities, and high sounding declamation—first, about the horrors of arbitrary power and lawless violence; then the supremacy of the laws, and the glorious privileges of the writ of habeas corpus. These things sound very well, and are right in their proper place. I do not wish to extenuate the one, or depreciate the other. But when I hear gentlemen attempting to justify this unrighteous fine upon General Jackson, upon the ground of noncompliance with rules of court and mere technical formalities, I must confess I cannot appreciate the force of the argument. In cases of war and desolation, in times of peril and disaster, we should look at the substance not the shadow of things. . . . Talk to me not about rules and forms in court, when the enemy's cannon are pointed at the door, and the flames encircle the cupola!

Beyond likening concerns over arbitrary power and the writ of habeas corpus to "the shadow of things," Douglas ended this powerful portion of his speech with a rather excessive announcement: "I care not whether his [Jackson's] proceedings were legal or illegal, constitutional or unconstitutional, with or without precedent, if they were necessary to the salvation of that city."[33] Stephen Douglas's first speech in Congress advocated ideas about the sanctity of the Constitution that he would never espouse in the coming years when the sectional crisis over slavery threatened the Union's existence.

Still, the congressman did receive some notice for his defense of Jackson. John Quincy Adams wrote in his diary that Douglas "made an eloquent, sophistical speech," adding that it was "prodigiously admired by the slave Democracy of the House." Another contemporary of the time wrote later, and somewhat prematurely, that the speech was "the first move made by Mr. Douglas in his canvas for the presidency." Even Andrew Jackson, when he met Douglas later in 1844, thanked the congressman for his advocacy.[34]

Whigs Respond: The Southern Wing

On the whole, Democrats did a remarkably good job of defending the general's use of martial law. Utilizing the law of nature, they challenged arguments that Jackson's conduct was unconstitutional and that it endangered the delicate republican balance between civil and military power. And though Democrats did not agree on the exact parameters of the law of nature, or whether advocating martial law set a future precedent, they did come together in determining that martial law was justified in New Orleans. Democrats also took the next logical step and denounced Judge Hall's fine, arguing that because martial law was in force, Hall had no authority to issue a writ of habeas corpus.[35] Other Democrats argued that in light of Jackson's heroic defense the fine was unjust.[36] Still others insisted that the fine was illegal.[37] Finally, some Democrats charged that the judge acted solely out of revenge rather than any anxiety over the safety and preservation of the Constitution.[38]

To the many variations of Democratic arguments, Whigs responded with constitutional authority, republican tradition, disdain, ridicule, and party invective. Most argued that martial law was contrary to the Constitution. Yet Whigs also split, to some degree, over whether or not Jackson was justified in imposing military rule. Southern Whigs, remembering the general's great services to the South, tended to decry his violation of the Constitution but acknowledged the necessity in New

Orleans. Northern Whigs, however, refused to accept necessity as a justification. Yet at the same time that some of these leading Whig orators trumpeted the sanctity of the nation's laws and the republican balance between civil liberty and military power, striking inconsistencies existed. Finally, both groups of Whigs offered a steadfast defense of the judiciary in general, and Judge Hall specifically.

One of the first Whig speakers was Senator John Jordan Crittenden of Kentucky. As a member of the Judiciary Committee that had given a negative report on the refund bill, Crittenden rose to defend both the report and the sanctity of the judiciary. Concerned over "military enthusiasm," the senator noted that he "could never consent to honor any man so far, to elevate any man so high, as to violate in his favor the regulations of the country, and to degrade everyone else to stand below him."[39] With this in mind, he insisted that he was very wary of invalidating the judgment of the court. Other southern senators expressed similar views. William C. Preston of South Carolina explained that his only reservation in supporting the refund bill lay in the possibility that it could be understood or construed as a reproach on Judge Hall. Reacting to negative remarks made by Democrat James Buchanan, Preston announced, "I cannot but believe that the Senator makes an unjust, as he certainly does an unnecessary imputation upon Judge Hall, when he attributes to him motives so paltry as personal pique and irritation. . . . The Judge could not have been prompted to, or sustained in so high and bold a course by motives so petty and unworthy." Yet Preston also expressed sentiments about civil and military relations that few if any northern Whigs would consider. Reminiscing about the Battle of New Orleans, he noted his "pure and generous feeling," as well as the "glory," "skill and courage" of the "illustrious chief," Andrew Jackson. Referring to the general's ultimate acquiescence to Judge Hall, Preston announced, "more than the battle, it swells my bosom to see him bend that laurelled brow before the seat of justice— patiently taking its censure, and submitting to its award. Indeed, it was a very noble spectacle, and has emblazoned the principle of our institutions, that the military is subordinate to the civil authority, and that all men are equal before the law." The Republic, Preston concluded, "may with equal truth congratulate herself upon having such a Judge and such a General."[40] The senator's respect for Jackson revealed a rather common southern view, but seeing the court battle between the general and Judge Hall as "noble" was something altogether different.

Many Whigs discussed the relationship between the civilian and military spheres; very few viewed Jackson's actions as an example of devotion to civilian rule.

Continuing the theme of support for Jackson but defense of Hall was John MacPherson Berrien, senator from Georgia and chairman of the Judiciary Committee. Berrien explained that he "had always felt the deepest debt of gratitude to Gen. Jackson for his triumphant protection of the South, and for the accession of national honor and glory which he had achieved for his country." Surprisingly, Berrien also acknowledged, "Gen. Jackson was perfectly excusable, under all the circumstances of the case, in declaring martial law; and that he was equally excusable for disobeying the writ of *habeas corpus*." Under similar circumstances, Berrien noted, he would have done exactly the same.

Where Berrien and Jackson differed, however, was in the arrest of Judge Hall. Though Jackson may have been justified in banishing Hall, insisted Berrien, the judge's arrest and confinement was unnecessary. Hall, continued the senator, was "asserting the right of the civil power, and maintaining the majesty of the laws."[41] The ultimate conclusion was that both men were engaged in their respective duties. In making these arguments Berrien did not bother to surmise how Hall might have reacted differently if he had merely been escorted out of New Orleans rather than arrested. Moreover, the contempt of court was for Jackson's refusal to abide by the writ of habeas corpus, not solely the judge's arrest. Berrien's scenario, therefore, was hardly realistic. The senator certainly did not acknowledge the concept of martial law described by Democrats if he believed that Judge Hall had the authority to issue the writ in the first place and thereby assert the "right of the civil power." Perhaps Berrien's larger goal was drawing distinctions between abstract questions of if and when emergency powers were ever justified versus the concern over the tangible violations of civil liberties that occurred under martial law. If this was the case, one could accept the imposition of military rule but still hold a commander responsible for unreasonable excesses. This, however, was not a clear distinction as outlined by Berrien. Moreover, such a scenario was decidedly subjective and would ultimately result in exactly the debate in which Democrats and Whigs were engaged. Many of Jackson's supporters believed the judge had no authority to interfere with the military and thus deserved arrest, whereas most Whigs viewed the general's arrest of Hall as excessive and unwarranted.

The southern appreciation for Jackson coupled with support of the judiciary prompted John Henderson of Mississippi to propose an amendment that "nothing in this act shall be construed to be an expression of the opinion of Congress as to the legality of the proceedings of the judge." The bill, instead, was an "additional expression," he suggested, "of the high consideration" Congress held for General Jackson.[42] The modification was not concerned with civil liberties much less a condemnation of martial law. Rather, the amendment lauded Jackson's victory. Another southern senator, William A. Graham of North Carolina, suggested outright that Congress leave the question of martial law "untouched."[43] Other Whigs did not agree. In a subsequent Judiciary Committee report, Berrien, the man who said he too would have declared martial law, stated that the committee did not want to censure either the judge or the general, and that they desired to "protect the Senate from the possible inference that, in passing this bill, it has acknowledged the legal authority of a military officer to establish martial law within the limits of this free republic."[44] Though this may have been the committee's intent, their failure to address the legality of martial law within an amendment was problematic. Berrien and his colleagues discerned that maintaining "the legality of the proceedings of the judge" somehow implied a disapproval of martial law. This was certainly how some Democrats viewed it, even going so far as to say that upholding Hall's conduct was a censure upon Jackson. Yet in reality, defending Hall's decision was not tantamount to a denial of martial law. The fine was not imposed for the general's declaration. It was the seizure of and failure to abide by the writ of habeas corpus along with the judge's arrest that landed Jackson in court. Thus the idea that defending judicial authority was the same as ruling on the legality of martial law was simply incorrect. The only way to make a Senate determination on the legality of martial law was to include specific language within the refund bill itself.

John Henderson's amendment made no grand statements that might protect the nation from future declarations of martial law. Nor did many southern Whigs feel that Jackson's conduct was so terrible, as evidenced by Berrien's initial statements. Even after the amendment, southern Whigs continued their laudatory views of the general. Willie Mangum of North Carolina believed that Jackson "did his duty nobly and well," and, accepting Democratic assertions regarding the necessary power to defend New Orleans, declared that "at all hazards, he was to defend the country from all possibility of danger from an invading enemy." As with other Whigs, the only sticking point for Mangum was upholding the judge's reputation. Thus, concluded the senator, "Gen. Jackson may be defended amply, and yet Judge Hall's conduct might be equally defensible."[45]

Of the southern Whig senators who actually engaged in debate over the refund bill, the vast majority were not opposed to Jackson's use of martial law. This, most likely, stemmed primarily from his heroic reputation and popularity throughout the region. He had not only saved New Orleans but had stopped the Creek threat on the Alabama and Mississippi frontier, as well as on the Georgia-Florida border. It was also no small matter that his negotiations at the Treaty of Fort Jackson in 1814 yielded millions of acres for white Americans, as did his removal of the Cherokees from Georgia. Many southern Whigs had, in fact, been former Democrats and only left the party as a result of Jackson's bank policy. This was certainly the case with John Berrien.[46] Senate voting on the refund bill provides further indication of southern Whig support. On major votes, those involving either amendments, readings of the bill, or its passage, southern Whigs voted almost three to one over northerners in favor of the refund.[47]

That most southern Whigs supported the general's use of martial law does not mean that all southern Whigs did so. William Archer of Virginia, for example, appreciated Jackson for his services to the country but believed that the fine was "legally imposed" and should not be removed. The senator was not opposed to a "munificent donation for his military services" but not a direct return of the fine. Though charitable toward Jackson, Archer's brief comments also revealed an underlying Whig partisanship that continued from Jackson's tenure as president. Archer "condemned his civil policy and general conduct" and described him "as a man in power, who disregarded both laws and Constitution."[48]

Whigs Respond: The Northern Wing

The initial Whig response to the refund bill's introduction in the Senate was almost completely dominated by southerners. Only one northern Whig spoke in the spring of 1842; even then, it was brief, though important. In May, Richard Henry Bayard of Delaware offered a futile amendment stating that the bill included no opinion on "any judicial proceeding or legal question growing out of the declaration of martial law."[49] When the debates began anew in December, Bayard rose to challenge Democrats, declaring, "this is not a light matter for Congress to sanction the idea that the lives of our citizens, their property, and their personal liberty, may, with impunity, be placed at the mercy of a military commander, and a court-martial of his officers, brought together at his summons." He then discussed the supposed authority by which the general invoked his decree. The Constitution gives to Congress the power to raise armies and declare war, but, insisted Bayard, nowhere does it allow martial law. At most, he continued, a state of war "authorizes the suspension of the privilege of the writ of *habeas corpus*, which is the sacred instrument of liberty in the hands of State authorities . . . and that can be done by Congress only—not by an officer of the Government without its authority." After satisfying himself that martial law was utterly foreign to the Constitution, Bayard actually acknowledged Democratic arguments of necessity. He did not cite the law of nature or engage in an extended discussion of the subject, but his remarks were nonetheless significant: "If an individual, no matter how high in commission, or how much impelled by necessity, usurps the power, he cannot be said to act rightfully, though he may be excused. A high and imperious necessity may exist, which can alone form his excuse; and whenever such a case is presented, he [Bayard] would sustain the officer. Whether such was the fact in the case of General Jackson, should be distinctly settled."[50] On one level it appeared that Bayard, no matter the constitutionality, was willing to excuse extraordinary measures in cases of extreme necessity. The senator, however, was certainly not yet convinced that this scenario fit Jackson's use of martial law and looked to the Judiciary Committee to settle the issue. They failed to do so, as John Berrien's weak report so amply revealed.

Other northern senators did not match Bayard's charity. Jacob Welsh Miller of New Jersey judged that Jackson had done grave damage to the Constitution by declaring martial law. This act was made even worse by the arrest of Dominick Hall, for that arrest, insisted Miller, was "to defeat, by means of tyrannical and irresistible force, the legal operation of the *habeas corpus*." Throughout his long speech, the senator continually hammered away on this point, referring to the writ of habeas corpus as a "cherished jewel." At times, Miller reached the height of bombastic oratory, opining, "Who that reveres the institutions of this country can sanction a wanton breach of its Constitution? Who that loves liberty can excuse the blow that strikes down the bulwarks of its defence?" He then addressed Democratic justifications of Jackson, announcing, "Yet we are told that there is a law superior to the Constitution—the law of war, called martial law! Do gentlemen mean to say that a declaration of war abrogates the Constitution? Was not our Constitution made for war and peace? Is its potency only to be felt in the quiet unresisting times of peace, but lost amid the din of arms and shouts of victory?" Miller, of course, concluded that the Constitution was made for every situation that faced the nation and, as Senator Bayard had concluded, provided very specific powers through which the nation could wage war. Martial law was not one of them. Thus Senator Miller concluded with a simple question to his Senate colleagues: "Now, sir, I ask, can we, the Senate of the United States, existing by and acting under the Constitution, excuse, and thereby justify, this suspension of the habeas corpus? No sir, we cannot; we dare not. . . . I cannot sacrifice a great constitutional principle—a principle more valuable to this people than a hundred cities, more glorious than a thousand victories."[51]

Joining Miller in his defense of the Constitution and writ of habeas corpus was William Woodbridge of Michigan, who trumpeted that the latter was "a writ which opened the door of every prison, and whose talismanic influence no tower, no dungeon, nor bastile could successfully resist." Jackson, exclaimed Woodbridge, was "seduced, in the intoxication of the moment," and forgot "that he was not a Roman dictator." The senator's powerful condemnation allowed no room for pleas of necessity or justified conduct. Woodbridge adhered strictly to the Constitution and concluded his remarks with an ominous declaration: "That high emblem of constitutional power [the writ of habeas corpus] is trampled under foot by your impassioned general; and the judge who has dared to do his duty, and to issue it, is himself sent ignominiously and in chains into exile. And now you are required to blot out this whole page from your country's history. No, sir, it is worse than that. What, what is the lesson such an act will teach?"[52]

Senator Miller's and Woodbridge's speeches were the most damning of those delivered by Whigs in the upper house. Yet they did not, just as Senate Democrats did not, reach the level of animosity and extreme invective witnessed in the House. For it was in the lower chamber that the two parties engaged in a more mean spirited partisan brawl. In looking at the first Whig to deliver an address, it is unmistakable why debate in the House degenerated so quickly. John Quincy Adams simply hated Andrew Jackson, and the perpetual Massachusetts representative took delight in hurling bombs at his nemesis and the refund bill.[53] Adams immediately zeroed in on the patriotic, nationalist fervor that fueled the refund movement, barking, "If you pass this bill it will not be for the honor and glory of the battle of New Orleans, but for the honor and glory of the exercise of despotic power over your own citizens; it would be for the exercise of the extreme of martial law, when there was no necessity for using it." The steely representative exploded at southerners who constantly lauded the battle, insisting that the issue of martial law should be "fully discussed" and "deliberated on without any of your gag-laws, to stop the investigation of the principles involved in it."[54] Adams's mention of "gag-laws" was a reference to House rules that automatically tabled antislavery petitions so that they could not be read. With this little slap at southerners firmly in place, Adams focused more specifically on the constitutionality involved in the refund issue: "Should the bill pass in the form asked for by General Jackson, it would, in effect, become the law of the land in all future time. Should it be passed, it would be recognizing the right of a commander of the army to declare martial law and prostrate every right of the citizen. . . . Sanction this, and your children to the latest day will be subject to martial law at the fiat not only of the President, but of a commander of the army. You must remit the fine, and at the same time recognize the punishment, or do as General Jackson demands—stigmatize the character of a dead man [Judge Hall] who had the courage and the nerve to discharge his duty."[55]

Adams's speech posed important constitutional questions, most important among them the issue of creating a precedent for martial law. Even here, however, Adams merely attempted to throw an obstacle into the path of Jackson's refund bill rather than express any heartfelt, ideological conviction regarding the sanctity of liberty and the Constitution. In contrast to his high-minded denunciation of military rule, "Old Man Eloquent," as he was often called, had only nine months early been a staunch advocate of martial law. During a speech about the continuation of full diplomatic missions to England and Mexico, Adams had discussed the possibility of armed conflict with other nations and in doing so argued that martial law was an inherent right of war:

> When your country is actually in war, whether it be a war of inva-
> sion or a war of insurrection, Congress has power to carry on the
> war, and must carry it on according to the laws of war; and, by the
> laws of war, an invaded country has all its laws and municipal regu-
> lations swept by the board, and martial law takes the place of them.
> . . . General Jackson was acting under the laws of war, and because
> the moment you place a military commander in a district that is the
> theater of war, the laws of war apply to that district. . . . I might
> furnish a thousand proofs to show that the pretensions of gentlemen
> to the sanctity of their municipal institutions, under a state of actual
> invasion and actual war, whether servile, civil, or foreign, is wholly
> unfounded, and that the laws of war do in all such cases take prece-
> dence. I lay this down as the law of nations. I say that the military
> authority takes for the time the place of all municipal institutions.[56]

Here was a contradictory bombshell. Adams not only advocated
martial law but also pointed to Jackson's use of military rule as a prime
example. Yet why would Adams engage in such an obvious inconsistency? The answer lay in ulterior motives, principally his devotion to
abolition. For Adams, the charm of martial law was a direct result of
the power that the military possessed in an occupied territory during
a time of war: "When a country is invaded, and two hostile armies are
met in martial array, the commanders of both armies have the power
to emancipate all the slaves in the invaded territory. . . . I say the military authority takes for the time the place of all municipal institutions
and of slavery among the rest, and that under that state of things, so
far from its being true, that the States where slavery exists, have the
exclusive management of the subject, not only the President of the
United States, but the commander of the army, has the power to order
the universal emancipation of the slaves."[57] Clearly, Adams's support
for martial law was wedded to establishing an edict for emancipating
slaves under the guise of military necessity. And if accepted, such a
rule posed a dire threat to slaveholders. If under martial law the military was in full control, and thus all civil law, the Constitution included,
was swept aside, a military commander might very well emancipate
slaves under the pretext of necessity. Jackson, in fact, had caused quite
a controversy in New Orleans by merely arming a battalion of free
blacks to defend the city.[58] Moreover, at the outset of the Civil War,
Gen. John C. Frémont did exactly what Adams advocated by emancipating the slaves of Confederate activists in Missouri. President

Lincoln quickly requested Frémont to revise the order because of the delicate political situation with Unionists in the South.[59]

Congressman Adams's doctrine clearly had import. Nor was his 1842 declaration the first time he broached the connection between war powers and emancipation. In 1836, while discussing a resolution for supplying rations to the victims of Indian hostilities in Alabama and Georgia, Adams launched into a tirade on the "slaveholding exterminators of Indians," insisting that the unquenchable thirst for more slave lands could result only in war with Mexico or even England and thus the southern masters should understand fully the war powers of Congress. "From the instant that your slaveholding States become the theater of war, civil, servile, or foreign," declared Adams, "the war powers of Congress extend to interference with the institution of slavery in every way by which it can be interfered with."[60] Over time, Adams's wartime manumission strategy underwent a clear broadening of powers. In 1836, he insisted that Congress held the power to "interfere" with slavery. In 1842, he extended the power of emancipation not only to the president but also to any military commander.[61] Adams even acknowledged his overriding goal to create precedents for emancipation. Realizing that the slavery issue would not be reconciled in his lifetime, he confided to his diary, "To open the way for others is all that I can do."[62] In a letter to Benjamin Lundy, the famed Quaker abolitionist, Adams confessed that he had used such a strategy in relation to his 1836 speech: "The ice is broken. . . . I have taken the occasion of another measure to throw out some reflections on [slavery]." He communicated the same information in another letter: "I was therefore compelled to make the Resolution for distributing rations to the fugitives from Indian revenge in Alabama and Georgia, the text for a commentary on Mexico, Texas, Indian Wars and Treaties, and Slavery."[63]

There is no doubt that John Quincy Adams held moral convictions regarding slavery, but personal vindication and politics also played an important part of his mission. He blamed his 1828 presidential election defeat on a lack of southern support and ultimately came to believe that southern proponents of the peculiar institution represented an especially dire threat to the Union. Yet there remained one slaveholder whom the congressman especially despised, and this too stemmed from the 1828 contest. Adams held a malicious contempt for Andrew Jackson, both personally and politically. To be sure, Jackson had no love for Adams either, remarking in an 1842 letter, "Is Mr. Adams demented, or is he perversely wicked. Both I think and Adams ought to be confined to a hospital."[64]

It was Adams's dual hatred of southerners and Jackson that explains inconsistencies regarding martial law. His animosity also clarifies other glaring contradictions concerning his views of both Jackson and war powers. In 1818–19, Adams, then secretary of state, had been the sole cabinet-level defender of Jackson's foray into Florida to chastise both the Spanish and Creeks for Indian depredations across the Georgia border. At the time, he argued that Jackson acted out of national self-defense and his conduct was sanctioned under the law of nature. Was this not one of the exact arguments put forth by Democrats to defend Jackson's use of martial law? Much time had passed, as well as motives, since Adams championed Old Hickory. On that early occasion, a defense of Jackson jibed perfectly with American-Spanish negotiations over the western boundary of the Louisiana Territory.[65] At the time Adams had confided to his diary that "General Jackson has rendered such services to this Nation that it is impossible for me to contemplate his character or conduct without veneration." Moreover, even when both men vied for the presidency in 1824, Secretary of State Adams held an extravagant ball in Jackson's honor on the ninth anniversary of the Battle of New Orleans.[66] Twenty years later, the two were devoted enemies, and thus Adams's earlier notions about the law of nature were as dead as any previous mark of respect between the two men. Yet there is no denying that Adams's previous arguments about self-defense actually fit New Orleans better than Florida. This fact certainly was not lost on a number of Democratic congressmen. William O. Butler, for example, noted that Adams "cannot consistently oppose it [martial law] on the usual grounds—the unwarrantable assumption of power—is manifest from the fact, that he has himself most triumphantly vindicated the same General from a similar exercise of power, on the ground of necessity, and in a much more questionable case. We are, therefore, to seek elsewhere for that gentleman's opposition, nor is it difficult to find."[67] Butler concluded it was the 1828 presidential defeat.

John Quincy Adams's constitutional arguments against martial law could easily be dismissed as personally motivated ranting, but other House Whig views are not so easily discounted. Hiram Hunt of New York insisted that no "military officer, even in time of war, [had] the right to proclaim martial law, and to suspend the civil proceedings of the tribunals of this country." As had previous speakers, Hunt acknowledged that the writ of habeas corpus could be suspended, but "it was the Legislature of the country that was the judge, and the only judge, of that necessity."[68] John Minor Botts of Virginia concurred, and in making a number of harsh determinations on Jackson's conduct broke with many southern Whigs who viewed with a degree of understanding the general's actions. Botts "denied that General Jackson had the power to declare martial law, and to substitute his own absolute will for the laws of the country." He did not have the right, insisted the congressman, "to constitute himself the supreme judge, both in his own camp, and over the civil tribunals of the land." Botts concluded that Jackson's conduct was "the most despotic, cruel, and tyrannical that had ever been perpetrated in any country."[69] In keeping with these constitutional objections, the northern Whig–dominated House Committee on the Judiciary for the Twenty-seventh Congress decreed that "it would be an anomaly to our system of government, disgraceful to us, and utterly subversive to our boasted freedom, if construction should obtain which would wrest from the representatives of the people one of their peculiar powers and confer it on a military commander, who, at his own uncontrolled discretion, upon any necessity of which he should be the sole judge, might reverse the fundamental maxim of our institutions, and set up the military above the civil power. . . . And if neither the Constitution nor the laws can protect the citizen against the exercise of such extraordinary, undefined, and undefinable powers, then is our frame of government a solemn mockery, then are our bills and declarations of rights idle and unmeaning forms, and the boasted liberty of an American citizen but an empty sound."[70] Here was the mainstream northern Whig view in a nutshell. Martial law was unconstitutional, was not justified by necessity, and violated the sacred republican axiom that the military shall remain subordinate to the civil authority.

With the start of a new congressional session dominated by Democrats, some House Whigs continued to decry a violated Constitution. Perhaps the most outspoken was Daniel Dewey Barnard of New York, the former chair of the previous House Judiciary Committee. He offered the rather standard Whig view that the writ of habeas corpus could be suspended only in times of emergency but also provided additional insights regarding martial law. "Congress cannot suspend the constitution itself," he declared, "a proclamation of such martial law by Congress or the executive would in itself be a dissolution of the government. It would be a revolution. And yet what Congress and the executive could not do, a general in the field may do!" Barnard continued, insisting that "a direct and arbitrary suppression of the civil power . . . admits of no justification, and no conceivable necessity ever can exist for it. No threat or prospect of invasion, however imminent—no suspicion of disaffection, however violent, can make such a necessity." Ultimately, he concluded that an American commander must defend the nation only with the means provided for by the Constitution: "And if, with such forces as the constitution and laws afford him, he cannot make good his defence, the constitution expects him to yield."[71]

Barnard took his adherence to the Constitution a step further than other Whig congressman by acknowledging that cities would be lost in times of war. Yet at the same time, he advocated some striking notions about when extraordinary military power may be used and when commanders may be forgiven when transgressing the laws. "I can imagine cases," explained the congressman, where a territory might already have been lost to the enemy and in attempting to take it back an American commander might "govern by the law of arms and the military power, awaiting the return of security and tranquility." Barnard's reasoning allowed a foreign power to invade a city and destroy the civil government, but the army responsible for the defense of that city could override the civil government only after it was already put under foot by the enemy. To many in Congress, this logic no doubt seemed rather bizarre. Moreover, Barnard acknowledged that there were times of war when military commanders might violate individual rights, "but these are individual cases, and, whatever may be the apparent or real necessity, they are all cases of trespass for which the law holds the commanders personally responsible. The government will relieve them, as it has often done, if it believes them to have been actuated by an honest sense of duty. . . . But in all this there is no analogy to the wholesale dealings of General Jackson, under his martial law." From a first reading one might conclude that Barnard engaged in wholesale contradiction. Some Democrats had argued that Jackson acted on the grounds of necessity, and Lewis Linn had certainly discussed previous cases in which officers had been indemnified by Congress. Yet Barnard's view was more a matter of arguing along fine lines. He did not oppose violations resulting from necessity; rather, he opposed Jackson justifying violations under the guise of martial law and especially fought Congress' acknowledgment of such martial law.

Barnard's refusal to accept martial law's legality is well taken and, in fact, was expressed by many other speakers, both Whig and Democrat. Yet his distinctions regarding necessity are unfulfilling. Barnard failed to make any distinction between the violation of individual rights and Jackson's "wholesale dealings." One might argue that the difference was seizing the writ of habeas corpus and imprisoning a federal judge, but Barnard did not make this distinction. Thus one wonders if Jackson's actions in New Orleans were not actually called "martial law," would Barnard have accepted them merely as violations for which the commander was legally responsible? Probably not, but the reason most likely stemmed more from the congressman's partisan antipathy toward Jackson than any ideological conviction. Barnard ultimately concluded his speech with a statement that betrayed much of his underlying animosity: "This fine now stands as the only just rebuke remaining of record on any of the numerous acts of lawless disregard of constitution and laws which have so much distinguished and illustrated his whole career."[72] Congressman Barnard's speech electrified the House, and Democrats quickly focused on it as the address to attack.[73]

With only a few days left before the planned January 8, 1844, refund vote, several more Whigs made passing comments concerning martial law. Like previous remarks these views varied greatly, with southerners such as Alexander Stephens of Georgia showing respect for Jackson but disapproving suspension of the writ of habeas corpus, and David Dickinson of Tennessee justifying martial law. Northern Whigs such as Luther Severence of Maine and Robert Cumming Schenck of Ohio denounced martial law as utterly illegal.[74] Schenck delivered the final House speech on the refund bill and made sure to go out with a bang by matching the harangue put forth by Democrats such as Lewis Steenrod and Stephen Douglas. "There were some things that struck me as I listened to them," he noted, "some novel, and I must be permitted to say, dangerous doctrines and propositions, in the speeches of the gentlemen who have spoken on the other side of the hall." The congressman then focused specifically on Douglas. "The gentleman from Illinois," announced Schenck, "has been a judge I am told. He is, however, in some things, a strange expounder of the law. 'Talk about illegality!' says he. 'Talk about formalities!' Why, he expresses the most sovereign and scornful contempt for all such restraints upon the free action of his favorite general. . . . He cared not he said—and I quote the very language in which he has been reported—'he cared not whether General Jackson violated the constitution or not. He cared not whether General Jackson suspended all civil authority or not.' And then he proceeds to justify all his violence on the ground of necessity— that universal plea for tyrants." Schenck concluded, "Give currency to the doctrines which that gentleman has preached here, and your have only to say that when a commander of an army gets a commission in his pocket, every authority, and all law in the land, but his unbridled will, are utterly at an end."[75] To Robert Cumming Schenck, Jackson was a despot and martial law an anomaly. The congressman's remarks did not fall on deaf ears. John Quincy Adams was amused with Schenck's speech, noting he "had got hold of Douglas, and was shaking him as a bull-dog shakes between his teeth a dead rat."[76]

The Dorr War Conundrum

Both Senate and House Whigs achieved wide latitude when it came to martial law. Southern Whigs tended to show a degree of respect for Andrew Jackson, whereas northern Whigs abhorred him. Very few northerners accepted the law of nature or necessity arguments, nor did they engage in a detailed analysis of either. They focused instead upon the Constitution. Yet in making their stand, some northern Whigs, especially John Quincy Adams and Daniel Barnard, contradicted their own arguments and in doing so revealed their partisan leanings. Nor were they alone. In fact, the entire Whig Party had a problem. For at the outset of the refund debates, in June 1842, the Whig-controlled government of Rhode Island had declared martial law in order to stop a revolt by Thomas Wilson Dorr.

The infamous Dorr War resulted from Rhode Island's restrictive suffrage policies outlined in its colonial charter. Following the Revolution, the tiny ocean state never created a Constitution, opting instead to continue operating under the charter issued by Charles II. Dorr and his followers held a state convention unsanctioned by the sitting legislature, drafted and ratified a Constitution, and attempted to take control of the state government. To end this challenge, the Whig charter government, as it was called, declared martial law and began arresting Dorr and his followers.[77] Rhode Island's actions should have added a dose of military reality to what were otherwise decidedly theoretical debates about civil/military relations. What made the state's imposition of martial law that much more interesting was that the legislature, not a military commander, enacted the measure.

Yet the subject of martial law in Rhode Island did not captivate the legislators engaged in the refund debates. Indeed, the first mention of the state's action came as a quip when Congressman Joseph Underwood of Kentucky announced in January 1843 that voting against the refund bill would be "setting an example to all military men that no such thing as martial law was even to be proclaimed in this country." From the chamber echoed a voice, "Except in Rhode Island."[78] This was the only comment on the affair in the entire Twenty-seventh Congress. Rather than confronting martial law in Rhode Island, the vast majority of Whigs and Democrats focused instead on the legality of Dorr calling a convention and ratifying a new Constitution without the permission of the existing state government. The Whig and Democratic silence is conspicuous and confounding.

Silence, however, did not last forever. Martial law in Rhode Island came up during the next congressional session. Surprisingly, Democrats did not pounce on Whig actions within the state even though doing so would have supported their case for General Jackson and showed northern Whigs that members of their own party utilized martial law. More amazingly, some Democrats denounced the Whig government's use of martial law in the Dorr case. Congressman Andrew Kennedy, a staunch defender of Jackson's conduct in New Orleans, went so far as to declare during the refund debates that the general "would have been justifiable in hanging [Judge Hall]." Yet when it came to Rhode Island, Kennedy supported Dorr's attempt to alter the state government and thus martial law became something horrible: "Martial law was declared and enforced by the chartists upon the entire people of the State, for a considerable length of time. Now, sir, to this fact I call the attention of the entire people of the confederacy. Let it be made known that the military was made superior, and the whole civil code of a State in the Union was trampled upon, annulled, and abrogated; the people of an entire State put under the heel of a few pampered despots." Kennedy had suddenly become the defender of republicanism. Yet he certainly did not forget his defense of martial law two months earlier. After making his remarks about the chartists raising the military above the civil authority, he actually pointed a finger of blame at Whigs by charging them with hypocrisy: "This thing has been done at least under the countenance of the very men who raised a piteous howl of violated law and outraged liberty, when General Jackson declared martial law at New Orleans to save that city from the sack of a rude, infuriated, and licentious soldiery! God save the liberty of the country over which such men bear rule!"[79]

Kennedy was not the only Democrat to dive headlong into paradox. Congressman John McClernand of Illinois had also championed Jackson's use of martial law, insisting that "he had declared martial law from the *necessity* of the case; martial law was the paramount law for the time. The civil authority . . . of course yielded." McClernand even thought that martial law should have been used extensively, remarking that Jackson's "was a glorious defence of the country's liberties" and "if martial law had been declared [in Washington], perhaps the Capitol would not have been destroyed."[80] McClernand's Rhode Island speech advocated a decidedly different view. "It is a well-known fact," he announced, "that the law of arms, inexorably enforced, was the supreme law of the State. The military was placed above the civil authorities; and under the triumph of this grim and terrible despotism, the blood of unoffending McKelby was shed, the citizens . . . captured, shackled, and exhibited through the public streets, and some of them thrown into prison, there to remain for months. Martial law—which is the substitution of force for civil authority; which is, in fact, the abrogation of all law—reigned supreme; and these were the practical illustrations of the beautiful theories of the 'law and order party' of Rhode Island. God save the mark!"[81] McClernand, of course, did not bother to address his speech in support of Jackson, given just two months earlier.

The last Democrat to engage in a discussion of Rhode Island had not participated in the refund debates and therefore could not contradict himself. Nor did Congressman George Rathbun of New York contradict Democratic support for martial law. He did, however, point out Whig hypocrisy on the subject. "Gentleman of the other side seem to have fallen suddenly in love with martial law," announced the New Yorker. "We hear of no arbitrary and despotic power now—no tyrants— no trampling upon the constitution and laws—no complaint of searches and seizures—no apostrophes to departed liberty—no bemoaning of arrests and imprisonments; but when Gen. Jackson proclaimed martial law to save New Orleans . . . the vault of heaven rang with denunciations and invectives. He was then denounced as a tyrant and a despot; there was no justification—there could be none; the laws and constitution were trampled upon by the iron heel of military power." Rathbun concluded his remarks on martial law by mocking Whigs, noting that "now their voices are hushed; not a whisper has been heard in defense of the laws, or in condemnation of military despots and tyrants; no tears are now shed over the grave of departed liberty."[82]

Whigs wisely avoided discussion of martial law in Rhode Island. Only one member of the party, Caleb Smith of Indiana, made any reference to the state's actions, and even then he did not use the term "martial law," explaining instead that "all the horrors of Civil War had only been averted by the firm, but temperate, action of the State authorities."[83] Additionally, none of the Rhode Island senators or representatives, all of whom were Whigs, appears to have engaged in a discussion of martial law regarding New Orleans or their own state. The only way to determine their views is through voting on the refund bill. The two senators split on the issue. James Simmons voted against the refund, whereas John Francis supported it. The same is true of the two representatives. Elisha Potter voted in favor of the refund bill, but Henry Cranston did not.[84]

Legislators in Congress may have remained fairly silent on the subject of martial law in Rhode Island, but the state's newspapers did not. The *Pawtucket Gazette and Chronicle* raised many of the issues that the nation's representatives wrestled with concerning Jackson's use of martial law:

> Martial law yet reigns throughout the State, and the general inquiry is, When is it to cease, and why has the State been kept under it so long? Was this law ever before enforced in a State in a time of peace? Is it a *republican* form of government? What acts under it by the government which enforces it are justifiable, and what unjustifiable? Is there any restraint placed upon such government? Is martial law any law at all, but does it not, on the contrary, create a state of affairs in which *power* may do what it pleases with impunity? Is it not a law which ought never to be imposed upon people except in cases of great necessity, and ought it not to be removed the moment such necessity ceases to exist? What, under its operation, becomes of those great safeguards of human rights and liberty, which have been cherished for ages? What becomes of the writ of *habeas corpus?*[85]

Rhode Island's Dorr War and the ensuing imposition of martial law add an extra twist to the refund debates over Andrew Jackson's fine. The ultimate conclusion seems to be that martial law was only beautiful, or at least justified, when in the eyes of the beholder. When the great champion of the Democratic Party utilized martial law it was in noble defense of the nation and justified by overwhelming necessity.

When Whigs in Rhode Island declared martial law, it suddenly became despotic and destroyed the sacred republican balance between civil and military power. The same paradox was true of Whigs, especially northern Whigs.

The Refund Debates outside of Congress

In the midst of these convoluted partisan dealings over Andrew Jackson and martial law, many in the nation kept a close watch on the happenings in Congress. Newspapers across the nation ran articles from the Washington-based Democratic *Globe* and Whig-backed *National Intelligencer*.[86] President Tyler also entered the fray by advising in his State of the Union Address to refund the fine. In doing so, he advocated the Democratic view of martial law in which an officer was responsible for violating the Constitution but should be indemnified if his motives were worthy.[87] Certainly not everyone in the public agreed with the president's views or those expressed by the nation's legislators, and without a doubt one of the most outspoken declamations came from a southerner who wrote under the pseudonym "A Kentuckian." In a series of articles published in the *Louisville Journal* titled *Martial Law, by a Kentuckian*, the author, soon to be known as Samuel Smith Nicholas, a former judge, vented his disgust over not only Jackson's conduct but also Whigs and Democrats in Congress.[88] "The first men in the nation are boldly advocating the doctrine of martial law," decried Nicholas, "and nearly half of the Senate [are] shamelessly approving an outrageous instance of its exercise." "The doctrine is now, for the first time in this country," he continued, "promulgated by eminent men in civil stations, that martial law is some[thing] other and different as to right from mob law; that it is not a mere unlawful violence which it is the right and duty of every citizen to resist; but it is a law paramount to the Constitution itself. . . . This doctrine is sheer madness. . . . [And] in after times, other Generals and Senators will quote these opinions."[89]

Nicholas insisted that the nation's leading legislators had forgotten the Revolution's legacy and thus abandoned America's republican ideals concerning the protection of liberty. The Kentuckian set out to reeducate these wayward politicians. "Listen ye degenerate sons," he admonished, "to the warning voices and commands of your fathers, whilst I evoke the very embodiment of all their patriotic virtues and intelligence." After quoting from some thirteen state constitutions in which the founding fathers outlined the civil power's supremacy, he declared that "the concurring import, of all this language, of all these men of the Revolution, is, that, *at no time, for no purpose, under no pretext, shall military supremacy ever have a foothold in this land.*" Still, notwithstanding the force of his own argument, Nicholas was ultimately discouraged, lamenting that "those men of the Revolution . . . are gone, all gone, leaving nothing of their spirit behind—none worthy to be called posterity."[90] In his view, America had abandoned republicanism.

Nicholas, however, had much in common with other speakers as it pertained to motives. John Quincy Adams had espoused a doctrine perhaps even more dangerous than a general use of martial law—that under its power slaves could be emancipated. Thus the Kentuckian spent approximately a third of his treatise denouncing Adams's argument and took pains to ensure that neither a military commander nor especially the president possessed the power to usurp the Constitution by ending slavery. "Unable to find anything in the Constitution to authorize the Federal Government to interfere with the question of negro slavery," announced Nicholas, Mr. Adams "is driven to a power dehors the Constitution, and conjures up this undefined and undefinable power of martial law." Though Nicholas dismissed such a theory as an "absurdity," his concern was betrayed by the amount of space spent on the subject.[91] The Kentuckian's pamphlet was read and referred to widely in Congress, and Jackson, at home in Tennessee, certainly took note of the publication, insisting that it was promulgated by his arch enemy, Henry Clay.[92]

The Partisan Complexities of Martial Law

Andrew Jackson's quest for vindication via the refund bill raised difficult ideological problems that were debated in an atmosphere of intense partisanship. The constitutional and ideological ramifications, as some Whigs pointed out, were immense. The Constitution embodied specified powers in times of emergency. Democratic arguments justifying martial law opened a door to future declarations by military commanders and presidents as well. It ultimately did not matter that some members of the party disavowed the constitutionality of the act, or that others maintained that martial law was completely constitutional or parallel to the Constitution. The fact that they acknowledged and justified its imposition was enough to create a precedent. Moreover, in arguing their case Democrats did a calculated end-run around the Constitution and the much-vaunted republican ideal that the military shall remain subordinate to civil authority. Rather than adhere to this notion of American political thought, they opted for the more advantageous yet equally revered natural law tradition. Self-defense justified everything that Jackson did. And because this was the case, Dominick Hall was obviously wrong, even vindictive, in fining the general.

Whig views of martial law reached an equal level of complexity. Southern Whigs showed a respect for Jackson that was expected for a man who had done so much for the South. Most of these Whigs accepted his use of martial law but stopped short of condoning his treatment of Hall by attempting to make a logical, though ultimately convoluted, distinction between military rule and the acts performed while it was in force. Northern Whigs, on the other hand, blasted the general for tyranny and despotism. Yet some of the loudest cries of a battered and bruised American liberty came from men who spoke with conviction from one side of their mouth and contradiction from the other. Always at the bottom of these inconsistencies lay a deep and abiding hatred of Jackson.

Challenging even further the ideological motivations of Democrats and Whigs was the Rhode Island fiasco. How ironic, or perhaps understandable, that the little ocean state declared martial law in the midst of a major debate on that very subject. Yet both parties virtually ignored the obvious parallel, and when some legislators did address the matter they exploded their, and to a degree their parties', previous arguments. Ultimately, the debates on the ideological complexities of martial law reveal the length to which some politicians would go when battling over Andrew Jackson. The result was that partisanship had a profound impact on legislators' opinions regarding the meaning and justification of using emergency powers in the United States. And lest one forget, it was Jackson himself who forced the debate in the hopes of securing his legacy and creating a precedent for the future defense of the nation.

CHAPTER 5

Jackson versus the Judiciary:
The Dispute over Contempt of Court

I t seems that Andrew Jackson perpetually battled the judiciary. Most infamous was his alleged statement in the aftermath of the Supreme Court's *Worcester v. Georgia* decision: "Well: John Marshall has made his decision: *now let him enforce it.*" A classic Jacksonian-sounding statement, historians have debated whether the iron-willed general ever uttered such a remark. Nevertheless, Jackson's willingness to accost judges, even though he too served on the bench, is well known. In 1821, while serving as territorial governor of Florida, Jackson forcibly summoned territorial judge Eligius Fromentin and, in the words of Robert Remini, "administered a verbal tongue-lashing" for issuing a writ of habeas corpus ordering the release of Spanish colonel José Callava, with whom Jackson was involved in a dispute.[1] Whether justified or not, it seems clear that Jackson had few qualms about chastising judges who infringed on his authority by issuing writs of habeas corpus. And first, of course, was the arrest of Judge Dominick Augustus Hall.

The congressional refund debates naturally involved discussion of Jackson's and Hall's encounter. Immediately following Lewis Linn's introduction of the refund legislation, Whigs expressed concern over criticizing the judge's decision to fine the general and in doing so denigrating the judiciary. Democrats argued that the bill said nothing about Hall or his decision and therefore insisted that all amendments regarding such matters were unnecessary. Justice, argued Jackson's followers, was the real issue. Yet the architect behind the refund, Old Hickory himself, possessed his own notions of justice, and it included vindication and the establishment of a precedent for the future use of martial law. Both of these necessarily meant that Jackson was right and Hall was wrong. Thus many Democrats attacked the judge's conduct in 1815.

The Democratic strategy incorporated three distinct components. The first followed the time honored tradition of heralding Jackson's New Orleans victory and devotion to the nation. In light of his heroism, announced Democrats, the fine was excessive and vindictive. The second argument was that because martial law superceded civilian authority, Hall had no power to issue the writ of habeas corpus. Because the writ was invalid, Jackson could not possibly have obstructed the court's process and therefore he was not liable for contempt. This point was by far the most compelling and logical put forth by the general's defenders. The only problem was in acknowledging martial law as the paramount authority. Not all members of Congress, especially northern Whigs, accepted such a premise. Still, Democrats based their assertion regarding Jackson's right to refuse obedience to the writ of habeas corpus on the belief that the military was in complete control. The Democrats' third strategy focused on Hall's use of the court's contempt power, arguing that the judge acted illegally and unconstitutionally by sitting in his own case and refusing to allow Jackson a jury trial. With these three arguments put forth, Democrats concluded that Hall's conduct was a more atrocious case of power and usurpation of the laws than was martial law.

As they had done from the outset of the debates, Whigs championed the sanctity and power of the nation's judiciary. Even southern members of the party, though lauding Jackson as a heroic defender, expressed concern over his treatment of the judge. Whigs certainly disagreed with Democratic perceptions of the judiciary's authority to punish contempt, arguing that the right of summary punishment was instrumental in order for a court to preserve its dignity and ability to operate. In light of Jackson's seizure of the writ and obstruction of the court, Whigs insisted that he was guilty of contempt and Judge Hall had every right to fine him.

As a result of the competing party views concerning the judiciary's right to punish contempt summarily and without a jury trial, Democrats and Whigs engaged in a historical debate over the judicial precedent of the contempt power. Doing so naturally entailed an investigation into English common law and its influence on American jurisprudence. Such a discussion might seem logical considering the importance of the case and the potential ramifications on civil and military relations. The problem was that Congress had already engaged in such a conversation, sorted out the historical confusion, and passed a new statute in 1831 clarifying a judge's authority to punish contempt summarily. Thus in an attempt to champion Jackson's cause and paint Hall as the worst sort of tyrant, some Democrats argued as if no law existed which defined the judiciary's power to punish contempt of court. Others were particularly selective in how they viewed the conflict between Jackson and Hall in order to make it appear that the judge had no power to impose a summary punishment. These facts are especially surprising con sidering that Democratic senator James Buchanan, a key spokesman in the refund debates, was also the principle architect behind the 1831 legislation which defined the judiciary's contempt power. Yet in the midst of the refund debates, even Buchanan clouded his arguments with convoluted reasoning and an apparent ignorance of the clear wording in the very statute that he authored. As a result of Democratic refusal to acknowledge the contempt statute accurately, Whigs correctly pointed out the clarity of the 1831 law and charged that the general's defenders would argue anything in their zeal to support the aging party chieftain.

Finally, the attacks on Judge Hall were not new to the congressional refund debates. Immediately following the imposition of the fine, Andrew Jackson had castigated Hall in local Louisiana newspapers, calling him unpatriotic and claiming that he had fled the city in a panic. Moreover, the general's defense counsel had insisted that the case required a jury trial because Jackson was defending against a criminal prosecution.[2] Hall quickly dismissed such points. It appears likely that Democrats in the 1840s simply picked up Jackson's defense papers, which he happily forwarded via Francis Blair, and renewed the arguments made in 1815.

Nor was this the limit of Jackson and Blair's involvement. As they had in every other aspect of the Democratic offensive, the two made sure that congressional supporters understood the arguments that needed to be made. Jackson wrote to Blair in July 1842, noting heatedly, "I wish the whole world to see the injustice and cruelty of the imposition of this fine upon me, and what a w [sic] wicked judge in combination with a few traitors to their country, whilst it was invaded has done."[3] This comment was just the beginning when it came to shaping Democratic doctrine regarding Hall. Jackson's and Blair's influence cannot be made clearer than in the correspondence between Blair and Charles Jared Ingersoll, who was Jackson's champion in the House and the author of the most extensive written account of the contempt power. Prior to beginning his treatise, *Gen. Jackson's Fine*, Ingersoll wrote to Blair requesting papers to aid the argument.

After receiving a packet from the editor, Ingersoll penned a second note: "I recd. your letter from the Hermitage: but still desire if attainable further proof of Judge Hall's malevolence."[4] Blair quickly informed Jackson of the problem, noting, "Ingersol [sic] seems at a loss to understand Hall's malicious motives. I think I will make him comprehend them before he has finished his piece." Evidently, it did not take long for Blair to "make" Ingersoll understand the general's point of view. Two weeks later, Blair sent another letter to Jackson: "I send you a letter from Ingersol by which you will perceive that he at last understands the fraud of Judge Hall. . . . I am glad I have at last one of our public men to seize on this point and fix the attention of Congress and the country on an act of the Judge which strips his conduct of that patriotic pretention [sic], of love for laws, under which he attempted and your enemies now attempt to disguise wrong and oppression visited on you." Only days later Ingersoll noted in a follow up letter to Blair, "I have become so bent on what you call carrying the war into Africa that it will delay the publication ten or fourteen days."[5]

There is no question that Ingersoll's treatise was directed by Jackson and Blair. Not only do the letters prove this, but in a biography of Ingersoll, his grandson, William Meigs, recorded that "in the end of June, 1842, Mr. Polk called on him [Ingersoll] with papers on the subject sent by General Jackson to Mr. Kendall; and Mr. Ingersoll in July of the next year published an elaborate pamphlet upon the subject." Meigs continued, "I presume from these facts that this pamphlet is to be considered as presenting with authority General Jackson's side of the question." In 1844, Jackson stated that Ingersoll's work revealed "the true ground upon which I acted" but disingenuously claimed the work was "unsolicited."[6] As a result of such facts, there is really little

GEN. JACKSON'S FINE.

AN EXAMINATION

INTO

THE QUESTION OF MARTIAL LAW;

WITH

AN EXPLANATION

LAW OF CONTEMPT OF COURT:

SUGGESTED BY

REFLECTIONS ON THE INJUSTICE OF THE FINE IMPOSED ON GENERAL JACKSON BY JUDGE HALL IN 1815.

BY CHARLES J. INGERSOLL.

WASHINGTON:
PRINTED BY BLAIR AND RIVES.
1843.

Title page of Gen. Jackson's Fine, *by Charles J. Ingersoll, 1843.*

question about Jackson's political involvement or his skill in working the political system.

The History of the Contempt Power

The disagreement between Democrats and Whigs over the history of the contempt power necessitates a brief explanation of its use in both England and America. The right of courts to punish for contempt, argue legal scholars, reaches back to the earliest days of the English empire. Related directly to the royal governing power, the term "contempt" included any act in violation of a direct order of the king or his government. With the establishment of the courts of justice, judges, who represented the king, inherited the right to punish contempt and thus defiance of the courts was viewed as defiance of royal authority. As the judiciary evolved, the power to punish disobedience, obstruction, or disrespect became an inherent right of English courts, separate from any imperial authority.[7] American law was in large part borrowed from England and it was therefore natural that the contempt power became established in American courts. Section seventeen of the 1789 Federal Judiciary Act declared that all courts have the power "to punish by fine or imprisonment, at the discretion of said courts, all contempt of authority in any cause or hearing before the same."[8]

Though the courts unquestionably had some power regarding contempt of court the statute did not clearly define the proper mode of punishment. Could judges act summarily, or did those accused of contempt have the right to a jury trial? Some legal scholars during the early twentieth century asserted that, by implication, the 1789 statute included whatever the power of contempt was in English common law.[9] This view, however, did little to clarify the issue, for the common law itself was ambiguous. Though many judges and historians assume that summary punishment had always been an inherent right of the court, the noted English legal historian John Charles Fox revealed in 1909 that in England, as far back as the fourteenth century, guilt for contempt was in fact determined by a jury trial. Thus universal summary punishment was not an inherent right of the judiciary. Judges could impose immediate punishment only in specific instances: when the contemptuous act was done in the presence of the said court, when individuals confessed the guilt of their contemptuous act, and when the case involved officers of the court, sheriffs, attorneys, or jurors and

was executed in the discharge of their official duties.[10] Thus the power
to punish summarily existed in cases of "direct" contempt only, those
instances in which an act was intimately connected to the court either
because the offensive act was done in or near the judge's presence
or by an officer of the court. "Constructive" contempt, those acts
done outside the court, such as libelous publications, was subject to a
jury trial.

Fox explained further that the historical confusion over contempt
originated during the eighteenth century and stemmed from the opinion of Sir William Blackstone, who declared that the right of attachment,
to bring an individual before the court and punish him for a contemptuous act, "must necessarily be as ancient as the laws themselves."[11] A
luminary in the English judiciary, Blackstone was thereafter cited as
authority on the subject. Yet his judgment was not based on historical
precedent. Rather, it was derived from the unpublished opinion of his
friend and colleague Chief Justice Wilmot. In *King v. Almon*, Wilmot concluded that the court's right to punish all contempt summarily "stands
upon immemorial usage as supports the whole fabric of the common
law." The problem, just as with Blackstone, was that Wilmot possessed
no historical justification for such a position. John Charles Fox clarified, noting that "both justices, ignoring the early cases [in which contempt was punished by juries], base their statement of the origin of the
[summary] practice on immemorial usage. The early cases prove that
this ground is untenable."[12] Nevertheless, the opinions of Blackstone and
Wilmot stood as the authority from which subsequent justices claimed
their power to punish contempt summarily. The result was uncertainty
within the English judiciary.

Confusion over English common law inevitably meant confusion in
American law. The nation's first judiciary act, passed in 1789, failed to
outline definitively the procedure for punishing contempt. As a result,
at least two states, Pennsylvania in 1809 and New York in 1829, attempted
to remedy the deficiency by passing legislation governing the judiciary's
power.[13] The nation, however, remained without clear guidelines.

The Peck Trial and Clarifying the Contempt Power

The lack of clarity regarding contempt of court proceedings changed
for all federal courts following the impeachment trial of Missouri
federal district judge James H. Peck. Certainly the most well known

contempt case during the early nineteenth century, the Peck trial illustrated the misunderstanding surrounding the contempt power. At issue
was the limit of a judge's authority to punish libelous publications. Also
of special importance was the relationship between English common
law and American criminal law.[14] The trial stemmed from Peck's summary punishment of Luke E. Lawless. Shortly after an 1825 ruling on
a case involving Spanish land grants, Peck published an article explaining his decision against the claimants. Lawless, the attorney for the
claimants, issued his own article pointing out the errors in Peck's decision. For that, Lawless was subsequently cited for contempt, jailed for
twenty-four hours, and suspended from practice for eighteen months.[15]
He sought vindication through the House of Representatives by requesting Peck's impeachment. That body ultimately accepted Lawless's
plea and, following the Committee on the Judiciary's report, ruled that
Peck treated Lawless "arbitrarily, oppressively, and unjustly." The
House then selected a prosecution committee and forwarded the case
to the Senate, where the impeachment trial took place.[16]

Arguments during the nearly year-long trial revealed disagreement over the judiciary's right to punish a libelous contempt committed outside the actual court. Moreover, the trial illustrated the inade-
quacy of the 1789 federal statute. Though members of the prosecution
and defense teams attempted to determine the origin and limits of
the contempt power, the trial failed to arrive at a conclusion. James
Buchanan, chairman of the Senate prosecution committee, acknowledged that judges had the power to punish summarily for a direct contempt that obstructed immediate operations of the court. He argued,
however, that constructive contempt, done in connection to the court
but not necessarily infringing upon its operation, must be punished
according to proper judicial procedures. This included the use of both
grand juries and trials by jury.[17] Judge Peck was ultimately acquitted
on January 31, 1831, by the narrow margin of twenty-two to twenty-
one votes, leaving the Senate's view of the judiciary's contempt power
largely unsettled. Legislators were, however, aware of the problem,
and the next day, February 1, Congressman Joseph Draper, a Jacksonian Democrat from Virginia, offered a resolution requesting that the
Judiciary Committee define the law of contempt.[18] Under the chairman-
ship of Senator Buchanan, the committee acted quickly. On March 2,
1831, Congress passed a new statute defining the power of American
judges to punish contempt of court, in which they clarified any questions regarding the judiciary's right to punish contempt summarily:

> That the power of the several courts of the United States to issue
> attachments and inflict summary punishments for contempt of
> court, shall not be construed to extend to any cases except misbe-
> havior of any person or persons in the presence of the said courts,
> or so near thereto as to obstruct the administration of justice, the
> misbehavior of any of the officers of the said courts in their official
> transactions, and the disobedience or resistance by any officer of
> the said courts, party, juror, witness, or any other person or per-
> sons, to any lawful writ, process, order, rule, decree, or command
> of the said courts.[19]

The new law could not be clearer. Judges had the right to punish summarily any contempt that interfered with the actual operation of the
court, whether that interference occurred within the court's presence or
was done in direct relation to a legal writ or order coming from the court.

Contempt of Court and the Refund Debates

There is no question that the 1831 statute outlining the authority of
judges to punish contempt summarily settled the confusion over the
judiciary's power, which had stemmed from both English and American law. Nevertheless, Democrats, revealing the extent to which they
would go in fighting for Andrew Jackson, essentially ignored the 1831
law by insisting that Judge Hall had acted improperly by failing to provide the general with a jury trial and thereby voiding his right to such
a trial under the Constitution. This selective legislative amnesia on the
part of Democrats was not the only strategy in dealing with Hall's ruling, though it was by far the weakest Democratic argument. Jackson's
partisans also insisted that the general was not guilty of contempt
because martial law had canceled Hall's authority. This was unquestionably the more powerful of the Democratic approaches, though its
validity ultimately revolved around the legality of martial law.[20]

When Jackson had originally been called before Hall's court in New
Orleans, it was to answer

> why an attachment should not be awarded against him for contempt
> of this Court, in having disrespectfully wrested from the Clerk afore-
> said an original order of the Honorable the Judge of this Court, for
> the issuing of a writ of habeas corpus in the case of a certain Louis
> Louallier [sic], then imprisoned by the said Major General Andrew
> Jackson, and for detaining the same; also, for disregarding the said

writ of habeas corpus, when issued and served; in having imprisoned the Honorable the Judge of this Court; and for other contempt, as stated by the witnesses.[21]

The first to speak on these points was Senator Benjamin Tappan, who argued that the superior authority of martial law suspended Hall's judicial capacity and therefore the contempt fine "was wrongfully and illegally exacted." Tappan stated further that "the conduct of Judge Hall was more preeminently censurable. He attempted to aid and assist in introducing disorder, insubordination and mutiny into a camp where he had no power, and failing in this, as soon as his authority as a judge was restored, he revenges his own fancied wrongs upon the General." Tappan's initial reasoning seemed to be that the contempt charge did not rightfully apply to Jackson because it was in direct relation to Hall's lack of authority under martial law. The judge was simply not empowered to issue a writ of habeas corpus.

Yet as the senator continued, it became clear that he focused on another matter entirely, Jackson's arrest of Hall, and in doing so he deviated from what was surely the most solid Democratic argument and one that justifiably challenged the 1831 contempt statute. For if Tappan could conclusively prove that Judge Hall had no authority to issue a writ, and that one of the essential purposes of martial law was keeping the legislative and judicial branches of government from interfering with military rule, he may have gone a long way in dismantling Whig arguments that the judge had a right to act. If Jackson still believed, as he did, that another attack was possible and that many inhabitants of New Orleans, members of the state government included, were potentially untrustworthy, saving Louaillier from jail was a threat to the security of New Orleans. Overly paranoid or not, Jackson, as the commander responsible for the city, had to make such decisions.

Instead of focusing on such points, Tappan wrongly asserted that "the principal complaint against General Jackson was for the imprisonment of the judge" and then insisted that Hall should not have sat in his own case. "This was truly and wholly the cause of the judge himself," he concluded, "if a law of Congress had existed which authorized him to sit in judgment upon any man for an injury inflicted upon himself, such a law would have been a mere dead letter and the judge would have been bound to disregard it." Tappan continued by engaging in a dissertation on the history of the judiciary's contempt power in the United States, alluding to the famous Peck trial, the subsequent law passed by Congress, and then, somewhat strangely, concluding that "no learned jurist who is civil, polite, and decorous in the discharge of his official duties, ever has occasion to resort to rules for contempt."[22] What exactly this final statement had to do with the case at hand is unclear, but it seems that Tappan did not consider Hall to possess any of these admirable qualities. Why else would he have lowered himself to charging Jackson with contempt?

Tappan was joined in his attack on Hall and the contempt fine by Thomas Hart Benton, the imposing senator from Missouri. "The legality, the justice, the propriety of the fine is the question," demanded Benton. "No one can doubt that General Jackson in saving the city of New Orleans, and in doing what he did to save it, was actuated by no other feeling but that of patriotic devotion to his country, unalloyed by a particle of ill-will, revenge, or malice, to any human being. . . . There is special evidence of absence of all ill-will to Judge Hall on this occasion, in the noble manner in which Gen. Jackson interposed to protect the Judge from the exasperation of the surrounding crowd." After reminding senators of Jackson's steadfast patriotism, Benton castigated Judge Hall for summarily punishing Jackson: "No jury trial intervened. That great bulwark of the liberty, the life, the property of the citizen— the bulwark of jury trial—was not resorted to. General Jackson was not placed before a jury of his countrymen. He stood before a judge, irritated, acting in his own case, and acting alone. . . . The Judge was acting illegally and tyrannically."[23]

Following Benton came perhaps the most important Senate speaker on the contempt of court issue. Senator James Buchanan, formerly the chairman of the Peck trial prosecution team and the primary author of the 1831 contempt statute, possessed special knowledge of the judiciary's contempt power and was therefore eminently prepared to expound upon the limits of judicial authority. He quickly discounted any ideological grounds upon which Judge Hall fined Jackson. It had little to do with writs or civil versus military power, averred Buchanan. Rather, Hall's ruling stemmed from a bruised ego. "After martial law had ceased," insisted the senator, "Judge Hall, under the influence of excited and impassioned feelings, resulting from what he believed to be a personal injury, brought the General before him for contempt." After making this point decidedly clear, Buchanan engaged in an extensive discussion of why Jackson was not liable for contempt. Insisting that martial law was a necessity in saving New Orleans, Buchanan surmised, "If, then, the necessity of the case justified the declaration of martial law—and this must be admitted by all—what followed as a necessary consequence? Why, that the exercise of the civil authority should cease, at least so far as was necessary to the defence of the city. . . . The same necessity, therefore, which justified martial law, equally justified its execution, in despite of all obstacles which might be interposed by any civil magistrate. . . . The moment the declaration [of martial law] was made, the official functions of Judge Hall ceased with regard to his power of issuing writs of *habeas corpus,* which might interfere with the defence of the city." The senator also clarified that the "very arrest of the writ of *habeas corpus* is the ostensible and main allegation with regard to which the fine was inflicted by Judge Hall. The principle contempt of court was in this disregard of the writ of *habeas corpus.*"[24]

Buchanan's focus on the primary reason for the contempt charge and the fact that the judiciary had been relieved of its power due to the declaration of martial law was clear and forceful. It also represented the most lucid and logical Democratic counter to Whig assertions that Jackson had acted contemptuously. If martial law was the supreme authority and hence canceled all civilian functions, Judge Hall should never have interfered with the general by issuing a writ. Had Buchanan stopped here, though the opposing parties could have continued to wrangle over the legality of martial law, Whigs could not have refuted the senator's reasoned conclusion. Southern Whigs, who acquiesced in the need for martial law yet also supported the authority of the judiciary, would have been particularly hard pressed to answer such an argument.

But Buchanan was not finished. Immediately after insisting that the contempt fine was specifically for disregarding the writ of habeas corpus, he shifted to a discussion of the Peck trial and noted that Jackson's contempt was in "refusal to obey the writ of *habeas corpus,* and his expulsion of the Judge from camp." Though Buchanan was correct, both causes were listed in the indictment, there was no reason to go into this after already providing a logical argument on the nullity of the writ. Still, Buchanan cited the 1831 Peck trial and explained that Jackson's banishment of the judge did not fall within the guidelines of the federal statute: "It appears, from the declatory law which passed Congress unanimously, after the trial of Judge Peck, that this expulsion could, under no circumstances, be considered a contempt of court.

The only proceeding which could have been instituted against the General for this cause, was an indictment for assault and battery and false imprisonment, and a civil action for damages!"[25]

Focusing specifically on the issue of a direct contempt, Buchanan concluded that Jackson was not guilty because the order removing Hall from New Orleans had nothing to do with the court's actual process. The proximity of the contemptuous act and the ultimate range of the court's jurisdiction was the question, insisted the senator, as "the judge out of court was not the court. . . . He could only be regarded as a private citizen,—*Judge* Hall, if you please; but Judge Hall only by title, and not, at the moment, the embodied court of which he was on the bench, the representative."[26]

Senator Buchanan also addressed briefly the issue of summary punishment, arguing that under no circumstances should Judge Hall have assumed the role of prosecutor and adjudicator in his own case: "What a spectacle did this court present! There sat an angry judge to decide his own cause and to avenge real or supposed insults against him."[27]

Seeing Buchanan as an authority on judicial power, many Democrats lined up behind the Pennsylvania senator, concurring with his opinion.[28] Yet there remained a number of critical problems with Buchanan's reasoning. Though he was technically correct about a contempt needing to take place in proximity to the court, Buchanan was guilty of reading the 1831 federal statute selectively, focusing on the preliminary section which stated, "summary punishments for contempt of court, shall not be construed to extend to any cases except misbehavior of any person or persons in the presence of the said courts, or so near thereto as to obstruct the administration of justice."[29] Additionally, Buchanan's reasoning separated the judge's arrest and banishment from the seizure of the writ, when in fact they were intimately connected. Hall was incarcerated and removed from the city so that he could not interfere again by potentially issuing another judicial decree. The issuing of the writ, as Buchanan had correctly pointed out in his initial argument, was critical because Jackson's seizure of the writ was one of the reasons he was held in contempt. It seems that he later ignored this point by artificially separating the Judge's arrest from the actual issuance of the writ.

Buchanan's separation of Hall's arrest and his creation of the writ led to another major flaw in the senator's position. In arguing that Hall had no right to sit in his own case and exact summary punishment,

Buchanan ignored the second half of the 1831 contempt law, which clearly allowed judges to impose immediate penalties for "disobedience or resistance by any officer of the said courts, party, juror, witness, or any other person or persons, *to any lawful writ,* process, order, rule, decree, or command of the said courts."[30] Not only did Hall have a right to hold Jackson in contempt for seizing the writ, but because the writ issue was tied directly to Hall's arrest and banishment, Jackson had actually "obstructed" the court's process and was liable under both sections of the 1831 statute. Buchanan, the Democratic authority in the Senate, was dead wrong and guilty of butchering his own legislation— all this for Andrew Jackson. Buchanan would have been much better off sticking to his very logical argument that martial law canceled the judge's authority to issue writs of habeas corpus. At least this argument, though Whigs could still debate the legality of martial law, was clean and decisive.

Democrats in the House of Representatives followed similar lines of argument to those presented in the Senate. The key spokesman in the lower chamber was Charles Jared Ingersoll, Blair's and Jackson's puppet. After being tutored by Blair, Ingersoll engaged in a lengthy diatribe on the contempt power. Speaking before his colleagues, Ingersoll bellowed, "What right had any judge in this country to take a man by his mandate, and, dispensing with the trial by jury, to put him to torture to compel him to answer, (for that was torture;) and if he did not, to inflict on him a fine *ad libilum*?" "If he could do that," continued Ingersoll, "he might imprison him as well as fine; and, sir, why not torture him? Why not torture him to death? Why not question him upon the rack?" After engaging in this bit of sensationalism, Ingersoll cited the Peck trial and the resulting federal statute outlining a judge's power in cases of contempt: "Every gentleman knew that, in 1831, an act of Congress was passed limiting the powers of the courts in cases of contempts, and restricting the exercise of their authority in such cases to their own officers, attorneys, and witnesses, or to direct obstruction of their administration."[31] Like Senator Buchanan, Ingersoll engaged in a selective reading of the federal statute. He made no mention of the section authorizing summary punishments. Nor did he even identify what he considered to be the principle reason for the contempt charge.

Congressman Ingersoll's House speech was short in comparison to many others made by his colleagues. Perhaps he saved his time and energies for the expansive treatise published by Francis Blair. In this

printed forum, Ingersoll had the opportunity to elaborate on the impending necessity and meaning of martial law as well as the history
and ultimate authority of the judiciary's contempt power. Still, he continued to ignore portions of the 1831 law and never identified why
exactly Hall cited Jackson for contempt. Instead, he engaged in a
learned though biased discourse on contempt of court. As had many
members of both parties, he maintained that contempt proceedings
were essentially judicial self-defense. Judges cited disruptive individuals out of necessity in order to protect and continue the court's operations. Yet the extent of a judge's power to engage in such a defense was
limited, argued Ingersoll. Judges could go only so far as removing
direct obstructions to the court's process, such as a disturbance within
the courtroom. Moreover, the right of self-defense existed only as long
as the threat to the court continued. Furthermore, Ingersoll again contradicted the 1831 federal contempt statute by arguing that judicial
self-defense in no way included summary punishment, an act antithetical to both the American Constitution and the nation's concept of liberty. One could be removed from the courtroom and cited for contempt,
but only a jury could determine guilt. "The plain letter of the Constitution is eluded by contending that summary and exceptional punishment of contempt, without jury trial or common proof, is conformable
to the law of the land," insisted Ingersoll.[32] Numerous Democrats
emphasized the same point, arguing that summary punishment was
illegal and the proper course was a jury trial as guaranteed by the
Constitution.[33]

In order to prove his point that summary punishment was illegal,
Ingersoll delved into a detailed history of the judiciary's authority in
cases of contempt. The mistaken notion that summary punishment belonged to judges, argued the congressman, stemmed from British chief
justice Wilmot's opinion in *King v. Almon*. Rather than a valid law or
precedent, insisted Ingersoll, Wilmot's decision and the subsequent
doctrine derived from it "is an unreasonable and unfounded innova-
tion." Summary punishment, therefore, was not based on wholesale
"immemorial usage." Wilmot's ruling, declared Ingersoll, not only set
a false precedent and confused the common law but also influenced
American judges, such as Dominick Hall, who wrongly inflicted summary punishment.[34]

Ingersoll also went to the extent of reviewing both the 1789 Judiciary Act and the 1831 contempt statute, concluding that the former
failed to define what constituted contempt, whereas the latter declared

what a contempt shall not be. The first act, he insisted, was "not a grant, but a limitation" and should "be interpreted as a shield for courts, not a sword for judges." The second act did not create a new definition; rather, it merely outlined more clearly the limits of the 1789 statute. Thus, declared Ingersoll, "no such summary power is to be found in either of the acts of Congress. The notion of power by an act of Congress for courts to proceed summarily to the punishment of contempts, is a radical mistake."[35] Ingersoll's conclusion is astounding. His arguments against summary punishment appear to be either a blatant misreading of the 1831 statute or a deliberate attempt to twist the law in favor of Andrew Jackson.

One other tactical point to which Ingersoll directed attention, in both his House speech and the published treatise, was the similarity between martial law and the courts' contempt power. Both, he insisted, were utilized for the purposes of self-defense, and as such "the law of contempt, as judicially recognized throughout the United States, is martial law in courts of justice."[36] Going a step further, Ingersoll determined that judicial power was actually a more dire threat to liberty, arguing that "if they did not refund this money, the Congress of the United States would sanction a judicial usurpation infinitely more dangerous than martial law in all its odious circumstances." A free citizen, he added, "ought never to hold his liberty, even for an hour, or the slightest portion of his property, at the will of any magistrate."[37] The assertion, that a judge with a decidedly limited purview could equal the power of a military commander at the head of an army, bordered on absurd. It was certainly a lame attempt to answer the Whig charge of one-man power and revealed the extent to which Ingersoll could divorce himself from logic in order to defend Andrew Jackson. Nor was the congressman alone. Other Democrats followed the same line of attack. Representative Ezra Dean of Ohio roared, "Let me tell those gentleman who pretend to have so much regard for the Constitution, and such horror of a military chieftain, that there is less danger to be apprehended to our rights from an army of citizen soldiers, led on by a gallant and chivalrous commander, boldly avowing his intentions, than there is from a malicious and vicious judge, who, in the plenitude of his power, under the solemn garb of justice, strikes his victim with an unseen arm, that admits not resistance, because he is shielded by the forms of law."[38]

Weighing the actions of a military commander who, in "boldly avowing his intentions," subverted all civilian authority and suspended civil liberties, versus a judge who exercised his federally sanctioned, though admittedly powerful authority, was both superficial and a little silly. Federal judges could not possibly create the same type of potential tyranny with the contempt power that generals could under martial law.

Notwithstanding this fact, Democrats continued to rail away, comparing martial law and the judiciary's authority to punish contempt, in an attempt to show that two men utilized excessive power in New Orleans. Congressman Stephen Douglas of Illinois noted, "I admit that the declaration of martial law is the exercise of a summary, arbitrary, and despotic power, like that of a judge punishing for contempt, without evidence, or trial, or jury, and without any other law than his own will, or any limit to the punishment but his own discretion. The power in the two cases is analogous; it rests upon the same principle, and is derivable from the same source—extreme necessity." Douglas also discussed the issue of when a judge could cite an individual for contempt, concluding, "The doctrine of contempts applies only to those acts which obstruct the proceedings of the court. . . . Judge Hall had no right to punish him by the summary process of the doctrine of contempts, without indictment, or jury, or evidence, or the forms of trial."[39]

The issue of summary punishment was rather common fare for those Democrats who engaged in the debate over the judiciary's authority. Yet Douglas also focused upon a tactic that few members of his party investigated.[40] Arguing a point that General Jackson had made when actually seizing the writ of habeas corpus, Douglas noted two items that made the writ void and thus the contempt charge invalid. First, he argued that the writ was actually served several hours after it was due to be returned to Judge Hall and therefore "had spent its force; had expired; was *functus officio* before it reached Gen. Jackson. There was no command of the court remaining that could be obeyed; the time had elapsed."[41] Douglas's assertion that the writ was not served in time to meet the court's decree was correct and as such might have been a good technical, lawyerly point for Democrats to follow.[42] The second argument concerning the writ involved Hall's changing of the date from March 5 to March 6. He had apparently mistaken the date and then changed it. Jackson considered the alteration "juggling" and believed that it revealed a conspiracy on the part of Hall and Louaillier. In his mind, Hall actually issued the writ prior to the formal request in order to prepare for a movement against military authority. There is no proof to support this allegation. Nevertheless, Douglas concluded, "These alterations of themselves rendered the papers void, even if they had been originally valid."[43]

If Democrats had maintained these types of technical points, or even better, stuck to the argument that the paramount authority of martial law canceled all civilian authority and thus Judge Hall was not within his rights to issue a writ of habeas corpus, they would have had a much more concise, logical plan of attack. Instead, they marched headlong into a legal morass that was simply untenable. The argument that summary punishment was illegal was worse than weak; it was wrong. General Jackson's defenders debated the subject as though the Peck trial and subsequent contempt statute had never occurred. Democrats were simply incorrect in their appraisal of a judge's right to punish summarily. This is particularly surprising considering James Buchanan's role as the lead prosecutor in the Peck trial and the primary author of the 1831 law.

In Defense of the Judiciary: The Whigs

In response to the various Democratic arguments about the contempt of court charge Whigs tackled not only the issue of their opponents misreading of the federal contempt statute but also the question of why Jackson was cited for contempt. Whigs also championed the sanctity of the judiciary and expressed outrage at the very idea that a judge could be imprisoned for issuing a writ of habeas corpus.

As chairman of the Senate Judiciary Committee, John Berrien responded to a variety of Democrats' statements about the source of the contempt charge, remarking that "how little the Senate is informed of the subject, is obvious from the fact that it is disputed here whether the fine was inflicted for the disobedience of the writ of *habeas corpus*, or for the indignity offer to the court by the arrest of its judge."[44] In making this point, Berrien was joined by Charles Conrad. "Every gentleman who had spoken had supposed, and based his argument on, a different state of facts," announced Conrad. "They did not even agree on the *cause* for which the fine was imposed. One says it was inflicted on General Jackson because *he declared martial law;* another, because he refused to obey the writ of *habeas corpus;* another, because he offered a personal indignity to the Judge; and all concur in censuring the Judge, and in supposing he was actuated by personal resentment alone." In order to correct these varied misconceptions of why Hall indicted and fined Jackson, Conrad listed why, in his view, the general had been held in contempt: "1st. By imprisoning the Judge, and thereby preventing him from discharging his official duties. 2d. By violently taking possession of a record of the court. 3d. By threatening the officers of the court. For this contempt of court, and for nothing else, was this fine imposed." Conrad thus surmised "it was the providence of the court to vindicate its own dignity, by punishing an open and avowed resistance to its authority, accompanied with the most wanton and unnecessary violence and insult to the person of the Judge."[45] Though the senator's list placed Hall's arrest at the top of the causes for the fine, it was properly connected to the judge's ability to discharge his duties, which included issuing the writ of habeas corpus.

Senator Jacob Miller followed exactly the same reasoning and style of presentation, insisting that the fine "was for a contempt of court, in resisting the authority of the writ of *habeas corpus*." Miller then focused specifically on the connection between the writ and Hall's arrest by providing his own list: "1. That the only act committed by Judge Hall, previous to his arrest, was the granting an order for a writ of habeas corpus, upon the sworn petition of a citizen, alleging that he was illegally imprisoned. 2. That for this act, and this alone, Gen. Jackson ordered the person of the Judge to be seized and imprisoned. 3. That the object of this arrest was to defeat the writ of habeas corpus." There was no question, argued Miller, that the writ's seizure and the incarceration of the judge were acts of contempt. Indeed, he continued, "this is, in fact, something more than a contempt. For a contempt is seldom so outrageous as to deprive the tribunal of its existence; but here the blow was so fierce and fatal, that the whole court, with all its functions and faculties, judicial, ministerial, executive, together with its record, process, and seal—all fell paralyzed in death beneath the arm of the hero of New Orleans."[46]

Miller's juxtaposition of Jackson's patriotic title with his authoritarian treatment of the court was a clever jibe that was certainly not lost on the Democratic members of the Senate who constantly touted the general's victory. In closing on the subject of Hall's arrest and the resulting contempt charge, Miller expressed awe at the circumstances of the case: "The awarding of a writ of habeas corpus declared to be proof of a mutinous act; the performing a of constitutional duty converted into a crime; the great bulwark of human liberty struck down at a blow, and made the cause of oppression and imprisonment! Does the record of any court, civil or military, upon the face of the earth, present an examination of an arrest of a freeman, upon proof like this?"[47]

Senator Miller's disdain was easily matched by Whigs in the House. Daniel Barnard attested to the "entire propriety, impartiality, deliberation, and dignity of the whole course of proceedings on the part of the judge" and lamented, "I am sorry that it should have been deemed necessary by the friends of this bill to make an assault either on the character of Judge Hall or on the well-settled law of contempts. No sacrifice seems to be too great or too costly for them to offer before the shrine of idolatry." That Barnard viewed the Democratic defense of Jackson and the lofty theories on contempt of court as mere "idolatry" is hardly surprising. Anyone with a degree of knowledge on the subject of the judiciary's authority to punish contempt summarily could quickly ascertain the feeble nature of Democratic arguments. Indeed, anyone who read the 1831 statute could draw such a conclusion. Thus Barnard set out to explode his opponent's arguments. Setting his sights on Charles Ingersoll, Barnard referred to the congressman's lengthy treatise on the contempt power, remarking that the "able and learned gentleman from Pennsylvania . . . has written a book to prove, amongst other things, that courts of justice in general, and Judge Hall in particular, had no right to punish for contempts." Yet, continued Barnard, "every court must necessarily have the power to protect itself against violent interruptions or disturbance, and to enforce obedience to its lawful commands"[48] To prove his argument, Barnard focused upon the history of the judiciary's right to punish contempt. Citing the Peck trial, as well as the 1789 Judiciary Act and 1831 federal statute, he noted that

> in the case of the courts of the United States the power to punish
> for contempts has, as we all know, been confirmed by express stat-
> utes. It is found in the judiciary act of 1789, passed in the first year
> of the government. And, at a later period, in 1831, after an instance
> of abuse of the power in the case of Judge Peck, and for which he
> was subjected to impeachment and trial, a declatory act was passed
> defining the authority of courts to punish contempts. The authority
> exercised by Judge Hall in the case before us, though long before
> the act last referred to was strictly within the definition and limita-
> tions of that act.[49]

Barnard clearly interpreted the contempt statutes differently than Democrats, viewing them as grants rather than limitations of judicial authority. Every court had the right, he insisted, to punish contempt

summarily. "The truth is," argued the Congressman, "that in the case
of contempts there is properly no trial—there can be none." Explaining
that the American contempt acts were borrowed from English common law, Barnard maintained that the "power to punish contempts in
a summary way has never, that I know of, been doubted in England."[50]
Here Barnard was not on solid footing. Congressman Ingersoll had correctly outlined the confusion over the common law origins of summary
punishment when explaining the *King v. Almon* decision. Barnard did
not bother to delve into this history or to challenge Ingersoll on this
point. There was no need. Barnard simply focused on the tangible and
clear laws passed by Congress, first in 1789 and again in 1831. Still,
Barnard was not the only Whig to mistake the English origins of summary punishment for contempt of court. In its official report on the
refund bill, the House Judiciary Committee reviewed the right to punish summarily prior to the 1831 contempt act and concluded "the power
of the courts, before this statute, was such as the English courts possessed; for, when the judiciary act [of 1789] gave to them the power to
punish for contempts, without limitation, it was from the English law
on the subject that they were to look for the rules of construction and
mode of proceeding."[51]

Like Barnard, other Whigs were incorrect when it came to the common law origins of summary punishment. Lack of historical knowledge,
however, was moot. American law answered the question concisely.
Reading directly from the 1789 federal statute, the Judiciary Committee report declared it "sufficient, that in the seventeenth section of the
judiciary act passed in 1789, the courts of the United States are empowered to 'punish, by fine or imprisonment, at their discretion, all contempts of authority in any cause or hearing before them.'" Though some
might argue, as a number of Democrats did, that Jackson was not "before" the court, the 1831 statute clarified further the power of the courts.
The committee noted that "by this statute, certain constructive contempts
were abolished; but the courts retained the power 'to inflict summary
punishment' for disobedience of their process, such as a writ of habeas
corpus."[52] The Judiciary Committee ultimately concluded, "General
Jackson's refusal to obey the writ of habeas corpus, and his imprisonment of the judge, was a violation of the most sacred right of the citizen, of the express provision of the Constitution, and of the judicial independence, and, together with his seizure of an original court paper, was
a contempt of court for which he was justly and legally fined."[53]

Whigs were lucky in that they had a fairly simple case to make. They clarified the reason for which Jackson was indicted and fined; a record that was readily available. Whigs also illustrated the weakness of the Democratic argument concerning the judiciary's right to punish contempt of court summarily. This too was an easy argument to win. One need only read the 1789 Judiciary Act as well as the subsequent 1831 contempt statute.

Concluding the Contempt Power

The Democratic and Whig argument over contempt of court is a prime example of how partisanship could direct political discourse. Even in the face of federal legislation that told them otherwise, Democrats persisted in arguing against the right of summary punishment for contempt of court. It was a position that lacked any basis in consideration of American law on the subject. Democrats also attempted to divert criticism of Jackson by heralding his patriotism and devotion to the nation. Appealing to Jackson's nationalism was a tactic that had worked for years and always resonated with voters. Once setting this picture in the minds of the people, Democrats opined that the fine was excessive and vindictive. After all, Jackson was the Hero of New Orleans. The best Democratic argument to combat the contempt charge was by far the theory that once declared, martial law canceled all civilian authority. Under this view, Hall could not possibly have issued a writ of habeas corpus on behalf of Louis Louaillier. James Buchanan forcefully explained this idea but ultimately clouded his argument by adding a feeble discussion on summary punishment. The supremacy of martial law theory was certainly not foolproof. One had to accept that military rule did indeed supercede civilian authority, but a large portion of the debates focused upon this and it would have been far better for the Democrats to maintain this line of attack than to open themselves up to Whig abuse with a weak argument about summary punishment. Part of the issue for Democrats, however, was to make Judge Hall look as tyrannical as possible. If they simply ignored the judge's proceedings by insisting that martial law canceled his authority, the opportunity to lambaste Hall would be lost. And Jackson unquestionably wanted Hall lambasted. This was clear from his letters to Blair and other supporters, and was perhaps one of Jackson's worst character traits; he could hate with passion.

For their part, Whigs quickly grasped the Democratic tactics concerning the contempt issue. Heralding the sanctity of the judiciary and writ of habeas corpus as well as the legality of Hall's actions, Whigs insisted that Jackson was a tyrant who should not have laid hands on a judge. Even southern Whigs lamented the general's treatment of Hall. Ultimately, the Whig's easiest and most convincing arguments were in relation to contempt of court and summary punishment. If they found it difficult to combat the constant fawning over Jackson's glorious victory, it was remarkably simple to prove the Democrats' twisting of the nation's contempt statutes. The battle over contempt of court revealed just how far politicians were willing to go when arguing over Andrew Jackson.

CHAPTER 6

The Evolution of Martial Law

E stablishing a precedent for the future use of emergency powers in times of immanent danger was an important component of Andrew Jackson's quest for recouping his one-thousand-dollar fine plus interest. The general made this point repeatedly, and in doing so assured that Lewis Linn would argue it within the halls of Congress. Jackson's devotion to the Union and firm belief that dangerous times required extraordinary defenses, lest the nation perish, drove his commitment to establishing a precedent. He never seemed concerned that such measures might threaten the very liberties and Constitution he ultimately wanted to protect. And though the final bill which returned Jackson's money said nothing about the legality or even the meaning of martial law, the debates nevertheless established an important change in the definition of martial law. Jackson's precedent was achieved. The debates, along with the infamous Dorr War in Rhode Island, did indeed establish a new meaning for martial law, one that allowed the military to take control of the civilian sphere.

In arguing about the constitutionality, necessity, and justification of General Jackson's conduct, some Democrats and Whigs discussed martial law as though a uniform definition existed. Yet this was hardly the case. In reality, there were at least two definitions. One referred to martial law interchangeably with military law as a code of conduct for the armed forces. The second embodied the more wholesale meaning of martial law as an extraordinary military power used in times of emergency. The central difference between the two meanings had to do with applicability and legality. Essentially, the legality of martial law depended on to whom it was applied. If martial law was merely another name for military law and was used solely as a code of conduct for the army and navy, it was entirely legal. If, however, martial law allowed the use of military power on civilians, it was illegal.

The definitional disparity over martial law stemmed directly from English origins. The earliest British writings on the subject utilized the terms "martial law" and "military law" interchangeably, defining both as rules for the armed forces. Yet the English also recognized the more extraordinary conception of martial law, and as the empire grew, so too did rebellion and the need for more rigorous military control. Thus by the 1840s, British legal treatises revealed a clear evolution of the term martial law; it was no longer confounded with military law. Rather, the two terms took on distinct meanings. Martial law was extraordinary and applied to civilians. Military law was solely for military personnel.

During the early years of the Republic, American courts and legal scholars made no such attempt to expand the meaning of martial law. Though aware of the more extraordinary conception of the term, Americans, even after Jackson's use of martial law in 1814–15, refused to formally acknowledge such a definition. To do so would have entailed an acceptance, even if temporary, of the military's supremacy over the civil power, an idea that was anathema to republican notions of liberty. Instead, jurists and legal treatises adhered unwaveringly to the traditional definition that martial law was a code of conduct for the military. This, however, changed immediately following the congressional refund debates. Whigs and Democrats wrangled over the meaning of martial law and in doing so revealed the term's historical duality. Moreover, in an attempt to justify and legalize Jackson's conduct some Democrats actually expanded the concept of martial law by combining the two historical definitions: martial law was a military code of conduct, but it traveled with an army and existed within a military camp. Any civilian within the sphere of that camp was subject to military authority.

The English Origins of Martial Law

Americans borrowed their original definition of martial law from the earliest English conceptions of the term, and thus any investigation must begin in Great Britain, where, over the centuries, legal and political theorists repeatedly employed the terms martial and military law interchangeably. Both expressions denoted a law or code of conduct for the armed forces. The earliest and most often quoted authority on the subject was the English jurist Sir Matthew Hale. Writing in 1713, he noted that "the kings of this realm, by advice of the constable and marshal, were used to compose a book of rules and orders for the due order and discipline of their officers and soldiers, together with certain penalties on the offenders; and this was called martial law." Such rules, however, were in fact not sanctioned by written law, insisted Hale. Rather, he explained, "in truth and reality it is not a law, but something indulged, rather than allowed, as a law. The necessity of government, order, and discipline, in an army, is that only which can give those laws a countenance."[1]

Acknowledged as an authority on the subject, Hale established the precedent of viewing martial law as a code of conduct for the military and it was this definition that subsequent scholars and theorists cited. Yet Hale also recognized another, often ignored, conception of the term: "With regard to his [the king's] subjects. . . . He may punish them by martial law during such insurrection or rebellion, but not after it is suppressed."[2] Though not sanctioned in the written laws of England, martial law's use on civilians was deemed by Hale as a royal prerogative. Thus from early on, the term martial law embodied a striking duality. Depending on the circumstances, it was a means of control for both the military as well as civilians. Still, it was primarily martial law's connection to the military that subsequent legal experts acknowledged. Fifty years after Hale, Sir William Blackstone confirmed that martial law was a code for the military and noted that when the army is "drawn into actual service, they are subject to the rigours of martial law, as necessary to keep them in order."[3] Blackstone also agreed that it was extralegal, remarking it was "in reality no law at all."

Over time, and with the use of military force to quell Irish insurrections in 1798, other theories appeared. They included a fuller, more refined evaluation of martial law and in the process challenged the opinions of both Hale and Blackstone. In 1800, Alexander Tytler, the judge advocate of England, explained that the understanding of military law suffered because it had "never been systematically treated." Criticizing Blackstone for deriving antiquated and erroneous views from Hale, Tytler insisted that Blackstone's work "teems with error, with inconsistency, and with misrepresentation." He insisted that mili tary, or martial law, was not extralegal. Rather, it was "certain, determinate, and immutable." Tytler made no distinction between martial and military law, using the terms interchangeably, but he did expand the idea of its use as an emergency power in the civilian sphere. In doing so he added to the term's confused duality. Affirming that during the normal operation of society the civil law remained supreme, Tytler allowed that "there are extraordinary seasons when the body-politic, like the natural, is affected by disease, and when absolute necessity authorises the application of extraordinary remedies. . . . In times of turbulence and danger, these securities of personal liberty must yield to the greater object, the security of the state; and the legislature authorises for the time a suspension of the *Habeas Corpus*."[4]

Tytler maintained that there existed an intrinsic connection between the suspension of the writ of habeas corpus and the use of martial law, a common association in later times. He held that in employing so extreme a measure as martial law, we "part with our liberty for a while, in order that we may preserve it for ever."[5]

Renewed turmoil in Ireland in 1803 and an 1805 rebellion in Barbados undoubtedly influenced the evolution of emergency powers in the British kingdom. Writing in 1805, John McArthur concurred with Alexander Tytler regarding the use of martial law on civilians but made a clear distinction between martial and military law by explaining that the latter was a code of conduct. Military law was for "the regulation of his majesty's troops," whereas the "royal prerogative denominated martial law . . . is only resorted to upon an emergency of invasion, rebellion, or insurrection."[6]

Throughout the next half century, England utilized martial law in response to continued uprisings in her colonies, and as a result numerous English military experts clarified "the distinction between Martial and Military Law is this—*Martial Law* extends to *all persons: Military Law* to all military persons, but not to those in a civil capacity."[7] Thus by the early to middle nineteenth century, the confusion over martial law in Great Britain had ceased. Scholars no longer confounded it with military law.[8]

The American Origins of Martial Law

The definitional clarity that martial law underwent in England did not take hold in America until after the debates over Andrew Jackson's conduct in New Orleans. From the nation's earliest years Americans refused to acknowledge the idea that the military could control the civilian sphere. In the years leading to the Revolution, colonists were outspoken in their condemnation of the king for attempting to render the military independent of and superior to civil authority. Such beliefs became the foundation of American political ideals, and therefore any definition of the term martial law excluded its applicability to civilians. Nor did Americans most likely believe that such an extraordinary power would ever be needed. They had created a Republic predicated on liberty, a society in which threats from power, especially military power, were cautiously guarded against.

Thus Americans, in their laws as well as in their military and legal treatises, failed to accord martial law any legitimacy except as a code for governing the military. Similar to the earliest English definitions, martial law for Americans was synonymous with military law. Some five state Constitutions written between 1780 and 1819 confirmed this usage.[9] So, too, did Nathan Dane's *Digest of American Laws* published in 1823, in which the author clarified that civilians were not subject to martial law.[10] In the highly acclaimed *Commentaries on American Law* published in 1826, James Kent failed even to mention martial or military law.[11] Joseph Story included the subject in his 1833 *Commentaries on the Constitution* but merely repeated the traditional military code definition.[12] The first American legal dictionary, John Bouvier's *Law Dictionary Adapted to the Constitution and Laws of the United States of America*, published in 1839, also defined martial law as "a code established for the government of the army and navy of the United States."[13] Official military sources gave the same definition. At the request of the House of Representatives in 1819, Secretary of War John C. Calhoun instructed Gen. Winfield Scott to compile a manual of military laws. Scott made no distinction between martial and military law and in fact discussed martial law in terms of a "base of discipline." The very title of Scott's work implied that martial law was a code for the military: *A Letter from the Secretary of War, Transmitting a System of Field Service & Police, and a System of Martial Law, for the Government of the Army of the United States.*[14]

One other military treatise, as well as a number of judicial sources, repeated the traditional code for the military definition. They did, however, note that confusion existed over the term martial law, explaining that it sometimes embodied a second meaning that authorized the imposition of military power over civilians. Addressing the duality of martial law was by no means done to legitimize or expand its use beyond the military sphere. On the contrary, American authors who discussed the possible subversion of the civil government by the military endeavored to eradicate such an idea. Brig. Gen. Isaac Maltby of the Massachusetts Militia addressed the subject in 1813. Discussing the application of martial law to civilians, he declared that "citizens are amenable to the *civil*, and not to the *military law*. . . . Neither by the constitution nor the laws of the country, are such trials [court-martials of civilians] authorized."[15] Maltby then commented on an alleged use of martial law on civilians by Col. Zebulon Montgomery Pike in 1813. Other than Maltby's mention of the case, no evidence has been found to support that Pike imposed military rule. Nonetheless, Maltby treated the episode as an important factor that touched on the delicate balance between liberty and power inherent in a republican nation: "If this *new doctrine* be established, that a military officer can, with impunity, declare martial law to exist; and put in execution his intention to 'enforce it with the utmost severity'; then indeed are our liberties fled— the *civil* is subject to the military power—and a complete military despotism prevails. . . . In a free country, the civil power must predominate. . . . It is the *soul* of liberty."[16]

Maltby's traditional code definition and his concern over the subversion of liberty by military power can be found in the nation's courts as well. In 1814, a South Carolina district judge, Elihu Hall Bay, in a case involving a civilian who ignored a militia muster order and was ultimately convicted by a court-martial, discussed briefly the history of martial law and the impossibility of such an arbitrary power being exercised in a republican nation:

> If by martial law is to be understood that dreadful system, the law
> of arms, which in former times was exercised by the King of Eng-
> land and his lieutenants, when his word was law, and his will the
> power by which it was exercised, I have no hesitation in saying that
> such a monster could not exist in this land of liberty and freedom.
> The political atmosphere of America would destroy it in embryo. . . .
> But if by this military code are to be understood the rules and regu-

lations for the government of our men in arms . . . then I am bound
to say, there is nothing unconstitutional in such a system.[17]

Bay's ruling illustrated not only the historical duality of martial
law but also the refusal of Americans to accept the broader, extraordinary meaning of the term. Nor was Bay the only judge who attempted to dispel the idea that martial law was applicable to civilians.
In *Johnson v. Duncan,* an 1815 case that is particularly significant
because it stemmed directly from Andrew Jackson's use of martial law
in New Orleans, two Louisiana Supreme Court justices denounced martial law as illegal. The actual case concerned the impairment of contracts, yet Judges Xavier Martin and Pierre Derbigny seized the opportunity to make a decree on General Jackson's use of military power
only months earlier. The Louisiana court, Martin declared, "is bound
utterly to disregard what is thus called martial law; if anything be
meant thereby but the strict enforcing of the rules and articles for the
government of the army of the United States." Derbigny agreed and,
as Bay had done, commented on the inherent clash between oppressive
military power and American liberty: "The proclamation of martial law,
therefore, cannot have had any other effect than that of placing under
military authority all the citizens subject to militia service. It is in that
sense alone that the vague expression of martial law ought to be understood among us. To give it any larger extent, would be trampling upon
the constitution and laws of our country."[18] To a limited extent, Derbigny
did broaden the traditional definition by acknowledging that civilians
subject to militia duty were also subject to martial law. Yet his description by no means accepted the wholesale use of martial law on a general civilian population, this even though he had witnessed it under
Jackson. Nevertheless, Derbigny's opinion upheld the military code
definition.

The Revolutionary era tradition of safeguarding civil liberty from
military power appeared entrenched in the writings of legal and military scholars, all of whom determined that martial law was solely a
code for the military and inapplicable to civilians. Even those authors
who discussed the more extraordinary meaning did so in order to deny
its legality. Notwithstanding this fact, martial law as a doctrine of extreme powers remained. Perhaps the recognition of martial law's
power came from its use at the hands of the British during the Revolution or from the continued evolution of the term in England. Whatever
the reason, there was an awareness that martial law embodied a more

wholesale meaning than a mere code for the military. Even the most unlikely sources confirmed that Americans remained conscious of martial law as an extraordinary power. In 1808, shortly after the infamous Burr conspiracy, a frustrated Thomas Jefferson, the apostle of freedom, argued that there existed times of necessity when the military should supplant the civil government: "Under the maxim of the law itself, that *inter arma silent leges,* that in an encampment expecting daily attack from a powerful enemy, self-preservation is paramount to all law. . . . There are extreme cases where the laws become inadequate even to their own preservation, and where the universal resource is a dictator, or martial law."[19]

Certainly, Jefferson's conception of martial law included military control of civilians. Yet the author of the Declaration of Independence expressed his opinion in a private letter, not in any widely published form that could influence the views of military and legal experts. Thus the traditional idea that martial law was strictly a code for the military remained, uninfluenced by the arguments of men like Jefferson. Still, his letter reveals that another understanding, one that included the military policing of civilians, existed. Andrew Jackson certainly knew of martial law as a means of civilian control during times of emergency. When in 1814 he faced the fractious, multiethnic community of New Orleans and received continual word of spies and traitors in his midst, the general looked to martial law as one option to solve the problem. Yet even Jackson had questions regarding the actual meaning and scope of martial law. Though Edward Livingston and Abner Duncan disagreed on its legality, they did agree that martial law placed all civilians under military control.[20] With this point settled, Jackson declared martial law and later, when called before Dominick Hall's court to defend his actions, gave a clear definition of the decree: "Martial law, being established, applies, as the commanding general believes, to all persons who remain within the sphere of its operations, and claims exclusive jurisdiction of all offences [*sic*] which aim at the disorganization and ruin of the army over which it extends. To a certain extent it is believed, it makes every man a *soldier;* to defend the spot where chance or choice has placed him, and to make him liable for any misconduct calculated to weaken its defence."[21]

Jackson's use of martial law in New Orleans surely removed any question concerning the existence of a more extraordinary definition in America. No one could mistake the totality of the general's proclamation. It could not be confused with a code of conduct for the military. Secretary of War Alexander Dallas, writing at President Madison's behest in 1815, certainly did not express any confusion. The secretary did, however, deny its legality.[22] Yet without a more formal decree on Jackson's conduct, something that Madison was unwilling to issue, martial law in New Orleans remained unchallenged. Unbelievable as it may seem, legal and military authors refused to acknowledge the very clear precedent established by Old Hickory. Indeed, they clung to the traditional, military code meaning. The proof lies in the publication dates of the leading American texts. Winfield Scott published a manual at the request of John Calhoun in 1819; Nathan Dane's *Digest of American Laws* appeared in 1823; James Kent's issued *Commentaries on American Law* in 1826; Joseph Story published *Commentaries on the Constitution* in 1833; and John Bouvier's introduced *A Law Dictionary Adapted to the Constitution and Laws of the United States of America* in 1839. All of these works failed to mention Jackson's use of martial law and instead upheld the military code definition. The judiciary was no different. In 1815, Judges Xavier Martin and Pierre Derbigny denied the existence of martial law's more extraordinary meaning even though it had occurred right under their noses. The evolution of martial law would have to wait until legislators in the 1840s debated Jackson's refund.

The Meaning of Martial Law: The Refund Debates

It should come as no surprise that many northern Whigs, those who vehemently denied the legality of Jackson's conduct, advocated the traditional code for the military definition of martial law. Senator Richard Bayard asserted that "even in time of war, the private citizen, the noncombatant, cannot be subjected to the code which governs those engaged in warfare, without a manifest violation of his civil rights." "The only power Government has to establish a code of martial law," he insisted, "is in relation to those who are enlisted in its land and naval forces, including the militia."[23] Senator Jacob Miller concurred, and also added a foreboding commentary on the threat to American liberty:

> If by this law is meant that code of laws which govern men in
> arms—the rules and regulations of an army and navy—we all under-
> stand it. But when you claim for this law a supremacy over the Con-
> stitution; when you extend its jurisdiction over the citizen—over the

> life, liberty, and property of the private individual, and subject him
> and all his rights to be dealt with according to the will or whim of a
> military commander—you present a monster, a tyrant, under whose
> government no freeman could live in safety for an hour.[24]

Miller's view was strikingly similar to those of Isaac Maltby in 1813
and Judge Elihu Bay in 1814. All three men denied the application of
a military code to civilians and insisted that doing so was antithetical
to the nature of American government.

Northern Whig members of the House were no less obstinate in
their military code definition. Daniel Barnard, a man who had proven
so distasteful to Democrats on virtually every aspect of the refund
debates, continued his onslaught against Jackson when it came to defining martial law. "We must not fail to distinguish between it [this sort
of martial law] and the military code of the country as recognized by
the constitution and established by statutes," announced Barnard.
"This code is very carefully limited in its application to officers and
soldiers of the regular army and to the militia when in the service of
the United States. . . . No citizen, not a soldier, or attached to the army,
of course is subject to this code, or ever can be. It is forbidden by the
constitution." Continuing, Barnard announced, "General Jackson's
martial law was something very different from all this. . . . Here, then,
was a complete overleaping, by one bound, not of the military code
only, but of all regular government, of all constituted authority."[25]

For Democrats, overthrowing the traditional code meaning of martial law was instrumental in defending Jackson and winning approval
of the refund bill. They had good evidence to support their view. Martial
law in New Orleans did occur. Of this no one could deny. The problem
with acknowledging the existence of martial law as a means of civilian
control was the question of legality. American legal treatises refused
to include the extraordinary definition because it ran counter to both
the Constitution and republican traditions. Yet acknowledging the existence of martial law as something other than a military code did not
automatically translate legality. Many Democrats, and some southern
Whigs, argued that Jackson's decree was necessary but not legal.

The Democratic mission entailed advocating not only the extraordinary meaning of martial law but also its supremacy once declared.
Senator Buchanan insisted that every citizen, including public offi-
cials, must submit to and obey the military. "For it was quite a plain
case," he explained, "that if martial law did not supersede, and, dur-

ing its continuance, put in abeyance, the civil power, it would be wholly inefficient." Benjamin Tappan agreed, noting that necessity alone justified the general's conduct, and "martial law did in fact exist, and of necessary consequence . . . Judge Hall's authority was suspended." Lewis Linn concurred: "From the moment of its adoption to that in which it ceased, the martial law was paramount."[26]

Other Democrats, while still upholding the use of martial law on civilians, focused more carefully on the extent of martial law's power. Rather than insisting that it included a wholesale cancellation of civilian authority, a number of Democrats discussed the geographical limits of martial law, insisting that a boundary to military control existed. A commander's authority under martial law, they contended, was limited to the confines of a military camp, an area within the theater of war that often included civilian dwellings. Any civilians within the encampment were automatically subject to martial law. In a sense, the Democratic argument fused the traditional, military code definition with the more extraordinary meaning. Martial law was not simply a set of rules for the military or a wholesale power pervasive in scope. Rather, it could be applied, with specific geographical limitations, to the civilian sphere.

This novel camp theory was most ably argued from outside the halls of Congress. The ingenious pen of Amos Kendall, Jackson's longtime friend and political advisor, had many times in the past been put to use in support of the general. Whereas Jackson was the man of action, Amos Kendall was one of many men who theorized, wrote, and ultimately justified that action. Kendall first advocated the camp theory in an 1843 article published in the *United States Magazine and Democratic Review,* arguing that "the city and its immediate environs became *his* [Jackson's] *camp.* . . . He had a right to prescribe rules for preserving order in his camp, to establish patrols to enforce them, to arrest any citizen violating them, to confine him or send him beyond his lines." Kendall's view was novel. He simply took the existing military code definition and allowed it to travel with the military and occupy any territory the military may inhabit. Any civilian that happened to fall within an encampment was by default subject to military authority. Kendall ultimately concluded that martial law was a preexisting code of conduct for the military and thus "to establish and enforce it, required no declaration of Martial Law, that being already the law of the camp, and consequently the law of the city."[27] More than devising a doctrine to excuse the imposition of martial law in a democratic Republic, Kendall conceived a way to make military rule of civilians legal and traditional. In the process he made a genuine contribution to the development of a constitutional doctrine on martial law.[28]

Democratic legislators read the *Democratic Review* religiously and were quick to employ the new camp theory. Congressmen Ezra Dean of Ohio explained that though the Constitution did not recognize martial law, it was an implied power "existing in every military commander in time of war and in the presence of the enemy, within the limits of his camp [and] all other laws must give way to martial law in a besieged camp."[29] Congressman Aaron Brown agreed: "Within the bounds of every encampment, military and not civil law must prevail." There could be no question, continued Brown, that New Orleans "and its environs were within the military encampment of General Jackson."[30] Dean and Brown clearly viewed martial law as a code of conduct for the military. Yet it was Kendall's military law with a twist; it could be applied to civilians within the camp. The congressmen insisted that the code of martial, or military law, traveled with the army and existed automatically. It was only the question of geography that remained. How large was a military camp? How far did martial law extend into civilian areas? Most important, who decided such questions? Surely it was the commanding general. Samuel McRoberts, a senator from Illinois, believed this to be the case, insisting that "the very power to declare war . . . carried with it necessarily the power of the General to command his own camp; and the General must be himself the judge as to the limits of his camp."[31]

Not all Democrats embraced the camp theory: Buchanan, Tappan, and Linn, for example. At the heart of the matter was martial law's legality. The camp theorists maintained that Jackson's declaration was legal. Other Democrats wanted to avoid such a discussion. They instead focused on justification through necessity. Only one member of the party addressed the inconsistency of these varying views. Charles Jared Ingersoll argued that a distinction existed between military and martial law. The latter, he argued, was "the law of mere and sheer necessity, substituted for all common, enacted, or judicial law—analogous to the cases of self-protection from personal violence." He disagreed with "Mr. Kendall's position, that martial law is always the law of a camp in time of war." Rather, insisted the congressman, "it was the occasional and temporary application of extreme force."[32] Expanding his argument in a pamphlet, Ingersoll insisted that Jackson's proclamation initiated "a momentary suspension of all rules, except the commander's arbitrary will, from stern necessity, which has no law, as the only remaining means of preventing the downfall of the country, and, with it, that of all rules, laws, and institutions. . . . Martial Law does not establish a code, enact a system of rules, or pretend to be permanent; but, like war itself, declared and waged by violating all rules and laws, as the only way to peace, is an exception, not a rule."[33] Ingersoll obtained his definition of martial law directly from English precedent. His argument echoed not only Sir Matthew Hale's statement that martial law "was no law at all" but also the Duke of Wellington's assertion that martial law was nothing more than "the will of the general."[34]

The most substantial difference between Kendall's camp theory and Ingersoll's extraordinary power argument was the issue of legality. They both, in fact, upheld martial law as legal. Kendall, however, based it on an expanded conception of the traditional military code, whereas Ingersoll focused on the supremacy of natural law. What the two theories had in common, and what was most important for expanding the definition of martial law, was that it could be applied to civilians. This was the key in acknowledging a new understanding of emergency military powers.

The Evolution of Martial Law

The varied arguments over the extraordinary meaning of martial law significantly influenced the term's evolution in America. Congress ultimately passed the refund legislation and one might argue that victory validated the Democratic definition. Yet Democrats proposed multiple arguments and it was not at all certain in the immediate aftermath of the debates what meaning was adopted or if the debates had any influence at all. Historians have remained divided on this point. Jackson's first major biographer, James Parton, insisted in 1860, "Congress thus notified the future commanders of armies, first, that they may place under martial law a city threatened by an enemy; and, secondly, that they may keep it under martial law for the space of two months after the enemy has been vanquished. . . . In other words, Congress invested the military commanders of cities, in time of war, with supreme authority."[35] In 1939, military historian Robert Rankin concurred with Parton's opinion: "Jackson's use of martial law was upheld by congress and the people and a precedent was thus created calculated to influence all subsequent use of martial law."[36] Numerous scholars have made the same assertion.[37]

At least one historian disagreed. George M. Dennison argued that the refund debates can be seen only "as at most a reflection of changing attitudes, but by no means as the ratification of new views on the law of emergency powers."[38] Dennison's point is well taken. The refund bill itself made no mention of martial law and as a result failed to legislatively define the term. The many arguments proposed by Democrats and Whigs were merely theories. The very deliberation on martial law was something of an abstraction. Legislators engaged in a rare discussion over what powers a military commander could assume during a time of war when in fact no war existed. Nevertheless, at least one person at the time asserted that the opinions of leading politicians regarding the meaning and legality of martial law would have negative ramifications. Insisting that the debates influenced Rhode Island's use of martial law during the Dorr War in 1842, Samuel Smith Nicholas, a former judge from Kentucky, denounced the proceedings in Congress and attacked the use of military power on civilians. He insisted that prior to the start of the debates a proclamation such as Jackson's could never have been condoned in America. "But, since then," he argued, "the conduct of the Rhode Island Legislature, with the tame acquiescence of the people of that State, and *the damnable heresies preached in the halls of Congress* . . . have raised a horrible doubt whether a large portion of the nation is not already in training for the yoke of the master."[39] Martial law in Rhode Island was, in essence, identical to that utilized by Jackson. Both sanctioned the arbitrary use of military power to control civilians; it was not merely a code for the military in either instance.[40] Moreover, immediately following the cessation of the Dorr insurrection, Rhode Island legislators drafted and ratified a new state Constitution including an important article: "The law martial shall be used in such and exercised in such cases only as occasion shall necessarily require it."[41] This new doctrine marked the first time that a state constitution included the more extraordinary definition of martial law.

It is particularly remarkable if Rhode Island took the steps of both imposing martial law and adopting a constitutional resolution in support of such an act without the Jackson precedent and the ongoing congressional debates in mind. The refund bill was introduced in March

1842, some three months prior to Rhode Island's June proclamation. Although legislators in Congress did not engage in serious discussion of the refund bill until mid-May, and the remainder of the debates occurred after the turmoil in Rhode Island had ceased, it was clear from the outset that many members of Congress supported Jackson's use of martial law. Additionally, Americans were abundantly aware of the famous Battle of New Orleans as well as the means utilized to win it. Martial law in Louisiana had always been a sensitive subject, but with the introduction of the refund bill and the backing of the Democratic Party, the extraordinary meaning of martial law became more legitimized than ever before. Thus Rhode Island most likely felt confident in both their decree and constitutional addition. Moreover, legal issues stemming from the Dorr War upheld the state's use of martial law. On November 15, 1843, Justice Joseph Story issued his decision in *Luther v. Borden,* a case resulting from a military arrest. Story sustained Rhode Island's right to declare martial law and gave a concise definition of the term:

> Martial law is the law of war. It is a resort to the military authority in cases where the civil authority is not sufficient for the maintenance of the laws, and it gives to legally appointed military officers summary power, for the purpose of restoring tranquility and sustaining the State. . . . They are to judge the degree of force which the necessity of the exigency demands; and there is no limit to their exercise of the power conferred upon them by the law martial, except the nature and character of the exigency.[42]

Here was no traditional code for the military definition of martial law. Rather, it embodied the extraordinary power of the military to place the civilian sphere under complete control. Story's view of martial law was new not only to the judicial system but also to his own convictions on the subject. When defining martial law just ten years earlier in his 1833 *Commentaries,* he had noted only that it was a code of conduct for the military.[43]

There is little doubt that Story's new understanding of martial law was directly influenced by the congressional refund debates. He referred to martial law as "the law of war," an argument introduced and advocated solely by John Quincy Adams.[44] Story also noted that "no court had ever decided that a military officer had the right, much less the exclusive right to declare martial law," yet added that "there are occasions in which a high military officer may be justified in taking the responsibility to save his country."[45] The confluence is striking between Justice Story's opinion and those expressed in Congress while the *Luther* case was ongoing. Ultimately, Story altered only one component concerning the declaration of martial law, insisting that for the decree to be legal it must come from the legislature. This view was, in actuality, keeping with the notion that only the legislature had the power to suspend the writ of habeas corpus, an action directly conected to martial law.

Joseph Story was not the only person involved in the *Luther* case who was influenced by the congressional refund debates. The plaintiff's attorney, Benjamin F. Hallet, utilized Amos Kendall's camp theory when insisting that martial law extended only to the limits of the camp and thus the entire state of Rhode Island was not subject to the proclamation. Story was not, however, swayed by Hallet's argument and ruled that "martial law does not extend merely to the camp, or the persons who are under arms."[46] Moreover, when *Luther v. Borden* came before the Supreme Court in 1848, the attorney for the state, the renowned Daniel Webster, also employed the camp theory. Yet this time it was utilized to show the limitless parameters of a military encampment. Webster insisted that when martial law has been proclaimed, "the land becomes a camp, and the law of the camp is the law of the land."[47]

The judicial decisions and arguments connected to the Dorr War were not the only sources that revealed an influence from the congressional refund debates. American military treatises also took up the issue of redefining martial law. William De Hart, a former judge advocate of the army, and John O'Brien, a military author, made clear distinctions between military and martial law. Publishing their works in 1846, both authors agreed that the former was a code respecting military discipline, whereas martial law was something very different: it could be applied to civilians. Yet the authors differed on certain points. De Hart maintained that martial law applied military law to all persons. Such an argument fused the traditional military code argument with the more extraordinary meaning and in fact paralleled the camp theory posed by Democrats. O'Brien made no such attempt to connect martial law to military rules, insisting that "despotic in its character and tyrannical in its application. . . . [Martial law bears] no analogy whatever to military law."[48] The authors also differed on the question of legality. De Hart wavered, remarking that martial law "is a very questionable proceeding." O'Brien left no doubt concerning the doctrine's legality, insisting that from the "principle of self-preservation the constitution of the United States has wisely, and indeed, necessarily permitted the proclamation of martial law."[49] There can be little doubt that both men's views, especially O'Brien's use of "self-preservation," came directly from the well-publicized refund debates.

Legal treatises also reflected the changing definition of martial law in the wake of the congressional debates. Joseph Kent's *Commentaries on American Law*, published in 1826, made no mention of military or martial law, yet the 1848 edition included a footnote making a distinction between the two terms: military law was a "system of regulations" for the army, whereas *"martial* law is quite a distinct thing, and is founded on paramount necessity, and proclaimed by a military chief."[50] The theories espoused during the debates inevitably made their entrance into law dictionaries as well. In 1839, John Bouvier defined martial law as a code for the government of the army and navy. In the 1848 edition, he added that "a military commander has not the power, by declaring a district to be under martial law, to subject all the citizens to that code."[51] Moreover, Bouvier expressed the same opinion three years later in *Institutes of American Law* and went further by declaring that only the legislature had the power to declare martial law.[52]

The first edition of *Burrill's Law Dictionary*, published in 1851, noted that martial law was a code for the military and "an arbitrary kind of law or rule" in which the civil authority is suspended by and subjected to military power.[53] In the 1856 edition of *Commentaries on the Criminal Law*, Joel Prentiss Bishop made a clear distinction between military and martial law stating that the latter could be proclaimed by a military commander and a legislature. Bishop cited the cases of both Jackson and Rhode Island.[54] More than the fact that the congressional refund debates had a significant impact on the evolution of the term martial law, it is evident that the Democratic and Whig disputes on the subject made their way into the new definitions. De Hart and O'Brien differed over the question of martial law's legality, the former insisting that it was a "questionable proceeding" and the latter justifying it on the grounds of "self-preservation" and noting that the Constitution "wisely" permitted such a declaration. Joseph Kent concluded that martial law was justified on the grounds of "paramount necessity" and imposed by a "military chieftain." John Bouvier bristled at the idea that civilians could be held to a military code and ultimately supported

Joseph Story's opinion that only the legislature could proclaim martial law. Alexander Burrill returned to the dual notion that martial law was both a code and something more extraordinary. Joel Bishop ultimately combined earlier views and decreed that both a military commander and a legislature had the power to declare martial law. In this steady evolution existed many of the ideas and disputes first enunciated during the congressional refund debates.

In the midst of this continual development from 1843 to the early 1850s, another example of martial law appeared. During the Mexican War, Gen. Winfield Scott proclaimed martial law in occupied Mexican territory. Yet other than dramatizing the use of the martial decree, Scott's 1847 order did little to advance the theory or use of the term. Imposing martial law on civilians in a subjugated, foreign country was, as one historian noted, "a superfluous and unnecessary proceeding, adding nothing to the military authority or jurisdiction."[55] Scott's use did not have to do with suspensions of habeas corpus or the use of military powers within one's own country. This is not to say that the use of martial law in Mexico was entirely without influence. It certainly strengthened the precedent that a military commander could make such a proclamation during war time.

The last major commentary on martial law prior to its use during the Civil War was rendered in 1857. Ruling on the legality of a martial law proclamation by the governor of the Washington Territory, Caleb Cushing, the attorney general for the United States, declared that "martial law is a thing not mentioned by name, and scarcely as much hinted at, in the Constitution."[56] Yet, concluded Cushing, this did not necessarily make it illegal. Discussing the grounds upon which the writ of habeas corpus could be suspended, he argued that if an emergency was such that it required a suspension of the writ, "surely that emergency must be not the less an essential prerequisite of the proclamation of martial law, and of its constitutional existence."[57] In making such a determination, Cushing came to the same conclusion that Andrew Jackson's legal counselor, Abner Duncan, had reached some forty-three years earlier and that which the Englishman Alexander Tytler had advocated in 1800.

Unlike Duncan and Tytler, however, Cushing acknowledged that only the legislature had the authority to suspend the writ and, by implication, proclaim martial law. In this sense, he supported the concept that Justice Story had advocated in the 1843 *Luther* decision. Yet

Cushing clarified that suspending the writ of habeas corpus was but one, and "by no means the largest or gravest," consequence of martial law. "According to every definition of martial law," he insisted, "it suspends, for the time being, all the laws of the land, and substitutes in their place no law, that is, the mere will of the military commander." Furthermore, he announced that cases may exist in which "emergencies of necessity" justify the suspension of laws and the omnipotence of the military. Cushing contended that in such circumstances, the proclamation is merely an expression of a fact that already exists, not its legal creation. For precedent, Cushing turned directly to Andrew Jackson, remarking that this "is the true explanation of the proclamation of martial law at New Orleans by General Jackson."[58] The attorney general's opinion both confirmed the Democratic argument of "paramount necessity" advocated in the debates and combined it with Amos Kendall's contention that martial law existed implicitly whether proclaimed or not.

Cushing was eminently familiar with such Democrat arguments because he had witnessed them firsthand as a participant in the refund debates. As a member of the House of Representatives during the early 1840s, though ostensibly a member of the Whig Party, he supported the refund of Jackson's fine.[59] As attorney general, he confirmed the Democratic theories espoused in the debates. Martial law was not merely a code for the military, but, rather, an exercise of extraordinary military authority decreed at a time of necessity. Cushing did attempt to combine martial law with a semblance of constitutionality by rather blandly insisted that it was only legal when issued by a legislature. But he understood that such a tidy occurrence was altogether unlikely in the midst of war and virtually nullified his own argument by acknowledging that a military commander was justified in "emergencies of necessity."

With opinions of men like Attorney General Cushing, as well as the numerous legal and military treatises that altered definitions of martial law in the aftermath of the refund debates, there is no doubt that Jackson's battle to reclaim his New Orleans fine served as a catalyst in the evolution of the term martial law. Prior to Democratic and Whig arguments over the meaning and legality of martial law, every source treated it strictly as a code for the conduct of military personnel. This concept was derived directly from English origins. But as the concept of martial law in Great Britain expanded, Americans, with their stringent notions of liberty and governmental power, clung tightly to the more traditional military code meaning. By the late 1850s, however, martial law as an extraordinary power was firmly entrenched in American law. All of this was due to the congressional refund debates and the Dorr War. As a result they both mark a significant turning point in the history of American civil liberties. Never before had legislators, judges, as well as legal and military commentators condoned the suspension of all rights and the subversion of civil authority by the military. Jackson had received his precedent.

CHAPTER 7

Andrew Jackson and Martial Law during the Civil War

A ndrew Jackson never had the opportunity to witness the evolution of martial law as it related to legal and military treatises. A little over a year after his refund victory in the Congress, the indomitable general succumbed to the illnesses that had dogged him for so many years of his life. On June 8, 1845, he passed away at the Hermitage in Nashville. Newspapers around the nation reported the news and in Nashville after city flags were lowered to half-mast, church bells rang out, and guns echoed in tribute. As with virtually everything else in Jackson's life, his death, too, was the source of tremendous partisan maneuvering. Democrats once again attempted to use the occasion for its potential election power and Whigs attacked Jackson for the same reasons. In New York City, some forty thousand people marched in the streets to pay homage to the Hero of New Orleans. Even some Whigs acknowledged the general's unflagging patriotism and military services to the country. Most let the issue of martial law rest.[1]

Yet it still remained in the minds of some. A Philadelphia artist named Charles (Christian) Schussele recorded on canvas the infamous court room scene in which Jackson stood in front of Judge Hall's court in New Orleans, and as his supporters harangued the judge, Jackson, with outstretched arm, exclaimed that he would defend the court as he

Andrew Jackson before Judge Hall, *by Charles Schuselle. Gilcrease Museum, Tulsa, Okla.*

had the city, or perish in the effort. The painting, *General Andrew Jackson before Judge Hall,* showed the general in civilian garb, and illuminated by a shaft of light. He mesmerized the eager onlookers, with a cold stare fixed on Judge Hall, who is relegated to the shadowy borders.[2]

The depiction is all Jackson. He is in charge. As with most artistic works related to the Battle of New Orleans, he is the illustrious hero.[3] Schussele's rendition is particularly significant because it is one of only two works that portray an event connected to martial law, and more important, because it represents General Jackson's submission to civilian authority.[4] Yet even though Schussele addressed the martial law episode, the significance of military rule and its importance to America's still-burgeoning constitutional government was essentially ignored.

Schussele's work was inspired directly by the refund debates and commissioned in 1849 by a Philadelphia shoe merchant and publisher, Charles J. Hedenberg. For the next nine years Hedenberg collected the portraits of some three dozen people present in the court room so that Schussele could portray them accurately. Hedenberg also printed a key to identify the various figures and wrote participants involved in the

EXPLANATION

OF

THE PICTURE

ANDREW JACKSON

BEFORE JUDGE HALL,

AT NEW-ORLEANS, 1815,

SUSTAINING THE LAWS OF HIS COUNTRY, AS HE HAD DE-
FENDED HER LIBERTIES IN THE FIELD.

PAINTED BY

C. SCHUSSELE, OF PHILADELPHIA

Reliable Portraits of all the parties herein named are given in the Painting,
having been carefully collected by the undersigned, for whom
the picture was painted

C. J. HEDENBERG,

1919 *Vine St. Philada.*

Quinn, Printer, Third and Market Sts. Phila.

Title page of Explanation of the Picture of Andrew Jackson before Judge Hall, *by C. J. Hedenberg.*

1840s debates, requesting their speeches in order to give Schussele more detailed descriptions of Jackson's conduct before Hall.[5] The end result was a portrait of the Democratic hero, a perpetuation of only half the New Orleans story.

When the painting was finally completed in 1858, Schussele and Hedenberg could not have imagined that only three years later all of the controversies that had surrounded Jackson's use of martial law would resurface once again. This time, however, military rule was invoked to save the Union in what became the most trying and bloody challenge the Republic had ever faced. The military realities of the Civil War caused both the Union and the Confederacy to suspend the writ of habeas corpus and impose martial law.[6] President Abraham Lincoln justified his violation of civil liberties in the North by turning directly to Andrew Jackson for precedent:

> After the Battle of New Orleans and while the fact that the treaty
> of peace had been concluded was well known in the city, but before
> official knowledge of it had arrived, General Jackson still main-
> tained martial or military law. . . . It may be remarked—first, that
> we had the same Constitution then as now; secondly, that we then
> had a case of invasion, and now have a case of rebellion; and, thirdly,
> that the permanent right of the people to public discussion, the lib-
> erty of speech and of the press, the trial by jury, the law of evi-
> dence, and the *habeas corpus* suffered no detriment whatever by
> the conduct of General Jackson, or its subsequent approval by the
> American Congress.[7]

The "approval" of Congress! Lincoln clearly looked back to the refund debates and took from them exactly what Jackson had originally desired and what Whigs had feared. Yet the refund bill itself had remained silent on the question of martial law's legality. No one, however, was fooled. All understood that the refund was a tacit, if not legislatively recognized, acceptance of Jackson's actions. This was certainly the effect on martial law's definitional evolution. The ultimate irony is that this development of a theory of emergency powers occurred in the midst of a political brawl that was influenced as much by partisan strategizing as it was by ideological conviction about republicanism and the sanctity of the Constitution. For many legislators, support or opposition to martial law in the 1840s was tied directly to one's party affiliation; little changed during the Civil War.

One must not miss the inherent irony in Abraham Lincoln, a for-mer Whig, holding up Andrew Jackson, the venerated leader of the

Democratic Party, as a justification for curtailing civil liberties. Lincoln was not a member of Congress during the 1842–44 congressional refund debates, but he surely knew of his former party's views on the subject and the intense arguments that surrounded Jackson's use of martial law in Louisiana. Lincoln's letter citing the New Orleans precedent went into considerable detail, revealing that the war president had researched the matter. In some ways, Lincoln must have relished the ability to shove Jackson in the faces of anti-administration Democrats who vigorously denounced the federal government's suspension of the writ of habeas corpus and imposition of martial law. These Democrats, some of whom had been able defenders of martial law under Jackson, had become in the midst of Lincoln's similar actions the guardians of injured rights and republican institutions. Their earlier views in support of martial law had been both theoretical and tied directly to Andrew Jackson, always with the hope of reaping political reward from an extended dispute over the refund.

The 1860s presented a decidedly different scenario. With the Democratic Party splintered into northern and southern wings, the rise of a new and formidable Republican Party bent on forcing the South into respect for federal authority, Abraham Lincoln's elevation to the executive chair, as well as the reality of war, Democrats were now the minority. As the opposition, they felt much of the Union sting when it came to curtailment of civil liberties. It is thus no surprise that Democrats quickly abandoned their former stance on the legality of martial law. This fact is seen not only in the altered opinions of those men who were either legislators at the time or expressed their views on the matter from outside the walls of Congress but also in the writings of prominent Democrats of the Civil War era who attempted to twist or dismiss the Jackson precedent. The result is clear: the Democratic Party abandoned the necessity, justification, and legality of martial law.

Whigs were not much better. Though the party had died a rather slow and debilitating death in the 1850s, many members found new life within the spirited and formidable Republican Party. With the onset of the war and President Lincoln's quick movement to impose military rule, some of these former Whigs abandoned their earlier views of martial law in much the same way that they had fled their defunct political party. As members of the dominant national party in the 1860s, these reinvigorated Republicans, no longer the beleaguered opposition, no longer in need of Andrew Jackson as an anti-symbol, no longer in fear of Democratic victory, now supported martial law as a necessary and justifiable resource for the nation's salvation. The degree to which the tables could turn regarding the legality of martial law is astounding.

The North was not the only place where disputes over martial law occurred. The Confederacy also suspended the writ of habeas corpus and imposed military rule in order to curb internal dissent. The opposition to such activities is, however, not nearly as well documented and without political parties the debate was not as well focused. Though Jefferson Davis never mirrored Lincoln's use of the Jackson precedent to justify Confederate military rule, there are nevertheless some instances of southerners who dealt with martial law in both the 1840s and 1860s. The fact that extensive violations of civil liberties occurred within the Confederacy may come as a surprise to some historians, most of whom have argued that southerners were more jealous of their rights and acted within the legal bounds of the Constitution. Scholarship has, however, recently exploded this myth.[8] In relation to the question of Confederate devotion to civil liberties, one must also not forget that the majority of southerners in the 1840s, whether Democrat or Whig, accepted Jackson's use of martial law during a time of national emergency. It comes as no surprise, therefore, that they would do so again in order to combat northern tyranny.

One might of course argue that there existed considerable differences between martial law in 1814–15 and martial law in the 1860s. As a result, the subsequent debates over military rule were different for the two time periods. An important point is that the refund debates were an abstraction, an argument about what a military commander might justifiably do during a time of war. The reality of war during the great rebellion was something all together different. In this later instance, the necessity was "real." Yet the true reality is that the threats facing Jackson in 1814–15 were also tangible. He was faced with a formidable British force that could have potentially taken over and kept New Orleans. Jackson did not know if or when the British would return in the aftermath of the New Orleans victory, and thus the issue of necessity was still a formidable one.

It is difficult to embrace another generation's dangers, and thus it is often rather easy to dismiss the sense of fear and pending doom that makes the resort to emergency military powers not only justified but welcome. This is certainly true when attempting to look back and determine whether Jackson should have acted as he did in New Orleans. The issue was even more problematic by the time the refund debates came around. Jackson had spent eight years as president, and the Whig Party had formed directly in opposition to his domineering command style. It was therefore virtually impossible that an unimpassioned, nonpartisan debate could occur over his conduct or the future use of martial law. One might therefore argue that the basis for discussing martial law was simply different some twenty years later during the Civil War. The original debates over martial law centered more around Jackson than the nation and focused on his application of military rule. In the 1860s, the reverse was true. The Union was now at risk, Jackson was no longer at the heart of the dispute and legislators therefore reset their political compasses accordingly.

There is unquestionably truth in the extent to which Jackson as the centerpiece of the debates influenced political views of martial law—indeed one theme of this book is to point out this reality—yet it does not logically follow that one can dismiss the glaring changes in opinion regarding civil liberty issues that occurred in the midst of the Civil War. Many of the politicians who argued during the refund debates made impassioned pleas to either justify martial law or condemn it, basing their arguments around fundamental republican principles and constitutionalism. Such views are difficult to dismiss twenty years later, especially when the political circumstances of altered opinions are once again paramount to the discussion. Finally, the point here is not merely to condemn the opinions of particular men for "flip-flopping," though this chapter necessarily focuses in part on individual participants of the refund debates. Rather, the issue is the dramatic shift in party thought, especially the Democrats, who had helped to cause an evolution in the nation's understanding of emergency powers.

In the 1860s, there remained alive only twelve legislators and three commentators from outside of Congress who had connection to the congressional refund debates. Of these, the majority, nine, engaged the subject of martial law during the Civil War.[9] Three of these men were Democrats both during the 1840s and in the 1860s. The remaining six men were former Whigs, only one of whom was a northerner and became a Republican. The rest of the old Whigs were southerners, only two of whom were secessionists. Out of the total nine, four revealed remarkable changes of opinion concerning martial law and the power of the military to suppress civil liberties. The remaining five expressed fairly consistent views on martial law, though most had very particular reasons that had little to do with ideological considerations.

Old Democrats with New Opinions of Martial Law

One of the remaining Democrats from the refund debate days was Senator William Allen of Ohio. He had always been a good Union man and a true Jacksonian. He often harkened back to the day when Andrew Jackson, fresh from the fields of his glorious victory in New Orleans, passed through Lynchburg, Virginia, on his way to the nation's capital and in doing so patted a young boy upon the head. With the touch and inspiring words of this great hero, the boy, William Allen, noted later that it was not to be wondered that he became "a Democrat dyed in the wool."[10] Allen's reminiscence revealed not only his unwavering admiration for Jackson but also a desire to be linked with the general's most celebrated achievement. And when it came time to refund Jackson's fine and defend his use of martial law, Allen again showed reverence for the aging hero, noting that his character was "resplendent, burnished, [and] sparkling with brilliancy."[11]

Allen took an immediate interest in the refund bill following its proposal by introducing it on a number of occasions and pushing for Senate votes. Notwithstanding his admiration of Jackson, Allen opted to allow his senior colleague, Benjamin Tappan, the honor of introducing their state's resolutions and speaking on the matter. "His age, his ability, the relations in which he has long stood with the illustrious personage to whom the resolutions related," insisted Allen, "all of these things made it peculiarly proper that he should present the resolutions, and take a more special charge of the subject."[12] Tappan argued forcefully that Judge Hall's actions "were not only exceedingly outrageous, but were wholly illegal and void" and that "the law of self-preservation is paramount to all other laws," adding, "'In the midst of arms the laws are silent.'" Allen declared that his colleague "gave clearly and forcibly all those reasons which may legitimately be brought to bear upon the case."[13]

As Whig opposition to the refund bill increased, Allen felt compelled to speak on the measure's behalf by denouncing Whig amendments calling for the protection of Judge Hall and the judiciary. "No," he declared, "you had better state in your bill the whole fact—that a military commander, almost in his very camp, shall be dragged before a civil authority, and fined, while in the act of guarding that very court and its members from a foreign enemy." Allen argued that amendments changed the very nature of the bill, a bill that he believed was meant to vindicate General Jackson: "You must either imply that General Jackson was guilty of an offence of great magnitude, or else the conduct of Judge Hall was inexcusable: one of these conclusions must be true." Senator Allen had no reservations regarding the answer. Jackson was correct; the judge unpardonable. Thus he harangued Whigs, announcing, "I have simply to say I shall vote against all manner of provisoes, and even against the very word 'provided'; I shall not vote for the bill, if there be any proviso attached to it, because I consider the hanging on of the word as a direct censure upon General Jackson."[14] William Allen's support for martial law could not be clearer.

When Civil War came, Allen did not immediately change his position on military rule and civil liberties. Rather, he showed true Jacksonian fervor for the Union by coming out of retirement and aiding the Lincoln administration. As a Union Democrat throughout 1861 and into the summer of 1862, Allen supported the Republican government and even made a speech in Chillicothe, Ohio, heralding the Union, the law, and the Constitution. He encouraged young men to enlist and, as soldiers, help in the great struggle. Allen noted particularly that the war was for Union, not abolition.[15] During this time there is no indication that he had reservations about President Lincoln's suspension of the writ of habeas corpus or his use of the military in early 1861. But in the late summer and fall of 1862, Allen's view of the war and the means to win it changed. In July, Congress passed an act that both permitted the confiscation of rebel owned estates and provided for the freedom of any slaves escaping to a free state or seeking refuge within Union lines. Then, in September, Lincoln announced the preliminary Emancipation Proclamation. Allen now believed that the war was waged primarily for abolition, a policy that he did not support. He quickly parted ways with the Lincoln administration and its use of military power. Allen joined the Peace Democrats of Ohio, who were in part guided by the infamous Clement Vallandigham, a former congressman who was later arrested by General Ambrose Burnside in 1863 for making a speech criticizing Lincoln's war policies, especially those regarding civil liberty issues.

Shortly after taking up league with Peace Democrats, Allen began denouncing Republican war strategies, especially suspension of the writ of habeas corpus and arrest of civilians. Speaking at a rally on behalf of Vallandigham's bid for the Ohio governorship in 1863, Allen condemned the administration's arbitrary arrests and insisted that "this nation was once free. . . . We are now endangered for no other crime than for our opinion; to have our houses entered at midnight by armed men and our people taken off to be tried, not before a jury, but before a military inquisition, and for the crime of thinking, and condemned to exile." For the cause of abolition, chastised Allen, Lincoln "has determined to silence this righteous indignation [of the Democratic Party]. He has put forth his Emancipation Proclamation and he has established martial law; he has divided up the free states and he has put us under military rule for this reason." "Remember," he counseled, "that in supporting Vallandigham you support your own rights and by neglecting to sustain him you open your own doors and invite an armed despotism into your own house."[16]

William Allen's new view of martial law, tied directly to his disgust for emancipation, in no way mirrored his earlier position. When Jackson utilized military rule to suppress personal opinion Allen considered it necessary and justified. When Lincoln suspended the hallowed writ of habeas corpus and put down the heel of military might at the outset of the war, Allen had nothing to say in defense of liberty. Yet when abolition entered the picture, martial law suddenly became "armed despotism." Allen was a steadfast Union man, but apparently his vision of Union did not include manumitted slaves roaming the nation. His decisions regarding martial law during the Civil War were based on ideology, but his preeminent views focused on ideals of race not liberty.

Other Democrats from the refund debate days did not emulate Allen's transparency. He, after all, reversed his convictions on martial law in the midst of the Union struggle. Amos Kendall did so at the start of the war and thus only those who paid close attention may have noticed his stark shift in thought. Of course, anyone who knew Kendall also knew that he acquired his fame and power directly in relation to Andrew Jackson. It was therefore no stretch to assume that the former Kitchen Cabinet advisor to Jackson supported his favorite general's use of martial law. One needed only pull an old issue of the *Democratic Review* and read Kendall's 1843 article, "General Jackson's Fine," in which he justified all that Jackson did in New Orleans. Kendall even devised the novel "camp theory," arguing that a military commander had the authority to extend the laws of the camp onto any adjacent area in a theater of war. In making such a claim, he effectively merged the traditional military code definition with the more extraordinary meaning of martial law. If this was not enough to convince the opponents of martial law, Kendall simply argued the preeminent authority of the military in cases of national emergency, noting, "there are occasions when the military power knows no superior among the inferior magistrates of the country. The law itself, for such emergencies, places it above the local civil magistracy, which is *silent* at its command." "*Silent leges inter arma,*" commanded Kendall, "is as true now as it was in the days of conquering Rome."[17]

For Kendall, as it turned out, the Latin maxim applied to Jackson only. When Union generals suspended civil liberties and imposed martial law under Lincoln's direction, the former advisor railed against "usurpations and abuses." Kendall's motto was "the Constitution as it is" and "the Union as it was." In 1864, he wrote a fiery denunciation of Lincoln's administration titled *Letters Exposing the Mismanagement of Public Affairs by Abraham Lincoln and the Political Combinations to Secure His Re-election.* Essentially a campaign pamphlet championing Gen. George B. McClellan's presidential bid, the letters touched briefly on Lincoln's lack of character, abuse of power, and inability to end the war. The president, he declared, "has neither the judgement, decision or courage which the crisis of the country requires in a chief magistrate," and we are left with "indefinite war and bloodshed . . . a nation clothed in mourning, agitated with internal throes and sinking at last under military despotism."[18] Insisting that McClellan's election was the only way "to rid the country of the Lincoln tyranny and open the door to peace and Union on the basis of the Constitution," Kendall condemned "*the destruction of the safeguards of liberty* by the general suspension of the writ of *habeas corpus,* thus exposing every citizen, loyal, as well as disloyal, with cause or without cause, to arbitrary arrest and indefinite imprisonment. This act and the outrages that have followed, would have produced a revolution among any people less devoted to peace and order and less hopeful of the future than the people of the United States."

Amos Kendall had suddenly become the great defender, the sage and protector of civil liberties. When Jackson had taken it upon his own authority to suspend the writ of habeas corpus, arrest civilians and ultimately a state senator and federal judge, Kendall justified such acts under the dictates of paramount military authority which became "superior" to "inferior magistrates." Like William Allen, however, Kendall's views of protecting civil liberties changed, in part, because of his opposition to the Emancipation Proclamation. He insisted that abolitionists controlled both Lincoln and the Republican Party. With General Jackson long gone and his own party in minority status, Kendall suddenly had a major problem with Union commanders arresting suspected traitors, ignoring writs of habeas corpus, and essentially placing the entire North under martial law. The camp could indeed be large. Abraham Lincoln's defense of the nation garnered no understanding on Kendall's part, and the former Jacksonian warned that Lincoln's reelection would result in "an end of all truly republican government, [and] the domination of unprincipled military chieftains."[19] How ironic, or perhaps fitting, that Kendall not only abandoned his views of martial law but also reapplied the negativity of a "military chieftain," an epithet most connected with Andrew Jackson and one that had become an attribute at the hands of Democrats in the 1820s and 1830s.

The last of the congressional refund debate era Democrats to engage the issue of martial law during the Civil War was actually something of an anomaly, not just because chief justice of the Supreme Court Roger B. Taney's support of Andrew Jackson's conduct was never made public in the 1840s, but because of the central and exceedingly important role he played regarding the defense of civil liberties at the outset of the Civil War. Taney was certainly no fan of the Lincoln administration. Nor was he much of a friend to the North in the years preceding the war. His infamous *Dred Scott* decision, in which he voided the Missouri Compromise, was universally hated by Republicans. Nevertheless, historians have largely heralded Taney's *Ex Parte Merryman* decision as a stalwart defense of civil liberties and constitutionalism in the midst of military oppression. As an early biographer shortly after the Civil War noted, "there is nothing more sublime in the acts of great magistrates that give dignity to governments, than this attempt of Chief Justice Taney to uphold the supremacy of the Constitution and the civil authority in the midst of arms." Twentieth-century scholars of the Supreme Court have concurred. In 1936, Charles W. Smith lauded Taney's "almost religious zeal for individual rights," noting that, "believing as he did in a government of law, Taney looked with abhorrence on anything that savored of military rule." Carl B. Swisher, in his 1974 *History of the Supreme Court of the United States: The Taney Period, 1836–64,* followed suit, declaring that the Merryman decision "rings clear for all who fear unnecessary expansion of executive power on the part of various military leaders."[20]

Such conclusions on the part of scholars are not entirely surprising considering the circumstances of the Merryman case, which stemmed from Lincoln's suspension of the writ of habeas corpus on April 27, 1861. Never before had a president authorized such an act. Jefferson attempted it during the infamous Burr affair in 1807, but the House of Representatives refused. With Congress not in session and Republicans in firm control when Congress did convene, Lincoln had no such difficulty. He took the authority upon himself, confident that the national legislature would sustain his decision. Arrests, of course, ensued, one of which was that of John Merryman, a Maryland citizen accused of destroying railroad bridges and preparing men to travel south and join the Confederate army. Apprehended on May 25, Merryman quickly petitioned Chief Justice Taney, on circuit as a federal district judge, for a writ of habeas corpus. The writ issued by Taney, done so as a Supreme Court justice from chambers, was promptly disobeyed by the commanding general, George Cadwalader, who cited Lincoln's order of April 27.

Taney followed with the *Ex Parte Merryman* decision, in which he denied the president's authority to suspend the writ of habeas corpus or to pass on such a power to military commanders. Taney also delivered a dissertation on the limits of military power within a constitutionally based Republic: "A military officer has no right to arrest and detain a person not subject to the rules and articles of war, for an offense against the laws of the United States, except in aid of judicial authority, and subject to its control; and if the party be arrested by the military, it is the duty of the officer to deliver him over immediately to the civil authority, to be dealt with according to law." Going still further, the chief justice declared that

> the military in this case has gone far beyond the mere suspension
> of the privilege of the writ of habeas corpus. It has, by force of arms,
> thrust aside the judicial authorities and officers to whom the constitu-
> tion has confided the power and duty of interpreting and administer-
> ing the laws, and substituted a military government in its place. . . .
> I can only say that if the authority which the constitution has con-
> fided to the judiciary department and judicial officers, may thus,
> upon any pretext or under any circumstances, be usurped by the
> military power, at its discretion, the people of the United States are
> no longer living under a government of laws, but every citizen holds
> life, liberty and property at the will and pleasure of the army officer
> in whose military district he may happen to be found.[21]

Is there any wonder why constitutional historians have championed the *Merryman* decision as the quintessential pronouncement on the supremacy of civil liberty? Taney attempted to nullify the notion that "in the midst of arms the laws are silent." Rather than acquiescing to extraordinary powers during times of national emergency, Taney discounted the authority of military rule "upon any pretext or under any circumstances."

Yet the chief justice's opinion was not always so. Appointed as lead justice on the Supreme Court in 1836 by Andrew Jackson, Taney had been loyal and obedient to the party chieftain. This was particularly evident in then–Secretary of the Treasury Taney's removal of the federal deposits from the Bank of the United States in 1833, Jackson's final blow to the besieged institution. Taney received the chief justice position, in part, for this steadfast adherence to Jackson's will. It is thus no surprise that in the midst of the 1840s congressional refund debates, Jackson would again receive Taney's support, if only as a friend through private correspondence. The means of the chief justice's support, however, do not matter. The fact is that he rendered striking opinions on the subject of military rule that ultimately ran counter to his much lauded Merryman decision.

In the spring of 1843, after Whigs had stymied the refund bill with amendments Taney wrote Jackson commiserating that treason within New Orleans "was prevented from shewing itself only by the vigor of your measures and the splendour of your victory." As for Judge Dominick Hall's issuance of the habeas writ and subsequent fine of Jackson, Taney bristled: "Future ages will be amazed that such conduct as that of Judge Hall could find defenders or apologists in this count[r]y, and how there could be any difficulty in stigmatizing the disgraceful proceeding in the manner it deserves." He concluded that Whig opposition was nothing more than blatant partisanship, remarking, "unfortunately the bitter feelings engendered by party conflicts too often render men blind to the principles of justice."[22] In the aftermath of the refund bill's passage, Taney wrote the general again, this time congratulating him on the victory and again chastising Hall's conduct as "*unjust* & in my judgement a grosser act of injustice was never perpetrated by any court, than the infliction of that fine upon you."[23]

It seems abundantly clear that Chief Justice Roger Taney supported Jackson's imposition of martial law and suspension of civilian authority. His comments to the general revolved directly around the actions that transpired as a result of military rule. "The vigor of your measures" necessarily included suspension of the writ of habeas corpus and Jackson's defiance of Hall's writ of habeas corpus. Taney rebuked Hall's "disgraceful proceedings," proceedings that included not only the contempt fine but also Hall's interference with military authority through the issuance of the writ. The chief justice, the great defender of civil liberties in *Ex Parte Merryman,* made no mention to Jackson that a "military officer has no right to arrest and detain a person not subject to the rules and articles of war," even though the general had arrested Louis Louallier, tried him by military court, then continued to detain him even after the court's ruling of innocence. Nor did Taney lament Jackson's thrusting aside of "judicial authorities" and substitution of "military government in its place." So much for the idea that military rule could not exist under "any pretext or under any circumstances." Taney was either disingenuous when writing Jackson, when there was really nothing to be gained by such an act, or *Ex Parte Merryman* reflected his own partisan motivations, the very motivation that he had accused Whigs of in the 1840s. This time, however, the stakes were much higher. Taney had already shown his defense of the South, in the *Dred Scott* decision, and thus he once again attempted to shield southerners by hampering Abraham Lincoln's war efforts. For if the president had felt constrained to obey the *Merryman* decision it would have effectively destroyed his ability to curtail internal dissent within the Union. Northern presses were certainly not remiss in recognizing Taney's thinly veiled actions. The *New York Times,* for example, noted, "too feeble to wield the sword against the Constitution, too old and palsied and weak to march in the ranks of rebellion and fight against the Union, he uses the powers of his office to serve the cause of traitors."[24]

Former Whigs and Martial Law

Democrats of the refund debate era had a particular problem when it came to martial law during the Civil War, yet they were not alone. Though former Whigs are unquestionably a more difficult lot to explain because the party ceased to exist by the time of the war, they too had some difficulties regarding former views of martial law. Of the five former Whigs who participated in the debates, only one, Robert

Cumming Schenck of Ohio, was from the North. He is also the most blatant example of Whig reversal. A newcomer to the House of Representatives in 1844, Schenck made his debut speech on the return of Jackson's fine; it was also the final speech of the House debates prior to the bill's passage. As such, the young congressman took special aim at some of the arguments posed by his Democratic opponents. "Give currency and sanction to the doctrines [of martial law] preached here," he declared, "and you have only to say that when a commander of an army gets a commission in his pocket, every other authority, and all law in the land but his unbridled will, are utterly at an end. . . . [Democrats] justify all of his [Jackson's] violence on the ground of necessity—that universal plea of tyrants." "Let us pray," insisted Schenck, that the "principle of safety and protection of all our rights may never be substituted by the unregulated caprice and arbitrary will of any man or set of men."[25] As the final speech in the House, Schenck sounded a defiant chord against military rule. This, however, was soon to change.

On June 30, 1863, acting as commander of the Middle Department, comprising Maryland and the surrounding areas, Maj. Gen. Robert C. Schenck declared martial law. In his proclamation, he stated that "the immediate presence of the rebel army within this department and in the State of Maryland requires as a military necessity a resort to all the proper and usual means of defense and security." He declared that the "suspension of the civil government . . . shall not extend beyond the necessities of the occasion." Furthermore, he warned that "traitorous and dangerous persons must expect to be dealt with as the public safety may seem to require. *'To save the country is paramount to all other considerations.'*"[26]

In the midst of a bloody war, with an enemy army pouring into Pennsylvania, Robert Schenck suddenly understood the need for martial law. It was now a "proper and usual means of defense" justified by necessity. Yet some twenty years earlier, when acting as a congressman, Schenck was outspoken in his defense of civil liberties and condemnation of martial law, scoffing that Democratic arguments of inherent necessity was "the universal plea of tyrants." Andrew Jackson had maintained that saving New Orleans was his paramount consideration. He reasserted this point in the midst of the debates, insisting "the safety of the republic became the supreme law."[27] Schenck, blinded by his Whig allegiance, brooked no tolerance for such excuses. His laments for the Constitution and civil liberty quickly faded, however, when he donned a general's uniform and faced a situation similar to Jackson's. Of Schenck's domineering command in the Middle Department, one historian noted that "the previous commands of this department had been so severe that most people were willing to believe that nothing could be worse. They would be surprised." With few restraints on his authority, Schenck engaged in wholesale arrests, shut down social and political clubs, closed newspapers and sent suspected editors south into rebel lines. "Citizens were arrested," explained a historian, "on the flimsiest of charges and held without bail or trial."[28]

General Schenck's words echoed Old Hickory's even more closely when the Union general resigned his post following his election to Congress in December, 1863. Issuing a proclamation to the citizens within his command and thanking them for their support and cooperation, Schenck declared,

> If I have succeeded at all, it has been, I am sure, only owing to the simple fact that I have been unwilling to compromise with treason in any form or expression it might assume. And if, as I am but too conscious may be the case, I have made mistakes, I have a good degree of confidence that in this community I will at least have credit for honesty of purpose in my efforts, at all times, to sustain the just authority of a great and blessed Government, whose existence has been imperiled by devilish and causeless conspiracy and insurrection.[29]

Jackson too had stressed the purity of his intentions, his refusal to bow to treason, and the existence of rampant disaffection and conspiracy within New Orleans.

After reentering the House of Representatives as a Republican member of the Thirty-eighth Congress, Schenck proved himself a zealous defender of martial law and Lincoln's suspension of the habeas corpus writ. Once again he sounded like the Hero of New Orleans: "We are, as I have stated, in the presence of the enemy. Every man in this Union is to-day, in one sense, a citizen soldier."[30] Jackson had insisted that, "the Republic being endangered, and its safety being the supreme law made all soldiers capable of bearing arms and all subject to martial law so long as it was in danger."[31] Most striking, however, were Schenck's comments concerning the sanctity of the Constitution. In 1844, he reacted passionately when Stephen Douglas declared, "I must confess that I cannot appreciate the force of the argument" when men attack Jackson "upon the ground of non-compliance with rules of court and mere technical formalities. . . . I care not whether his proceedings were legal or illegal, constitutional or unconstitutional, with or without precedent , *if they were necessary to the salvation of that city.*"[32] "Such doctrines," retorted an exasperated Schenck, "may do well enough for the meridian of St. Petersburg or Constantinople; but I take it they are rather startling to be asserted in this free country."[33] Yet when battling Democrats who upheld the inviolability of the Constitution during the Civil War, the Ohio congressman insisted,

> when gentlemen speak of such holy horror of the possibility of "over-leaping the Constitution in order to save the country," I must confess that I do not see anything so terrible in that figure. What is the Constitution? The form and framework of our system under and through which the people may carry on the Government. It is, after all, the form only, and not the life itself. . . . To those, then, who talk idly of permitting this nation to be destroyed rather than see any provision of the Constitution in the least exceeded, I say that under the pretext of saving the Constitution they are making war, or encouraging those who do make war, upon the very existence of the nation.[34]

The similarities between Schenck's and Douglas's speeches are so striking that one wonders if the Ohioan actually pulled the old refund debates to glean from his opponent's argument. In some respects Schenck's speech actually exceeded Douglas's by announcing that those who espoused the sanctity of the Constitution were traitors who were "making war" on the nation. One of the most radical of Jackson's Democratic defenders, Douglas was surpassed by the very Whig who so aggressively challenged his doctrines.

Though Schenck's reversal was absolute, not all Whigs are so easily explained. The remaining five from the refund debate era who commented on some aspect of military rule and civil liberties during the Civil War did not have a wholesale change of opinion on the subject. Rather, their opinions either shifted ever so slightly, and with a degree of discomfort, or they remained the same. Yet even in recognizing these factors, one must also understand that each case had its own peculiarities. Moreover, all of these former Whigs were southerners. Going a step further, they can be broken up into two distinct categories: border state men and those who lived within the Confederacy.

The first of the border state southerners was John Jordan Crittenden of Kentucky. Crittenden was one of those well-known Whig politicians who had ascended politically, both within his home state as well as nationally, alongside the ubiquitous Henry Clay. Crittenden and Clay were the perennial senators from Kentucky, and Crittenden, in fact, was present to participate in the congressional refund debates only because he returned to the upper chamber in order to finish out Clay's term after an 1841 resignation. As a member of the Senate Judiciary Committee and one of the first Whigs to speak on the refund bill, Crittenden was a decided departure from many of the Whigs who followed. Incorporating neither high invective nor writhing in the death throws of fated liberty, he displayed a reasoned and cool deliberation. Expressing concern over "military enthusiasm," the senator simply stated that he "could never consent to honor any man so far, to elevate any man so high, as to violate in his favor the regulations of the country, and to degrade everyone else to stand below him." He also warned that Congress "should be extremely cautious in doing an act which would degrade the judiciary of the country, or imply that the law is of little consequence." For, Crittenden explained, "the law was intended to protect the weak from the strong."[35]

Crittenden's concern for the sanctity of law did not change substantially when Civil War engulfed the nation. Nevertheless, though he certainly did not support martial law and the civilian arrests that accompanied it, Crittenden did at least come to recognize and ultimately did not rabidly oppose violations of civil liberties in times of emergency. This view, however, only materialized as the war progressed. In the immediate aftermath of the 1860 election, Crittenden was quite clear on his opposition to secession. Though a thorough-going Unionist, he nevertheless questioned the means utilized to save the country. Writing to his son Thomas in 1862, Crittenden declared, "I am inflexibly for the Union. . . . I can never subscribe to a separation of the United States." Yet devotion to the Union did not mean acquiescence to every policy that Lincoln devised to win the war. In the same letter, Crittenden insisted that the civil governments in both the states and Washington "are the primary guardians of public liberty and the Constitution." Moreover, he continued, "the case must be strong, indeed, to manifest . . . the *necessity* that would justify or excuse the military interfering with or resisting the authority of Civil government to which its rule of action is subordination." Keeping with this philosophy, Crittenden, serving once again as a Kentucky senator, wrote early on in the war to both President Lincoln and Secretary of State Seward in order to protest the widespread military arrests both in his home state and throughout the nation. Concerned that Radical Republicans threatened the very nature of the Union, in the summer of 1862 Crittenden helped organize a group of conservative congressman who ultimately proposed a resolution limiting the war to suppression of the rebellion and preservation of the Constitution.[36]

With his own family split over the war, one son served as a general in the Confederate army and the other as a general in the Union army, and as the war dragged on, with the blood letting on both sides becoming more extreme, Crittenden softened ever so slightly on his concerns over the measures necessary to win the war. He apparently came to understand that the "the case" was indeed "strong" and that the "*necessity*" existed for the "military interfering" with civil government. When friends and colleagues in Kentucky considered withdrawing their support of Lincoln because of anger regarding the Union conscription policy and the emancipation act, Crittenden dissuaded them by insisting that their duty was "to save the country first, and then turn around and save the Constitution."[37] Though Crittenden's admonition was in no way directly related to civil liberties, subsequent actions revealed that his sentiment on saving the Constitution fit the subject of violated civil liberties as well. When he received an 1863 letter from Samuel Smith Nicholas, an old friend from Kentucky and the author of an inflammatory 1842 pamphlet chastising Andrew Jackson for declaring martial law, Crittenden refused to take part in any type of protest against military usurpation. Nicholas had written to elicit support for a movement against the military in the aftermath of Clement Vallandigham's arrest in Ohio. "If we do not mean to submit without remonstrance to military despotism in permanency," he implored, "we ought to do, or rather say something in protest against tyranny." Nicholas then advised that Crittenden and a number of other senior statesmen protest Vallandigham's arrest and demand the dismissal of the military officers involved. Crittenden flatly refused, immediately telegraphing Nicholas that "*no good*" would come of it.[38]

John Crittenden was by all rights a sincere believer in the Constitution. He expressed his concern for the sanctity of law both in regards to Jackson's use of martial law as well as the Lincoln administration's suppression of civil liberties at the outset of the Civil War. Notwithstanding such views, however, the reality of the war tempered the degree to which he would strictly adhere to constitutional guidelines. It was not that Crittenden completely abandoned his earlier convictions on the subject. Rather, he seemed compelled to acquiesce on a matter of expediency in wartime. One must also not forget that Crittenden, neither during the refund debates nor during the Civil War, appeared as a partisan or extremist. He did not harangue Jackson or Lincoln as despots bent on destroying the Union. Crittenden seemed to understand that both men did what they thought was right even though he may have disagreed. It seems fairly clear that Crittenden felt discomfort with the military abusing civil authority but saw no alternative in the midst of the Civil War.

Though Crittenden refused to take part in Samuel Smith Nicholas's scheme to protest military arrests in the North, it by no means restrained Nicholas's ardor on the matter. As the only other border state southerner who had engaged the congressional refund debates, Nicholas, writing then under the pseudonym "A Kentuckian," lashed out against military rule at the hands of Andrew Jackson. "Martial law stood upon the precise same footing and none other, as lynch law, regulators law, or mob law," roared Nicholas in 1842. "For in a legal or moral sense, they all have the same precise basis. They are equally the same arbitrary usurpation of power, without a particle of law or right to sustain either." Nicholas also warned that in the future, "Generals and Senators" would quote the opinions of those who supported martial law during the refund debates.[39] When the Civil War began and Lincoln imposed martial law, Nicholas reminded the nation of his premonition by reprinting his 1842 article, "Martial Law, by a Kentuckian," to which was added a new appendix in which he announced, "It is high time our [military] officers should be informed, that so far from a President having the power to make or authorize the arbitrary arrest of a free citizen, if he were to attempt to aid in making such an arrest, the citizen would have a right to kill the President in self-defence." The extreme Nicholas added to this earlier work with the 1862 publication of *Habeas Corpus, the Law of War, and Confiscation.*[40] Both blasted away at the inviolable nature of the Constitution and the sanctity of civil liberty. And though Nicholas waved the republican banner of liberty until it was ragged, his underlying goal was a defense of slavery, as the inclusion of the word "confiscation" within his second treatise betrayed.

The defense of slavery was originally necessitated as a result of John Quincy Adams's provocative theory that during a time of war and when martial law was imposed, the president as well as a military commander possessed the authority to emancipate slaves.[41] Nicholas's 1842 pamphlet, and its reprint in 1861, was devoted directly to repudiating Adams's argument. The 1862 *Habeas Corpus* had the same goal. Nicholas began the piece by quoting then attacking Adams's speech on martial law and emancipation. The Kentuckian actually had good reason to do so. Lincoln's Emancipation Proclamation was only a little over a year away, and Gen. John C. Frémont had already revealed in an 1861 proclamation governing Confederate activists in Missouri that he deemed it within his authority to emancipate slaves.[42] Whether either Lincoln or Frémont ever read John Quincy Adams's arguments on war and emancipation is unknown, but it is evident that all three men were like-minded on the subject. It is also exceedingly clear that Samuel Smith Nicholas feared this very real possibility. He therefore attacked military abuses and emancipation.

Nicholas also attempted to increase his political effectiveness by joining the ranks of Peace Democrats. As a lone gun, he could do little to effect changes in the Lincoln administration's war policies. He therefore organized. One example was his letter to John Crittenden encouraging opposition by senior statesmen. Though he failed in this matter, Nicholas could be quite subtle and shrewd on other occasions. When military arrests first occurred at the outset of the war and were defended by Attorney General Edward Bates, Nicholas responded in the summer of 1861 with a thirty-eight-page review of the attorney general's argument in which not one mention of slavery appeared. Rather, Nicholas's piece was a surprisingly well ordered treatise on the sanctity of civil liberties and the president's lack of authority to suspend the writ of habeas corpus. He also wrote friends in Kentucky advocating a split with radicals from both North and South and suggested creating a confederacy of the Mississippi Valley states.[43] With no ringing defense of slavery or chastisement of emancipation in his response to Bates, Nicholas's writing might at first appear a stalwart defense of civil liberties. Yet one must not lose sight of timing and motivation in the Kentuckian's argument. In early 1861, the extent of secession in the South was uncertain. This was especially true in Nicholas's home state. Thus everyone, Northerners and Southerners alike, handled the border states with care. Nicholas was certainly no fool, and he, like Jefferson Davis and other Southerners, did not make the mistake of heralding slavery's defense as the focal point. Rather, they lamented the loss of liberty and the danger of tyranny at the hands of a despotic federal government.[44] By 1862, when the status of the border states was no longer a sensitive issue, the slavery-obsessed Nicholas returned to his primary focus by reprinting his *Martial Law* pamphlet and added to his disgust over military emancipation with the work on *Habeas Corpus, the Law of War, and Confiscation.*

To some extent, it appears fitting that Nicholas joined the Democratic ranks of men like Amos Kendall and William Allen. All three developed opinions on military rule in part because of their opposition to emancipation. To be sure, Nicholas, a Whig in the 1840s, attacked Jackson's use of martial law—or more correctly John Quincy Adams's manipulation of martial law—from the outset. His consistency on the matter was a self-serving defense of slavery. Kendall and Allen paid no attention to the provocative theories of Adams, whom many Democrats regarded as a cantankerous nut, and devoted themselves to Jackson's defense. It was only later, when martial law came at the hands of Lincoln, and especially for Allen, when emancipation became a policy of military rule, that the defense of civil liberties was necessary.

The remaining three Whigs from the congressional refund debate era were all Southerners who remained within the Confederacy during the Civil War. Originally opposed to secession, Alexander H. Stephens of Georgia did not fight the ordinance once it passed. Instead, he threw his support to the Confederacy. In both the 1840s and the 1860s, Stephens expressed his belief that martial law was illegal within America. On the first occasion he was a newly appointed congressional representative from Georgia, on the second, the vice-president of the Confederate States of America. Yet in both capacities, Stephens revealed a consistency on the subject of military rule within a constitutionally based Republic.

Like several other freshman congressmen, Stephens's first appearance on the national congressional stage involved Andrew Jackson's fine. And like so many of his Southern colleagues, the young Stephens paid homage to Jackson's popularity, remarking that he "detracted nothing from General Jackson, or his meritorious defense of New Orleans." Yet Stephens also focused upon the importance of maintaining the law and held up Judge Dominick Hall as a noble defender of civil authority. "The Judge deserved as much praise for his firmness in defending the laws, as the General did for defending the city," he insisted. "The judge, on that occasion, showed more moral firmness than did the General. . . . In future ages, the Judge would stand higher in the public

estimation for his defense of the laws than the General would for defending the city."⁴⁵ In addition to these very brief comments, Stephens
also proposed a last ditch amendment in the final moments before the
bill's passage in which he tried to shield Judge Hall from any implied
ccnsurc. This, of course, failed, and the congressman's only recourse
was to vote against the refund.⁴⁶

Stephens's comments on the relationship between military and
civilian authority on the occasion of the refund bill were decidedly
limited. Nonetheless, it is apparent that he believed a defense of the
civilian sphere against military encroachment was a noble and important act. When the Civil War arrived and the Confederate Congress
authorized the suspension of the writ of habeas corpus as well as the
imposition of martial law, Stephens gave a much fuller view on the
sanctity of constitutional government. Opposing his own government's
decision, Stephens denounced military rule and insisted that martial
law was illegal. After receiving a letter from James M. Calhoun, who
had recently been appointed civil governor of Atlanta by Gen. Braxton
Bragg and desired to know from the vice-president the extent of a civil
governor's authority, Stephens replied tersely, "General Bragg had no
more authority for appointing you Civil Governor of Atlanta than I
had; and I had, or have, no more authority than any street-walker in
your city." "We live under a Constitution," insisted Stephens, and "that
Constitution was made for War as well as peace. Under that Constitution we have civil laws and military laws; laws for the civil authorities and laws for the military." The separation, continued Stephens,
was very clear. The military could not legally dictate policy for the
civil government, nor could the military wantonly suppress the rights
of citizens. Perhaps most important, Vice-President Stephens refused
to accept the notion of martial law:

> In this country there is no such thing as Martial Law, and cannot
> be until the Constitution is set aside—if such an evil day shall ever
> come upon us. All the law-making power in the Confederate States
> of Government is vested in Congress. But Congress cannot declare
> Martial Law, which in its proper sense is nothing but the abrogation
> of all laws. If Congress cannot do it, much less can an officer of the
> Government, either civil or military, do it rightly, from the highest
> to the lowest. . . . I assure you, in my opinion, nothing is more essen-
> tial to the maintenance and preservation of Constitutional Liberty
> than that the Military be ever kept subordinate to Civil Authorities.⁴⁷

Here was a ringing defense of civil liberties and a refusal to accept the doctrine of martial law. Going a step further, Stephens worked with colleagues in Georgia to have the state's general assembly issue resolutions denouncing the suspension of the writ of habeas corpus.[48] What is perhaps most remarkable about Alexander Stephens's views is not only that they remained consistent from 1844 to the Civil War but actually increased in determination and clarity. Whereas so many other politicians from the refund debates had reversed their positions when confronted with the reality of war, Stephens did not. Still, some historians have questioned the degree to which Stephens and others in the South were motivated in their views of habeas corpus suspension directly as a result of their former partisan affiliations. In a study of the Confederate Congress, Thomas Alexander and Richard Beringer concluded that former party membership and, more important, one's position on secession, influenced Southern positions on suspension of the writ of habeas corpus. The authors found that Union Whigs, like Stephens, were more inclined to oppose suspension than were secession minded Democrats.[49] Historian Mark E. Neely Jr. made a similar argument: "In the Confederacy, where mostly former Democrats rather than former Whigs now ran the country, opposition to martial law and the suspension of the writ of habeas corpus came often from former Whigs."[50] As valid as these conclusions undoubtedly are, dismissing Stephens's views on martial law during the Civil War may be in error, both because of his past comments on the subject and because of the stand he took on the excesses of military and presidential authority in the midst of the Mexican War. Insisting that Congress was the only body authorized to declare war, Representative Stephens argued in 1847 that the war had commenced illegally. Speaking in metaphor, Stephens announced that "the enemy has not only entered the city, but has seized the citadel of liberty, and is fast battering down the Constitution itself." He also argued against "the charge of *treason*" for those who did not support the "Executive will," and lamented that "the oath of allegiance, at the point of a bayonet, may be administered to a mixed population" in Mexico.[51] Stephen's arguments on this occasion are not exactly analogous to those made in reference to martial law, and one could legitimately argue that these comments were merely another example of partisan rhetoric. Whigs almost universally opposed the Mexican War as a Democratic action. Still, Stephens's concerns over military power seem consistent on at least three occasions.

Alexander Stephens was not alone in remaining consistent on martial law. John Minor Botts of Virginia also maintained the anti–martial law views first expressed during the congressional refund debates. During the Civil War, however, Botts had a particularly good reason for opposing military arrest and loss of liberty. As a pro-Union Southerner, he refused to support secessionists and refused to leave his home state of Virginia. He also planned to expose what he called the "secret" Southern motivations for the war in a "tell all" book on the history of the conflict. For all of these reasons, Confederate forces arrested Botts on March 2, 1862 and, to use his own words, placed him in a "filthy negro jail" for eight weeks. During this time, authorities ransacked his home in search of the much vaunted manuscript, and ultimately removed him to another county where he remained under military supervision.[52]

When Botts originally expressed his views of martial law as imposed by Andrew Jackson, the Virginia congressman did not, like so many in the South, herald the general's victory. Rather, he railed against military abuses and charged the Democratic Party with partisan trickery in order to influence the electorate. "The conduct of General Jackson [w]as the most despotic, cruel, and tyrannical that had ever been perpetrated in any country," howled Botts, and this bill is nothing more than an attempt to "purchase the political support of General Jackson." Botts was so focused on this latter charge that he spent more than half his speech vilifying Democrats for "the imprudence of dragging this weak, if not superannuated, old man again into the political arena." Botts was so disgusted over the refund bill that he refused to comply with Virginia's resolutions calling for the return of Jackson's fine.[53]

Had John Botts never again spoken on the subject of martial law one would be inclined to dismiss much of his commentary as a mere partisan diatribe. The fact that he spent far more time pressing the issue of Democratic political machinations rather than civil liberties makes such a conclusion reasonable. Yet during the Civil War, Botts again criticized military rule, announcing that, "for the purpose of putting a padlock upon every man's mouth, and thus annihilating all freedom of speech, the Confederate Congress, on the 1st of March, 1862, suspended the writ of habeas corpus and declared martial law, thus conferring absolute and dictatorial powers on Mr. Jefferson Davis, perhaps the most unscrupulous despot that has appeared since the days of Nero."[54] The very next day Confederate forces arrested Botts, and thus it is not surprising that Davis quickly replaced Jackson, who had formerly been "the most despotic, cruel, and tyrannical." Botts complained that the Confederacy had "effectually sealed every man's lips; all were afraid to express opinions, under reign of terror and the demands of despotism that had been established in Richmond. Every man felt that his personal liberty and safety required silent submission to tyranny of the Confederacy." Even as a political prisoner, however, Botts did not submit quietly. He wrote the Confederate secretary of war, George W. Randolph, protesting that he had been "thrown in prison, without a hearing and without the privilege of counsel, under this *detestable, unwritten,* and *unknown* code called '*martial law.*'"[55]

Had Botts not been so directly affected by military rule, one might be inclined to see complete consistency in his views. Yet his abhorrence of martial law at the hands of the Confederacy stemmed at least in part from his own subjection to military arrest. Botts is therefore a difficult character. He did remain consistent on the subject, but on both occasions he was influenced by either partisan or personal motivations. To make matters even more perplexing, Botts was held in high esteem by many politicians surrounding Abraham Lincoln, and the president was encouraged that if Southerners were included in his cabinet, "the noble & gallant Botts, that every old Whig loves and the Republicans admire," would be essential. Moreover, in the midst of the war, Botts wrote Lincoln, declaring that "despite the horrors of a dungeon, [I] adhered with fidelity and tenacity to warmly cherished principles of a long life as I have done, *principles* in which I *know,* as well as I know that I exist, are inseparably involved the permanent peace, happiness, prosperity and freedom of the people of my own state as well as of the country at large."[56] Finally, at the behest of a friend, Botts wrote a detailed critique of Lincoln's policies in which he showed admiration for the president's honesty and noted that he was "indefatigable in the exercise of what he conceives to be the duties of his office." Notwithstanding such praise, Botts insisted that Lincoln had usurped the Constitution by emancipating slaves: "It is a Military right, growing out of the rebellion, if that be so, I must think it a very dangerous right, as I do not perceive any limit to its exercise, which depends solely on the will of the person who may happen to control the military at the time; and it is to say the least of it, a vagrant, rambling, unsettled & unfixed power, that would be very differently exercised by different persons who might be in a position to exercise power. . . . I confess that I do not like these unwritten & unknown and undefined laws, dependent alone on the arbitrary will of whomsoever might happen to fill the Presidential chair for the moment." Though Botts remained adamant that the Emancipation Proclamation was illegal, he acquiesced. If freeing the slaves would save the Union and its institutions, then "in the name of God let it go." Botts also insisted, "I will not quarrel about property until my own liberties, and the liberties of the people are restored to that condition of security, which we enjoyed before the rebellion." If one takes Botts's opinions to heart, he appeared a thoughtful critic of "Military right" and a sincere defender of liberty. Yet pushing matters one step further and throwing more confusion onto his views, he noted in the very same letter that, "for though I am not very certain, that if I were in his [Lincoln's] place, I would not do many things, that my own judgement might not entirely approve; we are all creatures of circumstances to a greater or less extent, and are more or less controlled by circumstances that surround us."[57]

On the one hand, John Minor Botts's consistency regarding military usurpation of civil liberties was directly connected to partisan and personal motivations, yet he also revealed an apparently thoughtful and not unreasonable view on the excesses of military authority in relation to Lincoln's presidential powers. At the same moment, Botts submitted that he too might be forced to abandon some of his libertarian convictions if he were in Lincoln's position. The Virginian's final comments may, in fact, provide the greatest insight into his views on martial law. Botts was unquestionably a "creature of circumstances." His views of military rule, though ultimately consistent, were largely formed by the situations in which he found himself.

The final Confederate who engaged martial law during both the congressional refund debates and the Civil War was William Graham of North Carolina. A Whig during the 1840s and an antisecessionist during the war, Graham's involvement in issues related to military rule was minor. As a Whig senator, he spoke to the matter on only two occasions. When the bill was originally introduced by Lewis Linn on March 10, 1842, Graham moved that it be referred to the Judiciary Committee. In February 1843, he proposed alterations to the wording of the bill, announcing that he "would not do anything to impeach the character of General Jackson, and, at the same time, nothing that would cast an imputation on Judge Hall for his conduct." True to his word, Graham moved a weak, worthless, and doomed amendment calling for a change in the bill's language. Instead of reading "A bill to indemnify Major General Andrew Jackson for the damage sustained by him in the discharge of his official duties," Graham moved to remove language that did not actually exist. He proposed that the Senate "strike from the original bill the words 'for official acts in that capacity,' and to insert the words 'an alleged contempt of court.'" Graham most likely meant to remove the statement "discharge of his official duties," intending that this would somehow connote that imposing martial law was not an official act. This meaningless suggestion was for the benefit of Whigs. Democrats were thrown a bone with the statement that Jackson's contempt was "alleged." Yet Graham's attempt to skirt the middle ground between the two parties was lame at best. In deference to Jackson, Graham also moved to change the Whig title of the bill from "relief" for General Jackson to "indemnity." The first made the old hero sound like a pauper, something at which he expressed rage. The most that can be made of Graham's "convictions" on martial law is that he was not all together opposed to military rule.[58]

Little more can be said about William Graham's views on martial law during the Civil War. He made no major declarations on the subject. Rather, his involvement was acting as legal counsel for two civilians arrested by Confederate military authorities. In one of the cases, Graham protested the military's removal of R. J. Graves from the state. Graham even introduced a resolution in the state legislature demanding Graves's return. There is little evidence that Graham expressed any more conviction on civil liberties in these cases than he did in the 1840s refund debates. One historian essentially chalked up Graham's actions as those of former Whig engaged in "political opposition to the government in Richmond."[59]

Civil War Era Politicians and the Jackson Precedent

Congressional refund debate era politicians were certainly not alone in reversing their opinions on martial law. With civil liberties threatened during the Civil War, a new generation of politicians and political commentators discussed the legality of military rule and arrived at conclusions that starkly contrasted their parties' earlier views. The Democrats survived the party reshuffle of the 1850s, and it is therefore easier to assess that party's overall shift in positions. The same is not true for Whigs, though individual members of the group can be evaluated.

Andrew Jackson's use of martial law and the subsequent congressional refund debates were a real problem for Civil War Democrats,
and Abraham Lincoln knew it. This is the very reason that he utilized
Jackson's military rule and the subsequent "approval" by Congress as
a justification for suspending the writ of habeas corpus and imposing
martial law on much of the North. Making the Democrats face the
actions of their party's chieftain as well as the precedent for which
many members of the party had expressly argued placed Democrats
in a sticky position. Yet in actuality, Lincoln merely emphasized an episode to which many politicians and commentators were already well
aware. In the aftermath of Chief Justice Roger Taney's *Ex Parte Merryman* decision, the *Illinois State Register*, based in Springfield, supported the limited use of martial law and cited Jackson's case as a precedent: "There is a great deal of reverence paid . . . at present to the old
maxim, that in the midst of war law should be silent. In a modified sense
this is true. In the presence of actual hostilities, in districts largely
infected by treason, measures of a very stringent nature may be justified by a paramount public necessity. Thus Jackson was right at New
Orleans, and it may be that martial law is essential to the peace and
loyalty of St. Louis and Baltimore."[60]

The *Register*'s support of martial law was something of an anomaly,
primarily because it was a Democratic organ and because it went against
mainstream Democratic views on civil liberty issues. As the minority
party, Democrats mounted a spirited defense against the administration's abuse of military rule. The first pamphlets came from the pen of
Samuel Smith Nicholas, the notorious Kentuckian who had criticized
martial law both in the 1840s and 1860s but did so in order to defend
slavery. Notwithstanding his motivations, Nicholas's diatribes had an
effect on subsequent authors. Reverend Robert L. Breck, for example,
a Democrat from Maysville, Kentucky, reproduced Nicholas's views.
In *The Habeas Corpus, and Martial Law*, published in the winter of
1861–62, Breck stated that martial law was "the highest treason against
the Constitution." For support of this view, he quoted large tracts from
Nicholas's pamphlets. Yet like the Kentuckian, Breck betrayed his
underlying motivation by quoting extensively from Nicholas's arguments on the emancipation theories espoused by John Quincy Adams.
The reverend ultimately concluded that the "present monstrous usurpation of power by the Executive and Military departments of the Government, are the full and complete development" of the doctrines espoused
by Adams.

Breck also wrangled with the Jackson precedent, arguing that Congress had never actually sanctioned Jackson's imposition of military rule. Rather, Breck insisted that the refund was merely "a tribute to a popular favorite, or a generous extenuation of an offense of one who had rendered eminent service to his country. It was not the judgement of Congress, or of the nation, upon the question in relation to martial law." Breck's view was entirely selective. Some Democrats had argued on the grounds of simple justice, but many had been just as clear, especially the bill's originator Lewis Linn, that passing the refund served as a message to future generals. There is no question that these Democrats meant the refund to be a precedent. The final bill was vague, however, and it therefore allowed Breck to engage in a beneficial, though disingenuous interpretation. Even a cursory reading of the long and intense refund debates divulged, especially for a Democrat, that the party meant the refund to be a justification of Jackson's conduct. Whigs certainly criticized it as such and Jackson himself was forceful in his desire for a precedent. Breck even acknowledged, though he denied its significance, that Jackson had threatened to refuse the money "unless it were understood to be an exoneration of himself."[61] Breck, quite simply, manipulated the issue.

Samuel Smith Nicholas's and Robert Breck's denunciations of martial law were actually ahead of the Democratic curve. More concentrated criticism of military rule did not come until mid-1862 and was directed in response to Philadelphia lawyer Horace Binney's pro-Lincoln pamphlet, *The Privilege of the Writ of Habeas Corpus Under the Constitution.*[62] Though Binney made no mention of the Jackson precedent, his defense of Lincoln's policies prompted a flood of responses from Democrats, many of whom either danced carefully around Jackson's actions or flatly opposed his conduct and, amazingly, quoted former Whigs to make their case.[63] John C. Bullitt, for example, a Democrat and also a Philadelphia lawyer, cited, as he described it, "a continuous stream of authority" to prove that suspension of the writ of habeas corpus was solely a legislative right. He argued that the president had no power to authorize such an act, and part of the ammunition for this argument was the opinions of Judges Xavier Martin and Pierre Derbigny of the Louisiana Supreme Court. In the 1815 *Johnson v. Duncan* case, explained Bullitt, the judges had ruled against "the legality of the martial law established by General Jackson in New Orleans during the memorable winter of 1815." Bullitt also made use of the congressional refund debates. Yet rather than follow the former arguments of his own party, Bullitt cited the 1844 speech of New York Whig Daniel D. Barnard, a man who had enraged Democrats. Based on Barnard, Bullitt determined that martial law was "a violation of the Constitution."[64]

John Bullitt was not the only Democrat who attempted to deflate the Jackson precedent. Tatlow Jackson, also from Philadelphia, published two tracts that stressed the illegality of Old Hickory's conduct. Noting that "General Jackson declared martial law in New Orleans, but seems to have been aware that he was transcending his authority," he determined that military rule was "despotic" and "unlawful." To support his arguments, he, like John Bullitt, turned to the congressional refund debates. And again like Bullitt, Tatlow Jackson used a Whig speech to make his case. The added irony, however, was that he quoted from none other than John Quincy Adams. He had, however, two diametrically opposite Adams speeches from which to choose. He of course utilized the one lambasting martial law as tyrannical. Jackson even had an answer for the discrepancy in Adams's contradictory arguments: "Mr. Adams was converted from the martial law, or despotic theory, by the very able writings of Judge Nicholas, of Kentucky." The absurdity of Tatlow Jackson's argument was paralleled only by the stereotypically negative view of a lawyer's ability to twist into a Gordian knot what was originally clear. Attorney Jackson did not, however, stop with John Quincy Adams. Also cited was the anti–martial law speech of Virginia Whig John Minor Botts. And to Tatlow Jackson's credit, he at least acknowledged the refund debate views of former Democrats Stephen Douglas and James Buchanan, but he dismissed them by scoffing, "So much for extra judicial opinions; they are, as must be all such where political feuds and alliances influence the speaker, contradictory and unsatisfactory."[65] The divorce from Democratic Party doctrine on martial law could not have been more complete.

Denunciation of martial law at the hands of Civil War era Democrats could also reveal rather intimate connections with the congressional refund debates. In the 1840s, Pennsylvania Democrat Charles Jared Ingersoll had not only introduced and championed the refund bill in the House, but wrote a detailed analysis of martial law and contempt of court.[66] Yet support for Jackson did not, apparently, run in the family. Ingersoll's son, Charles Robert, published a tract in 1862 that denounced martial law. It was no mystery why he did so. In August of that year he was the victim of military authority after criticizing the Lincoln administration at a Democratic rally. He also served as legal defense for John H. Cook, who was also arrested by the military. The young Ingersoll never had the opportunity to deliver his argument in court, so he instead opted for publication.[67] Referring to "the case of what is called General Jackson's fine," Ingersoll attempted to both rectify a Democratic error and provide an amazing revisionist history of the debates: "Time brings with it oblivion to our faults. This fine was by the way of Congress of the United States repaid . . . twenty nine years after. It was repaid by circumstances to produce the extremest sanction of Jackson's conduct which it was possible for a country to bestow: but without its occurring even to his most ardent admirers to go the length of pretending a legal justification of his act."[68]

Charles Robert Ingersoll's separation from reality could have been corrected had he merely looked at his father's defense of General Jackson, in which the congressman argued, "The blast of war stiffens the sinews to severer control, burns houses, seizes chattels, imprisons men; as danger increases, necessity keeps pace with it, till all common law may be superseded for self-preservation." "Self-defence," he insisted, "the primary law of nature, cannot be taken away by the law of society." If the elder Ingersoll's natural law theories were too complex, his son could have turned to Stephen Douglas's argument that, "in the exercise of this power, General Jackson did not violate the Constitution, nor assume to himself any authority which was not fully authorized by and legalized by his position, his duty, and the unavoidable necessity of the case."[69] Democrats certainly never viewed the refund bill as "the extremest sanction of Jackson's conduct," and many believed that it was a legal justification for martial law. Charles Robert Ingersoll had contradicted his father's and other Democratic arguments because he was not only angry over his own arrest but also hoped that the South would win the war.[70]

The Democratic reactions to Horace Binney's pro-Lincoln pamphlet came almost exclusively from commentators outside of Congress. Politicians did not engage the issue of suspending the writ of habeas corpus and imposing martial law until President Lincoln attempted to push through a bill formally suspending the writ in September 1862.[71]

The ensuing debates released a torrent of Democratic abuse. Surprisingly, the Jackson precedent went virtually untouched by both

Democrats and Republicans, even though it fit the occasion perfectly. Only one legislator mentioned Jackson's use of martial law, and he was a Democrat who cited it as a proper example of how martial law should be utilized. Garrett Davis, a pro-Union Democrat from Kentucky, insisted that "when forts, cities, and important places are beleaguered by an enemy, and there is probable cause to believe that persons are giving information or other aid to the enemy, the commander would be excusable to seize the suspected persons, and hold them in temporary confinement until the danger for the time and the occasion, the military necessity, had passed, as General Jackson acted during the investment of New Orleans by the English. But that is the *ultima thule* of military necessity."[72]

There existed considerable irony in Senator Davis supporting martial law and citing Jackson as a precedent at the same time Democratic commentators outside of Congress denounced both. Yet matters grew even more bizarre due to the fact that Davis cited John Quincy Adams of all people to prove that generals in America could declare martial law. Davis, of course, turned to Adams's speech on martial law and emancipation rather than his anti–martial law speech delivered during the refund debates. No effort was made to reconcile Adams's contradictions. That two Democrats, Tatlow Jackson and Garrett Davis, could both cite Adams to support their opposing views reveals the extent to which arguing about civil liberties became a rather tangled web of contradiction and questionable ideology. Nor did the problem stop there. Democratic senator James A. Bayard Jr. of Delaware insisted that martial law was totally illegal. In doing so, he ignored his brother's earlier refund debate arguments when they actually would have been helpful. Senator Richard H. Bayard, a Whig from Delaware, was an outspoken opponent of Jackson and martial law. The only substantial difference in the two brothers' speeches was that James and Richard belonged to opposing parties. Otherwise, their arguments were identical. In this respect, James's views were representative of many Democratic speeches denouncing martial law in 1863, any one of which could have been substituted for a Whig speech from the 1840s.[73] The party of Jackson had abandoned their former position on martial law. Inherent necessity was a thing of the past. Partisan animosity toward the Lincoln administration made sure of that.

The March 3, 1863, approval of the Habeas Corpus bill gave congressional sanction to what Lincoln had already done on numerous occasions: suspend the celebrated writ. It was really only a formality, but it no doubt set the minds of some Republicans at ease. Democrats, however, continued their opposition, and in May 1863 they organized an indignation rally in Albany, New York. Members of the rally passed a series of resolutions that were sent by Erastus Corning to President Lincoln, who responded with the famous Corning letter in which he cited Jackson's use of martial law and Congress' "approval." Not to be outdone, Democrats turned to John V. L. Pruyn, a railroad executive, former chancery lawyer, and member of the New York legislature, for a response to the president. Pruyn not only engaged in a well-written, tightly argued refutation of the administration's arrest policy but challenged Lincoln's understanding of the Jackson precedent. "You have referred to the arrest of Judge Hall, at New-Orleans, by order of General Jackson," he noted, "but that case differs widely from the case of Mr. Vallandigham. New-Orleans was then, as you truly state, under 'martial or military law.' This was not the case in Ohio, where Mr. Vallandigham was arrested. The administration of the civil law had not been disturbed in that Commonwealth."[74] Pruyn's assessment focused on the technical, or actual declaration, of martial law, which had not in fact been imposed throughout the North. Rather, Lincoln had suspended the writ of habeas corpus throughout the North. There was a slight difference, and it was on this that Pruyn seized. Yet the distinction was actually weak in light of what several commentators had previously asserted. Englishman Alexander Tytler, Jackson's counsel in New Orleans, Abner Duncan, and Attorney General Caleb Cushing had all argued that suspension of the writ and the imposition of martial law were intimately connected.[75]

If Pruyn proved vulnerable on this point, he did a better job of chipping away at other aspects of the Jackson precedent as an unassailable justification for martial law. Delivering his argument as a lesson for President Lincoln, Pruyn explained, "You seem also to have forgotten that General Jackson submitted implicitly to the judgement of the court which imposed the fine upon him; [and] that he promptly paid it." Pruyn also scoured James Parton's biography of Andrew Jackson in which the author recorded that President Madison had "'mildly but decidedly rebuked the proceedings of General Jackson,' and that the President viewed the subject with 'surprise and solicitude.'" Though this was as much as could possibly be said about Madison's treatment of the episode, Pruyn used it for all it was worth, noting, "Unlike

President Madison, you [Lincoln], in a case much more unwarranted, approve the proceedings of your subordinate officer, and in addition, justify your course by a carefully considered argument in its support."

Pruyn's greatest strategy was remaining focused on 1815. It was then that Jackson received punishment and admitted he had no authority to impose martial law. Dealing with the refund debates created problems because Democrats had steadfastly defended martial law. Pruyn nevertheless attempted to sap the debates of their meaning by acknowledging "it is true that after some thirty years, Congress, in consideration of the devoted and patriotic services of General Jackson, refunded the amount of the fine he had paid!" "But," insisted Pruyn, "the long delay in doing this proved how reluctant the American people were to do any thing which could be considered as in any way approving the disregard shown to the majesty of the law, even by one who so eminently enjoyed their confidence and regard."[76] Like so many other Democrats who mentioned the refund debates, John Pruyn engaged in selective amnesia regarding his own party's defense of Jackson and their advocacy of martial law.

How quickly Democrats could turn away from the Jackson precedent when they became the besieged minority, oppressed by Abraham Lincoln's war policies. Whereas they had once championed martial law and scoffed at Whig lamentations over endangered liberty, Civil War era Democrats now borrowed from the speeches of their former foes. Yet Democratic wailing over lost liberty was fairly short lived. After nominating Gen. George B. McClellan as their 1864 presidential hopeful, Democratic leaders repudiated the peace wing of the party and avoided the civil liberties issue at all costs. Not only did McClellan show no interest in the subject, but he was intimately connected to the 1861 military arrest of Maryland legislators and it would have looked foolish and hypocritical had he later denounced military rule. Thus when political expediency no longer required it, Democrats ceased to be the avid defenders of liberty. As one historian put it, "Democrats' opposition to military arrests of civilians during the Civil War was fairly short-lived and decidedly opportunistic."[77] It seems that little changed since politicians debated martial law in the 1840s.

Republicans did not fail to respond to Democratic attacks on martial law. Lincoln issued his Corning letter and other Republicans addressed the issue as well. Yet various factions within the president's party disagreed on the extent of martial law's power, just as some

Democrats had done during the refund debates. Joel Parker, though he justified martial law based on John Quincy Adams's 1840s speech, advocated what seemed to be a narrow application of military rule. Formerly a Whig and now a conservative Republican, Parker served as the Royal Professor of Law at Harvard University, where he offered a critical review of Roger Taney's *Ex Parte Merryman* decision: "In time of war, whether actual or domestic, there may be justifiable refusals to obey the command of the writ, without any act of Congress, or any order or authorization of the President, or any State legislation for that purpose; and the principle upon which such cases are based is, that the existence of martial law, so far as the operation of the law extends, is *ipso facto*, a suspension of the writ." Parker's opinion, though it came from the authority of a Harvard law professor, was hardly new. Alexander Tytler, Abner Duncan, and Caleb Cushing had all argued similar opinions long before Parker.[78] But the Harvard scholar added another component, one that he believed showed the restrictive nature of martial law. Focusing on the geographic extent of martial law, Parker announced "military rule and authority which exists in time of war, and is conferred by the laws of war, in relation to persons and things under and within the scope of active military operations in carrying on the war, and which extinguishes or suspends civil rights, and the remedies founded upon them, for the time being."[79] Parker's tortured legal prose translated into the belief that martial law was legal only within a military encampment or the geographical limits of an army's military operations. Thus there remained only one question regarding the *Merryman* decision: Was Fort McHenry, where John Merryman was incarcerated, within the limits of a military encampment? Parker believed that it was, and for this reason he insisted that Chief Justice Taney's writ had no authority. Just like Parker's decree on the connection between the suspension of the writ of habeas corpus and the imposition of martial law, the professor's determinations on the geographic limits of martial were nothing new. Amos Kendall had introduced the argument some twenty years earlier in his camp theory. Yet Parker viewed his judgment as a restriction on military rule. So too did the *Illinois State Register,* which described it in an October 1861 headline as "The Limited Range of Martial Law." In reality, the theory had no limitations except for those upon which a general decided, for it was the military commander who determined the extent of a camp.[80]

If Joel Parker attempted to place artificial restrictions on martial law, other Republican legal experts did not. New York lawyer Daniel Gardner upheld the unlimited use of martial law in war time and cited as proof not only Andrew Jackson but also the congressional refund debates. Gardner published two works on the subject, one of which declared that "the national and State courts have recognized the constitutional martial power of the President and his officers, in time of war, to supersede the civil code, including constitutional civil provisions to the extent of adjudged military necessities." Gardner's primary citation was the "declatory [sic] act of Congress, approving of General Jackson's declaration of martial law at New Orleans, in 1815." Gardner, like so many other Civil War era commentators, cited John Quincy Adams's early views, especially emancipation as "a war measure."[81]

Next to Abraham Lincoln, no other Republican was as connected to the issue of military rule as Secretary of State William H. Seward. He was both the author of the Habeas Corpus bill and, for a time, Lincoln's enforcer of martial law. The famed historian Frederick Bancroft wrote, "Lincoln was responsible for the suspension of the writ of *habeas corpus* and Seward for the system that developed there from."[82] Personally responsible for hundreds of arrests in the North, Seward's curtailment of civil liberties and zealous use of martial law were something of a contradiction considering that he disapproved Andrew Jackson's use of martial law. A Whig in 1828, Seward served as president for a state convention in New York that issued a formal pamphlet opposing Jackson's presidential candidacy and his past violations of civil liberties. The first resolution passed by the convention declared their support for "upholding the Constitution and securing the laws from the dangerous encroachments of misguided military ardour." Members of the meeting went on to note that Jackson's "first violation of the Constitution of his country was, unfortunately, destined to be exhibited in the arbitrary suspension of the habeas corpus (one of those privileges which form the principal distinction between a free and a despotic government)."[83] There is certainly no way to ascertain Seward's influence on this document, but the fact that he served as president of the convention provides at the very least support. It also reveals that former Whigs could reverse their positions on martial law just as easily as could the Democratic Party. The Civil War, with altered political circumstances for all involved, changed how political commentators and legislators debated the issue of civil liberties.

Partisan Motivations and Martial Law

Arguments over martial law during the Civil War reveal startling reversals from the opinions expressed during the 1840s congressional refund debates. Most striking are the abandonment of earlier views by such men as William Allen, Amos Kendall, Roger Taney, and Robert Cumming Schenck. Perhaps more amazing is the almost wholesale dismissal of the Jackson precedent by Democrats. Whereas the party had once championed the general's use of martial law as a great act of patriotism and insisted that his example would stand for future military leaders, Democrats suddenly ran from such notions. The debates were unceremoniously twisted into a reproach of Jackson's actions, and Democrats used Whig refund debate arguments to do it. They were especially fond of John Quincy Adams's doctrines on martial law and emancipation. Samuel Smith Nicholas could not have been more correct when in 1842 he warned that future legislators would latch onto Adam's arguments and use them to invoke despotism and free slaves. There is simply no other conclusion than the fact that Democrats turned their backs on Jackson and martial law. Thus there is no support for the conclusion by one Civil War historian who argued that the Democratic Party's protection of civil liberties during the war grew "out of an ideology rooted in their traditions and experiences and the perceptions developed in their past about the role and power of government, about the nature of the Constitution, and about the direction of racial and social policy within the nation."[84] The fact is that Democrats abandoned martial law.

Whigs were not much better. Though it is far more difficult to assess the party's view during the Civil War, mainly because the Whigs had disintegrated, it is no small matter that Abraham Lincoln, himself a former Whig, heralded the Jackson precedent and the congressional battle that his party lost. Changes in political circumstances could indeed have a strange effect on the defense of civil liberties and the denunciation of military rule in America. It seems particularly clear that, more often than not, partisanship outweighed ideology when it came to martial law.

CONCLUSION

N ew Orleans was a distinct beginning for Andrew Jackson. The unprecedented battle sky rocketed him to national fame. Even Henry Clay, who was soon to be one of the general's most virulent political foes, remarked as a Ghent peace commissioner that because of the victory he could travel to England with his head held high. Yet New Orleans held two distinct legacies for Old Hickory: national heroism and unprecedented despotism. No American military leader, not even the famed Washington, had achieved such a successful victory. Nor had Washington or any other general declared martial law and with it curtailed civil liberties. The two events went hand in hand. Jackson certainly believed that he could not have secured victory against such a formidable enemy without complete control of the factious population of New Orleans. Thus the Battle of New Orleans and martial law are inseparably linked. Yet as clear as this fact is, President James Madison wanted to pretend that military rule had never occurred. Rather than defending the nation's ideological convictions regarding the balance between military and civil authorities, Madison chose political expediency and thus let the matter rest. He chose to remain silent rather than confront a wildly popular national hero. Perhaps it was prudent at the time, but it promised ideological difficulties in the years to come.

It was not until Jackson made a move toward the presidency that criticism of martial law surfaced. The partisanship of a quickly evolving party system ensured rabid criticism of Jackson's conduct.

Heralding the language of republicanism, the general's detractors lamented fated liberty and warned against the power of a "military chieftain." These same cries rang throughout the halls of Congress when supporters proposed refunding Jackson's contempt fine. Arguments over martial law appeared to be a classic republican battle over the supremacy of civil authority to that of military power. What actually occurred was a partisanship that tipped the scales of ideological conviction. Democrats lauded the general's victory and insisted that he did only that which was necessary to save the nation. In the midst of the congressional refund debates, some party members even went to the extreme of discounting the Constitution's importance if it impeded Jackson's ability to safeguard New Orleans. Granted, this view was extreme and not universally held by Democrats, but the vast majority of the party supported Jackson's actions even though they violated both the nation's laws and the most cherished of ideological convictions. In order to do so, however, Democrats needed to chart a way around the ideological morass that faced them. During the 1820s, they effectively turned republicanism on its head by insisting that a military commander, traditionally the antithesis of liberty, was best suited to maintain the people's rights. During both the 1820s and 1840s, Democrats stepped around the republican conflict by focusing instead upon natural law. Doing so was a clever juxtaposition of two competing ideologies. The difficulty in accepting such professions is that Democrats went to seemingly ludicrous extremes in defense of Jackson and ultimately contradicted themselves. Not only were their arguments over contempt of court embarrassingly shallow, but some of the party faithful were contradictory when denouncing martial law in Rhode Island. More significantly, the mass of Democrats abandoned martial law and the Jackson precedent when faced with similar action on the part of Abraham Lincoln.

The answer to this wholesale reversal stems from the party's political circumstances. In the 1820s, Jackson was the man of the day and a real contender for the presidential office. In 1842, when Jackson's refund bill fell into their laps, Democrats were at the lowest point of their history. The general had not meant the legislation to be an election boon for the party, though he relished in that possibility when it arose. His focus was self-vindication and the establishment of a precedent for future military leaders should the nation once again be endangered. In this sense, Jackson's goal represented his steadfast Unionism but paradoxically threatened the very fabric of the Republic he was attempting to defend. Nevertheless, Jackson engaged in a political battle, from the first introduction of the refund bill in the Davezac letter to the bill's ultimate success, that revealed a sagacity and skill that some historians have doubted. Jackson was, quite simply, not the shallow, psychologically challenged nut he has been portrayed as. He was without question a powerful leader who held controversial views and engaged in equally controversial acts, but to dismiss him as little more than a "romanticized" figure is a gross misreading of the past.

Democrats understood the former president's political and military nationalism, his symbolic political appeal, and therefore raised the war-worn hero to their masthead. Doing so, however, required a careful manipulation of the issues. Military power had to be made acceptable in a nation obsessed with threats to liberty.

For their part, Whigs too engaged in partisan strategizing. Andrew Jackson polarized men and parties. Opposition to "King Andrew I" was the raison d'être of the Whig Party, the very reason they came into being. After finally achieving presidential victory in 1840, even though it was short lived with the death of William Henry Harrison, they did not relish the possibility of losing power to Democrats. When the refund bill surfaced in 1842, Whigs spied an issue that could bring their great nemesis back into the political arena and potentially vault his party to the head of government. Whigs therefore attempted to kill the legislation. Yet rather than extinguishing a Democratic fire, Whigs actually fanned it into a blaze. Many attempted to win the fight by decrying Jackson's destruction of liberty and the Constitution. Yet not all members of the party bought into this argument, splitting into northern and southern wings. The latter, for the most part, accepted Jackson's use of martial law. His popularity had always been immense in the South, where he had been the great defender against the British and Indians. It is no wonder that southern Whigs, many of whom had formerly been Democrats, failed to bemoan the tragedy to liberty. Many saw no dire threat to republicanism. Northern Whigs, however, always the general's staunchest foes, wailed over his destruction of the civilian sphere and refused to acknowledge the immense danger that faced New Orleans. Yet much of their argument was driven by partisan and at times personal animosity. John Quincy Adams certainly showed the extremes to which he could go in hatred of Jackson. Other members of the party, such as Daniel Barnard, also revealed that past battles with President Jackson shaped their views of the refund issue. Most Whigs simply wanted to deny Democrats an item that would aid their possible return to political power. Opposition to Jackson and his party was more of a driving force for Whigs than were ideological convictions concerning liberty. They certainly did not rise to the floor of Congress and denounce martial law when it appeared in Rhode Island. And twenty years later, when the Civil War bled the nation, former Whigs suddenly became lovers of military rule. Abraham Lincoln, himself a former Whig, actually heralded the Jackson precedent and Congress' "approval." Robert Cumming Schenck, a diehard opponent during the refund debates, became a Union general and imposed martial law. His decrees sounded remarkably like Andrew Jackson's.

The evolution of the second American party system with its carefully orchestrated political maneuverings engendered a rampant partisanship that often outweighed ideology. This is not to say that all conviction disappeared. Yet Democrats and Whigs, both of whom formed directly around the mighty Jackson, fought so fiercely over this general from the backwoods of South Carolina that they often went to extremes. In this Age of Party, battling over Jackson was often more important than policy or issues. In a strange way, devotion to or hatred of Old Hickory became an ideology of its own.

NOTES

INTRODUCTION

1. The original letter to Davezac was published in the Washington-based *Democratic Globe*. See "General Jackson's Fine," *Daily Globe*, Mar. 12, 1842. A Creole from Santo Domingo, Davezac served as a major in the New Orleans militia and acted as aide and judge advocate for Jackson during the occupation of the city. Upon becoming president, Jackson appointed Davezac secretary of legation to the Hague in 1829, chargé d'affaires to the Netherlands in 1831, and special diplomatic agent to the Two Sicilies in 1833. "Major Davezac," *United States Magazine and Democratic Review* 16 (1845): 110; Dumas Malone, ed., *Dictionary of American Biography*, vol. 5 (New York: Scribner, 1930), vol. 5: 89.

2. For Jackson's ill health, see Robert V. Remini, *Andrew Jackson: The Course of American Democracy* (New York: Harper & Row, 1984), 524; Robert V. Remini, "The Final Days and Hours in the Life of Andrew Jackson," *Tennessee Historical Quarterly* 39, no. 2 (1980): 167–77; and Ludwig M. Deppisch, "Andrew Jackson and American Medical Practice: Old Hickory and his Physicians," *Tennessee Historical Quarterly* 62, no. 2 (Summer 2003): 130–51.

3. "Andrew Jackson and Judge D. A. Hall, Report of the Committee of the Senate (Of the State of Louisiana, 1843)," *Louisiana Historical Quarterly* 5 (1922): 509–70.

4. "General Jackson's Fine." This was not the first occasion Jackson had mentioned the fine. In an 1839 letter to his nephew, Andrew Jackson Donelson, the general complained that he could not attend the annual Battle of New

Orleans celebration held in Louisiana due to insufficient funds, adding, "I have sacrificed both property and health in the salvation of Neworleans, paid $1000 fine and costs, and the Legislature thereof has never attempted to have that unjust sentence removed by resolutions and memorial to congress to have the fine and costs restored to me with interest." Andrew Jackson to Andrew Donelson, Dec. 10, 1839, in *Correspondence of Andrew Jackson*, vol. 6, ed. John Spencer Bassett (Washington, D.C.: Carnegie Institute, 1903), 41–42 (hereafter cited as *Correspondence of Andrew Jackson*).

5. "Major Davezac," 110. The New York House of Representatives passed a resolution on February 2, 1842, requesting their representatives and senators to procure the passage of a refund bill. See *Niles Weekly Register* 61 (Feb. 12, 1842): 384. John Quincy Adams did not miss the connection between the bill proposed in the Senate and that put forth in New York, noting in his diary that "this is a crumb of political swindling, got up by Davezac, a profligate French Creole of New Orleans, now commorant in the city of New York and disgracing it as one of its representatives in the State Legislature." Charles Adams, ed., *Memoirs of John Quincy Adams* (New York: AMS Press, 1970), 11:244. Congressman William Gwin also acknowledged that Davezac was "the prime mover on this subject." See House, Congressman Gwin of Mississippi on General Jackson's Fine, *Congressional Globe*, 27th Cong., 3d sess., Jan. 5, 1843, 12:123. Senator Lewis Linn's involvement in the congressional refund movement is discussed in detail in chapter 3, this volume. Senator Benjamin Tappan of Ohio also prepared a bill to refund the money and even noted that he had hoped to be first (see chapter 3).

6. This is a recurrent theme in Robert V. Remini's works, though it is perhaps most concisely argued in his first, one-volume biography, *Andrew Jackson* (1966; reprint, New York: Harper Collins, 1999). See also Robert V. Remini's three-volume biography: *Andrew Jackson: The Course of American Empire* (New York: Harper & Row, 1977), *Andrew Jackson: The Course of American Freedom* (New York: Harper & Row, 1981), and *Andrew Jackson: The Course of American Democracy*.

7. Andrew Burstein, *The Passions of Andrew Jackson* (New York: Knopf, 2003), 234, 240, 231, 237, 233. For other historians' views on Remini, see Donald B. Cole, "Honoring Andrew Jackson Before All Living Men," *Reviews in American History* 13 (Sept. 1985): 359–66; and Douglas R. Egerton, "An Update on Jacksonian Historiography: The Biographies," *Tennessee Historical Quarterly* 46 (1987): 79–85.

8. James C. Curtis, *Andrew Jackson and the Search for Vindication* (New York: Harper Collins, 1976.) At the same time Curtis worked on his psychological portrait of Jackson, Michael Paul Rogin, *Fathers and Children: Andrew Jackson and the Subjugation of the American Indian* (New York: Alfred Knopf, 1975), worked on a similar interpretation. Curtis read Rogin's manuscript prior to its publication and specifically thanks Rogin for this courtesy in the author's preface (xi). For more on the connection

between Curtis and Burstein, see Matthew Warshauer, "A Review Essay on Burstein, *The Passions of Andrew Jackson*," *Tennessee Historical Quarterly* 58 (Winter 2003): 366–72. What is particularly interesting about Curtis's book is that at the time of publication, a number of historians scoffed at his method and conclusions, yet more recent historians have seemed to embrace his "truths." One reviewer, for example, noted, "I genuinely do not mean to be unkind to Professor Curtis, but he has written a biography of Jackson which has little to commend it to the world of scholarship. . . . In short, the author has attempted psychohistory and retrospective analysis of motivation. This is dangerous ground for an historian, for whatever statement is made from this kind of approach must, necessarily, be in the nature of assumption. It is not susceptible to historical proof." See Sam B. Smith, "Review of *Andrew Jackson and the Search for Vindication*," *Tennessee Historical Quarterly* 36 (Spring 1977): 112–14. Charles M. Wiltse wrote that "as interpretive history . . . [Curtis's book] transcends its premises" and that the author was "not always successful [in his] effort to assign motives." See "Review of *Andrew Jackson and the Search for Vindication*," *American Historical Review* 82 (June 1977): 743–44. Another reviewer noted, "Perhaps the thesis has merit; but this book, lacking no documentation, merely asserts the argument instead of proving it." See "Review of *Andrew Jackson and the Search for Vindication*," *Choice* 13 (Mar.–Sept. 1976): 582. To be fair, a number of scholars commended the work. See John D. Haeger, "Review of *Andrew Jackson and the Search for Vindication*," *History Teacher* 10 (Nov. 1976): 144–45; and Nathan Miller, "Review of *Andrew Jackson and the Search for Vindication*," *Wisconsin Magazine of History* 60 (Winter 1976): 166–68. A number of reviews were mixed, asserting that Curtis's work offered new insights though his psychoanalytical techniques were questionable. See Edward Pessen, "Review of *Andrew Jackson and the Search for Vindication*," *New York History* 59 (1978): 80–82; Richard P. McCormick, "Review of *Andrew Jackson and the Search for Vindication*," *Journal of American History* 64 (June–Sept. 1977): 143–44; and William J. Gilmore, "Review of *Andrew Jackson and the Search for Vindication*," *Journal of Southern History* 42 (1976): 589–91.

9. Donald B. Cole, *The Presidency of Andrew Jackson* (Lawrence: Univ. Press of Kansas, 1993), x; John F. Marszalek, *The Petticoat Affair: Manners, Mutiny, and Sex in Andrew Jackson's White House* (New York: Free Press, 1997), 13. See, especially, chapter 1 of the present volume. For an additional example of Jackson as the product of his orphaned youth, see David S. Heidler and Jeanne T. Heidler, *Old Hickory's War: Andrew Jackson and the Quest for Empire* (Mechanicsburg, Pa.: Stackpole Books, 1996), 18–19.

10. Andrew Jackson to Samuel Swartwout, Mar. 25, 1824, in *The Papers of Andrew Jackson*, vol. 5, ed. Harold Moser et al. (Knoxville: Univ. of Tennessee Press, 1996), 381 (hereafter cited as *Papers of Andrew Jackson*).

11. See Andrew Jackson to Louis F. Linn, Mar. 12, 1842, *Correspondence of Andrew Jackson* 6:144. Jackson expressed the same sentiment in other letters. See Andrew Jackson to Lewis Linn, July 4, 1842, and Andrew Jackson

to Francis Blair, July 2, Oct. 29, 1842, and Feb. 20, 1843, all in *The Papers of Andrew Jackson,* Library of Congress microfilm edition (hereafter cited as *Jackson Papers,* LC).

12. Bernard Bailyn, *The Ideological Origins of the American Revolution* (1967; reprint, Cambridge, Mass.: Belknap Press, 1992), xiii, 43, 55, 56. Bailyn also insisted that the colonists' concerns over liberty and power were sincere beliefs. At its most fundamental level, republicanism identifies the system of government constructed by colonists in the aftermath of the Revolution. Differing from the common structure of governments found throughout Europe, a republic is a country without a king or some other form of monarchical, aristocratic rule. Americans established their system on a representational basis in which citizens participated in a limited capacity by electing representatives to nonhereditary offices. Citizens were then expected to support the society's leaders, deferring to their expertise, moral virtue, and promise of custodianship. In Federalist 39, James Madison defined a republic as "a government which derives all its powers directly or indirectly from the great body of the people; and is administered by persons holding their offices during pleasure, for a limited period of time, or during good behavior." James E. Cooke, ed., *The Federalist* (Middletown, Conn.: Wesleyan Univ. Press, 1961), 251.

13. For a good account of the Revolutionary generation's fear of the military, see Lois G. Schwoerer, *"No Standing Armies!": The Antiarmy Ideology in Seventeenth Century England* (Baltimore: Johns Hopkins Univ. Press, 1974), 195–200; Reginald C. Stuart, "'Engines of Tyranny': Recent Historiography on Standing Armies During the Era of the American Revolution," *Canadian Journal of History* 19 (1984): 182–99; and Bernard Bailyn, *The Origin of American Politics* (New York: Vintage Books, 1976). Jackson's supporters heralded the fact that he led a yeoman army; see John William Ward, *Andrew Jackson: Symbol for an Age* (New York: Oxford Univ. Press, 1953).

14. Some twenty-two states between 1776 and 1844 included articles declaring that the military shall remain subordinate to civil authority. See William F. Swindler, ed., *Sources and Documents of the United States Constitutions,* 11 vols. (Dobbs Ferry, N.Y.: Oceana Publications, 1973–79).

15. This issue is discussed in detail in chapter 1, this volume.

16. Lynn Hudson Parsons, *John Quincy Adams* (Madison, Wisc.: Madison House, 1998), 140–44; William Weeks, "John Quincy Adams's 'Great Gun' and the Rhetoric of American Empire," *Diplomatic History* 14 (Winter 1990): 25–42; James Chace and Caleb Carr, "The Odd Couple Who Won Florida and Half the West," *Smithsonian* 19 (Apr. 1988): 34–160; Philip Coolidge Brooks, *Diplomacy in the Borderlands: The Adams-Onis Treaty of 1819* (1939; reprint, New York: Octagon Books, 1970), 148–50; Remini, *Andrew Jackson: The Course of American Empire,* 367–77.

17. Frances Norene Ahl, *Andrew Jackson and the Constitution* (Boston: Christopher Publishing House, 1939), 80. For more on the Jefferson birthday celebration, see Remini, *Andrew Jackson: The Course of American Freedom,* 235. Richard E. Ellis raises questions concerning Jackson's lack of consistency on Union versus states' rights in his work *The Union at Risk:*

Jacksonian Democracy, States' Rights and the Nullification Crisis (New York: Oxford Univ. Press, 1987).

18. Leonard W. Levy, *Jefferson and Civil Liberties: The Darker Side* (Chicago: Ivan Dee Publishers, 1989), 22.

19. Andrew Jackson, "Farewell Address," in *Andrew Jackson versus Henry Clay: Democracy and Development in Antebellum America*, ed. Harry L. Watson (New York: Bedford, 1998), 238–50. Jackson bequeathed other swords, always with the same message. Jackson told the son of his long-time friend Gen. John Coffee to "wield it in the protection of the rights secured to the American citizens under our glorious constitution against all invaders whether foreign foes, or intestine traitors." He told his grand-son, Andrew Jackson III, to "always use it in defense of the constitution and our glorious Union and the perpetuation of our republican system, remembering the motto 'draw me not without occasion nor sheath me with-out honor.'" See "Jackson's Will, 7 June 1843," *Correspondence of Andrew Jackson* 6:221–22.

20. Ward, *Andrew Jackson*, 5,6.

21. For a further discussion of this point, see Matthew S. Warshauer, "Ridi-culing the Dead: Andrew Jackson and Connecticut Newspapers," *Connec-ticut History* 40, no. 1 (Spring 2001): 13–31.

22. Michael F. Holt, *The Political Crisis of the 1850s* (New York: W. W. Norton, 1978), 23.

23. For more on the campaign of 1840, see Robert G. Gunderson, *The Log Cabin Campaign* (Lexington: Univ. Press of Kentucky, 1957). For more on party formation, see Richard P. McCormick, *The Second American Party System: Party Formation in the Jacksonian Era* (Chapel Hill: Univ. of North Caro-lina Press, 1966.

24. Holt, *Political Crisis of the 1850s*, 42. Holt also makes the point that Jackson's retirement hurt the Democrats. A. Vandapell to Martin Van Buren, Apr. 13, 1844, in *Slavery and the American West: The Eclipse of Manifest Destiny and the Coming of the Civil War*, by Michael A. Morrison (Chapel Hill: Univ. of North Carolina Press, 1997), 26. Morrison provides a number of additional sources on the Democratic Party's problems.

25. Francis Preston Blair to Andrew Jackson, June 30,1842, *Jackson Papers*, LC. Blair and Jackson repeatedly referred to Whigs as Federalists, a name that was linked to elitism and, during the War of 1812, traitorous activity.

26. The citations for the many articles are too numerous to include. See the *Daily Globe* from March 12, 1842, to February 16, 1844, and the *National Intelligencer* for the same period. The *Globe* also included articles from the *Madisonian* as well as several Louisiana newspapers, including the *Planters' Advocate*, the *Plaquemine Planters' Gazette*, and the *New Orleans Herald*. Other newspapers throughout the nation undoubtedly followed the congres-sional debates.

27. Congressman William Gwin acknowledged that Davezac was "the prime mover on this subject." See House, Congressman Gwin of Mississippi on General Jackson's Fine, Jan. 5, 1843, 12:123. Resolutions and memorials in the House of Representatives, all in *House Journal*, 27th Cong., 2d sess.,

vol. 37: Congressman Medill of Ohio, Mar. 14, 1842, 534; Congressman Mathiot of Ohio, 541; Congressmen Brown and Keim of Pennsylvania, 534–35; and Congressman Ingersoll of Pennsylvania, 540; all in *House Journal*, 27th Cong., 3d sess.: Congressman Pickens of South Carolina, Dec. 29, 1842, 111; Congressman Cranston of Rhode Island, Jan. 24, 1843, 251; Congressman Littlefield of Maine, Feb. 1, 1843, 290; Congressman Ingersoll of Pennsylvania, Feb. 13, 1843, 355; and Congressman Cooper of Georgia, Mar. 1, 1843, 499; all in *House Journal*, 28th Cong., 1st sess.: Congressman Hale of New Hampshire, Dec. 16, 1843, 62; Congressman Slidell of Louisiana, Dec. 29, 1843, 138; Congressman Bidlack of Pennsylvania, Jan. 13, 1844, 224; Congressman Strong of New York, Jan. 22, 1844, 277; and Congressman Lyon of Michigan, Jan. 29, 1844, 320. Resolutions and memorials in the Senate, all in *Senate Journal*, 27th Cong., 2d sess.: Senator Buchanan of Pennsylvania, Mar. 11, 1842, 217; Senator Sturgeon of Pennsylvania, Mar. 11, 1842, 217; Senator Buchanan of Pennsylvania, Mar. 14, 1842, 220, and Mar. 16, 1842, 226; Senator Tappan of Ohio, Mar. 21, 1842, 233; Senator Buchanan of Pennsylvania, Apr. 9, 1842, 282; Senator Wright of New York, May 18, 1842, 348; all in *Senate Journal*, 27th Cong., 3d sess.: Dec. 19, 1842, 34; Senator Buchanan of Pennsylvania, Dec. 20, 1842, 49; Senator Smith of Connecticut, Jan. 3, 1843, 66; Senator Calhoun of South Carolina, Jan. 4, 1843, 72; Senator McRoberts of Illinois, Jan. 6, 1843, 78. Instructions from Arkansas, Jan. 9, 1843, 82; Senator Williams of Maine, Jan. 31, 1843, 138; Senator Sturgeon of Pennsylvania, March 11, 1842; Senator Linn of Missouri, Feb. 25, 1843, 218; all in *Senate Journal*, 28th Cong., 1st sess.: Senator Woodbury of New Hampshire, Dec. 5, 1843, 7; Senator Sturgeon of Pennsylvania, Jan. 16, 1844, 73; Senator Wright of New York, Jan. 19, 1844, 78; and Senator White of Indiana, Jan. 23, 1844, 84. At least one territory also debated sending a resolution. See David C. Mott, "Iowa Territory and General Jackson's Fine," *Annals of Iowa* 16 (July 1927): 58–64; and *Niles Weekly Register* 28, no. 63 (Jan. 1843): 352.

28. Thomas Brown, "From Old Hickory to Sly Fox: The Routinization of Charisma in the Early Democratic Party," *Journal of the Early Republic* 11, no. 3 (Fall 1991): 339–69. Brown further hints at my notion of Jackson as both a symbol and antisymbol, noting, "Even in their choice of a name, the Whigs paid tribute to how Jackson's personality and actions defined the issues of his time." For more on electioneering and symbolic devices related to Jackson, see Robert V. Remini, *The Election of Andrew Jackson* (Philadelphia: Lippincott, 1963). Holt, *Political Crisis of the 1850s*, 36.

29. Remini, *Andrew Jackson: The Course of American Freedom*, 78; Harry L. Watson, *Liberty and Power: The Politics of Jacksonian America* (New York: Noonday, 1990), 170. Two articles have also investigated republicanism within the Jacksonian era. Maj. L. Wilson, "Republicanism and the Idea of Party in the Jacksonian Period," *Journal of the Early Republic* 8 (Winter 1988): 419–41, focused primarily on antiparty sentiment within republican ideology in an attempt to explain the extent of party modernization within the period. Wilson argued that both Democrats and Whigs revealed aspects of republican beliefs in their attitudes toward parties and concluded that

"party spokesman used the language of republicanism to make sense of the rapidly changing world around them, and our understanding of the period must therefore take seriously the effort they made." Wilson also noted that "it might appear, the actual operation of the party system belied the republican claims on either side." Marc W. Kruman, "The Second American Party System and the Transformation of Revolutionary Republicanism," *Journal of the Early Republic* 12 (Winter 1992): 509–37, concluded that politicians recast republicanism into an ideology that "nourished partisanship." He argued further that "elections thus became surrogate battles to preserve republican government, as each party fought valiantly to save the republic from its iniquitous foe." Other historians have also considered the intersection between ideology and partisanship. Thomas Brown, *Politics and Statesmanship: Essays on the American Whig* (New York: Columbia Univ. Press, 1985), 8–12, questioned, "Could the men who were attracted into such institutions [parties] be independent and principled public servants? Would they not more likely be irresponsible spoilsmen and demagogues who were willing to go to any length to ensure the party (and themselves) success?" Brown concluded that statesmen, as opposed to politicians, were able to escape the traps of partisanship and retain their ideals. The statesmen, he insisted, were mostly Whigs. Marszalek, *Petticoat Affair*, 19, noted, "The Party system was born with a vengeance. . . . Party efforts revolved around electing candidates more than implementing ideology. Consequently, the era saw the birth of the politics of personality."

30. See, for example, Holt, *Political Crisis of the 1850s;* J. Mills Thornton, *Politics and Power in a Slave Society: Alabama, 1800–1860* (Baton Rouge: Louisiana State Univ. Press, 1978); and William E. Gienapp, *The Origins of the Republican Party, 1852–1856* (New York: Oxford Univ. Press, 1987).

31. Morrison, *Slavery and the American West*, 170, 7. In explaining how secessionists convinced Southern yeoman to fight, Morrison notes that "ambition" played a role and that "to insist that principles alone motivated them strains credulity" (254).

32. Holt, *Political Crisis of the 1850s*, 184.

33. Jean H. Baker, *Affairs of Party* (Ithaca, N.Y.: Cornell Univ. Press, 1983), 148, 151; Joel H. Silbey, *A Respectable Minority: The Democratic Party in the Civil War Era, 1860–1868* (New York: Norton, 1977), 70.

34. Abraham Lincoln to Erastus Corning and others, June 12, 1863, in *Collected Works of Abraham Lincoln*, vol. 6, ed. Roy P. Basler et al. (New Brunswick, N.J.: Rutgers Univ. Press, 1953–55), 268–69.

35. Few historians have discussed and none have investigated adequately Jackson's use of martial law. True, Old Hickory's chief modern biographer, Robert V. Remini, called the imposition of military rule and arrest of civilians "lunatic militarism," declaring that "Jackson established a police state with no other authority but his own" and that he "behaved in a highhanded, bizarre, and dangerous manner." Specifics of the "police state" were, nevertheless, absent from Remini's work. Moreover, Remini's chapter titled "The United States vs. Andrew Jackson," the title of the

court case, discussed the events leading up to Louaillier's and Hall's arrests rather than a detailed analysis of the court case, as the chapter title would seem to indicate. See Remini, *Andrew Jackson: The Course of American Empire*, 311–12. Remini's most recent work on the New Orleans victory barely mentions martial law. See Robert V. Remini, *The Battle of New Orleans: Andrew Jackson and America's First Military Victory* (New York: Viking Press, 1999). Even the best account of martial law, written by James Parton in 1861, failed to detail the numerous arrests, destruction of private property, or the court case with Judge Hall. See James Parton, *The Life of Andrew Jackson* (New York: Mason Brothers, 1861), 2:317. Many historians have retold Jackson's stupendous victory. See for example, Alexander Walker, *Jackson and New Orleans* (New York: J. C. Derby, 1856); John S. Jenkins, *The Life and Public Services of General Andrew Jackson* (New York: G. H. Derby, 1856); John Spencer Bassett, *The Life of Andrew Jackson* (New York: Macmillan, 1931); Marquis James, *Andrew Jackson: The Border Captain* (New York: Bobbs-Merrill, 1940); William Graham Sumner, *The Life and Times of Andrew Jackson: Soldier, Statesman, President* (New York: Houghton, Mifflin, 1882); Charles B. Brooks, *The Siege of New Orleans* (Seattle: Univ. of Washington Press, 1961); Donald Barr Chidsey, *The Battle of New Orleans* (New York: Crown, 1961); Samuel Carter III, *Blaze of Glory: The Fight for New Orleans, 1814–1815* (New York: St. Martin's Press, 1971); Robin Reilly, *The British at the Gates: The New Orleans Campaign in the War of 1812* (New York: Putnam, 1974); and Thomas Fleming, "Old Hickory's Finest Hour," *Military Historical Quarterly* 13 (2001): 6–17.

36. Some works on this subject do exist, though more needs to be done to connect military rule with nationalism and politics. See William E. Birkheimer, *Military Government and Martial Law* (Kansas City, Mo.: F. Hudson, 1904); Cassius M. Dowell, *Military Aid to the Civil Power* (Fort Leavenworth, Kans.: General Service School Press, 1925); Robert S. Rankin, *When Civil Law Fails: Martial Law and Its Legal Basis in the United States* (Durham, N.C.: Duke Univ. Press, 1939); Bennett Rich, *The President and Civil Disorder* (Washington, D.C.: Brookings Institute, 1941); Nathan D. Grundstein, *Presidential Delegation of Authority in Wartime* (Pittsburgh: Univ. of Pittsburgh Press, 1961); Jerry M. Cooper, *The Army and Civil Disorder* (Westport, Conn.: Greenwood Press, 1980); Merle T. Cole, "Martial Law in West Virginia and Major Davis as Emperor of the Tug River," *West Virginia History* 43 (Winter 1982): 125–36; Louis Fisher, *Presidential War Powers* (Lawrence: Univ. Press of Kansas, 1995); William H. Rehnquist, *All the Laws but One: Civil Liberties in Wartime* (New York: Knopf, 1998); Edward Berman, *Labor Disputes and the President of the United States* (New York: AMS Press, 1968); Harold C. Relyea, *National Emergency Powers: A Brief Overview of Presidential Suspensions of the Habeas Corpus Privilege and Invocations of Martial Law* (Washington, D.C.: Congressional Research Service, 1976); and Paul L. Murphy, *World War I and the Origin of Civil Liberties in the United States* (New York: W. W. Norton, 1979).

37. See, for example, the round table discussion, "Alternatives to the Party System in the 'Party Period,' 1830–1890," *Journal of American History* 86 (June 1999): Ronald Formisano, "The 'Party Period' Revisited," 93–120; Mark Voss-Hubbard, "The 'Third Party Tradition' Reconsidered: Third Parties and American Public Life, 1830–1900," 121–50; Michael F. Holt, "The Primacy of Party Reasserted," 151–57; and Paula Baker, "The Midlife Crisis of the New Political History," 158–66. See also William G. Shade, "Political Pluralism and Party Development: The Creation of a Modern Party System, 1815–1852," in *The Evolution of American Electoral Systems*, ed. Paul Kleppner et al. (Westport, Conn.: Greenwood Press, 1981), 77–111; Richard L. McCormick, *The Party Period and Public Policy: American Politics from the Age of Jackson to the Progressive Era* (New York: Oxford Univ. Press, 1986); Kruman, "Second American Party System"; and Gerald Leonard, *The Invention of Party Politics: Federalism, Popular Sovereignty, and Constitutional Development in Jacksonian Illinois* (Chapel Hill: Univ. of North Carolina Press, 2002).

38. Holt, *Political Crisis of the 1850s*.

39. Mark E. Neely Jr., *The Fate of Liberty: Abraham Lincoln and Civil Liberties* (New York: Oxford Univ. Press, 1991); Robert H. Jackson, *The Struggle for Judicial Supremacy: A Study of Crisis in American Power Politics* (New York: Vintage Books, 1941); Leonard Baker, *Back to Back: The Duel Between FDR and the Supreme Court* (New York: Macmillan, 1967); Robert Smith Thompson, *A Time for War: Franklin Delano Roosevelt and the Path to Pearl Harbor* (New York: Prentice-Hall, 1991); Robert B. Stinnett, *Day of Deceit: The Truth About FDR and Pearl Harbor* (New York: Free Press, 2000); Ivo H. Daalder, *America Unbound: The Bush Revolution in Foreign Policy* (Washington, D.C.: Brookings Institution, 2003); David Frum, *The Right Man: The Surprise Presidency of George W. Bush* (New York: Random House, 2003).

CHAPTER 1

1. Jackson reported to President Monroe that some 1,800 British soldiers were killed and wounded and another 400 were taken prisoner. The British reported 1,553 killed and 484 wounded. See Remini, *Battle of New Orleans*, 167.

2. Ward, *Andrew Jackson*.

3. William C. C. Claiborne to Andrew Jackson, Aug. 12, 1814, in *The Papers of Andrew Jackson*, vol. 3, ed. Harold Moser, Sharon McPherson, et al. (Knoxville: Univ. of Tennessee Press, 1991), 115–16 (hereafter cited as *Jackson Papers*). See also Claiborne to Jackson, a letter dated August 21, 1814, in which he states that he "strongly suspect, that some Spanish or English agent has made injurious impressions on the minds of these people." Claiborne's concerns were also expressed in a letter dated August 8, 1814; for both letters, see *Correspondence of Andrew Jackson* 6:437, 434. For an excellent account of foreign discontent, see Tom Kanon, "The Other Battle

of New Orleans: Andrew Jackson and the Louisianans," *Gulf South Historical Review* 2d ser., 10 (Spring 2002): 41–61.

4. William C. C. Claiborne to Andrew Jackson, Sept. 8, 1814, *Correspondence of Andrews Jackson* 6:438. By October, Claiborne's fears over disaffection had lessened. See William C. C. Claiborne to Eligius Fromentin, Oct. 24, 1814, in *The Official Letter Books of William C. C. Claiborne,* ed. Rowland Dunbar (Jackson, Miss.: State Department of Archives, 1917), 6:285 (hereafter cited as *Official Letter Books*); William C. C. Claiborne to James Monroe, Oct. 24, 1814, *Official Letter Books* 6:287; and William C. C. Claiborne to Andrew Jackson, Nov. 5, 16, 1814, *Correspondence of Andrew Jackson,* ed. John Spencer Bassett (Wash, D.C.: Carnegie Institution of Washington, 1927), vol. 2:100. For complaint against Claiborne, see Col. Samuel Fulton to Andrew Jackson, Sept. 20, 1814, *Correspondence of Andrew Jackson* 2:56; For additional complaints of disaffection, see Committee of Safety to Jackson, Sept. 18, 1814, *Correspondence of Andrew Jackson* 2:51–54; Edward Livingston to Andrew Jackson, Nov. 5, 1814, *Correspondence of Andrew Jackson* 2:90–91; on "vigilance," see Andrew Jackson to William C. C. Claiborne, Aug. 30, 1814, *Jackson Papers* 3:126.

5. There are a number of good works on the Burr conspiracy. See Melton F. Buckler, *Aaron Burr: Conspiracy to Treason* (New York: Wiley, 2002); Levy, *Jefferson and Civil Liberties;* and Thomas Perkins Abernathy, *The Burr Conspiracy* (New York: Oxford Univ. Press, 1954). *Ex parte Bollman and Swartwout,* 8 U.S. 75; 2 L. Ed. 554; 4 Cranch 75.

6. Andrew Jackson to William C. C. Claiborne, Dec. 10, 1814, *Jackson Papers* 3:202–3; Resolution of the Senate and House of Louisiana, Dec. 14, 1814, *Jackson Papers,* LC; Bassett, *Life of Andrew Jackson,* 173; Parton, *Life of Andrew Jackson* 2:61.

7. For concerns over Pensacola, see William C. C Claiborne to Andrew Jackson, Oct. 28, 1814, *Official Letter Books* 6:293; and Claiborne to Jackson, Nov. 4, 1814, *Jackson Papers* 3:178–79. See also Bassett, *Life of Andrew Jackson,* 147.

8. Thomas L. Butler, Aide-de-Camp to New Orleans Citizens and Soldiers, Dec. 15, 1814, *Jackson Papers* 3:204–5.

9. Livingston and Duncan opinions were provided orally to Jackson and were subsequently issued as written opinions in March 1815. See *Correspondence of Andrew Jackson* 2:197–99.

10. See note 5 above. For more on the evolution of martial law, see chapter 5, this volume.

11. Declaration of Martial Law, Dec. 16, 1814, in *The Papers of Andrew Jackson: A Microfilm Supplement,* ed. Harold D. Moser et al. (hereafter cited as *Jackson Papers, MS*). Also in Parton, *Life of Andrew Jackson* 2:60–61.

12. Andrew Jackson to Maj. Gen. Jacques P. Villeré, Dec. 19, 1814, *Jackson Papers, MS;* many of the bayous were blocked so thoroughly that the Louisiana legislature sent a resolution to the Thirty-fourth Congress requesting funds to remove the obstructions. See "Resolution of the Legislature of Louisiana," *United States Congressional Serial Set,* 34th Cong., 1st sess., S. Doc. 43; the requisition of carts was so extensive that the city's mayor

wrote Jackson requesting the return of some carts for public use. See
Nicholas Girod to Andrew Jackson, Jan. 2, 1815, *Jackson Papers*, LC;
Edward Livingston to Nicholas Girod, Dec. 29, 1814, *Jackson Papers* 3:225.
Vincent Nolte, one of the city's merchants, noted that 750 woolen covers
were confiscated from his warehouse to clothe the poorly clad Tennessee
and Kentucky troops; see Vincent O. Nolte, *Fifty Years in Both Hemispheres
or Reminiscences of the Life of a Former Merchant* (New York: Redfield,
1854), 223–24. For muster order, see Andrew Jackson to Colonel John
Constant, Dec. 22, 1814, *Jackson Papers*, LC, ser. 3; see also Andrew
Jackson to Philemon Thomas, Dec. 22, 1814, *Jackson Papers* 3:214; Edward
Livingston to Nicholas Girod, Dec. 29, 1814, *Jackson Papers* 3:225. For legislative and court actions, see Arsène Lacarrière Latour, *Historical Memoir
of the War in West Florida and Louisiana in 1814–185; with an Atlas* (1816;
reprint Gainesville: Univ. Press of Florida, 1999), appendix, xl–xlii; Parton,
Life of Andrew Jackson 2:61.

13. William C. C. Claiborne to James Monroe, Dec. 9, 1814, *Official Letter Books*
    6:321–23; William C. C. Claiborne to Andrew Jackson, Dec. 22, 1814, *Jackson
    Papers* 3:214–15; Andrew Jackson to Robert Hays, Dec. 26, 1814, *Jackson
    Papers*, MS. For Villeré, see *Jackson Papers* 3:211; see also "Decision of the
    Court Martial, in the Case of Major Villeré, March 15 1815," *Niles Weekly
    Register*, Apr. 29, 1815.

14. Latour, *Historical Memoir*, 146; "Report of the Commissioners Appointed
    to Examine and Assess the Damages Occasioned by the Troops of the United
    States in the Neighborhood of the City of New-Orleans," *United States
    Congressional Serial Set*, 18th Cong., 1st sess., S. Doc. 51; see also *American
    State Papers, Claims* 1:345, 347, 348, 356, 391, 416, 574 (Washington, D.C.:
    GPO, 1834); Nolte, *Fifty Years in Both Hemispheres*, 216; "The Memorial
    and Petition of John Rodriguez, Attorney at Law, Planter of the State of
    Louisiana, Citizen of the United States, to His Excellency Andrew Jackson,"
    Feb. 11, 1815, *Jackson Papers*, LC.

15. For a detailed description of the three major battles, see Remini, *Battle of
    New Orleans;* Reilly, *British at the Gates;* Andrew Jackson to General
    David Morgan, Jan. 8, 1815, *Jackson Papers*, LC, ser. 3; and Andrew
    Jackson to General David Morgan, Jan. 10, 1815, *Jackson Papers* 3:241.

16. "Answer of General Jackson to the Resolution of the 30th of December,
    1814, Report of the Committee of Inquiry on the Military Measures Exe-
    cuted Against the Legislature of the State of Louisiana, the 28th of Decem-
    ber 1814," *Louisiana Historical Quarterly* 9 (1926): 221–80; written on the
    envelope, Hatch Dent, chairman of the committee investigating the closing
    of the legislature, to Andrew Jackson, Jan. 11, 1815, *Jackson Papers*, LC;
    Latour, *Historical Memoir*, 205.

17. Reilly, *British at the Gates*, gives a good account of the British losses and
    subsequent retreat. Andrew Jackson to James Monroe, Jan. 19, 1815,
    Jackson Papers 3:250–51. For Jackson's concerns of another attack, see
    Andrew Jackson to William C. C. Claiborne, Jan. 21, 1815, *Jackson Papers*,
    LC; for continuation of fortifications, see the following letters in *Jackson
    Papers*, LC: Andrew Jackson to William Darby, engineer, Jan. 27, 1815;

Andrew Jackson to A. Lacarrière Latour and Howell Tatum, Jan. 27, 1815; Walter Gibbons, engineer, to Andrew Jackson, Feb. 1, 1815; William C. C. Claiborne to Andrew Jackson, Feb. 6, 1815; William Darby, engineer, to Andrew Jackson, Feb. 9, 1815; and Andrew Jackson to William Darby, engineer, Feb. 10, 1815.

18. Nicholas Girod to Andrew Jackson, Dec. 25, 1814, *Jackson Papers*, LC. For another example of men arrested for not having passes, see Pierre L. Duplesis to Andrew Jackson, Jan. 2, 1815, *Jackson Papers*, LC; for citizens who enrolled in the militia to gain release from prison, see General Jean Humbert to Andrew Jackson, Feb. 14, 1815, *Jackson Papers*, LC.

19. Brigadier Major Gordon to Brig. Gen. David B. Morgan, Jan. 14, 1815, *Jackson Papers*, LC; Court Martial Record of Joseph Suares, Private of the 3rd Company of the 3rd Regiment of the Louisiana Militia, Jan. 27, 1815, *Jackson Papers*, LC, ser. 5. For Suares's continued detainment, see "Morning Report of the Guard Mounted in Barracks New Orleans," Feb. 8–23, 1815, *Jackson Papers*, LC, ser. 5. Other citizens avoided charges of supplying the enemy by refusing payment offered by the British army for the seizure of cattle and other provisions. Maj. Gen. Jacques Villeré, in fact, sent a caustic note to the British commander rejecting a reimbursement of $490 for cattle, horses, and furniture used by enemy forces. Alceè Fortier, *A History of Louisiana* (New York: Goupil, 1904), 146; John Holland, keeper of the jail, to Andrew Jackson, Mar. 2, 1815, *Jackson Papers*, LC.

20. James Berns to Andrew Jackson, Feb. 8, 1815, *Jackson Papers* 3:275. Berns later enlisted in Jean Humbert's foreign legion of militia; J. Davidson to Andrew Jackson, Jan. 24, Feb.18, 1815, *Jackson Papers*, LC.

21. The number of prisoners is simply too many to list. See "Morning Report of the Guard Mounted in Barracks New Orleans," Jan. 31 to Mar. 11, 1815, *Jackson Papers*, LC, ser. 5. For "Citizens Without Charges," see "Report of the Guard Mounted at Barracks New Orleans," Feb. 23, 1815, *Jackson Papers*, LC. Civilians also had to contend with the misconduct of soldiers. See the correspondence between Andrew Jackson and Maj. Philemon Thomas, Feb. 7, 10, 1815, *Jackson Papers*, LC.

22. William D. Perry to Andrew Jackson, Feb. 17, 1815, *Jackson Papers*, LC. Perry's arrest may have stemmed from desertion or breach of orders. On January 27, 1815, he wrote Jackson requesting help because his wife had run off with money and plates; *Jackson Papers*, LC. One David C. Wallace tried Perry's strategy, writing the general that "the situation of your petitioner has become very irksome, as well as prejudicial to his business." Wallace noted that he knew of no charge but was willing to post bond and stand trial. See David C. Wallace to Andrew Jackson, Feb. 28, 1815, *Jackson Papers*, LC; Michel Fortier to Rachel Jackson, Feb. 28, 1815, *Jackson Papers*, LC. Fortier wrote on behalf of Peter Chavenet, arrested for "criminal intercourse with the enemy." Fortier did not argue Chavenet's innocence, only leniency. For Spanish prisoners, see Toaquin Provensal, Domingo Paj [?], José Garcia, and Pablo Sezanna to Andrew Jackson, Feb. 17, 1815, *Jackson Papers*, LC. The Spanish consul in New Orleans also

requested the men's release; see Diego Morphy to Andrew Jackson, Jan. 18, 1815, *Jackson Papers*, LC. One José Antonio de Riano also wrote Jackson in an effort to obtain release from prison; see Jan. 22, 1815, *Jackson Papers*, LC. Riano was ultimately tried as a spy; *Jackson Papers* 3:268 n. 7.

23. Disease was a major concern for any large army. Robert Young reported to Claiborne on February 1, 1815, that 136 men in his camp were on the sick list and 8 had died; *Jackson Papers*, LC. Gen. John Coffee notified Jackson on February 2, 1815, that "the diseases in my camp are every day becoming more fatal, not a day but several deaths"; *Jackson Papers*, LC. Alfred Hennen, secretary of the Louisiana Bible Society, reported on April 25 that some 360 men from the Louisiana militia were in the hospital; see Powell A. Casey, *Louisiana in the War of 1812* (Baton Rouge: Self-published, 1963), 101. For information on slave insurrections, see James Miller to Andrew Jackson, Dec. 29, 1814, *Jackson Papers*, LC; Thomas Butler to Captain Peter Ogden, Dec. 22, 1814, *Jackson Papers*, LC, ser. 3. For dismissal requests because of slave insurrections, see Louis DeBlanc et al. to Andrew Jackson, Jan. 1815, and Sgt. Adrian Dumartrait to Andrew Jackson, Mar. 4, 1815, both in *Jackson Papers*, LC. One insurrection resulted in the arrest of some 17 slaves; see Joshua Baker to Andrew Jackson, Feb. 2, 1815, *Jackson Papers* 3:264. For general dismissal requests, see William C. C. Claiborne to Andrew Jackson, Jan. 31, 1815, and Robert Butler to William C. C. Claiborne, Jan. 31, 1815, both in *Jackson Papers* 3:263. For desertions, see William C. C. Claiborne to Andrew Jackson, Feb. 1, 1815; Col. Pierre Delaronde to Andrew Jackson, Feb. 1, 1815; Col. Joshua Baker Sr. to Andrew Jackson, Feb. 2, 1815; and Maj. Daniel Hughes to Robert Butler, Feb. 2, 1815, all in *Jackson Papers*, LC. Jackson wrote to Maj. Gen. Jacques Villeré as early as January 23, ordering him to recall all absented soldiers; see *Jackson Papers*, MS. For punishments, see Andrew Jackson to William C. C. Claiborne, Feb. 3, 1815, *Jackson Papers* 3:266.

24. William C. C. Claiborne to Andrew Jackson, Feb. 3, 1815, *Jackson Papers* 3:267. For arrests, see guard house reports, Jan. to Mar., *Jackson Papers*, LC, ser. 5; James Harding to Andrew Jackson, Feb.13, 1815, *Jackson Papers*, LC; Citizens of Louisiana to Andrew Jackson, Feb. 27, 1815, *Jackson Papers* 3:291 and footnote 1; and the following in *Jackson Papers*, LC: William Winston to Daniel Patterson, Feb. 27, 1815; Richard Dealy, sailing master, to Daniel Patterson, Feb. 27, 1815; Daniel Patterson to Andrew Jackson, Feb. 27, 1815; and George Macquillen to Andrew Jackson, Feb. 28, 1815.

25. General Orders, Feb. 13, 1815, *Jackson Papers*, LC. For dismissal requests and refusals, see William C. C. Claiborne to Andrew Jackson, Feb. 13, 1815, *Jackson Papers*, LC; William H. Erwin to Andrew Jackson, Feb. 13, 1815, *Jackson Papers*, LC; Abbe William DuBourg to Andrew Jackson, Feb. 14, 1815, *Jackson Papers*, LC; Andrew Jackson to Valery Bordelon, Urban Plauche, and Charles Coppel, Feb. 18, 1815, *Jackson Papers*, LC, ser. 3; Andrew Jackson to the Veterans from the parishes of St. Jacques, La Fourche and Ibberville, Feb. 18, 1815, *Jackson Papers*, LC; William C. C. Claiborne to Andrew Jackson, Feb. 25, 1815, *Jackson Papers* 3:286.

26. Diego Morphy to Andrew Jackson, Feb. 17, 1815, *Jackson Papers* 3:282. In 1843, Jackson requested information from the collectors office of New Orleans on the number of Frenchman dismissed. See Thomas Gibbes Morgan to Andrew Jackson, Feb. 2, 1843, *Jackson Papers*, LC. Another example of Tousard's change of view is that he had previously written to Jackson complaining that a number of Frenchmen in the militia had insulted him for his allegiance to the new French government and insisted that the general was the only person who could remedy the problem. See Chevalier de Tousard to Andrew Jackson, Jan. 18, 1815, *Jackson Papers*, LC. For Tousard's statement concerning his duty as consul, see Norman B. Wilkinson, ed., "The Assaults on New Orleans, 1814–1815," *Louisiana History* 3 (Winter 1962): 43–53.

27. John H. Eaton, *The Life of Andrew Jackson* (Philadelphia: M. Carey, 1817; reprint, New York: Arno Press, 1971), 407; Order to the French Citizens of New Orleans, Feb. 28, 1815, *Jackson Papers* 3:294; Andrew Jackson to Chevalier de Tousard, Mar. 4, 1815, *Correspondence of Andrew Jackson* 2:182; Chevalier de Tousard to Andrew Jackson, Mar. 6, 1815, *Correspondence of Andrew Jackson* 2:186–87; Andrew Jackson to Chevalier de Tousard, Mar. 6, 1815, *Correspondence of Andrew Jackson* 2:187; see note 2, 188–89 for letter from Uniformed Battalion; see also Andrew Jackson to the Uniformed Battalion, Mar. 8, 1815, in *Niles Weekly Register*, Apr. 22, 1815.

28. John Reid to Godwin Brown Cotten, Feb. 21, 1815, *Jackson Papers* 3:284–85; for Cotton's reply, see note 1, p. 285.

29. On negotiations, see William C. C. Claiborne to Andrew Jackson, Jan. 31, 1815, *Jackson Papers* 3:268; Andrew Jackson to William C. C. Claiborne, *Jackson Papers* 3:268–69; William C. C. Claiborne to Stephen Marerceau, Feb. 24, 1815, *Official Letter Books* 6:338–39; William C. C. Claiborne to James Monroe, Feb. 1815, *Official Letter Books* 6:347. See also a number of letters from Claiborne to Monroe, Mar. 1815, *Official Letter Books* 6:344–49.

30. Andrew Jackson to Stephen Hopkins, Feb. 25, 1815, *Jackson Papers*, LC, ser. 3; "A Citizen of Louisiana of French Origin," *Louisiana Courier*, Mar. 3, 1815, in Parton, *Life of Andrew Jackson* 2:309–11.

31. Louaillier admitted in writing from prison that he was the author; see Louis Louaillier to Ferdinand Amelung, Mar. 5, 1815, *Jackson Papers*, LC. Jackson also noted that "the arrest and trial of Mr. Louaillier, will open to the view the extent to which his publication and other plans have been carried to excite mutiny and disaffection in my camp"; Andrew Jackson to Lt. Col. Mathew Arbuckle, Mar. 5, 1815, *Correspondence of Andrew Jackson* 2:183. For further evidence that Jackson believed a conspiracy existed, see Andrew Jackson to Capt. Thomas Beale, Mar. 6, 1815, *Jackson Papers* 3:301; Dumas Malone, ed., *Dictionary of American Biography*, vol. 8 (New York: Charles Scribner's Sons, 1932), 123–24; Francois-Xavier Martin, *The History of Louisiana from the Earliest Period* (New Orleans: Lyman and Beardslee, 1829), 2:394, 395.

32. Andrew Jackson to Lt. Col. Mathew Arbuckle, Mar. 5, 1815, *Correspondence of Andrew Jackson* 2:183; "Andrew Jackson and Judge D. A. Hall." Jackson

argued that Hall and Louaillier were working together and the writ was prepared prior to the senator's arrest. The judge thus had to change the date to fit the arrest. The day before, Jackson warned that all "found lurking as spies, in or about the fortifications or encampments of the armies of the United States . . . shall suffer death." General Orders, Mar. 5, 1815, *Niles Weekly Register*, Apr. 22, 1815. Hollander was arrested on March 12. See Nolte, *Fifty Years in Both Hemispheres*, 222.

33. Andrew Jackson to James Monroe, Mar. 6, 1815, *Jackson Papers*, LC.

34. For arrest orders, see Thomas Butler to Lt. Col. Mathew Arbuckle, Mar. 8, 1815, and Thomas Butler to Captain Thomas Beale, Mar. 8, 1815, both in *Jackson Papers*, LC, ser. 3. Later in his life, Jackson wrongly claimed that he did not order these arrests; see Andrew Jackson to Francis P. Blair, Sept. 9, 1842, *Correspondence of Andrew Jackson* 6:166. The question of whether Dick and Lewis were actually arrested has remained a point of confusion among historians. Two items support the assertion that they were not arrested. First, no arrest record on the guard house reports exist, as it did for both Louaillier and Hall. Second, even Judge Martin, a decided critic of the general, stated that Jackson countermanded the arrest order; see Martin, *History of Louisiana from the Earliest Period* 2:403. For release from duty, see General Orders, Mar. 8, 1815, *Niles Weekly Register*, Apr. 22, 1815.

35. *United States Congressional Serial Set*, 27th Cong., 3d sess., H. Doc. 69; Record of the Court Martial Prepared under the General's Authority by His Aide, Robert Butler, H. Doc. 69, 16–18.

36. Andrew Jackson to Dominick A. Hall, Mar. 11, 1815, *Correspondence of Andrew Jackson* 2:189; Proclamation of Peace, Mar. 13, 1815, *Jackson Papers* 3:310; "Andrew Jackson and Judge D. A. Hall," 509–70.

37. Jackson's defense and the court proceedings are in "Andrew Jackson and Judge D. A. Hall," 546; *Jackson Papers* 3:322–34; Eaton, *Life of Andrew Jackson*, 418.

38. Eaton, *Life of Andrew Jackson*, 422–23, 420–21. For newspaper accounts, see *Friends of the Laws*, Apr. 8, 11, 13, 15, 1815, *Niles Weekly Register*, June 3, 1815; for charges against Hall, see "Andrew Jackson and Judge D. A. Hall," 551, 558; Certificate of General David B. Morgan and Affidavit, Mar. 28, 1815, *Correspondence of Andrew Jackson* 2:199–200. When the Louisiana legislature investigated the case in 1843, a number of men testified that Hall approved martial law. See the affidavits of S. Hiriart, Maunsel White, and Clark Woodruff in "Andrew Jackson and Judge D. A. Hall," 518, 519, 524, respectively.

39. "Andrew Jackson and Judge D. A. Hall," 560; "A Note to General Jackson's Answer. Judge Hall," *Louisiana Gazette*, Apr. 15, 1815, in *Niles Weekly Register*, June 17, 1815.

40. Alexander J. Dallas to Andrew Jackson, Apr. 12, 1815, *Jackson Papers* 3:344, 345; Andrew Jackson to Alexander J. Dallas, May 23, 1815, *Jackson Papers* 3:358–59; Andrew Jackson to Daniel Todd Patterson, Apr. 2, 1815, *Jackson Papers*, MS. For Patterson's response, see Apr. 3, 1815, *Jackson Papers* 3:338–39.

41. On July 5, 1815, Jackson wrote Edward Livingston, "I have not lost sight of the impeachment—and an alteration in your Judiciary"; *Jackson Papers* 3:371. The *Niles Weekly Register*, July 15, 1815, noted that "general Jackson intends to impeach judge Hall, before the senate of the United States"; Alexander J. Dallas to Andrew Jackson, July 1, 1815, *Jackson Papers* 3:375.

42. Alexander J. Dallas to Andrew Jackson, July 1, 1815, *Jackson Papers* 3:375.

43. Ibid. 3:376–77; Andrew Jackson to Alexander J. Dallas, Sept. 5, 1815, *Jackson Papers* 3:384–85. See also Andrew Jackson to Edward Livingston, Sept. 5, 1815, *Jackson Papers, MS,* for the general's proposed trip to Washington.

44. John Reid to John Coffee, Nov. 21, 1815, *Jackson Papers* 3:395 n. 5; Andrew Jackson to John Coffee, Dec. 4, 1815, *Jackson Papers* 3:395.

CHAPTER 2

1. For the resolution, see House, Congressman Troup of Georgia on Battle of New Orleans, *Annals of the Congress of the United States, 1789–1824,* 42 vols. (Washington, D.C., 1834–56) (hereafter cited as *Annals of Congress*), 13th Cong., 3d sess., Feb. 6, 1815, 1123–24; for Troup's comment, see Defence of New Orleans, *Annals of Congress*, 13th Cong., 3d sess., Feb. 16, 1815, 1155; *National Intelligencer,* Mar. 18, 1815; Remini, *Andrew Jackson: The Course of American Empire,* 296; George Dangerfield, *The Awakening of American Nationalism, 1815–1828* (New York: Harper Torch Books, 1965).

2. Interestingly, James McPherson has argued that Abraham Lincoln championed a new conception of "positive liberty," in which the power of the government was utilized for the benefit of the nation. In many respects, this idea was developed by Democrats in regard to Jackson's defense of liberty through military power. See James McPherson, *Abraham Lincoln and the Second American Revolution* (New York: Oxford Univ. Press, 1991), 63–64.

3. Another episode in Jackson's military career was also scrutinized. His invasion of Florida on two separate occasions, in 1814 and 1818, sparked controversy within the United States and created tense relations with Spain. Additional incidents in Jackson's past were also attacked, his marriage to Rachel, duels, and the execution of militia men during the Creek War, for example. For the Florida episode, see Heidler and Heidler, *Old Hickory's War.* For the Florida episode and other campaign issues, see Remini, *Election of Andrew Jackson,* 159–70; Arthur Schlesinger, *The Age of Jackson* (Boston: Little, Brown, 1945), 36–43; Bassett, *Life of Andrew Jackson,* 393–94; Marquis James, *Andrew Jackson: Portrait of a President* (Indianapolis: Bobbs-Merrill, 1937), 153–54; Curtis, *Andrew Jackson and the Search for Vindication,* 48–63; Watson, *Liberty and Power,* 78, 92–93; and Michael J. Heale, *The Presidential Quest: Candidates and Images in American Political Culture, 1787–1852* (London: Longman, 1982), 74, 191.

4. Although martial law surfaced as an important campaign issue, it has remained conspicuously absent in histories on Jackson. Ward, *Andrew*

Jackson, 10. Old Hickory's first major biographer, James Parton, certainly realized the dichotomy of Jackson's image, noting that he "was a patriot and a traitor. . . . Two-thirds of his fellow citizens deified, and the other third vilified [him]." Parton, *Life of Andrew Jackson,* 1:vii.

5. Benjamin Watkin Leigh's authorship is identified in Mary W. M. Hargreaves and James F. Hopkins, eds., *The Papers of Henry Clay,* vol. 6 (Lexington: Univ. Press of Kentucky, 1981), 591 n. 1 (hereafter cited as *Papers of Henry Clay*). Francis T. Brooke mentions Leigh by name in a letter to Clay; see June 2, 1827, *Papers of Henry Clay* 6:636–37.

6. Dumas Malone, ed., *Dictionary of American Biography,* vol. 11 (New York: Scribner's, 1933), 152–53; for an excellent account of Leigh's aristocratic views, see William W. Freehling, *The Road to Disunion, 1776–1854* (New York: Oxford Univ. Press, 1990), 173.

7. *The Letters of Algernon Sydney in Defense of Civil Liberty and Against the Encroachments of Military Despotism, Written by an Eminent Citizen of Virginia, and First Published in the Richmond Enquirer in 1818–19* (Richmond: T. W. White, 1830), 3, 4, 10.

8. Ibid., 3.

9. Parsons, *John Quincy Adams,* 140–44; Brooks, *Diplomacy in the Borderlands,* 148–50; Remini, *Andrew Jackson: The Course of American Empire,* 367–77.

10. House, Congressman Smyth of Virginia on the Seminole War, *Annals of Congress,* 15th Cong., 2d sess., Jan. 21, 1819, 700, 703. Similar sentiments abound throughout the many speeches on the Seminole War.

11. House, Congressman Nelson of Virginia on the Seminole War, *Annals of Congress,* 15th Cong., 2d sess., Jan. 12, 1819, 518.

12. House, Congressman Smyth of Virginia on the Seminole War, 697.

13. House, Congressman Tallmadge of New York on the Seminole War, *Annals of Congress,* 15th Cong., 2d sess., Jan. 23, 1819, 742.

14. Remini, Andrew Jackson. *The Course of Am. Empire,* 370; see also Robert V. Remini, *Henry Clay: Statesman for the Union* (New York: W. W. Norton, 1991), 162.

15. House, Congressman Clay of Kentucky on the Seminole War, *Annals of Congress,* 15th Cong., 2d sess., Jan. 20, 1819, 631–55. Other congressmen also made statements about the protection of liberty and sanctity of the Constitution that could easily have been substituted for a speech on martial law. See, for example, House, Congressman Cobb of Georgia on the Seminole War, *Annals of Congress,* 15th Cong., 2d sess., Jan. 18, 1819, 589, 597; and Senate, Senator Lacock on Report on the Seminole War, *Annals of Congress,* 15th Cong., 2d sess., Feb. 24, 1819, 263.

16. James Morrison to Henry Clay, Feb. 17, 1819, in *The Papers of Henry Clay,* vol. 2, ed. Mary W. M. Hargreaves and James F. Hopkins (Lexington: Univ. Press of Kentucky, 1984), 671 (hereafter cited as *Papers of Henry Clay*).

17. Quoted in Remini, *Andrew Jackson,* 85.

18. Henry Clay to Peter B. Porter, Aug. 10, 1822, *Papers of Henry Clay* 2:274; Jonathon Meigs to Henry Clay, Sept. 3, 1822, *Papers of Henry Clay* 2:282.

19. John McKinley to Henry Clay, June 3, 1823, *Papers of Henry Clay* 2:427.
20. Some newspapers did mention the martial law episode prior to the 1824 election, but it was rare. See Robert P. Hay, "'The Presidential Question': Letters to Southern Editors, 1823–24," *Tennessee Historical Quarterly* 31 (1973): 170–86. Jackson was well aware that opponents wanted to present him in an unflattering light and stated such to John Coffee on June 18, 1824: "Great pains had been taken to represent me as having a savage disposition; who allways [*sic*] carried a Scalping Knife in one hand, & a tomahawk in the other; allways ready to knock down, & scalp, any & every person who differed with me in opinion." See *Papers of Andrew Jackson* 5:416.
21. Albert Gallatin to Walter Lowrie, May 22, 1824, in *The Writings of Albert Gallatin*, ed. Henry Adams (New York: Antiquarian Press, 1960), 2:289, 291.
22. Henry Clay to George McClure, Dec. 28, 1824, in *The Papers of Henry Clay*, vol. 3, ed. Mary W. M. Hargreaves and James F. Hopkins (Lexington: Univ. Press of Kentucky, 1963), 906 (hereafter cited as *Papers of Henry Clay*).
23. Henry Clay to Francis Preston Blair, Jan. 29, 1825, in *The Papers of Henry Clay*, vol. 4, ed. Mary W. M. Hargreaves and James F. Hopkins (Lexington: Univ. Press of Kentucky, 1972), 47 (hereafter cited as *Papers of Henry Clay*). Clay also used the "military chieftain" epithet in an earlier letter; see Clay to Francis T. Brooke, Jan. 28, 1825, *Papers of Henry Clay* 4:45. This letter was published in the *Daily National Intelligencer*, Feb. 12, 1825, as copied from the *Richmond Enquirer*, Feb. 8, 1825; it was also reprinted in the *Niles Weekly Register*, Feb. 19, 1825; (Lexington) *Kentucky Reporter*, Feb. 28, 1825; and (Lexington) *Kentucky Gazette*, Mar. 3, 1825; *Papers of Henry Clay* 4:46, footnote.
24. Andrew Jackson to Samuel Swartwout, Feb. 22, 1825, *Correspondence of Andrew Jackson*, ed. John Spencer Bassett, vol. 3, 1820–1828 (Washington, D.C.: Carnegie Institute of Washington, 1928), 3:279. This was not the first time that Jackson expressed such sentiments. Nearly a year earlier in a letter to Swartwout, the general wrote that he had been placed in situations of "a critical kind" and "there was imposed on me the necessity of Violating, or rather departing from, the constitution of the country; yet at no subsequent period has it produced to me a single pang, believing as I do now, & then did, that without it, security neither to myself or the great cause confided to me, could have been obtained." *Jackson Papers* 5:381.
25. Henry Clay to Francis T. Brooke, May 25, 1827, *Papers of Henry Clay* 6:591. Brooke apparently showed this letter to Benjamin Watkins Leigh, who was pleased with Clay's compliment; see Francis T. Brooke to Henry Clay, *Papers of Henry Clay* 6:636.
26. Louis Louaillier, *The Appeal of L. Louaillier, Sen., against the Charge of High Treason, and Explaining the Transactions at New Orleans* (New Orleans: n.p., 1827), 3–4; see also *Speech Delivered by Mr. Lewis [sic] Louaillier, at a Meeting of the Inhabitants of the County of Opelousas, State of Louisiana, Friendly to the Administration of the General Government* (New Orleans: n.p. 1827); Isaac Hill, *An Address, Delivered at Concord, N.H., January 8, 1828, Being the Thirteenth Anniversary of Jackson's Victory at New-Orleans* (Concord, N.H.: Manahan, Hoan, 1828), 41.

27. *An Address to the People of the United States, on the Subject of the Presidential Election: With a Special Reference to the Nomination of Andrew Jackson, Containing Public Sketches of His Public and Private Character.—By a citizen of the United States* (n.p., 1828), 9; Benjamin Watkins Leigh also remarked that Washington had never declared martial law. See *Letters of Algernon Sydney*, 5–6.

28. These arguments were introduced mainly for the 1828 campaign. To be sure, some issues extended into Jackson's reelection in 1832, but by then opponents enjoyed attacking the general for his stands on nullification and the Bank War and it was far more effective to capitalize on present difficulties than on Jackson's distant military career. Clay, however, never dropped his "military chieftain" charge during the election of 1832, and many pamphlets written for the elections of 1824 and 1828 were republished for the 1832 race. Few new works discussing martial law, however, were created for Jackson's last presidential bid.

29. J. Snelling, *A Brief and Impartial History of the Life and Actions of Andrew Jackson* (Boston: Stimpson and Clapp, 1831), 95; *A History of the Life and Public Services of Major General Andrew Jackson* (n.p., 1828), 37. Another writer stated that "from the irritability of his constitution, and an untoward disposition, he does not control the first impulse of his temper, but has indulged in repeated acts of violence." See *Address to the People of the United States*, 7.

30. *Proceedings and Address of the Republican Young Men of the State of New York* (Utica, N.Y.: Northway and Porter, 1828), 9, 16.

31. *Address to the People of the United States*, 7.

32. *Proceedings of the Anti-Jackson Convention, Held at the Capitol in the City of Richmond: With Their Address to the People of Virginia* (Richmond: Franklin Press, 1828), 18.

33. *Address to the People of the United States*, 13.

34. *New York Advertiser*, in *Proceedings of the Anti-Jackson Convention, Held at the Capitol in the City of Richmond*, Appendix G, 35.

35. Ibid., 20.

36. Ibid.

37. *An Impartial and True History of the Life and Services of Major-General Andrew Jackson* (n.p., 1828), 14.

38. *Address from a Meeting of Democratic Citizens of the City of Philadelphia, Opposed to the Election of General Jackson* (Philadelphia: John Binns, 1827), 9.

39. *Address to the People of the United States*, 15.

40. Ibid., 38.

41. Robert B. Hay, "The Case for Andrew Jackson in 1824: Eaton's Wyoming Letters," *Tennessee Historical Quarterly* 29 (1970): 139–51.

42. *The Letters of Wyoming, to the People of the United States, on the Presidential Election, and in Favour of Andrew Jackson* (Philadelphia: S. Simpson & J. Conrad, 1824), 14–15, 5, 103.

43. Ibid., 6–7.

44. Ibid., 36, 14, 29–30.

45. Ibid., 36, 5. John Hay notes Eaton's comparison of Jackson and Washington: "Eaton used one of the most powerful themes of American ideology to underline his pleas for Jackson. The moral goodness and political greatness of Washington were virtually unquestioned tenets of the American national faith in Eaton's day. Reverence for Washington permeated every part of the American consciousness." See Hay, "Case for Andrew Jackson in 1824," 146.

46. *Letters of Wyoming*, 87, 42–43.

47. Hay, "Case for Andrew Jackson in 1824," 140.

48. Isaac Watts Crane, *Address Delivered before the Jackson Convention of Delegates, from the Different Townships of the County of Cumberland Assembled at Bridgeton, July 27, 1824* (Philadelphia: n.p., 1824), 11, 7, 10.

49. See, for example, *A Concise Narrative of General Jackson's First Invasion of Florida, and of His Immortal Defense of New-Orleans: With Remarks, by Aristides* (New York: E. M. Murden & A. Ming, 1827), 37; *An Address Delivered at Jefferson Hall, Portsmouth, N.H., January 8, 1828, Being the Thirteenth Anniversary of Jackson's Victory at New Orleans, by Abner Greenleaf* (Portsmouth, N.H.: n.p., 1828), 11.

50. Crane, *Address Delivered before the Jackson Convention*, 11. Crane also stated that "we may find some security in having a President whose decision and firmness, and military character are so well known and highly respected, both at home and abroad" (12).

51. Of the twelve pro-Jackson pamphlets surveyed for the election of 1828, nine discussed the martial law episode and two of the three remaining pamphlets at least mentioned New Orleans and the "military chieftain" charge.

52. *Concise Narrative of General Jackson's First Invasion of Florida*, 4.

53. Ibid., 24.

54. Ibid., 11, 28, 23.

55. Hill, *Address, Delivered at Concord, N.H.*, 40–41.

56. Philo A. Goodwin, *Biography of Andrew Jackson, President of the United States, Formerly Major General in the Army of the United States* (Hartford, Conn.: Clapp and Benton, 1832), 175; *Civil and Military History of Andrew Jackson, Late Major-General in the Army of the United States, by an American Officer* (New York: P. M. Davis, 1825), 281–82; Maj. Henry Lee, *A Vindication of the Character and Public Services of Andrew Jackson; in Reply to the Richmond Address, Signed by Chapman Johnson, and to Other Electioneering Calumnies* (Boston: True and Greene, 1828), 16; Martin, *History of Louisiana from the Earliest Period* 2:394–95.

57. *Address of the Republican General Committee of Young Men of the City and County of New York, Friendly to the Election of Andrew Jackson* (New York: Alexander Ming Jr., 1828), 13; Lee, *Vindication of the Character and Public Services of Andrew Jackson*, 13.

58. Gabriel L. Lowe Jr., "John H. Eaton, Jackson's Campaign Manager," *Tennessee Historical Quarterly* 11 (1952): 99–147.

59. Lee, *Vindication of the Character and Public Services of Andrew Jackson*, 15.

60. Richard H. Cox, *Locke on War and Peace* (Washington, D.C.: Univ. Press of America, 1982), 112–14; James Tully, *An Approach to Political Philosophy: Locke in Contexts* (Cambridge: Cambridge Univ. Press, 1993), 143;

Emer de Vattel, *The Law of Nations; or, Principles of the Law of Nature; Applied to the Conduct and Affairs of Nations and Sovereigns* (New York: AMS Press, 1982).

61. Marcus Tullius Cicero, "Speech in Defence of Titus Annius Milo," in *Cicero: The Speeches*, ed. N. H. Watts (Cambridge: Univ. of Harvard Press, 1964), 17. Many works mention the Latin maxim *Inter arma silent leges*, but none give a historical account of its origin or growth. This is an important area of legal history that needs clarification. Chief Justice of the Supreme Court William Rehnquist even includes an entire chapter, titled "*Inter arma silent leges*," in his book *All the Laws But One*, though he provides no historical account of the term. See also Edward Keynes, *Undeclared War: The Twilight Zone of Constitutional Power* (University Park: Pennsylvania State Univ. Press, 1982). My thanks to Professor Elias Kapetanopoulos of Central Connecticut State University for aiding me with the Cicero quotation.

62. *Concise Narrative of General Jackson's First Invasion of Florida*, 23.

63. Hill, *Address, Delivered at Concord, N.H.*, 39.

64. *Concise Narrative of General Jackson's First Invasion of Florida*, 32, 25, 26.

65. *Proceedings, and Address of the New-Hampshire Republican State Convention of Delegates Friendly to the Election of Andrew Jackson . . . Assembled at Concord, June 11, and 12, 1828* (Concord, N.H.: Patriot Office, 1828), 25, 26.

66. Isaac Hill, *Brief Sketch of the Life, Character and Services of Major General Andrew Jackson, by a Citizen of New England* (Concord, N.H.: Manahan, Hoag, 1828), 11.

67. *Concise Narrative of General Jackson's First Invasion of Florida*, 13.

CHAPTER 3

1. Lewis Field Linn to Andrew Jackson, Feb. 28, 1842, *Jackson Papers*, LC.

2. See, for example, Remini, *Andrew Jackson: The Course of American Freedom*, 478–479; Burke Davis, *Old Hickory: A Life of Andrew Jackson* (New York: Dial Press, 1977), 372–72; James, *Andrew Jackson: Portrait*, 460; Bassett, *Life of Andrew Jackson*, 745–46; Parton, *Life of Andrew Jackson* 3:640.

3. Blair loaned Jackson ten thousand dollars in 1842. See Francis Blair to Andrew Jackson, May 24, 1842, *Jackson Papers*, MS. Plauche loaned Jackson six thousand dollars. See Remini, *Andrew Jackson: The Course of American Freedom*, 477.

4. For more on the expunging of the Senate censure, see Remini, *Andrew Jackson: The Course of American Democracy*, 376–81. The New York letter was written in 1841 and addressed to Maj. Auguste Davezac de Castera, a representative in the New York General Assembly. Reprinted in "General Jackson's Fine."

5. For an excellent discussion of the origins of Whiggery and republicanism, see Watson, *Liberty and Power*, chap. 2; for Jackson's importance as a

definer of party, see Holt, *Political Crisis of the 1850s,* 23–28. For Jackson's symbolism following his retirement, specifically at the time of his death, see Warshauer, "Ridiculing the Dead," 13–31; and Matthew Warshauer, "Contested Mourning: The New York Battle over Andrew Jackson's Death," forthcoming, *New York History.*

6. Francis Preston Blair to Andrew Jackson, June 30, 1842, *Jackson Papers,* LC . Blair and Jackson repeatedly referred to Whigs as Federalists, a name that was linked to elitism and, during the War of 1812, traitorous activity.

7. Norma Lois Peterson, *The Presidencies of William Henry Harrison and John Tyler* (Lawrence: Univ. Press of Kansas, 1989.) Michael Morrison has argued that the Democratic Party did not recover from its 1840 loss until the Texas issue revived their hopes for the 1844 presidential election. See her "Martin Van Buren, the Democracy, and the Partisan Politics of Texas Annexation," *Journal of Southern History* 61, no. 4 (1995): 694–724.

8. Andrew Jackson to Andrew Donelson, Dec. 10, 1839, *Correspondence of Andrew Jackson* 6:41–42.

9. A Creole from Santo Domingo, Davezac served as a major in the New Orleans Militia and acted as aide and judge advocate for Jackson during the occupation of the city. Upon becoming president, Jackson appointed Davezac secretary of legation to the Hague in 1829, chargé d'affaires to the Netherlands in 1831, and special diplomatic agent to the Two Sicilies in 1833. Davezac was also the brother-in-law of Edward Livingston, Jackson's longtime friend and former secretary of state. *Correspondence of Andrew Jackson* 2:20; Malone, ed., *Dictionary of American Biography* 5:89; "Major Davezac," *United States Magazine and Democratic Review* 16 (1845): 110.

10. "General Jackson's Fine."

11. Andrew Jackson to Lewis Field Linn, July 4, 1842, *Jackson Papers,* LC. During debate in the Senate, Thomas Hart Benton made it clear that the refund was not about money: "It is not an acquisition of money that he wishes this restoration, but as a condemnation of the judgment under which it was paid, and as an erasure from the records of the country of the censure which it implied." Senate, Senator Benton on General Jackson's Fine, *Congressional Globe,* 27th Cong., 2d sess., May 12, 1842, 11:492–93.

12. "Major Davezac," 110. The New York House of Representatives passed a resolution on February 2, 1842, requesting their representatives and senators to procure the passage of a refund bill. See *Niles Weekly Register* 61 (Feb. 12, 1842): 384.

13. Senate, Senator Linn of Missouri on the Introduction of a Bill to Indemnify Major General Andrew Jackson, *Congressional Globe,* 27th Cong., 2d sess., Mar. 10, 1842, 11:304.

14. Senate, Senator Tappan of Ohio on General Jackson's Fine, *Congressional Globe,* 27th Cong., 2d sess., Mar. 21, 1842, vol. 11, appendix, 221. Benjamin Tappan served as a presidential elector in 1832, and as Donald Ratcliff noted, he was "an ardent Jacksonian." Rewarded for his fidelity to the general with a nomination as a U.S. district judge, Tappan's prize was denied when the Whig-controlled Senate rejected him. Ultimately elected to Con-

gress in 1840, he proved to be among the most resolute defenders of the aging Jackson. See Donald J. Ratcliff, ed., "The Auto-biography of Benjamin Tappan," *Ohio History* 85 (Spring 1976): 109–57; Daniel Feller, "A Brother in Arms: Benjamin Tappan and the Antislavery Democracy," *Journal of American History* 88, no. 1 (June 2001): 48–74.

15. All figures determined from *Congressional Quarterly's Guide to Congress* (Washington, D.C.: GOP, 1991), 130–33. There existed a total of twenty-six states, resulting in fifty-two senators. One was listed as a Republican, and Tennessee had a vacant seat.

16. John Berrien spoke for the committee, declaring two grounds on which they ruled against the bill: (1) "The application for indemnity was not made by General Jackson, or by any person, legally authorized to do so"; and (2) lack of evidence before the committee. See Senate, Senator Berrien on the Adverse Report of the Judiciary Committee on the Bill to Refund to Major Gen. Andrew Jackson the Fine of $1000, *Congressional Globe*, 27th Cong., 2d sess., Apr. 22, 1842, vol. 11, appendix, 438. Committee members included John M. Berrien, Whig from Georgia; Thomas Clayton, Whig from Delaware; John J. Crittenden, Whig from Kentucky; Robert J. Walker, Democrat from Mississippi; and John L. Kerr, Whig from Maryland; see *Senate Journal*, 27th Cong., 2d sess., S. Doc., serial 389, 2.

17. Senate, Senator Walker of Mississippi on General Jackson's Fine, *Congressional Globe*, 27th Cong., 2d sess., May 12, 1842, vol. 11, appendix, 492.

18. Senate, Senator Benton of Missouri on General Jackson's Fine, Apr. 22, 1842, 11:438; Senate, Senator Crittenden of Kentucky on General Jackson's Fine, *Congressional Globe*, 27th Cong., 2d sess., May 12, 1842, vol. 11, appendix, 362.

19. Senate, Senator Henderson of Mississippi on General Jackson's Fine, *Congressional Globe*, 27th Cong., 2d sess., May 18, 1842, vol. 11, appendix, 374.

20. Senate, Senator Barrow of Louisiana on General Jackson's Fine, *Congressional Globe*, 27th Cong., 2d sess., May 18, 1842, 11:515; Senate, Senator Linn of Missouri on General Jackson's Fine, *Congressional Globe*, 27th Cong., 2d sess., May 18, 1842, 11:515.

21. *Congressional Globe* 11:515; Senate, Senator Archer of Virginia on General Jackson's Fine, *Congressional Globe*, 27th Cong., 2d sess., May 25, 1842, 11:515.

22. The two senators who crossed lines were Democrat Nathaniel Tallmadge of New York and Whig William Archer of Virginia. The final vote on engrossing was seventeen to twenty-four. *Congressional Globe* 11:515.

23. Senate, Senator King of Alabama on General Jackson's Fine, *Congressional Globe*, 27th Cong., 2d sess., May 12, 1842, vol. 11, appendix, 362.

24. Senate, Senator Buchanan of Pennsylvania on General Jackson's Fine, *Congressional Globe*, 27th Cong., 2d sess., May 12, 1842, vol. 11, appendix, 363. Levi Woodbury made a similar appeal to avoid party considerations; Senate, Senator Woodbury of New Hampshire on General Jackson's Fine, *Congressional Globe*, 27th Cong., 2d sess., May 12, 1842, vol. 11, appendix, 364.

25. Senate, Senator Conrad of Louisiana on General Jackson's Fine, 27th Cong., 2d sess., *Congressional Globe*, May 18, 1842, vol. 11, appendix, 373.

26. The second session did not end until August 31, 1842.

27. Andrew Jackson to Francis P. Blair, May 23, 1842, *Correspondence of Andrew Jackson* 6:153.

28. Andrew Jackson to Andrew J. Donelson, June 2, 1842, *Correspondence of Andrew Jackson* 6:155–56. Francis Blair wrote Jackson, declaring, "I told Linn and Benton that it [the bill] ought to be voted down by our side with any proviso whatever shielding the Judge." See Francis Blair to Andrew Jackson, May 24, 1842, *Correspondence of Andrew Jackson* 6:154.

29. Andrew Jackson to Francis Blair, June 4, 1842, *Jackson Papers, MS.*

30. Andrew Jackson to Francis Blair, Feb. 24, 1844, *Jackson Papers*, LC. For more on the Eaton Affair and Berrien's resignation, see Remini, *Andrew Jackson: The Course of American Freedom;* and Marszalek, *Petticoat Affair.*

31. Andrew Jackson to Francis Blair, June 16, 1842, *Jackson Papers*, LC.

32. James Breedlove wrote Jackson on July 18, 1842 (*Jackson Papers*, LC), noting that "Mr. Conrad was a zealous member of the Jackson party for many years, and brought himself some notoriety as a public speaker. . . . On all such occasions he approved of your course in relation to the defense of this city, and particularly that your declaring martial law, and the consequences that followed. Should it become necessary to shew up before the public Mr. Conrad's inconsistencies in this matter, many signatures of the highest respectability can be obtained here." See also James Breedlove to Andrew Jackson, Oct. 20, 1842; Jean-Baptiste Plauche to Andrew Jackson, Nov. 2, 1842; and H. D. Piere to Andrew Jackson, Jan. 9, 1843, all in *Jackson Papers*, LC. See also John M. Sacher, *A Perfect War of Politics: Parties, Politician, and Democracy in Louisiana, 1824–1861* (Baton Rouge: Louisiana State Univ. Press, 2003), 108.

33. For more on either of these episodes, see Remini, *Andrew Jackson: The Course of American Empire;* and Remini, *Andrew Jackson: The Course of American Freedom.* Other issues also contributed to Calhoun's expulsion.

34. Andrew Jackson to Francis Blair, June 16, 1842, *Jackson Papers*, LC. Jackson focused on Barrow as well because he had proposed an amendment insisting the bill did not impinge on the fidelity of Louisiana citizens.

35. Francis Blair to Andrew Jackson, June 30, 1842, *Jackson Papers, MS.*

36. Andrew Jackson to Francis Blair, July 8, 1842, *Jackson Papers*, LC; ibid, Aug. 1, 1842; ibid, Aug. 12, 1842, *Jackson Papers, MS;* Jackson also suspected that Henry Clay influenced Conrad in his attacks, writing that he had "little doubt that Mr. Clay and Mr. Berian [*sic*] stimulated Mr. Senator Conrad to his attack upon me in the Senate." Andrew Jackson to James W. Breedlove, Oct. 3, 1842, *Jackson Papers*, LC, 172.

37. Francis Blair to Andrew Jackson, June 30, 1842, *Jackson Papers, MS;* Sept. 28, 1842; Oct. 14, 1842.

38. Senate, Senator Linn of Missouri on General Jackson's Fine, *Congressional Globe*, 27th Cong., 3d sess., Dec. 14, 1842, 12:50. With the approach of a presidential election, Washington politics traditionally subordinated legislative business to campaign activity during the lame-duck session of one Congress and the first session of the succeeding Congress. The refund bill suffered

from the peculiarity of this congressional timetable. Thus many Whigs, viewing the refund bill as merely a campaign tactic, denounced Democrats for attempting to use Jackson's popularity to influence voters. For a superb explanation of this often confusing phenomenon, see David M. Potter, *The Impending Crisis, 1848–1861* (New York: Harper & Row, 1976), 375–76.

39. Senate, Senator Linn of Missouri on General Jackson's Fine, *Congressional Globe*, 27th Cong., 3d sess., Dec. 22, 1842, vol. 12, appendix, 68.

40. Senate, Senator Berrien on General Jackson's Fine, *Congressional Globe*, 27th Cong., 3d sess., Jan. 10, 1842, 12:141. Robert Walker of Mississippi certainly understood how Jackson would react to the change in title, remarking that "General Jackson has never solicited, nor will he ever receive, such relief." See Senate, Senator Walker of Mississippi on General Jackson's Fine, *Congressional Globe*, 27th Cong., 3d sess., Jan. 10, 1843, 12:141.

41. Senate, Senator Miller of New Jersey on General Jackson's Fine, *Congressional Globe*, 27th Cong., 3d sess., Feb. 17, 1843, 12:300–301. Miller even insinuated that Martin Van Buren was utilizing the refund to influence the election, noting that "from all that I have seen and heard, I cannot divest myself of the impression that a certain aspirant to the Presidency is attempting, through this measure, to use once more the name and influence of Gen. Jackson to obtain a second time the object of his ambition." *Congressional Globe*, vol. 12, appendix, 210. Daniel Barnard of New York made the same assertion: "This bill was to be passed for effect on the approaching Presidential election, and not because it was just." House, Congressman Barnard of New York on General Jackson's Fine, *Congressional Globe*, 28th Cong., 1st sess., Dec. 29, 1843, 13, pt. 1:89.

42. Senate, Senator Bagby of Alabama on General Jackson's Fine, *Congressional Globe*, 27th Cong., 3d sess., Feb. 17, 1843, 12:302.

43. House, Congressman Howard of Michigan, *House Journal*, 27th Cong., 2d sess., Feb. 28, 1842, 37:458.

44. Congressman William Gwin acknowledged that Davezac was "the prime mover on this subject." See House, Congressman Gwin of Mississippi on General Jackson's Fine, Jan. 5, 1843, 12:123. Resolutions and memorials in the House of Representatives, all in *House Journal*, 27th Cong., 2d sess., Mar. 14, 1842, vol. 37: Congressman Medill of Ohio, 534; Congressman Mathiot of Ohio, 541; Congressmen Brown and Keim of Pennsylvania, 534–35; Congressman Ingersoll of Pennsylvania, 540. Resolutions and memorial in the Senate, all in *Senate Journal*, 27th Cong., 2d sess.: Senator Buchanan of Pennsylvania, Mar. 11, 1842, 217; Senator Sturgeon of Pennsylvania, Mar. 11, 1842, 217; Senator Buchanan of Pennsylvania, Mar. 14, 1842, 220, and Mar. 16, 1842, 226; Senator Tappan of Ohio, Mar. 21, 1842, 233.

45. For other Whigs, see Congressman Wise of Virginia, *House Journal*, 27th Cong., 3d sess., Dec. 27, 1842, 98; Senator Graham of North Carolina, *Senate Journal*, 27th Cong., 3d sess., Feb. 13, 1843, 168; Senator Barrow of Louisiana, *Senate Journal*, 28th Cong., 1st sess., Dec. 20, 1843, 40; and Senator Dayton of New Jersey, *Senate Journal*, 28th Cong., 1st sess., Feb. 9, 1844, 111.

46. Resolutions and memorials in the House, all in *House Journal*, 27th Cong., 3d sess.: Congressman Pickens of South Carolina, Dec. 29, 1842, 111;

Congressman Cranston of Rhode Island, Jan. 24, 1843, 251; Congressman Littlefield of Maine, Feb. 1, 1843, 290; Congressman Ingersoll of Pennsylvania, Feb. 13, 1843, 355; and Congressman Cooper of Georgia, Mar. 1, 1843, 499; all in *House Journal,* 28th Cong., 1st. sess.: Congressman Hale of New Hampshire, Dec. 16, 1843, 62; Congressman Slidell of Louisiana, Dec. 29, 1843, 138; Congressman Bidlack of Pennsylvania, Jan. 13, 1844, 224; Congressman Strong of New York, Jan. 22, 1844, 277; and Congressman Lyon of Michigan, Jan. 29, 1844, 320. Resolutions and memorials in the Senate, all in *Senate Journal,* 27th Cong., 2d sess.: Senator Buchanan of Pennsylvania, Apr. 9, 1842, 282; and Senator Wright of New York, May 18, 1842, 348; all in *Senate Journal,* 27th Cong., 3d sess.: Senator McRoberts of Illinois, Dec. 19, 1842, 34; Senator Buchanan of Pennsylvania, Dec. 20, 1842, 49; Senator Smith of Connecticut, Jan. 3, 1843, 66; Senator Calhoun of South Carolina, Jan. 4, 1843, 72; Senator McRoberts of Illinois, Jan. 6, 1843, 78; Instructions from Arkansas, Jan. 9, 1843, 82; Senator Williams of Maine, Jan. 31, 1843, 138; Senator Sturgeon of Pennsylvania, Feb. 13, 1843; Senator Linn of Missouri, Feb. 25, 1843, 218; all in *Senate Journal,* 28th Cong., 1st sess.: Senator Woodbury of New Hampshire, Dec. 5, 1843, 71; Senator Sturgeon of Pennsylvania, Jan. 16, 1844, 73; Senator Wright of New York, Jan. 19, 1844, 78; and Senator White of Indiana, Jan. 23, 1844, 84. At least one territory also debated sending a resolution. See Mott, "Iowa Territory and General Jackson's Fine," 58–64; and *Niles Weekly Register* 28, no. 63 (Jan. 1843): 352.

47. House, Congressman Ingersoll of Pennsylvania, Committee on the Judiciary, H.R. 503, *House Journal,* 27th Cong., 2d sess., June 17, 1842, n.p.
48. Vote on Going into Committee of the Whole to Discuss H.R. 503, *Congressional Globe,* 27th Cong., 2d sess., Aug. 26, 1842, vol. 11, appendix, 947.
49. President John Tyler, Annual Message to Congress, *Congressional Globe,* Dec. 6, 1842, 12:33.
50. Vote on Going into Committee of the Whole to Discuss H.R. 503, *Congressional Globe,* 27th Cong., 2d sess., Dec. 12, 1842, vol. 11, appendix, 44.
51. House, Congressman Arnold of Tennessee on General Jackson's Fine, *Congressional Globe,* 27th Cong., 3d sess., Jan. 4, 1843, 12:114; House, Congressman Meriwhether of Georgia on the Fine of General Jackson, *Congressional Globe,* 27th Cong., 3d sess., Jan. 4, 1843, 12:114.
52. House, Congressman Gwin of Mississippi on General Jackson's Fine, Jan. 5, 1843, 12:122.
53. House, Congressman Cushing of Massachusetts on General Jackson's Fine, *Congressional Globe,* 27th Cong., 3d sess., Jan. 5, 1843, 12:122.
54. Ibid., 12:123.
55. House, Congressman Cushing of Massachusetts on General Jackson's Fine, *Congressional Globe,* 27th Cong., 3d sess., Jan. 6, 1843, 12:128.
56. Ibid. 12:129. See also Adams's comments in his diary. Adams, *Memoirs of John Quincy Adams* 11:244.
57. Robert V. Remini noted that "Tyler was a strong state's rights Southerner who had deserted the Democratic party on principle because he abhorred the tactics and programs of Andrew Jackson." See Remini, *Andrew Jackson:*

The Course of American Freedom, 464, 171, 151, 315. For Tyler's 1819 speech, see Robert Seager II, *And Tyler Too: A Biography of John and Julia Gardiner Tyler* (New York: McGraw Hill, 1963), 68.

58. Butler also speculated that the bill was proposed to Whigs "for the express purpose of affording that party the opportunity to prove to the world that justice and magnanimity are still to be found in its ranks; or it may be for precisely the opposite reason." House, Congressman Butler of Kentucky on the Fine to General Jackson, *Congressional Globe*, 27th Cong., 3d sess., Jan. 11, 1843, vol. 12, appendix, 117.

59. Ibid. 12:117, 118.

60. Ibid. 12:117.

61. Adams, *Memoirs of John Quincy Adams* 11:291, 286.

62. House, Congressman Botts of Virginia on General Jackson's Fine, *Congressional Globe*, 27th Cong., 3d sess., Jan. 24, 1843, 12:195.

63. Andrew Jackson to Francis Blair, July 2, 8, 1842, *Jackson Papers*, LC. Blair passed on the general's exact words, for on July 15, 1844, Charles Ingersoll wrote Blair that he had become "bent on what you call carrying the war in to Africa." See *Jackson Papers, MS*. Jackson's letters requesting and conveying various documents are simply too numerous to include. Listed, however, are some poignant examples of his deep involvement. All are located in *Jackson Papers*, LC: Andrew Jackson to Francis Blair, Aug. 1, 1842; Oct. 29, 1842; Jan. 11, 1843; and Feb. 20, 1843; Andrew Jackson to W. B. Lewis, Dec. 21, 1842; Andrew Jackson to J. Grimes, Jan. 24, 1843; James Breedlove to Andrew Jackson, Feb. 2, 1843; N. R. Jennings, clerk, U.S. District Court, Eastern District of Louisiana to Andrew Jackson, Feb. 10, 1843; and J. R. Grymes to Andrew Jackson, Feb. 15, 1843. See also Amos Kendall to Benjamin Tappan, Feb. 9, 1843, Papers of Benjamin Tappan, Library of Congress microfilm edition.

64. Francis P. Blair to Andrew Jackson, July 14, 1842, *Correspondence of Andrew Jackson* 6:160. Blair assured Jackson that he would republish Kendall's article in the *Daily Globe;* see Sept. 12, 1842, *Jackson Papers, MS.*

65. The Kitchen Cabinet was Jackson's unofficial group of advisors during the Eaton Affair; see Remini, *Andrew Jackson: The Course of American Freedom.* For Amos Kendall's article, see "General Jackson's Fine," *United States and Democratic Review* 12 (1843): 58–77; and Andrew Jackson to Amos Kendall, May 10, 1843, *Correspondence of Andrew Jackson* 6:217–18. For Polk's role as courier, see James K. Polk to Andrew Jackson, July 1, 1842, *Jackson Papers*, LC.

66. Andrew Jackson to Blair, July 25, 1842, *Jackson Papers*, LC. Jackson expressed the same sentiments in another letter to Blair, Oct. 29, 1842, *Jackson Papers*, LC: "I shall leave the whole of this matter to you & Mr. Kendall well aware of your friendship and in your hands that my fame is secure."

67. See, for example, *Daily Globe*, July 9, Dec. 23, 1842, and Mar. 2, 1843. Though it was never ultimately published, see also "Fine Surposed By Judge Hall," Andrew Jackson to the Editors of the Globe, Feb. 1843, *Correspondence of Andrew Jackson* 6:190; Francis Blair to Andrew Jackson, June 30, 1842,

Jackson Papers, LC; Andrew Jackson to Blair, Feb. 8, 1843, *Jackson Papers,* LC; Senate, Senator Linn of Missouri on General Jackson's Fine, *Congressional Globe,* 27th Cong., 2d sess., May 12, 1842, vol. 11, appendix, 364. See also a number of published letters from Jackson to Kendall in *Jackson Papers,* LC: May 23, June 17, June 18, and Oct. 26, 1842. See also Andrew Jackson to Blair, June 16 and June 28, 1842, in which he states, "I hope you have recd my letter on the subject, written for publication," *Jackson Papers, MS.*

68. Andrew Jackson to Andrew J. Donelson, June 2, 1842, *Correspondence of Andrew Jackson* 6:155–56.

69. Francis Blair to Andrew Jackson, Feb. 7, 1843, *Jackson Papers,* LC.

70. Francis Blair to Andrew Jackson, 22 Feb. 1843; *Jackson Papers,* LC, Mar. 22, 1843.

71. Louis Field Linn to Andrew Jackson, July 4, 1843, *Jackson Papers,* LC.

72. All figures determined from *Congressional Quarterly's Guide to Congress,* 134–37.

73. The Louisiana election took place on January 9, 1843. *New Orleans Daily Picayune,* in Robert Seager II, ed., *The Papers of Henry Clay* (Lexington: Univ. Press of Kentucky, 1988), 9:797 (hereafter cited as *Papers of Henry Clay*); Henry D. Piere to Andrew Jackson, Jan. 9, 1843, *Jackson Papers,* LC; House, Congressman Slidell of Louisiana on General Jackson's Fine, *Congressional Globe,* 28th Cong., 1st sess., Dec. 29, 1843, vol. 13, pt. 1:87. Henry Clay also commented on Conrad's loss, remarking that "Conrad has been sacrificed in consequence of a faithful discharge of his duty." See Henry Clay to John J. Crittenden, Jan. 14, 1843, *Papers of Henry Clay* 9:796. Clay never spoke on the refund issue, except to make an objection to a resolution to refund the fine. See Senate, Senator Clay of Kentucky, *Congressional Globe,* 27th Cong., 2d sess., Mar. 2, 1842, 340; Sacher, *Perfect War of Politics,* 108.

74. E. G. W. Butler to Charles Conrad, May 18, 1843, MSS 102, Folder 583, Butler Family Papers, Historic New Orleans Collection, Williams Research Center, New Orleans. It is impossible to confirm Butler's statement that the Louisiana legislature debated and approved martial law. Records within the state do not include entire speeches for this period, and it is unclear if an actual resolution or law was passed in relation to the matter.

75. Auguste Davezac to Andrew Jackson, Aug. 7, 1843, *Jackson Papers,* LC. Louisiana had three representatives: two were Whig, Edward D. White and John Moore, and one was a Democrat, John B. Dawson. In all votes pertaining to going into a committee on the whole to discuss the refund, Dawson voted in the affirmative. He retained his seat into the Twenty-eighth Congress. Both Whigs lost their seats, though it appears that on the four occasions during which the House had votes, White voted in the affirmative once, the negative twice, and either abstained or was not present on another occasion. Moore voted in the affirmative on three votes and either abstained or was not present on one occasion. See *Congressional Globe,* vol. 11, appendix, 947, 44; 12:124; vol. 13, pt. 1:87.

76. See vote in *Congressional Globe,* Feb. 14, 1844, 13:274.

77. Senate, Senator Calhoun of South Carolina Presenting Resolutions from the Legislature of That State, *Congressional Globe*, 27th Cong., 3d sess., Jan. 4, 1843, 12:110. On one other occasion Calhoun did make a comment regarding the refund, though it was not related to the actual debates. In a discussion over a relief bill for Gen. William Hull, a commander during the War of 1812 who surrendered the entire Michigan territory to the British, Calhoun remarked on the Judiciary Committee's support of the bill: "How strange that such unequal justice should be meted out by the committee to General Jackson, who terminated the war with glory, and General Hull, who commenced it with disgrace." It is difficult to determine why Calhoun made this comment but was unable to support Jackson's refund bill. See Senate, Senator Calhoun of South Carolina on Remarks on the Bill for the Relief of the Heirs of General William Hull, *Congressional Globe*, 27th Cong., 2d sess., July 12, 1842, 11:308.

78. Margaret L. Coit, *John C. Calhoun: American Portrait* (Boston: Houghton Mifflin, 1950), 350, 353.

79. Robert Barnwell Rhett to John C. Calhoun, Oct. 13, 1842, in *The Papers of John C. Calhoun*, ed. Clyde N. Wilson (Columbia: Univ. of South Carolina Press, 1984), 16:494–95 (hereafter cited as *Papers of John C. Calhoun*).

80. Calhoun gave no specific reason for his resignation, though most historians surmise that he quit the Senate to prepare for the presidential race. See for example, *Papers of John C. Calhoun* 16:439–40; and John Niven, *John C. Calhoun and the Price of Union: A Biography* (Baton Rouge: Louisiana State Univ. Press, 1988), 258. Charles M. Wiltse asserted that "Calhoun had probably decided early in the year to retire from the Senate at the end of the current Congress." Wiltse also cited the turmoil surrounding the refund bill but mistakenly identified it as an attempt by Jackson's opponents to revoke the expunging resolution that removed the Senate censure for removal of the federal deposits. The expunging resolution had actually passed in 1837. See Charles M. Wiltse, *John C. Calhoun: Sectionalist, 1840–1850* (Indianapolis: Bobbs-Merrill, 1944), 99–100.

81. Merrill D. Peterson, *The Great Triumvirate* (New York: Oxford Univ. Press, 1987), 335.

82. Ibid., 340.

83. House, Congressman Ingersoll of Pennsylvania on General Jackson's Fine, *Congressional Globe*, 28th Cong., 1st sess., Dec. 6, 1843, vol. 13, pt 1:18.

84. House, Congressman Slidell of Louisiana, *House Journal*, 28th Cong., 1st sess., Dec. 29, 1843, 137.

85. House, Congressman Stephens of Georgia on General Jackson's Fine, *Congressional Globe*, 28th Cong., 1st sess., Dec. 29, 1843, vol. 13, pt. 1:87; House, Congressman Ingersoll of Pennsylvania, *Congressional Globe*, 28th Cong., 1st sess., Dec. 29, 1843, vol. 13, pt. 1:87.

86. House, Congressman Barnard of New York on General Jackson's Fine, Dec. 29, 1843, vol. 13, pt. 1:89; Barnard added later that the bill was designed "to awaken anew the popular admiration for the heroic deeds of the favorite old chief in the hope of turning it to some good account in the their particular juncture of affairs. See House, Congressman Barnard of New

York, *Congressional Globe,* 28th Cong., 1st sess., Jan. 2, 1844, vol. 13, appendix, 206.

87. House, Congressman Dawson of Louisiana on General Jackson's Fine, *Congressional Globe,* 28th Cong., 1st sess., Dec. 29, 1843, vol. 13, pt 1:92.

88. House, Congressman Peyton of Tennessee on the Bill to Refund General Jackson's Fine, *Congressional Globe,* 28th Cong., 1st sess., Jan. 2, 1844, vol. 13, appendix, 46. David Dickinson, Peyton's colleague from Tennessee, argued along the same lines, stating that the Whigs succeeded in defeating the Democrats in 1840 and would do so again in 1844. Though Jackson was "the great tower of strength of the Democratic party," argued Dickinson, the general did not have the power to raise Van Buren to the presidential chair a second time. He warned that the Democrats "would not be able, with all their skill, to hide the fox of New York in the mane of the lion of Tennessee." See House, Congressman Dickinson of Tennessee on General Jackson's Fine, *Congressional Globe,* 28th Cong., 1st sess., Jan. 6, 1844, vol. 13, appendix, 3.

89. House, Congressman Schenck of Ohio on General Jackson's Fine, *Congressional Globe,* 28th Cong., 1st sess., Jan. 8, 1844, vol. 13, appendix, 228.

90. House, Congressman McClernand of Illinois on General Jackson's Fine, *Congressional Globe,* 28th Cong., 1st sess., Jan. 6, 1844, vol. 13, appendix, 27.

91. Steenrod continued, questioning, "Are they afraid the people will give the democratic party credit for doing their duty in passing this bill, or apprehensive that they will condemn the whig party of the last Congress, that omitted to do so, and refused to pass it?" House, Congressman Steenrod of Virginia on General Jackson's Fine, *Congressional Globe,* 28th Cong., 1st sess., Jan. 8, 1844, vol. 13, appendix, 88. Congressman John McClernand of Illinois made a similar assertion: "We will pass it here by the strength and force of Democratic votes. And the people of this country will be enabled to see, and to know, who are willing to give effect to their will, and who stand in the way of it." House, Congressman McClernand of Illinois on General Jackson's Fine, Jan. 6, 1844, 13, pt. 1:114.

92. For the final vote, see *Congressional Globe,* Jan. 8, 1844, 13, pt. 1:120

93. *Congressional Globe,* 28th Cong, 1st sess., Jan. 9, 1844, 13, pt. 1:121–22. Senate, Senator Sturgeon of Pennsylvania, *Congressional Globe,* Jan. 16, 1844, 148; Senate, Senator White of Indiana, *Congressional Globe,* Jan. 23, 1844, 175.

94. Senate, Senator Berrien of Georgia, *Congressional Globe,* Jan. 30, 1844, 206; Senate, Senator Allen of Ohio, *Congressional Globe,* Feb. 13, 1844, 278. For the vote on the amendment, see *Congressional Globe,* Feb. 13, 1844, 269.

95. For Democratic and Whig views of instruction, see Lawrence Frederick Kohl, *The Politics of Individualism: Parties and the American Character in the Jacksonian Era* (New York: Oxford Univ. Press, 1989), 124–25, 130–31; Cole, *Presidency of Andrew Jackson,* 252–53; Clement Eaton, "Southern Senators and the Right of Instruction, 1789–1860," *Journal of Southerner History* 18 (1952): 303–19; "Instructions to Senators," *United States Magazine and Democratic Review* 4 (1838): 169–70; "A Short Argument on the Doctrine of Instruction," *United States Magazine and Democratic Review* 9 (1841):

434-36; and "Instructions to Representatives," *American Jurist and Law Magazine* 4 (1830): 314–24.

96. Senate, Senator Dayton on General Jackson's Fine and the Right of Instruction, *Congressional Globe*, 28th Cong., 1st sess., Feb. 9, 1844, vol. 13, pt 1:250; Peter D. Levine, *The Behavior of State Legislative Parties in the Jacksonian Era: New Jersey, 1829–1844* (Rutherford, N.J.: Fairleigh Dickinson Univ. Press, 1977), 33; "Resolutions of the General Assembly of New Jersey," *United States Congressional Serial Set*, 28th Cong., 1st sess., S. Doc. 115, 433.

97. Senator Miller remarked, "I do not recognise the power in the legislature, even of my own State, to control my vote, as a senator of the United States." Senate, Senator Miller of New Jersey on the Fine Indemnity Bill, *Congressional Globe*, 28th Cong., 1st sess., Feb. 13, 1844, vol. 13, pt. 1:268. Senator Woodbridge spent the majority of his hour on the instruction issue, posing what he believed were important questions: "Are we all mere machines here? Is there no deliberation? no intellect? no wisdom in counsel? no concession? no moulding of opinions here? Are we sent here as puppets, to be moved as the wires are pulled by those behind us? No, sir, no! And such a doctrine is inconsistent with the spirit of the constitution." Senate, Senator Woodbridge of Michigan on the Bill to Refund General Jackson's Fine, *Congressional Globe*, 28th Cong., 1st sess., Feb. 14. 1844, vol. 13, appendix, 195.

98. Eaton, "Southerner Senators and the Right of Instruction."

99. Senate, Senator Foster of Tennessee on the Bill to Refund General Jackson's Fine, *Congressional Globe*, 28th Cong., 1st sess., Feb. 13, 1844, vol. 13, pt. 2, appendix, 113.

100. Final vote in *Congressional Globe*, vol. 13, pt. 1:282; see also the *Daily Globe*, Feb. 14, 1844. For notification of the president's signing, see *Senate Journal*, Feb. 16, 1844, 124. Jackson noted his dire need of the money in a letter to Blair, Feb. 24, 1844, *Correspondence of Andrew Jackson* 6:266. A. Redington wrote to Jackson on February 19, 1844, insisting that "the Nation spoke, Political hostility quailed under its mandate." One Henry Liebenan wrote on the same day that he organized a twenty-six gun salute and hanged a banner inscribed with "Justice to the Brave—Judge Hall's Sentence on gen. jackson repudiated by the nation Feb. 14th, 1844." *Jackson Papers*, LC.

101. Francis Blair to Andrew Jackson, Jan. 9, 1844, *Correspondence of Andrew Jackson* 6:254. Old Hickory also recognized the dire consequences awaiting Whigs if they refused to support the refund, remarking in a letter to Blair, "I want to see How our senators [from Tennessee] will vote upon the subject. The Whiggs here have got into a dilemma." Andrew Jackson to Francis Blair, Jan. 19, 1844, *Correspondence of Andrew Jackson* 6:257; Francis Blair to Andrew Jackson, Feb. 14, 1844, *Correspondence of Andrew Jackson* 6:259.

CHAPTER 4

1. Twenty-three of twenty-six state constitutions, written through 1842, address the issue of the civil government's superiority to the military. Alabama's 1819 constitution is a standard representation: "The military shall, in all cases, and at all times, be in strict subordination to the civil power." For various states, see Swindler, *Sources and Documents of the United States Constitutions.*

2. Livingston and Duncan provided written opinions in March 1815, *Correspondence of Andrew Jackson* 2:197–99; Declaration of Martial Law, Dec. 16, 1814, *Jackson Papers, MS.* Also in Parton, *Life of Andrew Jackson* 2:60–61. Dallas wrote Jackson, "The military power is clearly defined, and carefully limitted [*sic*], by the Constitution and laws of the United States; but the experience of the best regulated Governments teaches us, that exigencies may sometimes arise, when (as you have emphatically observed) 'Constitutional forms must be suspended, for the permanent preservation of Constitutional rights.' . . . To enforce the discipline and to ensure the safety of his garrison, or his camp, an American Commander possesses indeed, high and necessary powers; but all his powers are compatible with the rights of citizens, and the independence of the judicial authority. If, therefore, he undertake to suspend the writ of Habeas Corpus, to restrain the liberty of the Press, to inflict military punishments, upon citizens who are not military men, and generally to supersede the functions of the civil magistrate, he may be justified by the law of necessity, while he has the merit of saving his country, but he cannot resort to the established law of the land, for the means of vindication." Alexander J. Dallas to Andrew Jackson, July 1, 1815, *Jackson Papers* 3:375.

3. Senate, Senator Tappan of Ohio on General Jackson's Fine, *Congressional Globe,* 27th Cong., 2d sess., Mar. 22, 1842, vol. 11, appendix, 223.

4. For discussions of the extent to which Locke and Vattel influenced the minds of the Founding Fathers and subsequent generations of American leaders, see Peter S. Onuf and Nicholas G. Onuf, *Federal Union, Modern World: The Law of Nations in an Age of Revolutions, 1776–1814* (Madison, Wisc.: Madison House, 1993); and two articles by Charles G. Fenwick, "The Authority of Vattel," *American Political Science Review* 7, no. 3 (Aug. 1913): 395–410; 8, no. 3 (Aug. 1914): 375–92.

5. Senate, Senator Tappan of Ohio on General Jackson's Fine, Mar. 22, 1842, vol. 11, appendix, 223.

6. Senate, Senator Buchanan of Pennsylvania on General Jackson's Fine, May 12, 1842, 11:362, 365. Other Democrats also acknowledged the unconstitutionality of martial law; see Senate, Senator Woodbury of New Hampshire on General Jackson's Fine, *Congressional Globe,* May 12, 1842, 11:365.

7. Senate, Senator Linn of Missouri on General Jackson's Fine, May 18, 1842, vol. 11, appendix, 487.

8. "Beauty" and "booty" were the British code words during the invasion and pertained to the rape and pillage planned for New Orleans. Senate, Senator Linn of Missouri on General Jackson's Fine, May 12, 1842, 11:364.

9. Senate, Senator Linn of Missouri on General Jackson's Fine, May 18, 1842, vol. 11, appendix, 487. Senator William King of Alabama agreed on the issue of duty, remarking that "a commander who failed to declare martial law under the circumstances would fail to do his duty; he would be faithless to his country—a greater crime than a mere infringement of civil power. See Senate, Senator King of Alabama on General Jackson's Fine, *Congressional Globe*, 27th Cong., 2d sess., May 18, 1842, vol. 11, appendix, 376.

10. Senate, Senator Linn of Missouri on General Jackson's Fine, May 18, 1842, vol. 11, appendix, 488.

11. Ibid. Jefferson expressed his opinion in defense of General James Wilkinson, who ignored a writ of habeas corpus and relocated two prisoners from New Orleans to Washington to stand trial for treason; the writ was issued by Dominick Hall.

12. For the similarities, see Thomas Jefferson to John Breckinridge, Aug. 12, 1803, Thomas Jefferson Papers, Library of Congress, on line at American Memory web site, http://memory.loc.gov. See also Peter J. Kastor, *The Nation's Crucible: The Louisiana Purchase and the Creation of America* (New Haven: Yale Univ. Press, 2004).

13. Paul Leicester Ford, ed., *The Writings of Thomas Jefferson*, vol. 10 (New York: G. P. Putnam's Sons, 1899), 331.

14. Thomas Jefferson to James Brown, Oct. 27, 1808, in *Writings of Thomas Jefferson*, vol. 9, ed. Paul Leicester Ford (New York: G. P. Putnam's Sons, 1899), 211.

15. For the various cases listed by Linn, see Senate, Senator Louis Linn of Missouri on General Jackson's Fine, May 12, 1842, vol. 11, appendix, 364.

16. Ibid.

17. Senate, Senator Linn of Missouri on General Jackson's Fine, May 12, 1842, vol. 11, appendix, 364.

18. See Andrew Jackson to Louis F. Linn, Mar. 12, 1842, *Correspondence of Andrew Jackson* 6:144. Jackson expressed the same sentiment in other letters. See Andrew Jackson to Louis Linn, July 4, 1842; and Andrew Jackson to Francis Blair, July 2, Oct. 29, 1842, and Feb. 20, 1843, all in *Jackson Papers*, LC.

19. Senate, Senator Wright of New York on General Jackson's Fine, *Congressional Globe*, 27th Cong., 2d sess., May 18, 1842, vol. 11, appendix, 377; House, Congressman Payne of Alabama on General Jackson's Fine, *Congressional Globe*, 27th Cong., 3d sess., Jan. 28, 1843, 12:217.

20. House, Congressman Dawson of Louisiana on General Jackson's Fine, *Congressional Globe*, 28th Cong., 1st sess., Jan. 2, 1844, vol. 13, pt. 1:92.

21. Senate, Senator Walker of Mississippi the Fine on General Jackson, Jan. 10, 1843, 12:141. Samuel McRoberts made the same point about a general having the authority to control his own camp; see Senate, Senator McRoberts of Illinois on General Jackson's Fine, *Congressional Globe*, 27th Cong., 2d sess., Feb. 17, 1843, 12:301.

22. Charles Lanman, *Dictionary of the United States Congress Containing Biographical Sketches of Its Members from the Foundation of the Government* (Philadelphia: J. B. Lippincott, 1859), 439; *Congressional Quarterly's Guide to Congress*, 4th ed. (Washington, D.C.: GPO, 1991), 130.

23. Senate, Senator Smith of Connecticut on General Jackson's Fine, *Congressional Globe*, 27th Cong., 3d sess., Feb. 20, 1843, vol. 12, appendix, 220–21.

24. Ibid. In commenting on a Whig senator's speech, Lewis Linn also essentially argued that it was better to violate the Constitution than watch it be destroyed: "He [Jackson] was not the man voluntarily to abandon his duty to his country in such a crisis, and take refuge behind the letter of the Constitution for his excuse, after both country and Constitution were destroyed by an invading enemy." Senate, Senator Linn of Missouri on General Jackson's Fine, Dec. 22, 1842, vol. 12, appendix, 68.

25. The next chapter discusses the contempt of court issue. Charles Jared Ingersoll, *Gen. Jackson's Fine: An Examination into the Question of Martial Law; with an Explanation of the Law of Contempt of Court* (Washington, D.C.: Blair and Rives, 1843); Francis Blair to Andrew Jackson, June 22, 1843, *Jackson Papers*, LC.

26. In a biography of Ingersoll, the congressman's grandson, William Meigs, wrote that "in the end of June, 1842, Mr. Polk called on him [Ingersoll] with papers on the subject sent by General Jackson to Mr. Kendall; and Mr. Ingersoll in July of the next year published an elaborate pamphlet upon the subject." Meigs continued, "I presume from these facts that this pamphlet is to be considered as presenting with authority General Jackson's side of the question." See William M. Meigs, *The Life of C. J. Ingersoll* (Philadelphia: J. B. Lippincott, 1899), 250. Jackson stated that Ingersoll's pamphlet revealed "the true ground upon which I acted" but claimed the work was "unsolicited." See Andrew Jackson to Maunsel White, Jan. 12, 1844, *Correspondence of Andrew Jackson* 6:256. Correspondence between Jackson and his supporters confirm both Meigs's conclusion and Polk's role as courier. See James K. Polk to Andrew Jackson, July 1, 1842; Andrew Jackson to Francis Blair, July 2, 1842; and Andrew Jackson to Louis Linn, July 4, 1842, all in *Jackson Papers*, LC.

27. Ingersoll, "An Examination into the Question of Martial Law," 15.

28. House, Congressman Ingersoll of Pennsylvania on General Jackson's Fine, *Congressional Globe*, 27th Cong., 3d sess., Jan. 7, 1843, 12:132. William O. Butler supported Ingersoll on such points; see House, Congressman Butler of Kentucky on General Jackson's Fine, Jan. 11, 1843, vol. 12, appendix, 118, 120.

29. House, Congressman Brown of Tennessee on General Jackson's Fine, 28th Cong., *Congressional Globe*, 1st sess., Jan. 8, 1844, vol. 13, appendix, 47; House, Congressman Belser of Alabama on General Jackson's Fine, *Congressional Globe*, 28th Cong., 1st sess., Jan. 8, 1844, vol. 13, appendix, 35; House, Congressman Payne of Alabama on General Jackson's Fine, Jan. 28, 1843, 12:217.

30. House, Congressman Kennedy of Indiana on General Jackson's Fine, *Congressional Globe*, 28th Cong., 1st sess., Jan. 2, 1844, vol. 13, appendix, 46; House, Congressman Dawson of Louisiana on General Jackson's Fine, Jan. 2, 1844, 13, pt. 1:92.

31. House, Congressman Steenrod of Virginia on the Bill to Refund General Jackson's Fine, *Congressional Globe*, 28th Cong., 1st sess., Jan. 8, 1844, vol. 13, appendix, 88.

32. One source asserts that Hall was a native of South Carolina; see Malone, *Dictionary of American Biography* 8:123. Charles Gayarre insists that Hall was English born; see Charles Gayarre, *A History of Louisiana* (New York: W. J. Widdleton, 1867).

33. House, Congressman Douglas of Illinois on General Jackson's Fine, *Congressional Globe*, 28th Cong., 1st sess., Jan. 6, 1844, vol. 13, appendix, 43–44.

34. Adams, *Memoirs of John Quincy Adams* 11:478; Benjamin Perley Poor, *Reminiscences of Sixty Years in the National Metropolis* (Philadelphia: Hubbard Brothers, 1886), 1:316. Surprisingly, one historian noted that the speech "is not of much interest or importance now, though one cannot read it without feeling the power of the speaker." Louis Howland, *Stephen A. Douglas* (New York: Scribner, 1920), 35. Though Howland noted Douglas's discussion of the constitutionality of Jackson's actions and stated that "Douglas clearly was at that time no narrow constructionist," the author downplayed the importance of the congressman's arguments. To his credit, however, at least Howland discussed the constitutional aspect of the speech. Douglas's modern biographer, Robert W. Johannsen, did not mention the doctrines espoused by the young congressman or broach the constitutional nature of the speech. See Robert W. Johannsen, *Stephen A. Douglas* (New York: Oxford Univ. Press, 1973), 129–30. For Andrew Jackson's thanks, see a brief article relating the incident in the *New York Evening Post*, June 17, 1845.

35. Senate, Senator Buchanan of Pennsylvania on General Jackson's Fine, May 12, 1842, 11:365–66; Senate, Senator Woodbury of New Hampshire on General Jackson's Fine, May 12, 1842, 11:365; Senate, Senator Linn of Missouri on General Jackson's Fine, May 18, 1842, vol. 11, appendix, 487–90; House, Congressman Dean of Ohio on General Jackson's Fine, *Congressional Globe*, 28th Cong., 1st sess., Jan. 2, 1844, vol. 13, pt. 2:58; House, Congressman Weller of Ohio on General Jackson's Fine, *Congressional Globe*, 28th Cong., 1st sess., Jan. 6, 1844, vol. 13, pt. 1:111; House, Congressman Douglas of Illinois on General Jackson's Fine, Jan. 6, 1844, vol. 13, pt. 1: 115; House, Congressman McClernand of Illinois on General Jackson's Fine, Jan. 6, 1844, vol. 13, pt. 1:115; House, Congressman Belser of Alabama on General Jackson's Fine, Jan. 8, 1844, vol. 13, appendix, 35.

36. Senate, Senator Walker of Mississippi the Fine on General Jackson, May 12, 1842, 11:493; Senate, Senator King of Alabama on General Jackson's Fine, May 12, 1842, 11:362; Senate, Senator Smith of Connecticut on General Jackson's Fine, *Congressional Globe*, 27th Cong., 3d sess., Mar. 3, 1843, 12:315; House, Congressman Payne of Alabama on General Jackson's Fine, Jan. 28, 1843, 12:217.

37. Senate, Senator Tappan of Ohio on General Jackson's Fine, Mar. 22, 1842, vol. 11, appendix, 223; Senate, Senator Benton of Missouri on General Jackson's Fine, *Congressional Globe*, 27th Cong., 2d sess., May 12, 1842, 11:493; House, Congressman Kennedy of Indiana on General Jackson's Fine, Jan. 2, 1844, vol. 13, appendix, 46.

38. Senate, Senator Allen of Ohio on General Jackson's Fine, *Congressional Globe*, 27th Cong., 2d sess., May 18, 1842, vol. 11, appendix, 378; House, Congressman Slidell of Louisiana on General Jackson's Fine, Dec. 29, 1843,

vol. 13, pt. 1:88; House, Congressman Dawson of Louisiana on General Jackson's Fine, Jan. 2, 1844, vol. 13, pt. 1:92.

39. Senate, Senator Crittenden of Kentucky on General Jackson's Fine, May 12, 1842, vol. 11, appendix, 362.

40. Senate, Senator Preston of South Carolina on General Jackson's Fine, *Congressional Globe*, 27th Cong. 2d sess., May 12, 1842, vol. 11, appendix, 363. Some Democrats made the same assertion regarding Jackson bowing to the civil power. See Senate, Senator Walker of Mississippi the Fine on General Jackson, Jan. 10, 1843, 12:141; Senate, Senator Huger of South Carolina on General Jackson's Fine, *Congressional Globe*, 28th Cong., 1st sess., Feb. 14, 1844, vol. 13, pt. 1:274.

41. Senate, Senator Berrien of Georgia on General Jackson's Fine, *Congressional Globe*, 27th Cong., 2d sess., May 12, 1842, vol. 11, appendix, 363, 365.

42. The full amendment read: "*Provided always*, That nothing in this act shall be construed to be an expression of the opinion of Congress as the legality of the proceedings of the judge in inflicting the fine, but that this shall be deemed and taken to be an additional expression of the sense of Congress of the high consideration in which they hold the achievement of General Jackson in the defense of New Orleans, and of the services rendered by him and his companions in arms on that memorable occasion." See Senate, Senator Henderson of Mississippi on General Jackson's Fine, May 18, 1842, vol. 11, appendix, 374.

43. Senate, Senator Graham of North Carolina on General Jackson's Fine, *Congressional Globe*, 27th Cong., 3d sess., Feb. 20, 1843, 12:316.

44. Senate, Senator Berrien of Georgia on General Jackson's Fine, *Congressional Globe*, 27th Cong., 2d sess., Jan. 10, 1843, 12:141.

45. Senate, Senator Mangum of North Carolina on General Jackson's Fine, *Congressional Globe*, 27th Cong., 2d sess., May 18, 1842, vol. 11, appendix, 375.

46. Charles G. Sellers Jr. noted Jackson's popularity in the South, pointing out that out of some ninety southerners in the House of Representatives in the early 1830s, sixty-nine were elected as Jackson supporters. Twenty-five of these were later active in the Whig Party, leaving mainly because of the bank issue. See "Who Were the Southern Whigs?" *American Historical Review* 59 (1954): 335–46.

47. Numerous major and minor votes were taken on the refund bill, and for the most part, they reflect the three to one ratio. The most characteristic votes were taken during the Twenty-eighth Congress, first session. On a vote regarding censure of Judge Hall, some six southern Whigs and one northern Whig voted against any such amendment. See the Fine Indemnity Bill, *Congressional Globe*, 28th Cong., 1st sess., Feb. 13, 1844, vol. 13, pt. 1:269. The final vote on the bill showed seven southern Whig supporters and one northerner. These seven were out of twelve southerners total. Yet of the five who did not vote for the bill, two abstained. See Senate, *Senate on House of Representatives Bill 1*, 28th Cong., 1st sess., serial 430, 119.

48. Senate, Senator Archer of Virginia on General Jackson's Fine, May 25, 1842, 11:515.

49. Senate, Senator Bayard of Delaware on General Jackson's Fine, *Congressional Globe,* 27th Cong., 2d sess., May 25, 1842, 11:515.

50. Senate, Senator Bayard of Delaware on General Jackson's Fine, *Congressional Globe,* 27th Cong., 3d sess., Dec. 22, 1842, vol. 12, appendix, 67–68.

51. Senate, Senator Miller of New Jersey on General Jackson's Fine, Feb. 17, 1843, 12:208.

52. Senate, Senator Woodbridge of Michigan on the Bill to Refund General Jackson's Fine, Feb. 14, 1844, vol. 13, appendix, 194–68.

53. Some may take exception to calling Adams a Whig. He was certainly not a Whig of the Clay-Webster school, but he did side with the party on most issues. And because disgust with Jackson defined an important component of the Whig party, Adams certainly fit. For Adams siding with Whigs on most issues, see Leonard L. Richards, *The Life and Times of Congressman John Quincy Adams* (New York: Oxford Univ. Press, 1986), 54.

54. House, Congressman Adams of Massachusetts on General Jackson's Fine, *Congressional Globe,* 27th Cong., 3d sess., Jan. 5, 1843, 12:123.

55. House, Congressman Adams of Massachusctts on General Jackson's Fine, *Congressional Globe,* 27th Cong., 3d sess., Jan. 6, 1843, 12:129.

56. House, Congressman Adams of Massachusetts on the General Appropriation Bill, *Congressional Globe,* 27th Cong., 2d sess., Apr. 15, 1842, 11:429.

57. Ibid.

58. Remini, *Battle of New Orleans,* 37; see also William C. C. Claiborne to Andrew Jackson, Aug. 12, 1814, *Jackson Papers* 3:115–16.

59. James McPherson, *Battle Cry of Freedom: The Civil War Era* (New York: Oxford Univ. Press, 1988), 352–53.

60. House, Congressman Adams on Rations to the Inhabitants of Alabama, *Register of Debates,* 24th Cong. 1st sess., May 25, 1836, vol. 12, pt. 4:407.

61. Daniel Walker Howe's assertion that "Adams was not quite sure whether Congress, the Executive, or commanders in the field would be responsible for it," is incorrect. See Daniel Walker Howe, *Political Culture of the American Whigs* (Chicago: Univ. of Chicago Press, 1979), 64; David Herbert Donald's argument that Adams represented a "Whig creed" that strongly asserted war powers is not entirely correct. Adams advocated war powers abstractly and only when they served to facilitate his attack on slavery. See David Herbert Donald, "A Whig in the White House," in *Lincoln Reconsidered: Essays on the Civil War Era* (New York: Vintage Books, 1961), 204–7.

62. Charles Francis Adams, ed., *Memoirs of John Quincy Adams,* vol. 9 (New York: AMS Press, 1970), 298.

63. John Quincy Adams to Benjamin Lundy, June 2, 1836, and John Quincy Adams to Robert Walsh, June 3, 1836, in Charles Francis Adams, "John Quincy Adams and Martial Law," *Proceedings of the Massachusetts Historical Society* (1902): 450–51.

64. Andrew Jackson to William B. Lewis, Feb. 27, 1842, in *The Legacy of Andrew Jackson: Essays on Democracy, Indian Removal, and Slavery,* by Robert V. Remini (Baton Rouge: Louisiana State Univ. Press, 1988), 107.

Remini provides a very good, though brief, discussion of how Jacksonians viewed Adams's agitation of the slavery question as a payback for his loss in the 1828 presidential election (104–5). See also Richards, *Life and Times of Congressman John Quincy Adams*, 9; and Maj. L. Wilson, "The Concept of Time and the Political Dialogue in the United States, 1828–48," *American Quarterly* 19 (1976): 619–44.

65. Parsons, *John Quincy Adams*, 140–44; Weeks, "John Quincy Adams's 'Great Gun,'" 25–42; Chace and Carr, "Odd Couple Who Won Florida," 134–60; Brooks, *Diplomacy in the Borderlands*, 148–50; Remini, *Andrew Jackson: The Course of American Empire*, 367–77.

66. Lynn Hudson Parsons, "In Which the Political Becomes the Personal, and Vice Versa: The Last Ten Years of John Quincy Adams and Andrew Jackson," *Journal of the Early Republic* 23, no. 3 (Fall 2003): 421–43; Catherine Allgor, *Parlor Politics: In Which the Ladies of Washington Help Build a City and a Government* (Charlottesville: Univ. Press of Virginia, 2000), 177–82.

67. House, Congressman Butler of Kentucky on General Jackson's Fine, Jan. 11, 1843, vol. 12, appendix, 118. Charles Jared Ingersoll made the same point, remarking that "all the high handed, but justifiable proceedings of Gen. Jackson in his Seminole campaign, were justified by Mr. Adams, on the same plea of indispensable necessity for the public safety." See House, Congressman Ingersoll of Pennsylvania on General Jackson's Fine, Jan. 7, 1843, 12:132. William Payne asked "why was it that the distinguished gentleman from Massachusetts, who was formerly so able a champion of General Jackson, now turned round, and at the end of thirty years, to become—he had almost said, the reviler and slanderer of him whom he once so powerfully defended? He would not say that the feeling evinced by the gentleman had its origin in the political context of 1828; but he could tell the gentleman that others less charitable than himself not only thought such to be the fact, but were not backward in declaring so." House, Congressman Payne of Alabama on General Jackson's Fine, Jan. 28, 1843, 12:217.

68. House, Congressman Hunt of New York on General Jackson's Fine, *Congressional Globe*, 27th Cong., 3d sess., Jan. 14, 1843, 12:160.

69. House, Congressman Botts of Virginia on General Jackson's Fine, Jan. 24, 1843, 12:195.

70. "Mr. Pearce's Report from the Committee of the Judiciary of the House, Made on the 31st of January," *Nile's Weekly Register* 60 (Mar. 25, 1843): 62. Also contained in House, *Mr. Pearce's Report*, 27th Cong., 31 Jan. 1843, 3d sess., serial 426, 2–19. The committee was dominated by Whigs, six to three. Four of the six Whigs were from the North. See House, *Committee on the Judiciary*, 27th Cong., 3d sess., serial 400, 37–38.

71. House, Congressman Barnard of New York on General Jackson's Fine, Jan. 2, 1844, vol. 13, appendix, 206–11.

72. Ibid.

73. Aaron Brown, for example, stated, "I desire now to reply to the extraordinary speech of the gentleman from New York—extraordinary for its general bad temper. Why so hot and fiery on this occasion, and yet so cold, and even stoical, on all others? I fear the gentleman has grown jealous of

the venerable gentleman who sits next to him, [Mr. Adams,] [*Congressional Globe* addition] and is determined hereafter to outrival even him in turbulence and violence." House, Congressman Brown of Tennessee on General Jackson's Fine, Jan. 8, 1844, vol. 13, appendix, 47; see also House, Congressman Weller of Ohio on the Bill to Refund the Fine Assessed against General Jackson, *Congressional Globe*, 28th Cong., 1st sess., Jan. 6, 1844, vol. 13, appendix, 61.

74. House, Congressman Stephens of Georgia on General Jackson's Fine, Dec. 29, 1843, vol. 13, pt. 1:87; House, Congressman Dickinson of Tennessee on General Jackson's Fine, Jan. 6, 1844, vol. 13, appendix, 37; House, Congressman Severance of Maine on General Jackson's Fine, *Congressional Globe*, 28th Cong., 1st sess., Jan. 8, 1844, vol. 13, pt. 1:119.

75. House, Congressman Schenck of Ohio on General Jackson's Fine, Jan. 8, 1844, vol. 13, appendix, 227–30.

76. Adams, *Memoirs of John Quincy Adams* 11:479. For information on Schenck's background, see James R. Therry, "The Life of General Robert Cumming Schenck" (Ph.D. diss., Georgetown Univ., 1968) and Epiphanie Clara Kokkinou, "The Political Career of Robert Cumming Schenck" (master's thesis, Miami Univ., 1955).

77. For more on the Dorr War, see Arthur M. Mowry, *The Dorr War: Constitutional Struggle in Rhode Island* (New York: Chelsea House, 1970); Marvin E. Gettleman, *The Dorr Rebellion: A Study in American Radicalism, 1833–1849* (New York: Random House, 1973); and George M. Dennison, *The Dorr War: Republicanism on Trial, 1831–1861* (Lexington: Univ. Press of Kentucky, 1976).

78. House, Congressman Underwood of Kentucky on General Jackson's Fine, *Congressional Globe*, 27th Cong., 3d sess., Jan. 4, 1843, 12:114.

79. House, Congressman Kennedy of Indiana on the resolution authorizing the committee on the Rhode Island controversy to send for persons and papers, *Congressional Globe*, 28th Cong., 1st sess., Mar. 13, 1844, vol. 13, pt. 2:264.

80. House, Congressman McClernand of Illinois on General Jackson's Fine, Jan. 6, 1844, vol. 13, appendix, 28; vol. 13, pt 1:115.

81. House, Congressman McClernand of Illinois on the Rhode Island Memorial, *Congressional Globe*, 28th Cong., 1st sess., Mar. 19, 1844, vol. 13, pt. 2:329.

82. House, Congressman Rathbun of New York on the Rhode Island Memorial, *Congressional Globe*, 28th Cong., 1st sess., Mar. 9, 1844, vol. 13, pt. 2:335.

83. House, Congressman Smith of Indiana on the Rhode Island Memorial, *Congressional Globe*, 28th Cong., 1st sess., Mar. 14, 1844, vol. 13, pt. 2:463.

84. Senate, *Senate on House of Representatives Bill 1*, 119; House, House Bill 1, *Congressional Globe*, Jan. 8, 1844, vol. 13, pt. 1:120.

85. *Pawtucket Gazette and Chronicle*, July 15, 1842.

86. The cites for the many articles are too numerous to include. See the *Daily Globe* from March 12, 1842, to February 16, 1844, and the *National Intelligencer* for the same period. The *Globe* also included articles from the *Madisonian* as well as several Louisiana newspapers, including the *Planters' Advocate*, the *Plaquemine Planters' Gazette*, and the *New Orleans Herald*.

Other newspapers throughout the nation undoubtedly followed the congressional debates.

87. Tyler stated that an officer should be "relieved from the circumstances in which that judgment placed him. There are cases in which public functionaries may be called on to weigh the public interest against their own personal hazards; and, if the civil law be violated from praiseworthy motives, or an overruling sense of public danger and public necessity, punishment may well be restrained within that limit which asserts and maintains the authority of the law, and the subjection of the military to the civil power." See John Tyler, State of the Union Address, *Congressional Globe*, Dec. 14, 1842, 12:36.

88. Richard H. Collins, *The History of Kentucky*, 2 vols. (Covington, Ky.: Collins, 1883), 1:189, 498; 2:357, 376; James Grant Wilson and John Fiske, *Appleton's Cyclopedia of American Biography* (New York, D. Appleton, 1889–1900), 4:512.

89. Samuel Smith Nicholas, *Martial Law, by a Kentuckian*, republished from the *Louisville Journal* (Philadelphia: J. Campbell, 1862), 9, 10.

90. Ibid., 12.

91. Ibid., 7.

92. Jackson stated, "The moment I saw the Kentuckian on Martial Law, I was sure of the object & that Clay was *secretely* [sic] at the bottom of it." Andrew Jackson to Robert B. McAfee, Jan. 14, 1843, *Jackson Papers*, LC. Jackson made the same charge in a letter that he prepared for publication in the *Globe:* "The Kentuckian, just after Mr. Clay had left Louisville, Ky., lets fly his parthian arrow, sends it on to [Charles] Conrad, secretly without having the manly courage to furnish me a copy." The general continued, "This Kentuckian has made this publication for political purposes and to throw a dark shade over my fame whilst congress has the subject before them." Andrew Jackson to the Editors of the *Globe*, "The Fine Supposed by Judge Hall," Feb. 1842, *Correspondence of Andrew Jackson* 6:195, 197. Sam Houston supported Jackson's denunciation of Nicholas, remarking that "if the 'kentuckian' has any shame, he has abundant reason to blush for his foul slanders against you!" Sam Houston to Andrew Jackson, Jan. 31, 1843, in *Writings of Sam Houston*, ed. Amelia W. Williams and Eugene C. Barker (Austin: Univ. of Texas Press, 1940), 3:311–12. Jackson's indictment of Clay was not without merit. Clay traveled throughout the southwestern United States in 1842 and 1843, and in July of the former year the *National Intelligencer* reported that the "distinguished citizen [Clay] was to have left Louisville for the South on Saturday last" on his way to New Orleans. "Mr. Clay," *National Intelligencer*, Aug. 2, 1842. Though the exact publication date of the Kentuckian's pamphlet is unknown, it appeared in mid-1842 following the introduction of the refund bill in March. Excerpts from "Martial Law" were printed in the *National Intelligencer* on December 12, 1842, and January 4, 1843. Furthermore, there is little question of Clay and Nicholas's acquaintance. Both were members of the Free Grand Masonry Lodge of Louisville, and both were elected grand orator there. See Collins, *History of Kentucky* 1:526. Democrats argued that he had formerly been a member

of their party and supported Jackson's bid for the presidency. Nicholas allegedly changed his views only after Henry Clay secured him a judgeship. The *Daily Globe* reported on January 4, 1843 that Nicholas was "one of General Jackson's most ardent supporters for the Presidency." The paper added sarcastically that Nicholas "was extremely anxious to see this usurper, dictator, constitution-destroyer, put at the head of the Government." The author also charged that Nicholas was "a violent enemy of Mr. Clay at this time. . . . But became a judge, through the favor of Mr. Clay's friends in Kentucky." Nicholas therefore changed his allegiance, becoming "a new convert to the Federal creed."

CHAPTER 5

1. Remini, *Andrew Jackson: The Course of American Freedom*, 276; Remini, *Andrew Jackson: The Course of American Empire*, 409–15; see also Richard P. Longaker, "Andrew Jackson and the Judiciary," *Political Science Quarterly* 71 (Sept. 1956): 341–64.

2. For newspaper accounts, see *Friends of the Laws*, Apr. 8, 11, 13, 15, 1815, *Niles Weekly Register*, June 3, 1815; for other charges against Hall, see "Andrew Jackson and Judge D. A. Hall," 509–70. Jackson, in a letter to Francis Blair dated July 8, 1842, repeated his charge that Hall fled the city in panic; see *Jackson Papers, MS.*

3. Andrew Jackson to Francis Blair, July 2, 1842, *Jackson Papers, MS.*

4. Ingersoll, *Gen. Jackson's Fine*; Charles J. Ingersoll to Francis Blair, June 19, 1843, *Jackson Papers, MS.*

5. Charles J. Ingersoll to Francis Blair, June 19, 1843; Francis Blair to Andrew Jackson, June 22, 1843; Francis Blair to Andrew Jackson, July 4, 1843; Charles J. Ingersoll to Francis Blair, June 15, 1843. The phrase "carrying the war into Africa" came directly from a letter sent by Jackson to Blair on July 2, 1842, *Jackson Papers, LC.*

6. Meigs, *Life of C. J. Ingersoll*, 250; Andrew Jackson to Maunsel White, Jan. 12, 1844, *Correspondence of Andrew Jackson* 6:256.

7. Ronald L. Goldfarb, *The Contempt Power* (New York: Columbia Univ. Press, 1963), 9, 11–13; Joseph H. Beale, "Contempt of Court, Criminal and Civil," *Harvard Law Review* 21 (1908): 161–74; C. K. K., "Contempt of Court," *Tennessee Law Review* 2 (1923–24): 215–21.

8. Richard Peters, ed., *United States Statutes at Large, Containing the Laws and Concurrent Resolutions . . . and Reorganization Plan, Amendment to the Constitution, and Proclamations* (Washington, D.C.: GPO, 1845), 1:83.

9. Felix Frankfurter and James M. Landis, "Power of Congress Over Procedure in Criminal Contempts in 'Inferior' Federal Courts—A Study in Separation of Powers," *Harvard Law Review* 37 (1923–1924): 1010–58; Walter Nelles and Carol Weiss King, "Contempt by Publication in the United States," *Columbia Law Review* 28 (Apr. and May 1928): 401–31, 525–62; Goldfarb, *Contempt Power*, 20.

10. John Charles Fox, "The Summary Process to Punish Contempt," *Law Quarterly Review* 25 (1909): 238–52, 354–71.

11. Ibid.

12. The Almon case stemmed from a libelous publication involving the opinion of Chief Justice Lord Mansfield. Wilmot never delivered his opinion in court because of a technical error in the case. After studying both Wilmot's and Blackstone's decisions, John Fox concluded that "it is not improbable that Blackstone received advice from Wilmot on the subject." Fox, "Summary Process to Punish Contempt," 247, 250. See also Nelles and King, "Contempt by Publication," 408; John Charles Fox, "The King v. Almon," *Law Quarterly Review* 24 (1908): 184, 266; and John Charles Fox, *The History of Contempt of Court: The Form of Trial and the Mode of Punishment* (Oxford: Clarendon Press, 1927), 5–15.

13. Both the Pennsylvania and New York statutes stemmed from punishments for libelous publications and placed limits on the degree to which judges could punish contempt outside of the court. For a detailed history, see Frankfurter and Landis, "Power of Congress Over Procedure in Criminal Contempts," 1031–36; and Nelles and King, "Contempt by Publication," 409–22.

14. One legal historian argued that Peck's case was "probably the greatest abuse of the contempt power." See Cromwell H. Thomas, *Problems of Contempt of Court: A Study in Law and Public Policy* (Baltimore: Horn-Shafer, 1934), 25.

15. For the particulars of the case, see House, *Register of Debates*, 21st Cong., 1st sess., April 7, 1830, 6:411, 41; Thomas, *Problems of Contempt of Court*, 26; and "Speech on the Report of the Judiciary Committee Recommending the Impeachment of Judge Peck," in *The Works of James Buchanan*, ed. John Bassett Moore (New York: Antiquarian Press, 1960), 2:24–37.

16. Lawless's petition was first introduced by Congressman Scott of Missouri on December 8, 1826, but was opposed effectively by Daniel Webster. Three years later, on December 15, 1829, George McDuffie reintroduced the bill successfully. Thomas, *Problems of Contempt of Court*, 26–27. The members of the prosecution committee included the chairman, James Buchanan of Pennsylvania (Buchanan was also the chairman of the Committee on the Judiciary), Henry Storrs of New York, George McDuffie of South Carolina, Ambrose Spencer of New York, and Charles Wickliffe of Kentucky. House, "The Trial of Judge Peck," *Register of Debates*, 21st Cong., 1st. sess., May 3, 1830, 6:383.

17. Buchanan also argued that the common law of England had no place in the criminal statutes of America. The contempt power was derived from the Judiciary Act of 1789 exclusively, which had no relation to the common law. George McDuffie, Buchanan's co-counsel, expressed similar sentiments in regard to both the power of judges and the relationship of the common law. Counsel for the defense, William Wirt, argued that necessity, the need for a court to defend its operations, allowed every judge to punish summarily. And in contrast to Buchanan, Wirt insisted that the contempt power had a deep history related to the laws of England. Wirt relied greatly upon

King v. Almon as historical foundation. See "Argument in the Senate for
the Conviction of Judge Peck, January 28 and 29," in Moore, *Works of James
Buchanan* 2:81–161; Thomas Hart Benton, "George McDuffie on the Trial
of Judge Peck," in *Abridgement of the Debates of Congress*, by Thomas
Hart Benton (New York: D. Appleton, 1859), 11:125–31; Arthur J. Stansbury,
Report on the Trial of Judge Peck (1833; reprint, New York: De Capo Press,
1972). See also Nelles and King, "Contempt by Publication," 525, for the
view that Peck's acquittal determined nothing in regard to the power of
contempt.

18. Thomas Hart Benton, *Abridgement of the Debates of Congress* (New York:
    D. Appleton, 1859), 11:307–8; Goldfarb, in *Contempt Power*, stated incor-
    rectly that James Buchanan presented the bill to Congress. Draper was
    the original proponent of the measure, but Buchanan, acting as chairman
    of the Committee on the Judiciary, played a large role in drafting the bill
    (see p. 21).

19. Richard Peters, ed., *Statutes at Large of the United States of America* (1860;
    microfilm edition, Ann Arbor: University Microfilms, 1973), 6:487–88. For
    an excellent account of the legislative process regarding the contempt act
    bill, see Frankfurter and Landis, "Power of Congress over Procedure in
    Criminal Contempts," 1026 n. 75.

20. Not all Democrats attacked Hall and the judiciary. Some members of the
    party downplayed Judge Hall's involvement, insisting that his name was
    not even mentioned in the legislation and it was therefore unnecessary to
    involve the judge or to question his judicial authority. See, for example,
    Senate, Senator Linn of Missouri on General Jackson's Fine, May 18, 1842,
    11:487; and Senate, Senator Woodbury of New Hampshire on General
    Jackson's Fine, May 12, 1842, vol. 12, appendix, 365.

21. "Andrew Jackson and Judge D. A. Hall."

22. Senate, Senator Tappan of Ohio on General Jackson's Fine, Mar. 22, 1842,
    vol. 11, appendix, 223.

23. Senate, Senator Benton of Missouri on General Jackson's Fine, May 12,
    1842, 11:493.

24. Senate, Senator Buchanan of Pennsylvania on General Jackson's Fine,
    May 12, 1842, vol. 11, appendix, 363, 365.

25. Ibid.

26. Ibid., 366. This was a point that Buchanan made forcefully during the Peck
    trial. For Buchanan's discussion of direct versus constructive contempt
    during the trial, see Moore, *Works of James Buchanan* 2:33.

27. Senate, Senator Buchanan of Pennsylvania on General Jackson's Fine,
    May 12, 1842, vol. 11, appendix, 366. For Buchanan's argument in the Peck
    trial, see Moore, *Works of James Buchanan* 2:33, 115.

28. Senator Samuel McRoberts of Illinois, Jackson's former attorney general,
    made the same assertion: "What is a contempt of court? It was some act
    done in the presence of the court—some act which reflected directly upon
    the court as a court. Was it pretended that such was the case here? Judge
    Hall admitted himself that no court was held from the time martial law
    was declared until the army was disbanded. It could have been, therefore,

no contempt of court; and if it were held that Judge Hall could punish for a mere contempt of his person, he [McRoberts] must be permitted to say it was a new doctrine." Senate, Senator McRoberts of Illinois on General Jackson's Fine, Feb. 17, 1843, 12:301. See also House, Congressman Dean of Ohio on General Jackson's Fine, Jan. 2, 1844, vol. 13, pt. 1:95; and House, Congressman Douglas of Illinois on General Jackson's Fine, Jan. 6, 1844, vol. 13, appendix, 44.

29. Peters, *Statutes at Large of the United States of America* 6:487–88.

30. Ibid.; emphasis added.

31. House, Congressman Ingersoll of Pennsylvania on General Jackson's Fine, Jan. 7, 1843, 12:131.

32. Citing a work by Edward Livingston, the author of New York's 1829 contempt statute (and Jackson's aide during the battle of New Orleans and defense counsel during the Hall episode in 1815), Ingersoll stated, "Courts ought to be empowered to remove all obstructions to their proceeding. . . . Everything, then, that is necessary and proper to defend its existence, and secure the free performance of its functions, can with no greater propriety be denied to a court, than there would be in forbidding an individual to defend his life against the attack of an assassin." (James Buchanan quoted the same passage by Livingston during the Peck trial). The right of self-defense, however, existed only so long as a threat to the court remained. Once again utilizing Livingston's argument, and that which Buchanan had quoted so liberally in 1831, Ingersoll questioned, "Is the violence over?—has the interruption ceased?—is the intruder removed?—has the order which was disobeyed been complied with?" Ingersoll, *Gen. Jackson's Fine*, 36; Moore, *Works of James Buchanan* 2:112–13.

33. Senator William King averred that "acting in his own case, being prosecutor and judge, he [Hall] imposed upon the patriot soldier a fine of a thousand dollars for contempt of his mandate. . . . The judge was so lost to all sense of what was due to himself, and to the high station he occupied, as to preside in his own case, and impose a heavy fine on the man by whom he believed himself to be injured. Can you sanction such a procedure?" See Senate, Senator King of Alabama on General Jackson's Fine, May 12, 1842, vol. 11, appendix, 362. For similar opinions, see Senate, Senator Tappan of Ohio on General Jackson's Fine, Mar. 1842, vol. 11, appendix, 221; Senate, Senator Walker of Mississippi on General Jackson's Fine, Jan. 10, 1843, 12:141; House, Congressman Butler of Kentucky on General Jackson's Fine, Jan. 11, 1843, vol. 12, appendix, 121; House, Congressman Slidell of Louisiana on General Jackson's Fine, Dec. 29, 1843, vol. 13, pt. 1:89; House, Congressman Douglas of Illinois on General Jackson's Fine, Jan. 6, 1844, vol. 13, appendix, 44, 45; and House, Congressman Dean of Ohio on General Jackson's Fine, Jan. 2, 1844, vol. 13, appendix, 60.

34. Ingersoll, *Gen. Jackson's Fine*, 32–34.

35. Ibid., 37–39. Buchanan made the same distinction regarding the 1789 and 1831 statutes, stating the latter law "was a declatory act: an act declaring not what the law should be thereafter, but what it had always been in time past, as well as what it would be in time to come." See Senate, Senator

Buchanan of Pennsylvania on General Jackson's Fine, May 12, 1842, vol. 11, appendix, 364.

36. Ingersoll also stated that "the law of contempt is, like martial law, inherent and aboriginal necessity of self-preservation, which immemorial usage may attest, but preceding and transcending usage." Ibid., 16, 29.

37. House, Congressman Ingersoll of Pennsylvania on General Jackson's Fine, Jan. 7, 1843, 12:131; Ingersoll, *Gen. Jackson's Fine*, 35.

38. House, Congressman Dean of Ohio on General Jackson's Fine, Jan. 2, 1844, vol. 13, appendix, 60–61.

39. House, Congressman Douglas of Illinois on General Jackson's Fine, Jan. 6, 1844, vol. 13, appendix, 44.

40. Ingersoll discussed this briefly. See Ingersoll, *Gen. Jackson's Fine*, 31; see also House, Congressman Dean of Ohio on General Jackson's Fine, Jan. 2, 1844, vol. 13, appendix, 61.

41. House, Congressman Douglas of Illinois on General Jackson's Fine, Jan. 6, 1844, vol. 13, appendix, 45.

42. The writ commanded Jackson to bring Louaillier before the court by 11:00 a.m., but it was not served until 6:15 p.m. See the original records in the appendix of Ingersoll, *Gen. Jackson's Fine*, 61.

43. House, Congressman Douglas of Illinois on General Jackson's Fine, Jan. 6, 1844, vol. 13, appendix, 45.

44. Senate, Senator Berrien of Georgia on General Jackson's Fine, May 12, 1842, vol. 11, appendix, 364.

45. Senate, Senator Conrad of Louisiana on General Jackson's Fine, May 18, 1842, vol. 11, appendix, 373–74.

46. Senate, Senator Miller of New Jersey on General Jackson's Fine, Feb. 17, 1843, 12:209–10.

47. Ibid.

48. House, Congressman Barnard of New York on General Jackson's Fine, Jan. 2, 1844, vol. 13, appendix, 207.

49. Ibid.

50. Ibid., 207, 208.

51. *United States Congressional Serial Set*, 27th Cong., 1843, H. Rept. 122, 26:15.

52. Ibid.

53. Ibid., 26:16.

CHAPTER 6

1. Sir Matthew Hale, *The History of the Common Law of England and an Analysis of the Civil Part of the Law* (Stafford: J. Nutt & J. Walthoe, 1713), 42. Originally, the term "martial law" was derived from the law administered by the Court of the Marshall and the constable of England. W. S. Holdsworth, "Martial Law Historically Considered," *Law Quarterly Review* 18 (1902): 117.

2. Hale, *History of the Common Law*, 11.

3. Sir William Blackstone, *Commentaries of the Laws of England* (Oxford: Clarendon Press, 1765–69), 1:323. Stephen Payne Adye also included a portion of Hale's definition, noting that martial law was a "book of rules and orders" for the discipline of the army. See Stephen Payne Adye, *A Treatise on Courts Martial* (London: T. Maiden & Sherbourn-Lane, 1769), 5.

4. Alexander Fraser Tytler, *An Essay on Military Law and the Practice of Courts Martial* (Edinburgh: Murray & Cochrane, 1800), vi, 13, 15, 374.

5. Ibid., 378, 379.

6. John McArthur, *Principles and Practices of Naval and Military Courts Martial* (London: J. Butterworth, 1805), 1:32.

7. Quote from William Hough, *The Practice of Courts-Martial* (London: Kingsbury, Parbury, and Allen, 1825), 383–84; see also Frederick Augustus Griffiths, *Notes on Military Law; Proceedings of Courts Martial* (Woolwich: E. Jones, 1841), 20. Both Hough and Griffiths cite McArthur, *Principles and Practices*, when making the distinction between military and martial law; some English authors continued to use martial and military interchangeably. See E. Samuel, *An Historical Account of the British Army, and of the Law Military* (London: William Clowes, 1816), 179, 183–85; and Charles J. Napier, *Remarks on Military Law and the Punishment of Flogging* (London: T. and W. Boone, 1837), 1, 2, 10. Napier notes that using the "expression" martial law to describe the control of the civilian population is "inaccurate": "The term for such a lawless state is *despotism.*" England utilized martial law throughout her colonies on a number of occasions: Ireland, 1798 and 1803; Barbados, 1805 and 1816; Demerara, 1823; Canada, 1837–38; Ceylon, 1848; Cephalonia, 1849; Cape of Good Hope, 1835, 1849–51, and 1852; St. Vincent, 1963; and Jamaica, 1831–32 and 1865. See Charles Townshend, "Martial Law and Administrative Problems of Civil Emergency in Britain and the Empire, 1800–1940," *Historical Journal* 25, no. 1 (1982): 167–95.

8. Though most English authors differentiated between martial and military law, the controversy regarding the use of martial law was by no means over. The British courts and Parliament addressed the nature and legality of martial law on numerous occasions throughout the nineteenth and into the twentieth centuries. See Townshend, "Martial Law and Administrative Problems," 167–95.

9. State constitutions are in Swindler, *Sources and Documents of the United States Constitutions*. The pertinent states, years, volumes, and pages are as follows: Maine, 1819, 4:315; Massachusetts, 1780, 5:108; New Hampshire, 1784, 6:347; Ohio, 1802 (which actually uses the term "military law"), 7:555; and Tennessee, 1796, 9:149.

10. Nathan Dane, *Digest of American Laws* (Boston: Cummings and Hilliard, 1823), 6:725–26, 338.

11. James Kent, *Commentaries on American Law* (New York: O. Halstead, 1826). George M. Dennison argued incorrectly that Kent commented on and made a distinction between martial and military law in 1826. This, however, was not the case. The error was due to utilizing an 1884 edition of Kent's work and assuming the author's distinction regarding martial law

was also present in the original edition. See George M. Dennison, "Martial Law: The Development of a Theory of Emergency Powers, 1776–1861," *American Journal of Legal History* 1 (1974): 65 n. 46.

12. Joseph Story, *Commentaries on the Constitution of the United States* (Boston: Hilliard, Gray, 1833), 3:94.

13. John Bouvier, *A Law Dictionary Adapted to the Constitution and Laws of the United States of America* (Philadelphia: T & J. W. Johnson, 1839), 2:9. George Dennison made a similar mistake to that of citing Kent's 1884 edition when utilizing an 1856 edition of Bouvier's law dictionary. Dennison used a definition of martial law from the 1856 work and assumed that it was the same as the original 1839 edition. This, however, was not the case. The 1856 edition contained a third definition that stated a military commander could not declare martial law over a city and suspend the writ of habeas corpus. See Dennison, "Martial Law," 66 n. 49.

14. House, *A Letter from the Secretary of War, Transmitting a System of Field Service & Police, and a System of Martial Law, for the Government of the Army of the United States; Submitted in Obedience to a Resolution of the House of Representatives of the United States, of the 22d of December, 1819,* 16th Cong., 1st sess., Dec. 26, 1820, H. Doc. 45, serial 51, 13, 115. See also same title, AM State Papers, 16th Cong., 2d sess.—Military Affairs—vol. 2, p. 199–274.

15. Isaac Maltby, *A Treatise on Courts Martial and Military Law* (Boston: Thomas B. Waite, 1813), 38, 39.

16. Ibid., 40, 161. Maltby made this mention of Pike in regard to his command of the Fifteenth Regiment in West Lake Champlain, New York. Maltby's was the first and only mention of this incident that I have found. See Maltby, *Treatise on Courts Martial and Military Law,* 37–38.

17. "Judge Bay's Opinion," 1 Car. Law Rep., 330.

18. *Johnson v. Duncan et al.,* Supreme Court of the State of Louisiana, 1815, in Thomas C. Manning, ed., *Unreported Cases Heard and Determined by the Supreme Court of Louisiana* (St. Paul, Minn.: West Publishing, 1913), 198, 192.

19. Thomas Jefferson to James Brown, Oct. 27, 1808, in Ford, *Writings of Thomas Jefferson* 9:211.

20. "Opinion of Edward Livingston on Martial Law," *Correspondence of Andrew Jackson* 2:197–98; "Opinion of Abner L. Duncan on Martial Law," *Correspondence of Andrew Jackson* 2:199.

21. Record of the Court Martial Prepared under the General's Authority by His Aide, Robert Butler, 16–18.

22. Alexander J. Dallas to Andrew Jackson, Apr. 12, 1815, *Jackson Papers* 3:344, 345.

23. Senate, Senator Bayard of Delaware on General Jackson's Fine, Dec. 22, 1842, vol. 12, appendix, 68.

24. Senate, Senator Miller of New Jersey on General Jackson's Fine, Feb. 17, 1843, 12, appendix: 210.

25. See, for example, House, Congressman Barnard of New York on General Jackson's Fine, Jan. 2, 1844, vol. 13, appendix, 206.

26. Senate, Senator James Buchanan of Pennsylvania on General Jackson's Fine, May 12, 1842, 11: 364; Senate, Senator Benjamin Tappan of Ohio on General Jackson's Fine, Mar. 22, 1842, 11:222; Senate, Senator Linn of Missouri on General Jackson's Fine, May 18, 1842, 11:488.

27. Kendall, "General Jackson's Fine," 71, 72.

28. The idea that a camp created by a military force was under the commander's complete control was in fact nothing new. In Secretary of War Calhoun's letter "transmitting a system of field service & police," there is an extensive discussion of a camp's laws and the right of a military force to protect and police its camp. This work, however, says nothing about imposing military authority upon civilians. This is the aspect of the camp theory, as expressed in regard to Jackson's fine, that is entirely new. See "Letters from the Secretary of War," 72–73, 81–82, 109. One English author did note that certain laws applied to the camp and involved civilians. This law was, however, described as a redress for civilians rather than one imposing military rules upon them. See Hough, *Practice of Courts-Martial*, 384. George M. Dennison also discussed the role of civilians in relation to a theater of war, though he did not actually use the term "camp." He infers that Sir Matthew Hale "indicated" civilians who served in defense of the realm were automatically subject to martial law. This inference is speculative and does not address the situation of civilians who were not engaged in defense. See Dennison, "Martial Law," 53.

29. House, Congressman Ezra Dean of Ohio on General Jackson's Fine, Jan. 2, 1844, vol. 13, appendix, 59. Dean was not the first to discuss martial law in terms of it being an implied power. Abner Duncan had done so in regard to suspending the writ of habeas corpus. See note 23 above.

30. House, Congressman Brown of Tennessee on General Jackson's Fine, Jan. 8, 1844, vol. 13, appendix, 47.

31. McRoberts served as attorney general from 1830 to 1832; *Biographical Directory of the United States Congress, 1774–1989* (Washington, D.C., 1989); Senate, Senator McRoberts of Illinois on General Jackson's Fine, Feb. 17, 1843, 12:301.

32. House, Congressman Ingersoll of Pennsylvania on General Jackson's Fine, Jan. 7, 1843, 12:132. Ingersoll's mention of Kendall's theory confirms that his article was read by the members of Congress.

33. Ingersoll, *Gen. Jackson's Fine*, 14, 16.

34. Though Wellington is usually cited as having made this statement in 1851, he originally made the remark on April 19, 1810. See William Hough, *Precedents in Military Law: Including the Practice of Courts Martial* (London: William H. Allen, 1855), 514 n. 5.

35. Parton, *Life of Andrew Jackson* 3:641.

36. Rankin, *When Civil Law Fails*, 25.

37. J. W. French, *Law and Military Law; with an Analysis, by Subjects, of the Rules and Articles of War* (New York: John F. Baldwin, 1861), 18; Jenkins, *Life and Public Services of General Andrew Jackson*, 161; Birkheimer, *Military Government and Martial Law*, 356–57; Simeon E. Baldwin, *The American Judiciary* (New York: Century, 1914), 301; Frederick Bernays

Wiener, *A Practical Manual of Military Law* (Harrisburg, Pa.: Military
Service Publishing, 1940), 63; Tom W. Campbell, *Two Fighters and Two Fines:
Sketches of the Lives of Matthew Lyon and Andrew Jackson* (Little Rock,
Ark.: Pioneer Publishing, 1941), 311; Abraham D. Sofaer, "Emergency
Powers and the Hero of New Orleans," *Cardoza Law Review* 2, no. 2 (Winter
1981): 233–53; Badsah K. Mian, *American Habeas Corpus: Law, History, and
Politics* (San Francisco: Cosmos of Humanists Press, 1984), 119.

38. Dennison, "Martial Law," 53.
39. Emphasis added; Nicholas, *Martial Law, by a Kentuckian*, 12.
40. Though the use of martial law in both instances was, by strict definition,
    the same, Dennison pointed out correctly that Rhode Island's was the first
    instance in which martial law was "used simply as a means of insuring the
    continuance of governmental authority." Dennison, "Martial Law," 69.
41. Swindler, *Sources and Documents of the United States Constitutions* 8:388.
42. House, *Report of the Case of Luther vs. Borden, Tried before Judge Story, in
    the United States Circuit Court*, 28th Cong. 1st sess., June 17, 1844, H. Rept.
    581, serial 447, 159, 163–64.
43. Story, *Commentaries on the Constitution of the United States* 3:94. R. Kent
    Newmyer noted that Story was extremely concerned about the precedent of
    the Dorr War, in citizens altering a state Constitution without following the
    proper amendment procedures. Upholding the proclamation of martial law
    through the *Luther* decision supported what Story believed to be the legiti-
    mate state government and subsequently defeated radical social change at
    the hands of mob rule. Newmyer argued that Story's defeat of "mobocracy"
    through the *Luther* decision was conservative. Though Newmyer's observa-
    tion on this account is valid, he did not address the ramifications of legaliz-
    ing martial law. See R. Kent Newmyer, *Supreme Court Justice Joseph Story:
    Statesman of the Old Republic* (Chapel Hill: Univ. of North Carolina Press,
    1985), 365, 360.
44. House, Congressman Adams of Massachusetts on the General Appropria-
    tion Bill, *Congressional Globe*, 27th Cong., 2d sess., Apr. 15, 1842, 11:429. The
    author has found no other literature on the subject of martial law in which
    it is described as "the law of war." Adams alone did this, and it therefore
    seems logical to assume that Story was influenced by Adams's argument.
45. Ibid. 11:161.
46. Ibid. 11:160.
47. Daniel Webster, "The Rhode Island Government," *Works of Daniel Webster*
    (Boston: Little, Brown, 1853), 6:240.
48. De Hart was influenced by English precedent, citing William Hough's def-
    inition of martial law. William C. De Hart, *Observations on Military Law
    and the Constitution and Practice of Courts Martial* (New York: Wiley and
    Putnam, 1846), 17; John O'Brien, *A Treatise on American Military Laws
    and the Practice of Courts Martial; with Suggestions for Improvement*
    (Philadelphia: Lea & Blanchard, 1846), 26.
49. De Hart, *Observations on Military Law*, 17; O'Brien, *Treatise on American
    Military Laws*, 26. George Dennison not only stated incorrectly that both
    authors believed martial law was legal but also insisted that "De Hart

obviously preferred to make martial law more palatable by transforming it into known law—the Articles of War—whereas O'Brien refused any precise definition of law once declared." De Hart's comments regarding the imposition of "military law" did not imply using the articles of war so much as it recognized the absolute authority of a military commander within a theater of war. Martial law went into effect automatically by virtue of a state of war existing. Again, such a theory stemmed from the camp theory advocated during the debates. See Dennison, "Martial Law," 72.

50. James Kent, *Commentaries on American Law* (New York: William Kent, 1848), 1:341. It is not entirely clear whether the footnote was added by Kent or an editor. Revision of the work commenced in October 1847 but was completed by an editor because of Kent's death on December 12, 1847.

51. John Bouvier, *A Law Dictionary Adapted to the Constitution and Laws of the United States of America* (Philadelphia: T. & J. W. Johnson, 1848), 2:10. George Dennison incorrectly asserted that Bouvier's 1839 edition contained this passage. It was, however, not added until the 1848 edition. See Dennison, "Martial Law," 66.

52. Bouvier stated that "whether this writ ought to be suspended depends on political considerations, of which the legislature is to decide. The proclamation of a military chief, declaring martial law, cannot, therefore, suspend the operation of the law." John Bouvier, *Institutes of American Law* (Philadelphia: Robert E. Peterson, 1851), 1:91.

53. Alexander M. Burrill, *Burrill's Law Dictionary* (New York: John S. Voorhies, 1851), 2:708.

54. Joel Prentiss Bishop, *Commentaries on the Criminal Law* (Boston: Little, Brown, 1856), 1:47–48.

55. William Winthrop, *Military Law and Precedents* (Washington, D.C.: GPO, 1920), 823.

56. The governor of the Washington Territory made his proclamation in response to an Indian scare, and the very fact that he made such a decision reveals that the use of martial law as an extraordinary power had become common knowledge among Americans. Cushing ruled the governor's decree illegal; see Senate, *Executive Documents,* 34th Cong., 1st sess., Feb. 1857, S. Doc 98, serial 823, and S. Doc. 41 and 47, serial 881; Caleb Cushing, *Opinions of the Attorneys General* (Washington, D.C.: Harcourt, Brace, 1858), 8:368.

57. Cushing, *Opinions of the Attorneys General* 8:372. Cushing did not necessarily combine the two acts. The suspension of habeas corpus was not an automatic declaration of martial law. Rather, he asserted if an emergency of such magnitude existed, calling for the suspension of the writ, then it was reasonable to presume that further emergency powers could be declared.

58. Ibid. 8:374.

59. Though elected as a Whig, Cushing was essentially read out of the party because of his allegiance to John Tyler following the death of William Henry Harrison. M. Michael Catherine Hodgson, *Caleb Cushing: Attorney General of the United States, 1853–1857* (Washington, D.C.: Catholic Univ. of America Press, 1955), 41; Claude M. Fuess, *The Life of Caleb Cushing*

(New York: Harcourt, Brace, 1923), 1:327, 395; and Allen Johnson and Dumas Malone, eds., *Dictionary of American Biography*, vol. 4 (New York: Charles Scribner's Sons, 1930), 624. For Cushing's views in the debates, see House, Congressman Cushing of Massachusetts on General Jackson's Fine, Jan. 5, 1843, 12:122–23.

CHAPTER 7

1. For more on the partisanship at the time of Jackson's death, see Warshauer, "Ridiculing the Dead," 13–31; and Warshauer, "Contested Mourning."
2. The painting was directly inspired by the comments made by those who discussed the scene in the 1820s and 1840s. See *Concise Narrative of General Jackson's First Invasion of Florida*, 23; and Senate, Senator Conrad of Louisiana on General Jackson's Fine, May 18, 1842, vol. 11, appendix, 374. Jackson's supporters in fact liked Conrad's suggestion about placing a painting in the rotunda. Francis P. Blair wrote Jackson on December 25, 1843, stating, "I will get someone to move the filling of the niche in the rotunda opposite to the surrender of the British of York with the battle of New Orleans portraying the death of their Generals and overthrow of their army." Jackson replied on January 19, 1844, remarking, "You are always projecting something to add to my fame, the Whiggs and Federalists never can swallow any thing to be placed in the rotunda that will add to my memory." *Jackson Papers, MS;* Senate, Senator Linn of Missouri on General Jackson's Fine, May 18, 1842, vol. 11, appendix, 489. See also House, Congressman Dickinson of Tennessee on General Jackson's Fine, Jan. 6, 1844, vol. 13, appendix, 37. Dickinson declared, "Let them follow out the suggestions of the Senator from Louisiana, who proposed a painting of the scene in the court room when his fine was imposed and paid. The warrior, fresh from the field of battle, in his military dress, bowing in submission to the decree of the court; thus teaching posterity, by his example, that great truth which they should not fail to learn—which should be deeply impressed upon their hearts, and which lies at the basis of our institutions—'that the military should always be subordinate to the civil authority.'"
3. For a brief discussion of the portrait, see James G. Barber, *Andrew Jackson: A Portrait Study* (Washington, D.C.: National Portrait Gallery, 1991), 217–18, 221. Schussele also made two charcoal sketches of the courtroom scene. Both are owned by the Pennsylvania Academy of the Fine Arts.
4. The other is a sketch of General Jackson signing the order that imposed martial law. See John Frost, *Pictorial Life of Andrew Jackson* (Hartford, Conn.: Belknap and Hamersley, 1847).
5. Hedenberg's first name, never published in his printings, was found in McElroy's *Philadelphia Directory for 1860* (Philadelphia: A. McElroy, 1860), 422. The directory listed him, in alternate years, as both a shoe merchant and a publisher. See McElroy's directories from 1849 to 1862. See also

Barber, *Andrew Jackson,* 218; and C. J. Hedenberg, *Explanation of the Picture of Andrew Jackson before Judge Hall, at New Orleans, 1815, Sustaining the Laws of His Country, as He Had Defended Her Liberties in the Field* (Philadelphia: C. J. Hedenberg, n.d.). For an example of Hedenberg's correspondence with politicians, see J. Madison Cutts [Stephen Douglas's father-in-law] to C. J. Hedenberg, May 4, 1858, in *The Letters of Stephen A. Douglas,* ed. Robert J. Johannsen (Urbana: Univ. of Illinois Press, 1961), 420.

6. For more on the suspension of habeas corpus and martial law during the Civil War, see Neely, *Fate of Liberty;* and Mark E. Neely Jr., *Southern Rights: Political Prisoners and the Myth of Confederate Constitutionalism* (Charlottesville: Univ. of Virginia Press, 1999).

7. Abraham Lincoln to Erastus Corning and others, June 12, 1863, in Basler, *Collected Works of Abraham Lincoln* 6:268–69.

8. Neely, *Southern Rights.*

9. The men who remained alive but did not speak on martial law during the Civil War included the following Democrats: Robert James Walker of Mississippi supported the Union throughout the Civil War and in 1863–64 served as a financial agent in Europe for the United States; John A. McClernand of Illinois became a Union general under Ulysses Grant; John Slidell of Louisiana, though originally a pro-Union Democrat, ultimately sided with the South and became a Confederate ambassador to France (he achieved a degree of fame as a result of the "Trent Affair," in which he and his fellow ambassador, James M. Mason, were removed from a British ship by Union forces); and Lewis Steenrod of Virginia died early in 1862. Two Whigs survived into the Civil War era: William Dayton of New Jersey served as U.S. minister to France from 1861 until his death in 1864, and Charles M. Conrad of Louisiana served his state as a representative to the Confederate Congress from 1862 to 1864.

10. Howard Carroll, *Twelve Americans: Their Lives and Times* (New York: Harper & Brothers, 1883), 301.

11. Senate, Senator Allen of Ohio on General Jackson's Fine, May 18, 1842, vol. 11, appendix, 378.

12. Ibid.

13. Senate, Senator Tappan of Ohio on General Jackson's Fine, Mar. 22, 1842, vol. 11, appendix, 221, 222; Senate, Senator Allen of Ohio on General Jackson's Fine, May 18, 1842, vol. 11, appendix, 378.

14. Ibid., 379.

15. Reginald C. McGrane, *William Allen: A Study in Western Democracy* (Columbus, Ohio: F. J. Heer, 1925), 151, 153.

16. Ibid., 145–46, 150, 152, 163, 165, 166.

17. Kendall, "General Jackson's Fine," 58–77.

18. Amos Kendall, *Letters Exposing the Mismanagement of Public Affairs by Abraham Lincoln and the Political Combinations to Secure His Re-election* (Washington, D.C.: Constitutional Union Office, 1864), 6.

19. Ibid., 6, 32.

20. Samuel Tyler, *Memoir of Roger Brooke Taney, LL.D., Chief Justice of the Supreme Court of the United States* (Baltimore: J. Murphy, 1872), 427; Charles W. Smith, *Roger B. Taney: Jacksonian Jurist* (Chapel Hill: Univ. of

North Carolina Press, 1936), 177, 189; Carl B. Swisher, *History of the Supreme Court of the United States: The Taney Period, 1836–64* (New York: Macmillan, 1974), 852. Bernard C. Steiner stressed Taney's nonpartisanship; see his *Life of Roger Brooke Taney* (Westport, Conn.: Greenwood Press, 1970), 495, 500–503. See also Charles Warren, who described Taney as a "fearless Judge" in *The Supreme Court in United States History, 1836–1918* (Boston: Little, Brown, 1926), 2:374.

21. *Ex Parte Merryman*, in Martin Siegel, *The Supreme Court in American Life: The Taney Court, 1836–1864* (New York: Associate Faculty Press, 1986), 3:229, 232.

22. Roger Taney to Andrew Jackson, Apr. 28, 1843, *Correspondence of Andrew Jackson* 6:217.

23. Roger Taney to Andrew Jackson, Mar. 15, 1844, *Jackson Papers, MS.*

24. For Taney's southern leanings in the Scott case, see Don E. Fehrenbacher, *Slavery, Law, and Politics: The Dred Scott Case in Historical Perspective* (Oxford: Oxford Univ. Press, 1978), 287–88. The *New York Evening Post* added that Taney was using "his authority and position to the advantage of those who are armed against the Union [and] to serve treason, and embarrass and injure the Government." See Warren, *Supreme Court in United States History* 2:370.

25. House, Congressman Schenck of Ohio on General Jackson's Fine, Jan. 8, 1844, vol. 13, appendix, 230.

26. Emphasis added; "Proclamation of Martial Law in Baltimore and the Western Counties of Maryland," *War of the Rebellion: A Compilation of the Official Records of the Union and Confederate Armies*, 70 vols. in 128 vols. (Washington, D.C.: GPO, 1884), ser. 1, vol. 27, pt. 3:437–38 (hereafter cited as *OR*, with all citations referring to series 1). In General Order no. 1, in which Schenck assumed command of the Middle Department, he made a similar statement concerning civil liberties: "Nobody who loves our free institutions will pretend that thought or opinions, if that were possible, should be suppressed, or would desire to invade or disturb the sacredness of private life or conversation; but in this view of civil obligation, it must not be complained of if any public or open demonstrations or declarations of sympathy with treason should provoke strict and needful observation of the conduct of the party offending, and lead even to punishment, or restraint, if accompanied by acts of complicity or anything tending to danger or disorder." See General Order no. 1, Dec. 22, 1862, *OR* 21:873.

27. "Fine Surposed [*sic*] by Judge Hall," Andrew Jackson to the Editors of the *Globe* (Feb. 1843), *Correspondence of Andrew Jackson* 6:191.

28. Therry, "Life of General Robert Cumming Schenck," 266, 271. For more on Schenck's command of the Middle Department, see, especially, chapter 9, titled "No compromise with Treason." See also Donald Eugene Day, "The Military Career of Robert Cumming Schenck, 1861–1863" (master's thesis, Miami Univ., 1963); and Kokkinou, "Political Career of Robert Cumming Schenck."

29. General Order no. 66, Dec. 5, 1863, *OR*, vol. 29, pt. 2:548.

30. House, Congressman Schenck of Ohio on the Expulsion of Mr. Long, *Congressional Globe*, 38th Cong., 1st sess., Apr. 11, 1864, vol. 34, pt. 2:1539.

31. "Fine Surposed [*sic*] By Judge Hall," 6:194.

32. House, Congressman Douglas of Illinois on General Jackson's Fine, 28th Cong., 1st Sess., *Congressional Globe*, Jan. 6, 1844, vol. 13, appendix, 45.

33. House, Congressman Schenck of Ohio on General Jackson's Fine, 28th Cong. 1st Sess., *Congressional Globe*, Jan. 8, 1844, vol. 13, appendix, 230.

34. House, Congressman Schenck of Ohio on the Expulsion of Mr. Long, 38th Cong., 1st Sess., *Congressional Globe*, Apr. 11, 1864, vol. 34, pt. 2:1540.

35. Senate, Senator Crittenden of Kentucky on General Jackson's Fine, 27th Cong. 2d Sess., *Congressional Globe*, May 12, 1842, vol. 11, appendix, 362.

36. John J. Crittenden to Thomas Crittenden, Nov. 28, 1862, in Albert D. Kirwan, *John J. Crittenden: The Struggle for the Union* (Lexington: Univ. Press of Kentucky, 1962), 459, 456–57.

37. Ibid., 470.

38. Samuel Smith Nicholas to John J. Crittenden, 1861, in *The Life of John J. Crittenden*, by Mrs. Chapman Coleman (Philadelphia: J. B. Lippincott, 1871), 2:318.

39. Nicholas, *Martial Law, by a Kentuckian*, 6.

40. Nicholas, *Martial Law, by a Kentuckian*, 27; Samuel Smith Nicholas, *Habeas Corpus, the Law of War, and Confiscation* (Louisville: Bradley & Gilbert, 1862).

41. For Adams's speech, see House, Congressman Adams of Massachusetts on General Appropriation Bill, 27th cong., 2d Sess., *Congressional Globe*, Apr. 15, 1842, 11:429.

42. For Fremont's actions, see McPherson, *Battle Cry of Freedom*, 352.

43. Samuel Smith Nicholas, *A Review of the Argument of President Lincoln and Attorney General Bates in Favor of Presidential Power to Suspend the Privilege of the Writ of Habeas Corpus* (Louisville: Bradley & Gilbert, 1861); E. Merton Coulter, *The Civil War and Readjustment in Kentucky* (Chapel Hill: Univ. of North Carolina Press, 1926), 32–33, 53.

44. For more on Jefferson Davis's civil libertarian strategy, see Neely, *Southern Rights*, chap. 9.

45. House, Congressman Stephens of Georgia on General Jackson's Fine, Dec. 29, 1843, vol. 13, pt. 1:87.

46. For the final vote and voting record, see *Congressional Globe*, 28th Cong. 1st sess., Jan. 8, 1844, vol. 13, pt. 1:120.

47. Alexander H. Stephens, *A Constitutional View of the Late War Between the States* (Philadelphia: National Publishing, 1870), 2:786–88.

48. See "Resolutions on the Writ of Habeas Corpus," in Stephens, *Constitutional View of the Late War* 2:478–79; see also letters from Robert Toombs to Stephens, in which the former discusses Stephens's efforts against suspension of the writ of habeas corpus and the imposition of martial law. See, especially, Toombs to Stephens, Apr. 1, 1864, and Benjamin H. Hill to Alexander Stephens, Mar. 14, 1864, in *The Correspondence of Robert Toombs, Alexander H. Stephens, and Howell Cobb*, ed. Ulrich B. Phillips (New York: De Capo Press, 1970), 637–38, 636.

49. Thomas B. Alexander and Richard E. Beringer, *The Anatomy of the Confederate Congress: A Case Study of the Influences of Member Character-*

istics on Legislative Voting Behavior, 1861–1865 (Nashville: Vanderbilt Univ. Press, 1972), 173–87.

50. Neely, *Southern Rights*, 26.

51. House, Congressman Stephens of Georgia on the Mexican War, *Congressional Globe*, 29th Cong. 2d sess., Feb. 12, 1847, 351.

52. John Minor Botts, *The Great Rebellion: Its Secret History, Rise, Progress, and Disastrous Failure* (New York: Harper & Brothers, 1866), 279.

53. House, Congressman Botts of Virginia on General Jackson's Fine, Jan. 24, 1843, 12:195.

54. Botts, *Great Rebellion*, 279.

55. Ibid., 280, 286.

56. Josiah M. Lucas to Abraham Lincoln, Dec. 5, 1860, in the Abraham Lincoln Letters, Library of Congress, on line at American Memory web site, http://memory.loc.gov (hereafter cited as Lincoln Papers, LC Web). Numerous letters to Lincoln show support for Botts as a cabinet member; John Minor Botts to Abraham Lincoln, Sept. 30, 1863, Lincoln Papers, LC Web.

57. John Minor Botts to John B. Fry, Jan. 22, 1864, Lincoln Papers, LC Web.

58. Senate, Senator Graham of North Carolina on General Jackson's Fine, *Congressional Globe*, 27th Cong., 2d sess., Mar. 10, 1842, vol. 11, appendix, 304; Senate, Senator Graham of North Carolina on General Jackson's Fine, Feb. 20, 1843, 12:315.

59. Neely, *Southern Rights*, 56.

60. *Illinois State Register*, Sept. 2, 1861, in Neely, *Fate of Liberty*, 186.

61. Robert L. Breck, *The Habeas Corpus and Martial Law* (Cincinnati: Richard H. Collins, 1862), 37, 11, 84.

62. Horace Binney, *The Privilege of the Writ of Habeas Corpus Under the Constitution* (Philadelphia: C. Sherman & Son, 1862).

63. A number of works were published in opposition to Binney's pamphlet that made no mention of Jackson. See, for example, George Mifflin Wharton, *Remarks on Mr. Binney's Treatise on the Writ of Habeas Corpus by a Member of the Philadelphia Bar* (Philadelphia: n.p., 1862); D. B. Brown, *Reply to Horace Binney on the Privilege of the Writ of Habeas Corpus under the Constitution by a Member of the Philadelphia Bar* (Philadelphia: J. Challen, 1862); C. H. Cross, *A Reply to Horace Binney's Pamphlet on the Habeas Corpus* (Philadelphia: n.p., 1862); James F. Johnston, *The Suspending Power and the Writ of Habeas Corpus* (Philadelphia: J. Campbell, 1862); John Teackle Montgomery, *The Writ of Habeas Corpus and Mr. Binney* (Philadelphia: n.p., 1862); and R. Vaux, *The Habeas Corpus: (The Act, the Writ, and the Privilege): Its Death, and How It Came by It* (Philadelphia: John Doe, Office of the Public Advertiser, 1862).

64. John C. Bullitt, *A Review of Mr. Binney's Pamphlet on "The Privilege of the Writ of Habeas Corpus Under the Constitution"* (Philadelphia: John Campbell, 1862), 34, 23, 33..

65. Tatlow Jackson, *Martial Law: What Is It? And Who Can Declare It?* (Philadelphia: J. Campbell, 1862), 13, 15, 16. In his second work, and more limited overview of martial law, Jackson noted simply that "when imperious

necessity commands, let the department usurping do as did General Jackson at New Orleans—take the responsibility; and hope that, in the attainment of the end, the people will pardon or justify the means. But leave intact the Constitution as our fathers construed and adopted it." See Tatlow Jackson, *Authorities Cited Antagonistic to Horace Binney's Conclusions on the Writ of Habeas Corpus* (Philadelphia: J. Campbell, 1862), 7. One other Democratic pamphleteer made exactly the same assertion. See Isaac Myer, *Presidential Power Over Personal Liberty: A Review of Horace Binney's Essay on the Writ of Habeas Corpus* (Imprinted for the Author, 1862), 2.

66. Ingersoll, *Gen. Jackson's Fine.*
67. Neely, *Fate of Liberty*, 201.
68. Charles Edward Ingersoll, *An Undelivered Speech on Executive Arrests* (Philadelphia: n.p., 1862), 89, 91. In another pamphlet, Ingersoll argued that there existed no such thing as martial law; see his *Personal Liberty and Martial Law: A Review of Some Pamphlets of the Day* (Philadelphia: n.p., 1862), 30.
69. Ingersoll, *Gen. Jackson's Fine*, 15; House, Congressman Douglas of Illinois on General Jackson's Fine, Jan. 6, 1844, vol. 13, appendix, 44.
70. Neely, *Fate of Liberty*, 201, 190.
71. The September 1862 act was intended primarily to enforce the administration's conscription act of July 17, 1862. Neely, *Fate of Liberty*, 52; see 191–92 for the timing of the Democratic opposition.
72. Senate, Senator Garrett Davis of Kentucky on the Habeas Corpus Bill, *Congressional Globe*, 37th Cong., 3d sess., Jan. 27, 1863, vol. 33, pt. 1:532.
73. Senate, Senator James A. Bayard of Delaware on the Habeas Corpus Bill, *Congressional Globe*, 37th Cong., 3d sess., Jan. 27, 1863, vol. 33, pt. 1:547–54. For Democratic speeches that are virtually identical to those delivered by Whigs in the 1840s, see Senate, Senator Powell Lazarus of Kentucky on the Habeas Corpus Bill, *Congressional Globe*, 37th Cong., 3d sess., Mar. 2, 1863, vol. 33, pt. 2:1465; and House, Congressman Daniel Voorhees of Indiana on the Habeas Corpus Bill, *Congressional Globe*, 37th Cong., 3d sess., Feb. 19, 1863, vol. 33, pt. 2:1057–62.
74. John V. L. Pruyn et al., *Reply to President Lincoln's Letter of 12th June, 1863*, in *Union Pamphlets of the Civil War, 1861–1865*, ed. Frank Freidel (Cambridge: Harvard Univ. Press, 1967), 2:762.
75. See chapter 6, this volume.
76. Pruyn et al., *Reply to President Lincoln's Letter*, 763.
77. Neely, *Fate of Liberty*, 203, 207.
78. Joel Parker, *Habeas Corpus and Martial Law: A Review of the opinion of Chief Justice Taney in the Case of John Merryman* (Cambridge, Mass.: Welch, Bigelow, 1861), 24; Neely, *Fate of Liberty*, 188. For the earlier opinions, see chapter 6, this volume.
79. Parker, *Habeas Corpus and Martial Law*, 32.
80. Ibid., 40; *Illinois State Register*, Oct. 29, 1861, in Neely, *Fate of Liberty*, 189.
81. John Gardner, *A Treatise on the Law of the American Rebellion, Our True Policy, Domestic and Foreign* (New York: John W. Amerman, 1862), 6, 7.

    Gardner made the same assertions in his *Treatise on the Martial Power of the President of the United States* (n.p., n.d.), 4, 5.

82. Frederick Bancroft, *The Life of William H. Seward* (Gloucester, Mass.: Peter Smith, 1967), 2:259; for more on Bancroft's account of Seward's activities, see the chapter titled "Seward and the Political Prisoners." See also John M. Taylor, *William Henry Seward: Lincoln's Right Hand* (New York: Harper Collins, 1991), 169.

83. *Proceedings and Address of the Republican Young Men of the State of New-York*, 7, 15–16.

84. Silbey, *Respectable Minority*, 70.

INDEX

Whigs (cont.)
    battling Democrats over
        Jackson's suspension of civil
        liberties, 16
    championing power and sanctity
        of judiciary, 153–54
    contradictory views on martial
        law, 151
    control of Twenty-seventh Con-
        gress, 83
    declaring martial law in Rhode
        Island, 145–49, 151
    defending judiciary in contempt
        of court issue, 170–74, 175
    disagreed on precedent for mar-
        tial law, 116–17
    employing party tactics against
        refund bill, 83–84, 91–92
    evolution of, in response to
        Jackson's perceived abuse of
        power, 79
    focusing on problem of voiding a
        judicial decision, 87–88
    former, abandoning views of
        martial law, 201–2
    issues separating, from Demo-
        crats, 80–81
    northern wing, general response
        to refund bill and martial law
        questions, 132, 135–45
    opposition to refund bill, 79–80
    party's hatred of Jackson, 116
    politicizing refund debates, 11–12
    questioning Jackson's conduct in
        New Orleans, 120

reaction against refund bill, 13
    southern wing, general response
        to refund bill and martial law
        questions, 131–35
    southern wing, leaving
Democratic Party over Jackson's
    bank policy, 135
    split on geographic lines, 117
    summary of response to martial
        law, 239–40
    support for Judge Hall, 132
    tiring of refund bill debate, 110–11
    view of Jackson, 10, 11
White, Albert, involvement in refund
    bill debate, 109
White, Edward D., 268n75
Wickliffe, Charles, 282n16
Wilkinson, James, attempting to
    proclaim martial law in New
    Orleans, 21
Wilmot (British chief justice), 159,
    167
Wiltse, Charles M., on Calhoun's
    resignation, 269n80
Wirt, William, 282–83n16
Woodbridge, William
    defending Constitution and writ
        of habeus corpus, 137
    on instruction issue, 271n97
Worcester v. Georgia, 153
Workman, James, 21
Wright, Silas, 88

Andrew Jackson and the Politics of Martial Law was designed and typeset on a Macintosh computer system using QuarkXPress software. The body text (9/13) and display type are set in Olympian. This book was designed and typeset by Barbara Karwhite and manufactured by Thomson-Shore, Inc.